Contemporary Political Thought

Issues in Scope, Value, and Direction

Contemporary Political Thought

Issues in Scope, Value, and Direction

James A. Gould
University of South Florida

Vincent V. Thursby
The Florida State University

Holt, Rinehart and Winston, Inc.

New York   Chicago   San Francisco   Atlanta
Dallas   Montreal   Toronto   London   Sydney

Professor Gould
dedicates his efforts in
this book to Jean Gould Schuler

Copyright © 1969 by Holt, Rinehart and Winston, Inc.
All rights reserved
Library of Congress Catalog Card Number: 69–12562
SBN: 03–073605–6
Printed in the United States of America
0123 40 9876543

PREFACE

The purpose of this text is to bring together tracts upon four central and controversial issues in contemporary political thought. Every professor who teaches political thought, whether he terms his course political theory or political philosophy, talks about these issues. They are: the *nature*, the *methods*, the *value issues*, and the *condition* of political thought, and the articles present opposing points of view. Their juxtaposition should improve teaching and stimulate class discussion. Both the general introduction to the parts and the head-notes to articles have been written to aid the student to understand the particular position of each author. The bibliographies at the end of each topic contain references, both favorable and critical, for further reading.

Part II, the section on methodology, presents each position along with a specific criticism of that position (the exception to this is in the section on existentialism, where the positions of Sartre and Camus are presented without opposing articles). The editors hope that this approach will help to clarify the different approaches to methodology for the student.

A professor of government and a professor of philosophy have collaborated on this work and it is suitable for both political science and philosophy courses. The text is meant to be a supplementary book for such courses, although it can be combined with selected works of political thinkers and the combination used as a substitute for the usual textbook.

November 1968
J. A. G.
V. V. T.

CONTENTS

PREFACE   v

PART I. THE NATURE OF POLITICAL THOUGHT   1

1. *George H. Sabine,* What Is a Political Theory?   7
2. *George E. G. Catlin,* Political Theory: What Is It?   21
3. *Leo Strauss,* What Is Political Philosophy?   46
4. *William A. Glaser,* The Types and Uses of Political
     Theory   70
Further Readings   89

PART II. METHODOLOGIES IN POLITICAL
THOUGHT   91

5. *Andrew Hacker, CAPITAL* and Carbuncles   102

Behavioralism
6. *Robert A. Dahl,* The Behavioral Approach in
     Political Science   118
7. *Christian Bay,* A Critical Evaluation of Behavioral
     Literature   137
Further Readings   161

Analytic Political Philosophy
8. *T. D. Weldon,* Analytic Political Philosophy   162
9. *Joseph Margolis,* Difficulties in Analytic Political
    Philosophy   175
Further Readings   185

Functionalism
10. *W. G. Runciman,* Functionalism as a Method in
    Political Thought   186
11. *David Easton,* Systems Analysis: An Example of
    Functionalism   198
12. *Paul F. Kress,* A Critique of Easton's Systems Analysis   211
Further Readings   228

Existentialism
13. *Jean-Paul Sartre,* Marxism and Existentialism   230
14. *T. L. Thorson,* The Political Philosophy of Camus   256
Further Readings   272

**PART III. VALUE JUDGMENTS IN POLITICAL
THOUGHT**   273

15. *Gabriel A. Almond,* Politics, Science, and Ethics   276
16. *Alfred Cobban,* Ethics and the Decline of Political
    Theory   289
Further Readings   304

**PART IV. THE CONDITION AND PROSPECT OF
POLITICAL THOUGHT**   305

17. *David Easton,* The Decline of Modern Political
    Theory   307
18. *Isaiah Berlin,* Does Political Theory Still Exist?   328
19. *Harry Eckstein,* The Condition and Prospect of
    Political Thought   358
Further Readings   373

INDEX   375

Part I

THE NATURE
OF POLITICAL THOUGHT

What properly constitutes the subject matter of political thought is a matter of great debate. The different interests of the first three essayists of this book—all prominent political writers—reflect this debate. Sabine thinks statements about historical events should be included; Catlin emphasizes subject matter amenable to scientific analysis; and Strauss is strongly concerned with value presuppositions.

Not only is there difference of opinion upon the scope of the subject matter of political thought, but there is also difference as to the proper name to be given to the subject matter field itself. The term *political science*, which usually is meant to cover all aspects of the subject matter, is often—and reasonably—reserved for those aspects of the subject which are completely amenable to scientific analysis. The term *political theory* could also be reserved as well for aspects of political thought amenable to scientific analysis. But readers of the following pages will discover that reserving the name political theory for this one aspect of the subject matter is contrary to both Sabine's and Catlin's designations; they use this term to cover the entire subject matter. The multiple current meanings of political theory range from a synonym for political philosophy to the designation of "if . . . then" propositions and formal model construction. It must be admitted, therefore, that *political science, political theory, political thought,* and *political philosophy* have not been used consistently in the same sense by all scholars of the subject field; use in different senses can be cited for each of them. Sometimes the three latter terms are used as synonyms; sometimes they are distinguished. One is reminded of the exchange between Alice and Humpty Dumpty in *Through the Looking-Glass:*

> "The question is," said Alice, "whether you *can* make words mean so many different things."
> "The question is," said Humpty Dumpty, "which is to be master— that's all."

Such mastery within a scholarly discipline entails either inefficiency or failure in communication. Short of consensus in usage, each writer must specify the meaning he intends for each of these terms or impose upon his reader the additional burden of ascertaining the intended meaning.

For two reasons *political thought* would seem to be the best term for encompassing all subject matter within the discipline's province. First, *thought* is a general term that can appropriately encompass the entire subject matter. Second, use of *political thought* for the whole makes possible reservation of political science and political philosophy for relatively unambiguous subcategories. *Political science* is the analysis of actual political behavior. *Political philosophy,* as Eckstein points out in his article below, differs from political science on at least three different bases: subject, scope, and criteria of validity. As to subject matter political philosophy is concerned not only with matters of fact (as is political science), but also with moral matters in the political dimension, such as questions of political ends. In addition, the subject matter of political philosophy includes metatheory, that is, the study of the language used by theorists, the methods employed, and the epistemological and metaphysical implications of particular theories. In short, metatheory is the comparative and evaluative study of theories. The scope of political philosophy is therefore greater than that of political science: it encompasses the attempts to construct comprehensive theories such as those of Locke, Marx, Bernstein, and others. Finally, the criteria of proof differ for political science and political philosophy. Political science emphasizes correspondence while political philosophy emphasizes consistency and the study of reasons (especially in moral theory). Therefore, it is proposed that the entire subject matter be called *political thought* and that this be subdivided into *political science* and *political philosophy* on the bases of subject, scope, and criteria of proof. Differentiating political science from political philosophy in this way is more adequate than the frequently-made distinction that the former deals with the is and the latter deals with the ought. This latter way of distinguishing deals with only one part of one of three bases for distinction—namely subject matter: it ignores both scope and criteria of validity.

There are two basic approaches for the determination of the nature of political thought. The first approach is to list the books traditionally acknowledged as belonging to the subject—for example, Plato's *Republic*, Aristotle's *Politics*, Machiavelli's *The Prince*, Hobbes's *Leviathan*, Hegel's *Philosophy of Right*, Hobhouse's *The Metaphysical Theory of the State*—and then to note the recurrent questions, problems, and approaches encountered in them. Such questions would include: What goods or ideals ought to be realized in or through the state? What is the meaning of freedom? Why should men obey the government at all? What is the province of government? What does democracy mean? How important is consent? What does equality mean? How do we go about determining the answers to these questions? An obvious limitation of this method is lack of agreement as to the acknowledged classics: do Marx's *Capital* and Weldon's *Vocabulary of Politics*[1] belong? Hence this approach does not necessarily lead to agreement in identification of the important matters.

The second approach assumes a general philosophical methodology and then applies it to political matters. It is advantageous in that the method can yield a consistent system—although undoubtedly a rash system—one productive of ardent adherents in yielding certain truths and sharply demarcating the area of political thought. Weldon's *Vocabulary of Politics* is such a book. Its disadvantages are typical of this approach: it buys consistency at the expense of richness. Almost without exception, many of the important matters of traditional political thought are necessarily omitted by the very methodology of the approach. Hence it is the opinion of the editors that the first approach is better for defining political thought. This involves culling from the acknowledged classics of political thought the central concepts, problems, methods, questions, and so on, supplementing this list with suggested important omissions in the classics. The list-plus-supplementation would constitute the subject matter of political thought. The items selected should then be arranged in a hierarchy from general principles

[1]T. D. Weldon, *The Vocabulary of Politics* (London: Penguin Books Ltd., 1953).

to specific ones on the basis of relative importance, thus providing a comprehensive, coherent, and general account of political thought.

That this approach to determining the subject matter of political thought is not above criticism has already been recognized here. Some would go farther in their criticism than we have here. Assuming agreement as to the list of acknowledged classics, they might still count the approach too deferential to tradition and seek a better justification for the determination of the subject matter than that it has been considered as such since time out of mind. That something is old, or even that it exists, they would say, affords no justification for its continuance: it remains necessary to distinguish between what is well-worn and what is outworn—and how are we to make this distinction? Also, to say that the list of central concepts, problems, methods, and questions, culled from the acknowledged classics of political thought should be supplemented by suggested important omissions in the classics is easy enough; but both the culling and the supplementation require judgment, if the result is to be a comprehensive, coherent, and general account of political thought. Part of that judgment is the capacity to recognize the boundaries of the subject field; but what criteria are to tell us when the account is comprehensive, coherent, and general? And what is to be comprehended? Principles cohere in the light of an overarching conception, and classification suits the purposes of the classifier: What are the particular purposes of political thought? What distinguishes the units of this subject field from the units of others? What is general to those units? The merit of such criticisms is evident. The point is, however, that the approach favored here is less fraught with risk than its alternatives.

It may be instructive to consider briefly some definitions that have been suggested in the past and the present indicating what is added to thought by the qualifying adjective *political*. Catlin makes the point that he is "content provisionally to use the word 'politics' as Aristotle used it. This includes the operations of the *polis* . . . , the structure of the family, the control of slaves, the morphology of revolutions and comments on . . . 'pure democracy.' . . . It includes national politics, municipal and international, patriarchy, 'ecclesiastical polity,' and the structure of trade unions and employee organizations. It is the business of the political theorist to consider all these things. . . ."[2] Catlin returns to Aristotle in an attempt, by considering the etymology and original meaning of the word politics, to remove some of the term's ambiguity. He contends that acceptance of the wider description of

[2]George E.G. Catlin, "Political Theory: What Is It?" *Political Science Quarterly*, LXXII (1: March, 1957), p. 3.

politics which is the classical one can "save us from being gripped by the dead hand of the seventeenth century and paralyzed by the totalitarianism of Leviathan or even by the false (and correlative) individualism of Hobbes. It will emancipate us from Bodin and the lawyers." Whether the hand of the seventeenth century is dead obviously can be considered and argued from various vantage points and whether we should be emancipated from Bodin and the lawyers is debatable.

Apart from these and other points that might be raised in rejoinder, it should be noted that not all would agree with conceptual boundaries that included something like the family control system or ecclesiastical polity in the political category. Some would contend that such a conception was so broad as to be meaningless—preclusive of discipline. Selection of a narrower conceptual framework would be preferable to such critics. But a narrower conception is no less subject to challenge. A few examples should suffice to demonstrate the difficulties of the approach.

The first example concerns the significance of *political* in the definitions of political science and political theory in an early dictionary of political terms. Political science is defined there as "a branch of the social sciences dealing with the theory, organization, government, and practice of the state" and political theory as "generally the entire body of doctrine relating to the origin, form, behavior, and purpose of the state."[3] That the exclusive use of *political* in reference to the state would be unsatisfactory to Catlin is obvious from the quotation above. Readers of his article will find that he considers "delimitation of the field . . . as 'study of the state' . . . unconsciously biased and prejudiced in terms of a nationalist *Zeitgeist*," as well as inadequate. The state conceived by present-day students of politics, moreover, is a modern phenomenon. Does this mean that politics did not exist prior to the modern period?

A second example sees politics as competition for power. In the words of a well-known scholar who advances this view, "international politics, like all politics, is a struggle for power."[4] At least the definition avoids the former example's identification with a static and abstract concept. Wherever and whenever the "struggle for power" occurs there is politics. But is the discipline restricted to the "struggle" for power? What of cooperative, even consensual, activity that is productive of power: is this not political? Heinz Eulau observes, moreover,

[3]Edward C. Smith and Arnold J. Zurcher, eds., A *Dictionary of American Politics* (Richmond, Virginia: Johnson Publishing Co., 1944), p. 238.
[4]Hans J. Morgenthau, *Politics among Nations: The Struggle for Power and Peace* (4th ed.; New York: Alfred A. Knopf, Inc., 1967), p. 25.

that "power, long accepted as the central organizing concept of politics," seems "rapidly losing ground from the point of view of its operational, if not analytical, utility. . . . For as it is used in empirical research, it proves increasingly useless."[5] The concept becomes more and more elusive in application.

A third exemplary definition is afforded in Easton's article on the systems analysis of politics, wherein the author distinguishes a political system as "those interactions through which values are authoritatively allocated for a society." Kress' article is a criticism of Easton's conceptual scheme that renders clear its difficulties in connection with the boundaries and units problems of the discipline.[6]

Enough has been said in these fragmentary criticisms of definitions based upon assumptions about the special characteristic of "political" institutions or behavior to indicate the risk inherent in the approach. Perhaps Professor Eulau is correct in his observation that "*political* seems to be a residual rather than a generic term." He thinks "this makes it futile to search for characteristic features of political behavior apart from an institutional or situational environment that shapes and patterns certain types of interpersonal relations."[7] This conception brings us full circle.

The classic articles on the nature of political thought are reproduced in this volume. In them leading scholars propound the views they consider most tenable. The views expressed in this introductory note should be set in the perspective of their various statements and judged critically by the reader.

[5]Heinz Eulau, *The Behavioral Persuasion in Politics* (New York: Random House, Inc., 1963), p. 29.

[6]See also Eulau, pp. 28–29, for a critical commentary upon the conception of politics as "authoritative allocation of values," indicating some of the conception's premises and "empirical referents."

[7]Eulau, p. 17.

1

George H. Sabine

WHAT IS
A POLITICAL THEORY?*

George H. Sabine answers the question What is a political theory? by reference to the history of political thought to ascertain its "salient characteristics." His essay has a twofold purpose: (1) enumeration of the "properties that political theories have actually had" and (2) consideration of "a variety of questions about the truth or validity of political theories." As a political theory is always advanced in "reference to a pretty specific situation," reconstruction of "the time, the place, and the circumstances in which it was produced" is essential to understanding it. But great political theorizing excels both in "analysis of a present situation and in suggestiveness for other situations." Professor Sabine finds that the typical political theory includes "factual statements about the posture of affairs that gave rise to it," statements of "what may be roughly called a causal nature," and statements that "something ought to happen or is the right and desirable thing to have happen." He thinks all three elements—the factual, the causal, and the valuational—are subject to the requirement of logical consistency but perceives no other common logical measure for their judgment.

Another criterion applicable to political theories is the adequacy of scope of the particular theory, a point that can be formulated in the question, Does the theory cover all the aspects it should cover to explain and justify what it purports to explain and justify?

*Reprinted by permission of the publisher from *Journal of Politics,* I (1: February, 1939), pp. 1–16.

Sabine notes further that theories "play a double role" in that they are of the abstract world of thought and simultaneously influential beliefs serving as causal events in historical situations.

Professor Sabine uses the term *political theory* to include both the conception advanced for it by the editors in the introduction to Part I and the conception there attributed to political philosophy, so that it is a synonym for *political thought* as it also was discussed there. He neither eschews the consideration of values nor limits his consideration thereof to the consequences for human behavior of acceptance of one value or another.

For many centuries the philosophy of Western Europe has included as one of its accustomed parts a study of the nature and well-being of civic societies, a kind of companion-piece to its study, in psychology and ethics, of the nature and well-being of the human individual. Like so much else in European philosophy, this interest in the political community was, at the beginning, a creature of Greek civilization. It began with that humanistic reaction, fostered by the Sophists and crystallized in the overpowering personality of Socrates, which so completely changed the course of Greek philosophy at the end of the fifth century before Christ. Political philosophy began in Athens at the same time with the birth of social studies, such as linguistics, the history and criticism of literature, the descriptive analysis of political and economic institutions, and a critical as distinguished from a merely narrative history. This humanistic relationship, which dominated philosophy for many centuries, was not dissolved even when the rise of the modern natural sciences in the seventeenth century restored subjects like physics and mathematics to a place of foremost interest in the minds of philosophical scholars. Perhaps marginal, in the sense that it has existed on the edges of the more precise and more technical disciplines, political philosophy has still maintained its standing as a subject of perennial philosophical concern.

It is usually unprofitable to argue, speculatively and *a priori,* about the form or the purposes that a branch of science or philosophy ought to have. The discussion of scientific methods, like any other discussion, needs a subject matter, and in the case of political philosophy, this must be provided by the history of the subject. The question, What is a political theory, ought to be answered descriptively, since in fact political philosophy *is* whatever philosophers have thought about civil society and called by that name. Evidently, any practicable description will not be complete, for in the course of history political philosophy has assumed many forms, has served many purposes, and has answered to many conceptions of scientific and philosophical reliability. Still, the subject has to some extent been a unit throughout its history, and some description of its salient characteristics is possible. But though the description must depend on history, the object of seeking such a description at all is not historical. A person who wants to know what a political philosophy is, if he is not an antiquarian, means to ask about its truth, its certainty, or its reliability, and about the kind of criticism that should be applied in order to test these qualities. Obviously these are not historical questions, for the occurrence of a theory says nothing whatever about its truth.

This essay, therefore, has a twofold purpose. In the first place, it will enumerate some of the properties that political theories have actually had. Though this involves selection and concentration on a few properties that have recurred frequently and that seem important, it is intended to be quite factual, depending upon the analysis of what have figured as political theories in the literature of philosophy. In the second place, however, it is the intention to keep in view a variety of questions about the truth or validity of political theories. How far can they be described as simply true or false? In what sense can words like *sound, true, valid, reliable* be applied to them? And finally, the practical question, by what kind of criticism can elements of truth in them be discriminated from elements of falsehood?

When one runs his eye over the historical literature that belongs traditionally to political philosophy, he is struck at once by the fact that this literature is not typically the product of the study or the laboratory. Even when it is produced by scholars, its authors have one eye fixed on the forum; and when political philosophy is produced in quantities, it is a sure symptom that society itself is going through a period of stress and strain. It is a remarkable fact that, in a history extending over nearly twenty-five hundred years, a considerable part of the most significant writing on political philosophy was done in two periods of only about fifty years each and in two places of quite restricted area. The first of these places was Athens, and the period was the two middle quarters of the fourth century before Christ, which saw the production of Plato's *Republic* and *Laws* and Aristotle's *Politics*. The second place was England, and the period was the half century between 1640 and 1690, which produced the works of Hobbes and Locke, together with the works of a host of lesser figures. Both these periods, it should be noted, witnessed changes of the most momentous importance in the course of European social and intellectual history. The first period saw the lapse of the Greek city from its place of cultural leadership—surely the major moral upheaval of the ancient world—and the preparation of that amalgam of Greek and Asiatic civilization which determined the whole future course of European culture. The second period saw the formation of the first constitutional state on national lines and the preparation of those intellectual and scientific changes that governed the Western World down at least until 1914.

These two cases are major examples of a quality in political philosophy which might be illustrated almost without end and which is indeed typical. Political theories are secreted, to paraphrase a famous comparison of substantive and procedural law, in the interstices of political and social crisis. They are produced, not indeed by the crisis as such, but by its reaction on minds that have the sensitivity and the intellectual penetration to be aware of crisis. Hence there is in every political theory a reference to a pretty specific situation, which needs to be grasped in order to understand what the philosopher is thinking about. Always he is thinking about something that has actually occurred and that has been the stimulus of his thought. To recover this situation and its power of intellectual stimulation may, if the theory belongs to a remote time and place, be a difficult task set to the historical imagination. But to reconstruct, as nearly as one can, the time, the place, and the circumstance in which it was produced is always an important factor in understanding a political philosophy. For it is one of the characteristics of such a philosophy that it occurs as a part of or an incident in politics itself. It is an element of the same intellectual and social life within which politics is another element.

It is true, of course, that this reference to a specific situation should not be overemphasized. Because a political theory refers to the historical occasion from which it originated, it need not be applicable to that alone. Political problems and situations are more or less alike from time to time and from place to place; what has been thought on one occasion is a factor in what is thought on another. For obvious reasons the political philosophy that remains alive is just that which can weave itself into the developing tradition of the subject. The greatest political theorizing is that which excels in both respects, in analysis of a present situation and in suggestiveness for other situations. Judged by this standard, Aristotle's *Politics* was probably the most important treatise on the subject that was ever written. Rarely has a form of government been subjected to a more penetrating examination than the Greek city received in the Fourth and Fifth Books of the *Politics;* probably never has a political treatise written in one age played so great a part in another as the *Politics* played in the fourteenth century, or again even in the nineteenth.

Since a political theory depends upon a special configuration of facts, it is to that extent turned toward the past. It is also, however, turned toward the future, for the kind of interest that produces political theory is in general quite different from that of an antiquarian. Characteristically political theories are bred of the interest that makes men want to do something about a situation which they believe to be bad. But even the most violently conservative theory—a theory directed to the merest preservation of the *status quo*—would still be directed, in the mind of its maker, toward the future, since a policy of doing nothing is still a policy. Quite regularly a political theory does contain or imply a policy. It commends some way of doing or criticizes some other; it defends or attacks what has been done and argues for the continuance or the reversal of a line of conduct. Examples might be multiplied at any length. Locke, as everyone knows, wrote "to establish the throne of our great restorer, our present King William," and to show the validity of representative government founded in the consent of the people. Quite regularly his version of natural rights served to consolidate the gains of successful revolution or to defend the legitimacy of revolutionary programs. With equal regularity the great opponent of Locke's theory, the theory of dynastic legitimacy or royal divine right, was used to commend the values of political stability and national unity, or to neutralize revolutionary propaganda. Very often, perhaps usually, political theories have had some sort of partisan bias, revolutionary, liberal, conservative, or reactionary. Even the most detached philosophies have grown from some interested reading of the facts, some estimate of what the facts signify for the future, and some concern with the way events should shape themselves.

There is, then, no such thing as a disinterested political theory, if that word be used to mean literally something that is bred of indifference. For those who are genuinely indifferent about the future do not take the trouble to make political theories, and those who do take that trouble usually care intensely about something. This attitude of regard for the future itself needs to be analyzed and divided. It always must include, either expressly or by implication, both a judgment about what is likely and a judgment about what is desirable. In short, a political theory includes an estimate of probabilities and an estimate of values. It can scarcely lack the former because any responsible attitude toward the future must take account of the possibilities, or, more accurately, the varying degrees of likelihood that belong to different projects for action, unless indeed a theorist is the complete doctrinaire. It certainly cannot lack the latter because any interested attitude toward the future involves preferences, choices, the sense of moral imperatives, the belief that one outcome is better than another. The word *policy* is quite meaningless without some assumptions about what is desirable or obligatory—however one chooses to name this act of evaluation.

A political theory, then, as thus far analyzed, covers three kinds of factors: it includes factual statements about the posture of affairs that gave rise to it; it contains statements of what may be roughly called a causal nature, to the effect that one kind of thing is more likely to happen, or may be more easily brought about, than another; and it contains statements that something ought to happen or is the right and desirable thing to have happen. This analysis, it will be perceived, follows pretty closely the description of reflective thinking given by the pragmatists, particularly by Professor Dewey and George H. Mead. The pragmatists, indeed, would generalize the description, asserting that the joint reference to past and future, and the joint reference to causes and values, are characteristic of every complete act of thought, whether about politics or anything else. Any theory, for the pragmatist, is a plan of action designed to adjust a tension between actually conflicting but potentially harmonizable needs, and this definition is defended on the still more general principle that no concept could be meaningful at all except as a factor in behavior. Whether this general psychological theory of thinking is true or not, the description is reasonably accurate so far as theories of politics are concerned.

Granting that political theories have characteristically contained factors of the three kinds mentioned—the factual, the causal, and the valuational —it still remains a question what logical relation holds between these three types of proposition. The pragmatist infers that because the three sometimes (or, as he thinks, always) occur in the same psychological situation, they must therefore be united in some logical form of synthesis. In other words, what he calls a complete act of thought claims to be complete in a logical as well as a psychological sense. The validity of this conclusion is the philosophical problem (or one current form of it) that this essay is meant to pose, because it appears to be a major issue in contemporary thought. The conclusion herein defended is that logically the three kinds of propositions are quite distinct; in short, that the likelihood of an event's happening and the desirability of its happening are quite without any logical correlation. And this conclusion implies a destructive criticism of pragmatism, in so far as pragmatism has claimed to be more than a chapter in social psychology. This general conclusion will be made a little clearer, and perhaps a little more convincing, in the latter part of the essay, but at present it will be better to finish describing a political theory.

The description so far given applies to what might be called the logical structure of a political theory, the elements in it that make propositions and that might, in consequence, be affirmed or denied. Very often, however—perhaps usually—political theories have, and are intended to have, psychological as well as logical effects. Because they deal with practical social issues and are created as incidents of conflict, they are intended to persuade as well as to convince. Even the most abstract political theory probably never altogether lays aside some such purpose, and even the coolest scholar can hardly be indifferent to the adoption of courses that he believes to be wise and good. In popular political theorizing the element of persuasion is usually very much in the foreground. When Thomas Jefferson wrote the famous second paragraph of the Declaration of Independence, he set down the main axioms of the philosophy of natural rights as a justification, to America and to the world, of the action that the Congress had already taken in voting a resolution that "these United Colonies are, and of right ought to be, free and independent states." Years afterward, when John Adams testily declared that there was not an idea in the document which was not a generally accepted commonplace, Jefferson very reasonably replied that he had not been deputed by the Congress to "invent new ideas." He was to state the case for Congress and the Colonies in a form that would carry conviction to all men of intelligence and good will. The doctrine that men have indefeasible rights and are justified in protecting them by armed resistance was persuasive just because it had a familiarity and an emotional warmth bred by centuries of belief.

The project of persuading, however, opens up larger possibilities than are immediately evident. In form at least, the Declaration of Independence, though certainly biased, was still essentially argumentative, possibly because it was addressed to an age in which the love of rationality was itself a major passion. But passion of any sort is inherently persuasive. It generates its own belief in the fulfillment of its own wishes and projects its own loves and hates into the perception of facts both past and future. If the object of a political theory were merely to generate belief, it would probably be a waste of time to spend much effort on either facts or arguments. The obvious—and, it must be acknowledged, the effective— short-cut is to generate the passions and supply them with the psychological apparatus of uncritical belief that perpetuates them and gives them effect. The part that political philosophy has been made to play in the modern dictatorships might be described as an elaborate experiment in applied psychiatry, and they show that this art is not only feasible but comparatively easy. One thinks at once of the part that the conception of race has played in recent German political writing. On scientific grounds no competent anthropologist for a moment takes seriously the idea that any European race is pure. Neither is it possible to believe that the persecution of the Jews resulted from any of the actual characteristics of that group in Germany, such as their greater prosperity or their alleged inability to think, feel, or act like other Germans. They were merely suitable—for emotional, not for actual reasons—to be cast in the role of national scapegoat. The ideal of racial purity has a strictly mystical significance. It serves as a symbol, and object of veneration, to solidify a party, to release its energies, and to foster that "more savage will to power" which Hitler has described as the key to national greatness. Race is a "myth," in the sense that Georges Sorel attached to that word.

In truth, however, it is not the dictatorships alone that have discovered what might be called the folklore of political philosophy. The Freudian psychologists, and indeed psychologists of many other schools, have explored the influence that interests, wishes, and desires exert upon belief and their tendency to produce "rationalizations" that can masquerade as valid theories. As a mode of attacking an opponent's position this sort of criticism has become a standard part of the modern controversialists' equipment, witness the prevalence of a word like "ideology" in our modern vocabulary of political criticism. There is no denying that partisan interests do generate partisan beliefs, and that partisan beliefs do claim the certainty of fact or the necessity of logic. Probably it is true that no man, whatever his honesty of purpose or his desire to be fair, can always weigh his own interests on an equal scale with interests that he dislikes or distrusts. But it is one thing to say that political theories have sometimes served the same purposes as folklore, and another to imply, as enthusiastic psychologists and sociologists sometimes seem to do, that they never serve any other purpose, or that a theory is nothing but a tactical manoeuvre in the class-struggle or in the national struggle for power. This game of ideological criticism permits of any number of players, and when the game is all played out and every view has been shown to be equally nonsensical, then the serious business of politics as thus conceived can begin, namely, breaking heads instead of answering arguments.

It is true, of course, that every political theory is a fact, a quite substantial fact that occurs in the gamut of facts that makes up a particular political situation. As such, it had its causes and may, no doubt, have its effects. Moreover, it has its effects whether it be true or false, because in either case it exists in a quite objective sense, as a thing that may affect men's conduct. It is always possible that men behave differently in any given situation, merely because they entertain some theory about their own existence and the situation in which they find themselves. This is a curious involution that occurs in all social theories and that has no precise analogue in the theories of natural science, unless it be in those cases, recently brought to light by the principle of indeterminism, where the mere fact of observation operates to change the very state of affairs which is under observation. Where this occurs, the natural scientist admits with all modesty that he has reached a limit beyond which he cannot conceive a refinement of his theory. And the social scientist must surely, in all intellectual honesty, do the same. In so far as theories figure as facts, standing in causal relations with other facts, and in so far as they appear as the data of human behavior which a theorist must himself count among the data of the situation that he is studying, they must of course be accepted as all data are, simply as elements of the reality studied. Their effects are in no way correlated with their truth, for even false theories may influence men's conduct. Their causal influence as existing facts is simply irrelevant to their truth or falsity. But in any given time and place one must make up his mind which language he elects to speak. If he accepts a theory as itself a *bona fide* effort to speak the truth, he must accord it that respect which belongs to such an effort. He must meet it on the plane of logic, must confirm or refute it on that level, by showing its consistency or inconsistency and its ability or inability to explain the facts. When he begins to discuss its influence, he puts it among existing things in the world of events and objects, and events are not themselves true or false; they simply occur.

An example will make the meaning clearer. A critic may deal in two quite different ways with the doctrine that Jefferson wrote into the Declaration of Independence. It is possible to discuss the validity of those propositions about inalienable and indefeasible natural rights, to apply a rational criticism to the assertion that all men are created equal, to analyze their meaning, to show how they agreed with a prevalent conception of scientific method, and to point out wherein they fall short of the self-evidence that Jefferson attributed to them. But such criticism is possible only so far as the critic is willing to discuss the factual truth or logical consistency of the theory examined. Quite apart from all such questions, however, it is still a fact that Jefferson and his fellow-members of the Continental Congress did believe in the theory of natural rights. It is quite possible that they would not have acted as they did had their beliefs been otherwise. It is credible that in so believing they may have been unconsciously the agents of a militant middle-class, intent upon rising to the political power that their economic importance warranted. If such causal influences swayed their action, it is of no consequence whatever whether what they believed was true or false. As Bishop Butler said, "Everything is what it is, and not another thing," and beliefs may have their effects however false they are. But surely no critic can apply both criteria at once. He may be concerned to assess the correctness of a doctrine, and if so its consequences are irrelevant; or he may be concerned with its actual effects and influences, and then its truth is irrelevant.

Political theories, therefore, live on two planes or play a double role. They are theories, or logical entities belonging to the abstract world of thought, but they are also beliefs, events in people's minds and factors in their conduct. In this latter role they are influential (if they are) not because they are true but because they are believed. On this plane they operate as events, or as actual factors in historical situations, and as such are part of the data which the historian of politics has to deal with. But this historical reality is obviously not what interests those persons who sincerely believe a theory to be true; such persons are not interested in a theory because it exists but because they believe it to be a valid explanation of something else. What the framers of the Declaration of Independence meant to do was "to declare the causes" that impelled them to dissolve the political bands which had connected the Colonies with England, an explanation required by "a decent respect to the opinions of mankind." In this they set down as a major premise the claim of indefeasible natural rights and as a minor premise a long list of aggressions, which they attributed to the King of England and interpreted as evidence of a settled determination to tyrannize. For them these claims were not merely beliefs; they were parts of what purported to be a correct statement of facts and a valid inference from them. A rational criticism, as distinguished from a study of historical causes, would have to take these claims as *bona fide,* even though it might end with the conclusion that they were utterly fallacious.

To return now to the beginning of this essay, it will be apparent that the questions there raised referred to the rational criticism of political theories, the question whether, or in what sense, they can claim the logical attributes of truth or validity. It will be remembered also that in the description there given of political theories it was said that they regularly unite two kinds of factors. In the first place, there are elements of a factual and causal nature: the apprehension of a state of affairs actually existing, an estimate of the relative importance of different factors in this situation, and a weighing of future possibilities. In the second place, there are elements of valuation: an estimation of importance, not in the sense of what is likely to happen, but of what ought to happen, the discrimination of a better from a worse way, the conviction that some courses of action are morally obligatory, an expression of choice or preference growing from an attitude of desire, or fear, or confidence toward what the present holds and what the future may bring forth. The question, then, is whether a theory uniting these two kinds of factors can be rationally judged to be true or false; in short, whether there is any common measure that can extend over and validate the theory as a whole.

Now the only absolutely general standard of rational criticism is the rule that a theory must not contain propositions that are mutually contradictory. A person who thinks about politics is under the same obligation to think consistently as one who thinks about any other subject, and to be convicted of an inconsistency is as damaging to a political theorist as to any other kind of theorist. Moreover, the standard of straight, coherent thinking is applicable both to thought which has facts for its subject-matter and to thought which has values for its subject-matter. A thinker can argue for mutually contradictory obligations as easily as he can attribute mutually incompatible properties to objects, and when he does the first he is as certainly wrong as when he does the second, for the avoidance of contradiction is a general principle that applies to all valid intellectual operations whatsoever. Nevertheless, the mere absence of contradiction cannot be regarded as equivalent to truth, except perhaps in pure logic and mathematics. For even if a theory were altogether self-consistent, there would still be the question whether what actually happens is the same as what the theory contemplates, and even if a theory of values were entirely coherent, there would still be the question whether the values which it contemplates are really acceptable as ends to be striven for and, if possible, attained. After making every admission possible to the binding-force of logical consistency, one must still agree that it goes only a little way toward validating a theory of any kind, whether in politics or any other subject.

If non-contradiction, though indispensable, is still not a sufficient principle of criticism, is there any other principle that can bridge the two kinds of propositions—allegations of fact and ascriptions of value—that occur together in every political theory? Apparently the answer must be, No. In combining these two kinds of factor a political theory puts together propositions for which there is no common logical measure and which all the dictates of clear thinking require to be distinguished. In so far as a political theory depends on the assertion, expressed or implied, that some state of the facts is so and so, the only test applicable to it consists in inquiring whether the facts really were as alleged or different. In so far as it presumes that one course of events is more likely to occur than another, it can be tested only in the light of the actual probabilities and perhaps in part by seeing whether the event seems to justify the expectation. In either case the assertion that an event has happened and the assertion that it ought to have happened are simply different and therefore ought not to be confused. And similarly, to say that a future event is probable is quite different from saying that it is desirable, or good, or the reverse. The two kinds of propositions are logically disparate in the sense that any statement containing such a copulative verb as "ought to be" requires the assumption of a standard of value which is never present as such in any purely actual situation or any purely causal sequence of events. When the two kinds of statement occur in conjunction, as they continually do in political theories, the beginning of critical judgment is analysis, the discrimination of the two kinds and the application to each of the tests appropriate to it.

Analysis and discrimination in this matter do not imply the superficial idea that political theories can be made "scientific" by the omission of references to moral and other forms of valuation. This idea usually depends not at all on discrimination of values as one element in a theory, but only on a simple-minded unconsciousness of valuations that have become habitual. It depends upon the kind of intellectual simplicity that Schopenhauer once attributed to an opponent: he imagined, Schopenhauer said, that whatever he had learned before he was fifteen years old was an innate principle of human reason. In truth it is humanly impossible even to describe a political or social situation without at least implicit assumptions about the importance of the elements that are to go into the description; the choice is between implicit assumptions and the explicit avowal of what is assumed. Moreover, there is no objection, at least on the score of logic, to making explicit assumptions about what is desirable; a policy or an end can be discussed as reasonably as anything else. It is probably not true even that men disagree more about values than they do about other matters. In any case there is no logical reason why a social philosopher should not postulate any value he chooses, provided only that he avows what he is doing and does not pretend to prove what he is merely taking for granted. What he cannot do logically (or even honestly, if he knows what he is doing) is to pass off his valuations as if they were inescapable facts.

The practical question, of course, remains, whether it is really possible to perform this act of analysis, at least so long as a political theory is still an element in a living situation. Looking back to the past one easily perceives how often men's judgment of facts is swayed by their interests or misled by the intensity of their moral convictions, but in one's own thinking it must be admitted that one does not, and probably cannot, always avoid the same kind of error. The common usages of language conspire to make such confusions. The most ordinary words, like *is* and *must be,* have regularly a twofold use, to signify indifferently logical or moral necessity, existence or predication, and the precise meaning must be gathered, if at all, from the context. Thus, to refer again to the Declaration of Independence, when Jefferson declared it to be "self-evident that all men are created equal," he may have thought that the proposition was analogous to the alleged self-evident propositions that stand on the opening pages of Euclid. In the light of an exact analysis of those propositions, however, no one can imagine that he was merely giving a rule for handling symbols. It is hardly likely that Jefferson thought that all men are as a matter of fact equal; certainly the moral effect of the sentence is spoiled if one takes it to be parallel with some literally true statement about the way men are created, such as, All men are created babies. As everyone knows, Jefferson was really expressing a moral conviction to the effect that, in some matters of vital human importance, it is wrong to deprive men of their freedom of choice. One may accept or reject this assertion, but he cannot intelligently do either unless he sees what is really intended. In a sense the inevitability of confusion or error is irrelevant, even if it is a fact. No one wholly avoids inconsistency, but inconsistency is an error just the same. If there is a confusion inherent in the conflation of facts and values, it is still a confusion even if the whole world conspires to do it. Of course, no one doubts that, in this as in other respects, men do think more clearly when they try resolutely to avoid confusion.

It would be altogether unfair, however, to imply that the coalescence of judgments of value with judgments of fact or of logical implication has only the standing of a frequent, but admitted, popular confusion. On the contrary this coalescence is undertaken systematically in certain philosophies which, together, cover a considerable part of current philosophical opinion. A representative of one of these views would enter an exception against the statement made above, that propositions stating facts and propositions ascribing values are logically disparate and would hold that it is possible to include both within a single logical synthesis. Historically this contention goes back to Hegel, who believed that the idea of a self-developing totality in logic could sublate the duality of rationalism and empiricism and refute at once the revolutionary doctrine of natural rights and the conventionalism or positivism implied by Hume's critique of natural rights. This was the purpose which Hegel thought that dialectic could fulfill. By means of dialectic he supposed it possible to show that certain values must emerge in the course of history and, conversely, that the causal processes of history are regulated by an inherent tendency to realize and conserve values. The dialectic was at once, therefore, a causal exploration and an immanent ethical criticism. However it may be formulated, the belief that some such dovetailing of value and fact is a soluble problem remains the best index of Hegel's influence over later philosophy. It continued to characterize the English Neo-Hegelians, and with all their differences it remains the fundamental claim of the Marxists, whose dialectical materialism is still in essence a claim that causal and moral necessity can be synthetized. In a milder form the purposes, if not the apparatus, of Hegel's dialectic perpetuated themselves in the pragmatism of Professor Dewey and Professor Mead, already referred to. For from the allegation that meanings can occur only in the fulfillment of purposes and that reflective thought is only a directive agency in behavior, it appears to follow that logical adequacy must include both factual efficiency and the fulfillment of purpose.

It would be silly to embark upon a thumb-nail refutation of Hegelianism, with all its ramifications, at the end of an essay already too long. The purpose has been to outline a problem and to suggest a type of solution but not to offer a refutation of other types of solution that have been attempted. Its intention has been to suggest that here is one of the systematic differences between philosophical points of view, rooted as such differences are likely to be in diverse theories of knowledge. Descriptively one finds in human thinking about a concrete problem—say the problem attacked by a political theory—what seems to be a variety of factors answering to a variety of critical standards. There are allegations of fact and cause; there are imputations of value or obligation; there are the consequences, for human behavior, of believing or disbelieving the theory. Now must it be the case that there is some criterion of truth large enough to stretch over all these factors in the problem? If some such criterion is proposed—say "coherence"—does it cover the ground because it affords a really applicable standard for all types of problem, or does it seem to do so merely because it is so vague and ambiguous that no one knows with certainty what it means? Or, on the other hand, is it possible that the drawing of distinctions is both the beginning and the end of wisdom? In short, is it possible that truth is a word with several different meanings and that no one can say what it means unless he is allowed to discriminate at least what Leibniz called truths of reason and truths of fact, and perhaps several other kinds beside? With this reference to Leibniz it will be well to stop. For it suggests the obvious line of criticism, namely, that this paper illustrates a kind of philosophic atavism, the nostalgia for clear and distinct ideas that was more typical of the seventeenth than of the nineteenth century.

2

George E. G. Catlin

POLITICAL THEORY: WHAT IS IT?*

George Catlin contends that politics, like Gaul, is divided into three parts: "from the *practice* of politics, at least in theory, we distinguish the *theory*. But the theory itself is divided into *political science* and *political philosophy*." He thinks that "more logical analysis in politics would be a good thing, attending to the precise use of words and relating these words, not first to metaphysical abstractions such as sovereignty, independence, liberty, democracy and socialism or capitalism, but to the objects of sensuous experience."

Politics should be conceived broadly, as Aristotle conceived it, to include the operations of the *polis*, of the family, of slaves, of revolutions, and of "pure democracy." Politics is national politics, municipal and international, patriarchal, ecclesiastical, and economical. In returning to this broad conception, the political theorist will be less likely to err.

Professor Catlin holds political science (the first of his three parts of political theory) "indistinguishable . . . on any intellectually respectable grounds from sociology" and maintains that the sociologists' study of "myriads of individual acts and thousands of relations between groups" affords the basis "for authentic comparisons and, in the best tradition of Aristotle and Machiavelli, for the observation of constants."

*Reprinted by permission of the publisher from *Political Science Quarterly*, LXXII (1: March, 1957), pp. 1–29.

Catlin directs our attention as political scientists to the *"phenomena of control* in its many forms, over all the processes of the whole social field" and suggests that the "unit" for our study be the *"act of control,"* that is, "acts of individuals." Moreover we must check "abstract schemata . . . by the amassment, through field work, of accurate facts." He considers the "quantitative approach to politics . . . important to professional progress as distinct from anecdote and rhetoric"; yet he warns that "collection of statistics of measurements, as it were for their own sake, can end in the sterile, trivial and misleading."

Catlin's second part of political theory is political philosophy, which he considers "a branch of ethics." Here the concern is with "ends or final values": when a man asks " 'What is for the national good?' or 'what is the good society?' he is asking questions in philosophy." Catlin perceives a close relationship between ethics and aesthetics: "It is noteworthy how many of our ethical adjectives of appraisal are also aesthetic." Catlin favors basing political philosophy "on judgments which are in their fundamentals or axioms aesthetic, whatever the rational or logical deductions, instead of upon anthropological mores and their ecological or historical relativism or upon ethical situationalism," in the conviction that this will be more likely to save us from the inhuman error of totalitarianism. It is obvious at this point that Catlin disagrees with both Sabine and Strauss, neither of whom would accept a theory ultimately basing political philosophy on aesthetic values. Yet Catlin is not alone among twentieth-century empiricists in this view.

1

The answer, in a brief space, to so large a question as "What Is Political Theory?" can only be sketched in broad outline. The purpose here is rather to challenge criticism than to end it, and to restate with emphasis the theme of a revolution in approach begun three decades ago, a revolution which can be said to have had as its keynote "taking political science seriously."[1]

The first and patent distinction in politics is between political theory and political action. The distinction is yet perhaps not quite so patent as some people suppose. It is questionable whether anyone is competent as a teacher in political theory who has taken no part in political practice, and this with a fairly wide perspective—any more than an economist is likely to be a safe guide in practice who knows nothing of the inside of a

[1]This paper was delivered as the Inaugural Lecture of the Bronman Professor of Political Science, McGill University, on October 22, 1956.

bank, a factory or a trade union. This does not, therefore, mean that he has to be a banker or manager, still less a partisan of labor or management. It does not mean that the act and direct experience are all. It does not mean, by analogy, that no surgeon should practice until he has had an operation performed on him. But we can agree with Lenin, following Marx, on the fusion of theory and practice. Graham Wallas, whose tradition I wish to exalt (since it has been perhaps too much forgotten where it should have most been commemorated), was probably right in stressing the value of practical experience, for example, in local government. Too many academic textbooks are indeed compiled from blue books, and are even misleading about what actually and particularly does happen. In the strong words of John Dewey, in his *Reconstruction of Philosophy,* "forbidden by conditions and held back by lack of courage from making their knowledge a factor in the determination of events," these exponents of the spectator theory "have sought a refuge of complacency." Conversely, in the words of a former President of Columbia University who is President of the United States, there is an untapped and unapplied "reservoir of knowledge."

Amid so many hysterical laments about "the end of civilization," it is yet the atomic scientist and not the supposedly constructive social scientist who remains in demand. When the public asks to have its problems answered "by a scientist," what is meant is usually a physicist, although his views here professionally may be of little more weight than any layman's. The so-called "great issues" are dealt with by rhetoric. Not only in popular parlance, but in assessing allocations from the budgets of governments for research, the term "scientists" means "the physical scientists," pure and impure. The others are felt to be concerned with speculation, description and anecdote. The atom-splitter and the orthodontist collect the fees.

Politics, like Gaul, is divided into three parts. From the *practice* of politics, at least in theory, we distinguish the theory. But the *theory* itself is divided into *political science* and *political philosophy.* Uncertain usage darkens counsel. Perhaps it does not matter what terms we adopt; but it does matter that the usage should be consistent.

The utmost caution is yet required, at the very beginning, in defining our "field" of politics, with which theory as a whole has to deal. There is the gravest risk that, explicitly or tacitly, we shall adopt a definition which will illicitly affect our conclusions. Given the character of the hat, we can know what rabbits can be first packed in and then brought out of it. Less logical positivism in philosophy and more logical analysis in politics would be a good thing, attending to the precise use of words and relating these words, not first to metaphysical abstractions such as sovereignty, independence, liberty, democracy and socialism or capitalism, but to the objects of sensuous experience. Let us attend to the actual activities and avoid what has been termed "metapolitics."

When the popular use of words is ambiguous it is prudent to turn back to etymology and origins. I am content provisionally to use the word "politics" as Aristotle used it. This includes the operations of the *polis* (which, as Professor Robert M. MacIver has stressed, is not "the Modern State"), the structure of the family, the control of slaves, the morphology of revolutions and comments on that "pure democracy" which, until Dr. Gallup, we had come to forget all about. It includes national politics, municipal and international, patriarchy, "ecclesiastical polity," and the structure of trade unions and employee organizations. It is the business of the political theorist to consider all these things and perhaps to reach startling and overlooked conclusions, and thus to keep his subject fresh. Genius (such as Rousseau had, who was otherwise a creature ill-educated, misleading, sentimental, confused and dishonest) consists in doing just this. The wider description, which is the classical one, will save us from being gripped by the dead hand of the seventeenth century and paralyzed by the totalitarianism of Leviathan or even by the false (and correlative) individualism of Hobbes. It will emancipate us from Bodin and the lawyers. Let us get back to Aristotle.

2

Political science, which is one part of political theory, is indistinguishable, in my view, on any intellectually respectible grounds from sociology. Academically, of course, they have been distinguished because the younger discipline (to this day unrepresented by any chair in some of Britain's ancient universities) was left with the unconsidered trifles of divorce, juvenile delinquency, collections of comic strips (as Professor David Riesman records) and talk of princes and propaganda, pressure groups and matriarchs and things. All that was really "dignified" was appropriated by political scientists, shaped in the schools of history and law. This, however, was merely an unhappy accident, like the bondage in Germany, illustrated by Professor Theodore Abel, of the sociologists to the philosophers. The preservation of this distinction of sociology and political science, at a time when some of the most fascinating developments in the sciences came from the border-line areas, has a sterilizing effect. The repudiation of this artificial distinction (a distinction recently remade in one great American university), as not neutral but actively pernicious for students, has certain healthy consequences. First, it directs the attention of the student to relations and structure of society as a whole, and rids him of the illusion that a particular form or organization of society, arising between the fifteenth and the seventeenth century in part of Europe and called the "modern state," is a form static, eternal, unalterable and worshipful. However, much contemporary political theory, not least that which has to do with the balance of power, is in fact still static and vitiated in this way. It repeatedly forgets that human society has innumerable forms, functionally distinguishable or historically succeeding each other, and that every human being is a member of many social organizations, not only the state or nation, no one of which is *perfecta* in the sense of being completely independent of the other functioning forms.

We are all practicing political pluralists; and the development of human choice and responsibility depends upon this social practice. Error arises from the tacit "axioms" and unexamined premises of political theorists. It arises from this too casual and uncritical delimitation of the field itself as "study of the state," which delimitation is unconsciously biased and prejudiced in terms of a nationalist *Zeitgeist*.

Secondly, the assimilation of fields brings into proper harmony the sociologists' and the politicists' general theory of society. At a recent faculty seminar in the University of Minnesota it was interesting to observe political scientists, when discussing laws, regularities of conduct and the formulation of constants, readily adducing in evidence the formulations of such a sociologist as Max Weber; nor can any political theorist worth his salt afford to remain ignorant of the work of Durkheim,[2] Pareto and Weber, or, indeed, of Talcott Parsons and Robert K. Merton. Thirdly, as Professor David Easton, in *The Political System,* has recently pointed out, the scientific handicap in the recently fashionable treatment of politics (I do not think that Bentham and the Utilitarians were guilty) is that it has become a matter of discussing cabinets and wars and treaties, so that the instances which the student has to observe comparatively are few and, even so, owing to distances of time, place and environment, not strictly comparable. There are only about eighty sovereign states to deal with as specimens or, again, if we follow Professors Toynbee and Teggart, between twenty-one and twenty-six separable "cultures." Occasionally the student is bedeviled, in terms of social organisms, by false analogies from biology, and the eighty sovereign states become eighty mammal Leviathans. Even comparisons of parties, so well conducted, for example, by Professor Maurice Duverger, who has supplied us, if not with laws, yet with rules, can become a field of false analogues in less masterly hands. The curse of politics, as of many

[2]See the writer's introduction to Durkheim's *Rules of Sociological Method* (1938, translation by S. A. Solovay and J. H.Mueller), and Durkheim's *Division du Travail Social,* translated by my friend and sometime student, Professor George Simpson.

ancient disciplines such as law, is that it has tended to be altogether too grand in treatment for its good, and to neglect the trivial and common detail of circumstance. A return to the Utilitarian modest outlook, before the neo-Hegelians took over, would be beneficial—a return to Sidgwick instead of Bosanquet, Bentham instead of Hegel and (as newest fashion) of Marx. Alternatively, attention is concentrated upon the mere description of institutions to the disregard of theory, the kind of thing that Lenin anathematized. Thanks to a false start, no progress is made. The sociologist, on the contrary, rightly takes for his study myriads of individual acts and thousands of relations between groups. Here are bases for authentic comparisons and, in the best tradition of Aristotle and Machiavelli, for the observation of constants. We might do well to get back yet further than Sidgwick, to Machiavelli, especially to the *Discorsi.*

Fourthly, it is the supreme virtue of the fusion of sociology and political science that it could enable us to be sharp-eyed for *the phenomena of control* in its many forms, over all the processes of the whole social field. Instead of a static description, whether comparative or not, of objects (and this exact Linnaean task is, of course, strictly necessary, but yet requires selection and direction, and not merely what it is the vogue to call "serendipity"), this new fusion points forward to detect a process and a function, in a dynamic field, going beyond mere schematic definition of limits. First is the control process; then the resulting systems and their specific functions; then the more detailed organization and institutionalization of these systems in history. We have to watch scrupulously and to state overtly what we are taking as the *unit* for study in our system or society. I suggest that it is the *act of control;* "the acts of individuals." As D.C. Somervell says, abridging Toynbee: "Society is a system of relations between individuals."

The doctrine of equilibrium, which has value as to ideal norms and which Professor Easton perhaps too flatteringly attributes to myself, needs to be used critically. The political norm or functional model is indeed the moving equilibrium of contentment—whether or not contentment is "a good thing"—and, as Pareto and Freud indicate, societies tend to revert, from disturbance, to tried equilibria in the political market. But, too easily, we can fall into a complacent Spencerian theory of "adjustment to social environment" (known or assumed), which could be even fascist and certainly cooperative in implication. Lionel Trilling has recently emphasized the dangers of this sociological heresy.

We can call politics, if we like (along with Professor V. O. Key), "the study of government," provided that we bear in mind that "government" here must be used merely as a synonym for "control," and carries no necessary implication of presidents and cabinets; that our theory has to cover the arguments of anarchism; and that we must beware of the fallacy of loaded terms and of packing into our definition an authoritarianism at the beginning which we hope, as I have said, to pull out of the hat at the end. We can also call it "the study of power and influence" if, with George Washington, we bear in mind that "influence is not government." "Politics," writes Max Weber in *Politik als Beruf*, "is the struggle for power or the influencing of those in power, and embraces the struggle between states as such and between organized groups within the state." (One of the most brilliant and original contributors in this field, Professor Harold D. Lasswell, also uses this word "influence.") But Weber's work, too long unnoticed and now perhaps by compensation overpraised, also includes a typological treatment by social rôles, as that of the King, of the Premier, of the Old Man, of the Housewife—maybe of the Premier as the Old Man! Sociologically, I regard this as dangerous ground. I am frank to say that I find this route leads to the *tief* and "squashy" as of a marsh, so that a man thinking he stands on firm ground finds that he sinks. It may be suited to *Geisteswissenschaft*. It may well be suggestive for the social historian, like "the sociology of knowledge" of Max Weber and Scheler, praised by Mannheim and properly criticized by Dr. K. R. Popper. But it lacks the precise edges of lucidity; and for the advancement of learning by clear lights may be substituted only the pale academic glow of a Weberian jack-o'-lantern.

Further, we can choose to say, with Parsons and Shils, that "political science" is concerned only with "a class of concrete phenomena" of government, without tarrying to analyze or define precisely what "government" may be. But this contention both is the precise opposite of that here urged and, in ordinary terminology, presents difficulties in seeing how Plato's *Republic* or Hobbes's *Leviathan* or Rousseau's *Social Contract* could, for the most part, be brought under the caption of "politics," which is here described as a matter of study of a subsidiary species of concrete phenomena. Of course, if it is suggested that all these social themes, so far as they are not proper to anthropologist, psychologist and historian, should be regarded as sociology, and the political scientists given a semi-honorable discharge as *defuncti officio*, this writer will have no objection. The difficulty, on the contrary, with some sociologists is that they are so modest and absorbed in detail as to be unhelpful. In all this I do not wish to criticize or even to seem to correct the careful definitions of the sociologists; but rather to put on the defensive the politcial scientists, and to suggest that most of them have become too content to allow the sociologists to do their work in general theory for them.

3

However, to note the relations between political theory and practice, or to say that he who professes the subject must be at once sociologist and political scientist, is not yet to define what we regard as *the field* of political science.[3] It has been outstandingly done by members of what I have elsewhere called the Chicago School, who here lead the world, especially the late Professor Charles E. Merriam and Professor Harold D. Lasswell (although today there seems to be a "Chicago School" of a markedly different temper, illustrated, for example, by the somewhat Treitschkean views of Professor Hans J. Morgenthau and by the anti-intellectualism of Professor Daniel Boorstin and, in his Walgreen Lecture, by Professor Eric Voegelin). Reference may be made to Professor Lasswell's *Psychopathology and Politics* (1930) and to Lord Russell's much later book, entitled *Power* (1938). Briefly and schematically, the field of political science is *the field of study of social controls,* or, more specifically, of the control relationship of human, and even animal, wills. (A study of ants gives us comparative notions on totalitarianism; that of apes can give us, without false analogy, notions of a society ruled by the dominant male; that of swallows ideas of an ordered and ritualistic anarchism as in a free dance; and that of rats and hens comparisons with the learning behavior and pecking system among men!)

Nothing can be nearer to the core of political studies, or of greater quotidian practical importance, than the observation of the conditions most suited to obedience to law. And yet a study of such a significant question as whether men obey with less resistance under a system of a few laws of general character, or under a multiplicity of detailed regulations, would probably be far better carried out by comparison of obedience to regulations in two factories (perhaps in different communities) or to traffic regulations or to local government by-laws, yielding a multiplicity of instances, than in the field of statute laws where, in two comparative communities, other factors will more readily enter in and the specimens be less numerous and less pure. We owe to Professor G. C. Homans' *The Human Group* numerous examples of detailed studies illustrating, by modest instances, our actual practices in obedience or disobedience to rules, of the highest normative interest alike to lawyer, student of industrial relations and political scientist. Likewise the study of groups need not necessarily be limited, as Professor David Truman points out,

[3]This the present writer is endeavoring to do in a longer study on Political Elements, a general theory of politics; but in some measure he also did it in work in 1927 and 1930 in *The Science and Method of Politics* (New York, 1926) and *The Principles of Politics* (New York, 1930), both of which it is hoped will be republished.

to civil groups. Distinguished work on the relation of the power structure and interest groups has been done by Professors Odegard, Herring and Truman, as it has been done in the more formal (although not always constitutionally recognized) case of parties, from Ostrogorski and Michels to Duverger. This work is all part of what the latest UNESCO *Report on the Teaching of Political Science* (1956) calls "politicization," that is, the extension of the approach by study of the distinctive political function of control, in areas other than civil dominion. This and the use of the power hypothesis are perhaps the two revolutionary changes in political science in the last thirty years—they have, in the words of the *Report,* "affected the *nature* of political science."

If we take a plunge into abstraction—both the abstraction which follows practice, of supposing that ends can be selected to the extent of disregarding discussion of alternatives, and the abstraction which selects certain behavior, as in *homo politicus,* as likely to be a schema of primary emphasis or interest for this study of means—then we do no more than does any other science. In the words of Professor Morris Cohen (perhaps with a slight overemphasis), "every branch of science aims to assume the norm of rational mechanics or geometry, in which we do not directly deal with the realm of existence but with the realm of validity." The abstract schemata must be checked by the amassment, through field work, of accurate facts. For example, such a socio-legal issue as prohibition could not be confronted until in lieu of moral generalities we broke up the problem and engaged upon a precise sociological analysis. The sole test is whether these abstractions or paradigms will be useful from the point of view of systematic understanding, insight and foresight.

The concept of political science as concerned with *means,* as distinct from political philosophy as concerned with *ends* (thereby clarifying, by the distinction, what it is that theorists may be talking about) I have not developed here.[4] Precisely, we are not so much concerned with the historical "person" in his embarrassing individual riches, or with the abstract person or "actor *qua* actor," but with the "act." The unit of political science is the individual act of control. The only danger will be the quite reprehensible one of certain economists, and especially of certain tract-writing divines among the classical economists, that we may confuse the abstract schemata, the abstractions of the subject, with Natural Law, and then confound this in turn with moral imperatives. Professor Durkheim's sociological hypotheses or laws were sometimes fitted into the secularist educational propaganda of the Third French Republic; but I would not suppose that sociologists and political scientists

[4]I have touched on this in my article in the *Western Political Quarterly,* for December 1956.

(called by Sir John Seeley "politicists") in general would be so foolish. A hypothesis is a hypothesis, and an abstract definition is an abstract definition. The test is interpretative utility.

No science (and we shall later discuss whether we should say "no philosophy") is much interested in its own past errors. What matters is the contemporary situation of the discipline; and how far it has evolved that systematic general theory, or what Lasswell and Kaplan call "conceptual framework," which is one of the best indications of scientific maturity, and which is far removed from preoccupation with institutional anecdote or with political pamphleteering and such rhetoric.

4

We have here sought to provide a general definition of the field of political science, and have broken down certain otiose barriers and ancient obstructions. But a definition, even if of a dynamic process and not of static skeletons—that "politics is the study of the control relationship of wills" ("persons" would be too historically rich a term not to be misleading and even Carlylean, as well as obscuring the activities of groups)—is itself static and dead. It indicates to us *where* to look, but not *for what* to look. If the field is to come to life and if great progress, as with Adam Smith and Ricardo, or even with Marx, is to be made, we require certain vitalizing and, I may say, "lucky" hypotheses, often put forward almost arbitrarily and wilfully, looking at the data from the angle of "as if." We have to see patterns in the wallpaper which were there all the time; which no one had seen before; but which no one can fail to see again. We need sudden flashlights. On the other hand, we need the humility to recognize that the hypothesis is only a hypothesis and not a dogma; that there are no "single causes" or simple explanatory keys to the whole matter; and that when the secondary laws become altogether too complex to reconcile in experience with the primary law, we shall have to find some new broader hypothesis, as Henri Poincaré said, scientifically to cover the whole.

The hypotheses with which I personally have worked I do not propose to develop or to discuss at length here. Professor Thomas I. Cook, of Johns Hopkins, in the UNESCO survey has described my approach as "postulational" or hypothetical, and that of Professor Lasswell as "psychological." He has also elsewhere designated us both as "the dead-end kids" of contemporary political theory.[5] On the other hand, an eminent Canadian colleague has averred that I have earned the damning appellation of "the

---

[5] He was, however, elsewhere good enough to refer to us as "founding fathers."

contemporary Machiavelli." I confess that I do not know which of these appellations to accept. Maybe Machiavelli himself was also "a dead-end kid." I also would not venture to provide a defense of Professor Lasswell's position because he is far more competent than I to do that himself. It may be that he is less patently "psychological" and Freudian in his later works than in his former.

I have from the beginning always been unashamedly "psychological" in the sense of Graham Wallas and James Bryce, although I would be the first to admit that the doctrines of the Freudians and Adlerians today are modified from what was so confidently asserted thirty years ago (and even that the Master changed and saturninely ate his own offspring, Freud adding Adler's "power-lust," now called "death-instinct," to his own plain lust). The days when, as it has been said, the psychoanalysts were excitedly sniffing like hounds at the trunk of the Tree of Knowledge are now long ago. And so it was really perhaps wiser to proceed by hypothesis than by any one psychological school, although perhaps the "hypothesis" was an egg no fuller of meat than was the direct study, by Lasswell, of *Psychopathology and Politics*. What is at least true is that my hypothesis was much the same as the theme of Professors Merriam and Lasswell, who were among "the founding fathers" (although of a restatement and renaissance), which so much preceded the popularization by Bertrand Russell, in *Power,* but of which some germs were yet in Lord Russell's *A.B.C. of Bolshevism.* It sought to advance systematically (while paying appropriate homage) beyond mere Hobbesian guesswork and pseudo-geometry to the empiric test and prediction.

The theory was that, as stated by Lasswell, "political science is the study of the sharing and shaping of power"—or, as I would say, "of the phenomena of control, with the provisional hypothesis of some basic but ill-understood urge to power as a determinant." It is within the strict limits of hypothesis in the process of testing that we may properly refer to politics as the science of power. In the early days this doctrine, which theory has now attained its quarter century or jubilee, was a very suspect, heretical and unpopular one. Today the number of books on politics bearing the word "power" in their title has become almost fantastic, so that the thesis, at this level of popular usage, may be alleged to have vindicated itself. Rather today what may be required is, not a denial of the proposition, but a much closer analysis of what is meant by "power" than has, in all cases, been undertaken. It may be that major species of the urge to power are neurotic and can be allayed, without the stability of social control being lost or even diminished. The view that all politics is power politics, as well as the reaction against the moral views of Archbishop Fénelon and of Lord Acton, in his famous letter to Bishop

Creighton, that "power is poison" and that "power tends to corrupt," has passed from novelty to platitude and from platitude to distortion. In the sequence stated by Dean Inge, first men said it was impossible or untrue; then that it was immoral; and then that they themselves had said it all along.

The power theory of politics operates, it must be insisted, as a hypothesis about *homo politicus,* not as a dogma about political means. It may be that, if the facts of control are sustained by a widespread, although not universal, urge to control, some species of this urge are pathological rather than normally psychological. We must not expose the theory to the criticism made by Bishop Butler on Hobbes, that words were distorted so as to enable power to explain everything. Unlike the Marxian materialist or economic explanation of history (if indeed this is, as I think, the substantial Marxian position), it is not uni-causal. There are many factors at work. It is a hypothesis built upon the fusion between the theory of Hobbes (and, in part, Machiavelli) and the clinical experience of Adler, and of Freud in some phases. It is encouraged by the early attempts of Aristotle to propound a science of revolutions. So far as I personally am concerned, the work of A. F. Bentley, with his protest against what is now called "metapolitics," entered into the development not at all. I had not read his work, except most casually, or appreciated his weight. The hypothesis must be judged by its utility in illuminating the field on the assumption of certain major factors, and by showing up certain primary constants. It will have to be modified as our psychological knowledge develops. Clearly the theory of the power-urge does not directly cover the psychological behaviors of "withdrawal" and "passivity," in so far as these are not mere tactical pretenses; but it can assume that actors adopting these behaviors do not shape the political scene, but are material moved about upon it—or are even persons in flight from responsibility, at the best negatively influential by tending to *anomie.* These can be persons desirous only of being controlled or of escaping from this whole web of responsibilities, as well as persons constructively seeking to maintain rational and confidence-giving controls, as distinct from neurotic and distrustful controls or Caliban resistances. Max Weber indeed insists that the problem is of the study of "leadership." Very different yet is behavior (such as the Gandhian) which seeks to master the situation by conduct which involves a subtler, although very ancient, interpretation of the meaning of power.

It is one thing to take as our field all that conduct and functioning concerned with control of one man over another, or of the group over the individual, or of group over group—and, although these configurations may be dissimilar in attitude, they are not so dissimilar as to lack psychological continuity in explanation (or moral continuity). Upon these controls or stable order all social organization rests, and to ensure them institutional organizations came into being. "The characteristic act of 'power politics' may be defined as an activity that builds, consolidates and keeps in being aggregates of men," writes Bertrand de Jouvenel in a recent suggestive little essay in the *Cambridge Journal*. It is another, and further, thing to suggest that these controls arise from the normal demands of human beings, even in seeking their own fuller liberty, and do not simply come into being because society has to impose them, as a kind of mechanism or artifact of civilization, upon the unspoiled nature of instinctive or nobly savage man—although the anarchists and some passages in the works of Rousseau and of Condorcet may support this belief. If so many institutions, statecraft, priestcraft and the rest, are corrupting and evil, how then, we may ask, did they spring from a human nature so entirely good? And Freud (here like Hobbes), in reply, can point out to us that these controls arise, not because of some artificial social or legal "institutions" of authority, as external as Hume supposed, but because human nature not only requires but, despite schizophrenic revolts of which Freud speaks in *Civilization and Its Discontents*, even demands these controls.

This proposition, moreover, does not spring from the arbitrary or abstract delimitation of a field by prima facie inspection, but is a hypothesis debatable and needing empiric test. The linked relation of the dual polar demands for freedom and for authority is, indeed, the *fons et origo* of political science and, as such, comparable to the linked relations in economics of demand, supply and competitive price. The superficially paradoxical relation sets a problem for which, by one hypothesis or another, we have to offer to the politician indications of some scientifically satisfactory and practically tolerable solution of predictive use. That "internal freedom to fulfil demand in a society varies, *ceteris paribus,* inversely with external pressure" seems to me to be one of those observations, perhaps as commonplace as the laws of physics, which yet remains, on my analysis, the statement of a constant and the formulation of a *law,* not isolated but logically coherent with our general theory. A corollary would be that when the need for protection against external pressure is removed, the suppression of internal freedom produces (as in Poland) an unbalance, chemically explosive and impossible to be maintained except by direct force. Even the law of gravitation itself merely states a tendency,. circumstantially confuted in particular cases, as is shown by the fact that we debate these issues where we do, and not in the center of the earth or, as yet, in the focal hell of the sun's interior. It is not my view that what I would choose to call this "law of inverse ratio" is so superficially based upon human nature as to be merely a statistical statement of frequent accident or a kind of useful gadget which happens to hold true under particular conditions of the *faits socials*, as in the case of certain working rules, such as the so-called "law of the cube" in party elections. Moreover, it has the closest practical bearing upon the evolution of tyranny. Any dullard or defeatist can, of course, say that along these lines we have not got very far. The question rather is: What has he done to get us farther?

5

The Power Theory I am content to have developed, and to hope to continue to develop, elsewhere. What I am concerned more to do now is to utter a warning against what seem to me to be certain dangerous abuses or misunderstandings of it. In a preface to *World in a Trance*, by a distinguished German writer, Dr. Leopold Schwarzschild, Professor Denis Brogan wrote: "Power, military power, is as important in world history as it has ever been, and it has not been and it will not be abolished by pious opinions, by sermons and resolutions," of the kind upon which George Kennan has commented at length as too characteristic of the American tradition and scene. This was well said and I am sure that, by it, Professor Brogan did not propose to identify power with military power. A more ambiguous passage is to be found in *American Strategy in World Politics* by the late Professor Nicholas J. Spykman, of Yale. He writes: "International society is a society without a central authority to perceive law and order, and without an official agency to protect its members in the enjoyment of their rights. The result is that individual states must make the preservation and improvement of their power position a primary objective of their foreign policy." This kind of power, which is to be "improved" or enlarged, is here becoming identified with that peculiar species of control, or of the power position, which we may call "dominance." It is a point upon which Machiavelli himself uttered certain warnings.

We may note, at this juncture, the views of another eminent writer whose opinions are, in many respects, consonant with the well-known and traditional German philosophy of the historian, von Treitschke, as expressed in his *Politics*. Here we have almost the antithesis of the sentimental and irresponsible rhetoric, designed to please an electorate which is content merely to regard wars as a species of accident, disturbing, expensive and foolish, a rhetoric condemned so downrightly by George Kennan. We have the antithesis of contentment with a United Nations which is "not even a like-minded club," as an alleged executive organ to enforce peace. I refer to the work of Professor Hans J. Morgenthau, with which I must confess to finding myself pretty markedly in disagreement. Professor Morgenthau, indeed, quite properly deplores what he terms "the state of political thought of our time" (1952). But I would submit that this is not to be remedied by a common confusion (of which the practical consequences will not be the less grave because they are common) between the genus "power" and the species "domination" or dominative power. Even, of all people, Hobbes, with his distinction between government by conquest and government by compact—which howbeit he did not, like Dante, carry through to its logical conclusion in sovereignty in the international sphere—was more circumspect.

In his *Politics Among Nations* (1948) Professor Morgenthau admirably writes: "The natural purpose of all scientific undertakings is to discover the forces underlying social phenomena and how they operate. . . . Social forces are the product of human nature in action." (Likewise John Plamenatz, of Nuffield College, Oxford, says: "This does not of course mean that there are no sociological laws. Social phenomena are to be studied like any other part of the natural world"—an area "still tainted with philosophy.") Morgenthau also says: "International politics, like all politics, is a struggle for power. Whatever the ultimate aims of international politics, power is always the immediate aim." (He would not agree with a certain Member of Parliament for the Ince division of Lancashire, England, who said that "Mr. Nehru does not play at power politics.") Many of us indeed feel that America's reluctance to confront the responsible problem of power, which involves great costs, may end in military defeat; and that her quixotic and unconditional destruction of the balance of power and undue, illusionary building up of the power of the Russian dictatorship, in the later years of the Second World War, were a crime against democracy and herself. So far we may agree with what seems to be Professor Morgenthau's position. But how far, from the nature of the case, he is able sympathetically to enter into the distinctively American tradition is something which could merit further comment.

In his earlier *Scientific Man vs. Power Politics* (1947) Professor Morgenthau is even more explicit.

This re-examination [of the Western tradition] must start with the assumption that power-politics, rooted in this lust for power which is common to all men, is for this reason inseparable from social life itself. In order to eliminate from the political sphere not power politics—which is beyond the ability of any political philosopher or system—but the destructiveness of power politics, rational faculties are needed which are different from, and superior to, the reason of the scientific age. . . . Contemptuous of power politics and incapable of the statesmanship which alone is able to master it, the age has tried to make politics a science. By doing so, it has demonstrated its intellectual confusion, moral blindness, and political decay.

Certain passages here recall the important but ambiguous *Das Dämonie der Macht* (1940) of Professor Gerhard Ritter, of Freiburg. As remedy for the deplorable situation, Professor Morgenthau forthwith volunteers to write a book (that under discussion) which will "lift a veil from a truth"—perhaps relative, since he has underwritten the credit of historical relativity in truth—"once known," and "do for theory and, in the long run, for the practice of politics all that a book can do." Few can say fairer than that.

The present writer would submit that, properly understood, political science need be no such exercise in "scientific humanism" or "rationalism" as Professor Morgenthau supposes; and further that, properly analyzed, cooperation may also be a form of power, perhaps more subtle and difficult to construct, but also more stable than domination—although in ethics we may have to add that this cooperation, if it· is to be in any valuable way preferable to domination, ought to be around certain principles, and not merely from the "desire to be liked." Nor must it be based upon masochism or lack of animal energy. But that it can be effective power in its own right—power to assure control both of consent in divers degrees within the group as well as by dominative power outside it—seems patent, and involves certain consequences limiting the undisciplined lust for domination, springing from fear and distrust. This important theme, however, which involves major syntheses of thought, cannot be further developed here. Once the theory here has been matured, it will be practical to start work on the collection of relevant data—for example, in criminology, how far do we find a power structure set up, to protect themselves, in trades or professions by "brigands retired from business," and become respectable? How far is this historically true of the conduct of nations?

Within the field of political science, properly so called, one additional remark can appropriately be made here. In my *Principles* (1930) I endeavored to outline the concept of *a political market*. So far as useful, in constructing the political scheme, I indicated the analogous techniques of the so-successful methodological development of the sister science of economics. Professors Talcott Parsons and E. Shils have indeed recently spoken in terms, which they describe as economic, of "allocation," primarily on a psychological level; Professor George C. Homans, in *The Human Group,* has done the same; and Professor Sir Ernest Barker, in his latest works, has used the pattern of the market politically, but rather by way of analogy. However Parsons and Shils speak, strictly and not by analogy, of "making allocations [of facilities and rewards] among sectors of the population, most of whose claims"—they add in an optimistic sense, forgetting Hobbes's warning about the desire, without surcease, "for power after power until they be dead"—"will not too greatly exceed what they are receiving. Without a solution of this problem there can be no social system." Out of this problem of the market I developed the doctrine of a moving equilibrium, upon which Professor Easton comments and to which I have already referred, yielding pragmatic contentment as an optimum, and itself providing as in economics a norm, not in the sense of a moral imperative, but of a schematic ideal and recurrent tendency.

The mechanism of the market arises from the basic fact that every man wants as much fulfilment or gratification of his own will as he can, and would prefer both "to eat his cake and keep it," to have political goods and services without cost; but that freedom, rigidly defined,[6] and authority, although not contradictory, are complementarily balanced. To secure the freedom that, for particular gratification, I want, I have in turn to give support, which must have its costs, to the relevant authority. In brief, I cannot eat my cake and keep it: I am confronted (and even sovereign peoples are confronted) by the law of political choice. Balance is achieved when a man is getting, in the scheme of social controls, just as much as he can expect without feeling he is paying too much for it. The problem is, of course, simplified when there is that kind of "agreement on fundamentals" which the Marxists, for example, deny in existing society; and when culturally we have educationally "built in" the kind of desire, will and demand for which the social gratifications can readily be supplied by a benevolent and obliging authority. But this raises a subsidiary issue of education, and of what Walter Lippmann calls a "public philosophy" about expectations and rôles. Today too often "we don't know what to expect"; but the market goes on.

It may be objected that this schema, comparable to that of economics, is "only a method of talking," of linguistic style; and this is patently true when we use such terms as "market," "costs" and the like. However, although to avoid the multiplication of jargon our terms of description may be economic, the processes of exchange and covenant stand in their own right, asking for description. The terminology, whether economic or legal, is justified if it illuminates and serves in the analysis of the process.

Moreover, there is a practical justification. If, as free traders, we look at

[6]"Freedom," which I agree with Professor K. J. Scott also includes moral "license," must be sharply distinguished from "liberty within the law" which, authorized and approved, may carry those ethical overtones of "dignity" which M. de Jouvenel, in "A Discussion of Freedom," demands.

the higgling of the market without alarm, employers bidding against trade unions for legislation, and political parties offering their competitive legislative wares like Sears, Roebuck or Marshall Field catalogues to the elector-consumer, we are less likely to get into a frenzy of pseudo principles about the whole matter. We are more likely to take a detached and tolerant view, amid the party and national propaganda, of the objective claims which in fact have got to be met, in any given age (whatever we may personally think about them) owing to the quantitatively assessable volume of demand. We should rather expect to find political cycles, from stress upon liberty to stress upon security or authority, and back. Here is a school for diplomats. Incidentally, when we come to measure "volume of demand," we approximate to that quantitative approach to politics which, without going as far as Lord Kelvin's words— "only that is knowledge which can be weighed and measured"—in the famous inscription in Chicago University, is yet so wise and important to professional progress as distinct from anecdote and rhetoric. I would, however, warn that the collection of statistics of measurements, as it were for their own sake, can end in the sterile, trivial and misleading.

6

This leads us to a further point, where we can pass across the border from political science to political philosophy. How far is there not only a pragmatic chaffering on the political market, striking various balances of power between individuals, groups and nations, if not an ideal equilibrium of contentment? How far is there also a rational quality of "just price" and of proper demand, volume apart, which if gratified could lead to a contentment that some hold has the character of being almost a moral imperative, end or goal—and, conversely, which if ungratified leads to assured discontent and to social "dysphoria" and ill-health? This is the issue of Natural Law and is, of course, an entire theme in itself. It is, however, noteworthy that such a publicist as Walter Lippmann has an obvious nostalgia for Natural Law as a basis for his public philosophy"; that it has been the consistent contention of the Papacy and Catholic scholars; and that such a professional lawyer as Professor H. Lauterpacht, of Cambridge and now of the Permanent Court, has pointed to it as the required basis for a jurisprudence underlying all positive law. Recent jurisprudence has been befuddled by a school, lately fashionable in America, which, in the last resort, as Mr. Justice Holmes cynically pointed out, reduces the bases of law to the question "who can kill whom?" My personal position is that this age desperately needs a revival of Natural Law.

Properly stated, *the theory of Natural Law is not only defensible but essential,* and is the meeting ground between law and fundamental politics, sociology and, I would add, psychology. But it is important not to misunderstand what is implied. The subjectivism and wishful idealism, the notion of "natural rights" spattered around as from a metaphysical pepper pot, which did service for Natural Law from after Aquinas, or from the Reformation, to John Austin or later, must be dismissed. It is true that, in so far as the human being is a creature exercising choice, of latent powers and creative gifts, the Natural Law operative in the relevant segment of conduct must be rational and ethical, according to objective rules. Here the Catholic position stands. There are, however, vast segments of human conduct which depend upon the demands of the physiological system or of the psyche, conducting itself according to recognizable rules of behavior. These rules can be stated. They are empiric and can be tested; and with increasing medical and psychological knowledge we can know more about them.

This is not, as with Stammler, a matter of "natural law with changeable content," save so far as patently circumstances alter cases; but of development of knowledge about detail. We can, of course, defy these rules, constants of reaction or laws, if we choose—and here we are considering a far older concept of law than the statute law of jumped-up modern sovereign states. But, as with the law of gravitation for a man who leaps over a precipice, so here, if we break them, inevitably we pay the penalty. The formula for π remains π, whatever a legislator from Texas, according to the legend, may suggest it would more conveniently be, leaving out the decimal points and as enacted by the sovereign authority of Texas. Pavlov tells us that the impulse to freedom is indeed an instinct, because its total repression results in death. I owe to my old friend James Maxton, Clydeside M.P., the illustration that a Glasgow by-law which prohibits children playing in the streets when no playground provision is made, since it is of the nature and good health of children to play, is bad law, *nulla et vana.* Positive law with its instant sanctions aspires to be the *simulacrum* and implementation in detail of natural law with its final sanctions. The laws of political science are but the formulation of constants in social relations—formulations which, in so far as they are abstractions, are not to be confounded with natural law (an error made by some economists), but which, where they are adequate formulations of what happens, are identical with it. Thus, so far as we may choose to regard them as prudential commands, they can be broken at will. But the penalty will be paid. Positive law may, of course, formulate much else, which can even be quite effective, but has no sociological foundation in the constants of human nature. And, in reply to a criticism of what I have written, made by Dr. K. R. Popper, in *The Open Society and Its Enemies*,[7] I would say that this rational law is natural and indeed "naturalistic," in the sense of susceptible to empiric tests. But, as in medicine, those who think—as they need not—that there is any ethical imperative to keep healthy will observe this law as *also* a moral rule or moral norm.

7

The second great field or division of political theory is political philosophy. If I may quote Dr. Albert Schweitzer, "Intoxicated as I was with the delight of dealing with realities which could be determined with exactitude, I was far from any inclination to undervalue the humanities as others in a similar position often did." Just as I have suggested that political science is theoretically indistinguishable from sociology (unless maybe we identify the latter with anthropology), so I hold that political (and legal) philosophy is merely a part of the seamless robe of philosophy. It is Philosophy speaking with a social emphasis. Although I totally disagree, for the reasons already stated, with the dictum of Harold J. Laski, a great pamphleteer, that "Politics is a branch of Ethics," I entirely concur that Political Philosophy is this. Indeed Political Philosophy is more closely allied with Ethics in its content than Ethics is with either Logic or Ontology, which are traditionally regarded as parts of Philosophy. And for this reason, since I do not wish to involve myself here in a sweeping discussion of Philosophy, my remarks will be terse, even at the risk of seeming dogmatic. Actually they will be, not dogmatic, but highly speculative. Our concern here, as I have said earlier, is with the kingdom of ends or final values, with its instant practical bearing upon our policy in education. I would add that practical men would be ill advised to conclude that, if agreement cannot be reached here, the subject is unimportant. So soon as a man begins to ask, "what is for the national good?" or "what is the good society?," he is asking questions in philosophy. And, even if we cannot and will not all agree (although I understand that Professor Julian Huxley holds that we ultimately will), at least there is value in being able to state our own views lucidly; in educating ourselves out of a picayune provincialism; and in not arguing in favor of a self-contradictory position, unless we do so consciously because we hold the law of contradiction to be irrelevant.

I would begin by submitting the view, maintained in almost gnomic fashion by Wittgenstein, that "ethics is aesthetics." The view that the aesthetics, for example of the drama, must be an aesthetics only of

[7]Vol. I, pp. 208–209.

contemplation and not of the will and *action* and that, in turn, we never contemplatively judge ethical fitness seems to me incapable of being sustained. I am sure that Wittgenstein did not mean, and I do not, that one should judge moral actions as if they were the smell of a rose, or any such "aestheticism" or "pretty-pretty." I do not think that even John Dewey, with his instrumental view of ethics, instrumental to success and progress, would have so supposed. What presumably was meant was that what Albrecht Ritschl called "value-judgments" and aesthetic judgments are both of the same genus, despite Ritschl's own view to the contrary. These judgments, I submit, are not solely subjective, but are based upon some objective condition which human beings as such agree to call beautiful. It is noteworthy how many of our ethical adjectives of appraisal are also aesthetic. I am prepared to be told even that this common quality of the aesthetic judgment, as in the relation of music to the mathematics of sound waves, has some correlation to the physio-electric functioning of the human brain and its harmonies. It is a field of which we know little and which offers an immense area for early and revolutionary exploration. There is, of course, in the history of art a vast record, equal to that of anthropology itself, of the eccentric variations of human taste. Nevertheless there is something called the beautiful, either in contemplation or action. In terms of it we directly and *individually* appraise disinterestedly even such a humdrum matter as duty. But there is also a canon of beauty about which people may be *educated;* and this has recently been stated by authors as dissimilar as the unorthodox Miss Gertrude Stein and the academic Sir Kenneth Clark. It is those who are recognized masters in art who form an Areopagus of taste. Students in philosophy who are looking for a new approach might be well advised to study that adopted from Shaftesbury to Schiller and Goethe, and from Hutcheson and Schelling to A. J. Balfour and Malraux. Actually theologians have been more appreciative of this route than philosophers, the Platonists apart.

Whatever may be the scarlet errors of the Existentialists, they will yet save us from the totalitarian monstrosity of supposing values to be based upon a built-in valuational system corresponding with "the social expectances" of the Joneses, with Big Brother enshrined within our own heads as the Super-Ego. The basing of ethics on judgments which are in their fundamentals or axioms aesthetic, whatever the rational or logical deductions, instead of upon anthropological mores and their ecological or historical relativism or upon ethical situationalism, is even more likely than Existentialism to be free from this inhuman error. This error can reduce the "respect for personality," about which we talk so much, to "our orientation towards another's 'orientation of action' towards the socially convenient and effectively functioning organization"—functioning, like rats, for survival or for gratification in ends unknown. I submit that this is a travesty of sound philosophy, despite my sincere respect for some of the scientists who have chosen this path. Inspecting the bath water, they have omitted to notice the baby. For the followers, however, of Durkheim who, for political reasons (if I may change metaphors), found Heaven in a sociological skyward projection of the unhappy Third Republic of France, an opiate for discontent found in a new secular and sociological religion of scientific humanism, it comes much too easy.

If my general philosophical approach is conceded, which could give us aesthetic absolutes, then certain consequences will follow. These values move on their own plane and are not to be confused with the important schema of positivist political science preoccupied with control-as-a-means and power (a positivism which yet is properly limited in historical application by its own abstractions and mechanical models). Elsewhere we can discuss whether power itself—for example, collective power for the human race to reach the stars—may not be far from ethically neutral as means, but actually valuable as collective end, and to be admired—in some measure. (It raised the nice theological point whether the omnipotence of God is part of the virtue of God.) We can appeal, as the Roman lawyers traditionally did in their quest for norms, to reason and instinct. But logic will lead us back to its own presuppositions or axioms—here, as we assert, aesthetic—which are not themselves consequences of logic. And instinct provides too limited guidance in so much of the casuistry and actual moral behavior of life.

There is, however, besides "reason and instinct," a third criterion of our ethical judgments. We have referred to certain aesthetic perceptions which, in the admirable words of the Stoics, "seize us with conviction as by the hair of the head." But there is also an Areopagus of judgment and education about these individual convictions, which save them from becoming crude, culturally unintegrated and provincial. The word "culture," it will be noted, has an ambiguous meaning—as when we speak of "an aboriginal culture" and when we speak (in almost a precisely opposite sense) of a "cultured person." *This third and corrective criterion is to be found in history,* but in history of a certain kind. History, which has no end of itself, may yet display a record of human evaluations. This is sharply different from regarding history as a philosophic saga of success, speaking by examples. I owe to my old and revered tutor, Professor Sir Ernest Barker, one of the best expositions of it in a recent book, his *Traditions of Civility,* where he did briefly what I endeavored to do at much greater length, in what was intended as a modest philosophy of history and values.[8] While allowing for what is rather pretentiously called the "sociology of knowledge," in this case the modest influence of the biography of the thinkers upon their thought and the difficulty of interpreting their scholastic thought and abstract errors without acquaintance with their living emotions and concealed prejudices, I was primarily concerned whether there were not a continuous main stream of human judgment of values, what I called a *Grand Tradition of Values*. The merit of the work of Sir Ernest Barker is that, picking up the best in Burke and avoiding the error of making Burke merely "patriotic," local, provincial and unexportable (as some now try to do), he ascended to the heights of a full humanism and not a secular humanism. We approximate to the great spirit of Goethe (who provided, through Wilhelm von Humboldt, some of the best insights of J. S. Mill), and even perceive how we can reach to yet more catholic and oecumenic heights.

8

Does it, then, follow that we arrive at what is called "a public philosophy?" I can only reply in the words of a certain Warden of New College, Oxford, Dr. Archibald Spooner, a great humanist but a poor mathematician, who, being asked as a student how he had done in a geometry examination, replied: "I don't think I *proved* anything, but I rendered it very probable." In other words, in the necessary conditions of human ignorance, we cannot, in my view (as distinct from Dr. Huxley's), and must not expect uniform human agreement on any philosophy of ends and values. Such agreement, as the great Dr. Rashdall once said, will "depend upon whether there is an Inquisition or not." The compensation is that, whereas in heaven indeed ideally, with omniscience, we should have no need for freedom which then becomes a "perfect service," here we enjoy the pleasures of choice and error. But educated men can commend, like Bishop Butler, to the public a tradition as "very probable." And, although there is the healthy right to disagree and even be a sectary, *haereses opportet esse*, it is those who disagree who have the intellectual duty to inform their consciences and to give reasons for divergence. Societies can be expected to move along the broad lines.

 I should state that I find myself in almost total disagreement with what Archibald MacLeish calls "the American Proposition," which I suspect may, by contrasuggestion, have stimulated Mr. Lippmann into writing his

---

[8]My *History of the Political Philosophers*, a necessary counterpart, and third volume in a trilogy, to my earlier methodological and scientific work.

Public Philosophy. Naturally I do not agree that this American Proposition is indeed such, and is not merely Mr. MacLeish's Proposition, which is to the effect that men are not only free to think for themselves, are right to have thoughts on their own—Hobbes said no one could prevent that—but also "to believe as they think and to say as they believe . . . and to do as they say." The conclusion of this could be, not only that in a free country everybody is entitled to express his own opinion (as the saying is, "to shoot his mouth," short of obscenity) but also that—and this is, I suggest, the trend of Mr. MacLeish's argument—reversing the basic, prudent views of the Liberals about our "educated democracy," everybody is entitled to decide what is sound or convenient in education, and responsibly to respect no one man's views more than another's. Facts and opinions become "all born equal and democratic." This is contrary to common sense. Mathematics, for example, is not democratic; within its framework its conclusions hold firm whatever the vote may be. Opinions are not born free and equal, and sixty million Frenchmen or even six million Scotsmen can be wrong. What we can say is that, in judgments of taste and value, uniformity is improbable and, in a developing world, not even in totality desirable. I suppose the philosophical position sketched here, as much as those of Hume and Pascal and Newman, can be called conservative and (in some measure) skeptical. I am not sure that I would accept either description as adequate for what is a form of traditional humanism; but this cannot be argued here. It is more important to add that even such a conservative philosophy can be revolutionary, and that, for example, pure democracy, as understood from Aristotle to Rousseau, seems to me perhaps to involve the welcoming of a perpetual plebiscitary system, referred to by Renan and of which the apostle is Dr. Gallup, maybe operating in a world of very small states or cantons (the true benefactors of civilization) joined into very large regions, but which is scarcely discussed by politicians today, so preoccupied with the national power state.

Two last points. It is, I submit, implicit in what I have said that the rôle of the educator or teacher, endeavoring to instill a public philosophy, is an advisory and not an imposed rôle—just as parents today have learned not to impose marriage partners on their children but to be content to advise. We would rather be without élites holding the secular sword; but this does not mean that divine right lies automatically in the majority or that we have no need for instruction. To put the matter differently, I find myself in agreement with what I understand to be now the major contention of Professor Arnold Toynbee, that societies evolve, by virtue of the power of ideas; and that our own civilization is likely to evolve into a social form, of the administration of things (not of the reduction to objects of men by them) and of the cohesion of those of common values, more comparable—as also Augustine said—to a church than to a state, which latter has the *vis coactiva* as its distinctive characteristic and hallmark, stamped by the domination of men. Such a true community of values could, at least in some or other living form, persist whether under a totalitarian or under an individualistic and morally nihilistic or secularly indifferentist governmental régime, seeking to operate on it just as Greece, or Christianity, tutored Rome. However, such a community could not flower save in a culture unchilled by force and united in power-guarded freedom from tyranny.

Further, I wish to put on record my respect for the work of the late Professor Ernst Cassirer, especially in his *Essay on Man.* It is not enough to do as I have done, and to endeavor to state a tradition of values only in terms of the history of ideas, even if it be of what Plato called the architectonic ones. The tradition of values is expressed more broadly in folk customs and, perhaps most richly of all, in the art forms, the drama and indeed, as with the Greeks, the sacred drama of civilizations. Professor G. C. Homans has also remarked on this rôle of religion. Here the culture comes symbolically to a focal point, and a social culture which is poor here is psychologically poor indeed. Sometimes, of course, this folk drama and symbolism does not transcend the province or nation. It is a vast triumph of the human spirit when it does, and passes into some catholic world-order. It is noteworthy how, in Dr. Ruth Benedict's description, the Amerindians of the Northwest are nurtured in an aggressive and dominative psychology, which is written large in their culture. The matter is of more than local interest since, in some measure, the West and, certainly, both the Marxists and their *frères ennemies,* the capitalists of the period of that classical economy in which Marx was nurtured, conditioned and indeed "dated," suffered from a markedly aggressive and dominative psychology and culture. On the other hand, as Dr. Benedict pointed out, the pacific Pueblo Indian, without being unauthoritative, diverted his energies into a daily and everyday dramatic *ritus* and ritual which kept him busy, cooperative and peaceful. But to explore the consequences of these reflections would carry us well beyond the boundaries of a philosophy merely political, and of political theory, and must be left to other occasions.

3

Leo Strauss

WHAT IS
POLITICAL PHILOSOPHY?*

Leo Strauss, in the tradition of the classical political philosophy of
Plato and Aristotle, contends that political thought can not eschew
values, that a "value-free" political science is impossible. Even in determining the meaning of the word *political* one must refer to purpose and
in his statement of the purpose that is distinctively political he establishes a standard for the judgment of political actions and institutions.
Also, political philosophy is part of a larger whole: philosophy, or the
"quest for wisdom," that is, the "quest for universal knowledge, for
knowledge of the whole." As such, political philosophy is "the attempt
truly to know both the nature of political things and the right, or the
good, political order." Political thought must extend both to what was
termed political theory ("the attempt truly to know . . . the nature of
political things") and to what was termed political philosophy ("the
attempt truly to know . . . the right, or the good, political order") in
the introductory note of Part I. In sum, the one is inconceivable apart
from the other: "generally speaking, it is impossible to understand
thought or action or work without evaluating it."

*Reprinted by permission of the author and publisher from *Journal of Pol-
itics,* XIX (3: August, 1957), pp. 343–68. This is a revised version of a
portion of the Judah L. Magnes Lectures which were delivered at the Hebrew
University in Jerusalem in December, 1954, and January, 1955. A Hebrew
translation with English summary of this version appeared in *Iyyun,* April,
1955.

Professor Strauss answers the question, What is political philosophy? in terms of the consequences of adopting one or another alternative conception, specifically in the light of the inadequacies of "social science positivism" and of "historicism" (the latter being in his view "the serious antagonist of political philosophy"), and through recapitulation and extension of the "classical political philosophy." Differing from Sabine in that he bases his position much more upon Plato and Aristotle, he also disagrees with Catlin's sociological and aesthetically grounded political thought.

THE PROBLEM OF POLITICAL PHILOSOPHY

The meaning of political philosophy and its meaningful character are as evident today as they have been since the time when political philosophy first made its appearance in Athens. All political action aims at either preservation or change. When desiring to preserve, we wish to prevent a change to the worse; when desiring to change, we wish to bring about something better. All political action is, then, guided by some thought of better or worse. But thought of better or worse implies thought of the good. The awareness of the good which guides all our actions, has the character of opinion: it is no longer questioned but, on reflection, it proves to be questionable. The very fact that we can question it, directs us towards such a thought of the good as is no longer questionable—towards a thought which is no longer opinion but knowledge. All political action has then in itself a directedness towards knowledge of the good: of the good life, or the good society. For the good society is the complete political good.

If this directedness becomes explicit, if men make it their explicit goal to acquire knowledge of the good life and of the good society, political philosophy emerges. By calling this pursuit political philosophy, we imply that it forms a part of a larger whole: of philosophy. Since political philosophy is a branch of philosophy, even the most provisional explanation of what political philosophy is, cannot dispense with an explanation, however provisional, of what philosophy is. Philosophy, as quest for wisdom, is quest for universal knowledge, for knowledge of the whole. The quest would not be necessary if such knowledge were immediately available. The absence of knowledge of the whole does not mean, however, that men do not have thoughts about the whole: philosophy is necessarily preceded by opinions about the whole. It is, therefore, the attempt to replace opinions about the whole by knowledge of the whole. Instead of "the whole" philosophers also say "all things"; the whole is not a pure ether or an unrelieved darkness in which one cannot distinguish one part from the other, or in which one cannot discern anything. A quest for knowledge of "all things" means quest for knowledge of God, the world, and man—or rather quest for knowledge of the natures of all things: the natures in their totality are "the whole."

Philosophy is essentially not possession of the truth, but quest for the truth. The distinctive trait of the philosopher is that "he knows that he knows nothing," and that his insight into our ignorance concerning the most important things induces him to strive with all his power for knowledge. He would cease to be a philosopher by evading the questions concerning those things or by disregarding them because they cannot be answered. It may be that as regards the possible answers to these questions, the pros and cons will always be in a more or less even balance, and, therefore, the stage of discussion or disputation will never reach the stage of decision. This would not make philosophy futile. For the clear grasp of a fundamental question requires understanding of the nature of the subject matter with which the question is concerned. Genuine knowledge of a fundamental question, thorough understanding of it, is better than blindness to it, or indifference to it, be that indifference or blindness accompanied by knowledge of the answers to a vast number of peripheral or ephemeral questions or not. *Minimum quod potest haberi de cognitione rerum altissimarum, desiderabilius est quam certissima cognitio quae habetur de minimis rebus.* (Thomas Aquinas, *Summa Theologica, I,* qu. 1 a.5.)

Of philosophy thus understood, political philosophy is a branch. Political philosophy will then be the attempt to replace opinion about the nature of political things by knowledge of the nature of political things. Political things are by their nature subject to approval and disapproval, to choice and rejection, to praise and blame. It is of their essence not to be neutral but to raise a claim to men's obedience, allegiance, decision or judgment. One does not understand them as what they are, as political things, if one does not take seriously their explicit or implicit claim to be judged in terms of goodness or badness, of justice or injustice, *i.e.,* if one does not measure them by some standard of goodness or justice. To judge soundly one must know the true standards. If political philosophy wishes to do justice to its subject matter, it must strive for genuine knowledge of these standards. Political philosophy is the attempt truly to know both the nature of political things and the right, or the good, political order.

All knowledge of political things implies assumptions concerning the nature of political things, *i.e.,* assumptions which concern not merely the given political situation but political life or human life as such. One cannot know anything about a war going on at a given time without having some notion, however dim and hazy, of war as such and its place within human life as such. One cannot see a policeman as a policeman without having made an assumption about law and government as such. The assumptions concerning the nature of political things, which are implied in all knowledge of political things, have the character of opinions. It is only when these assumptions are made the theme of critical and coherent analysis that a philosophic or scientific approach to politics emerges.

The cognitive status of political knowledge is not different from that of the knowledge possessed by the shepherd, the husband, the general, or the cook. Yet the pursuits of these types of man do not give rise to pastoral, marital, military, or culinary philosophy because their ultimate goals are sufficiently clear and unambiguous. The ultimate political goal, on the other hand, urgently calls for coherent reflection. The goal of the general is victory, whereas the goal of the statesman is the common good. What victory means is not essentially controversial, but the meaning of the common good is essentially controversial. The ambiguity of the political goal is due to its comprehensive character. Thus the temptation arises to deny, or to evade, the comprehensive character of politics and to treat politics as one compartment among many. This temptation must be resisted if we are to face our situation as human beings, *i.e.*, the whole situation.

Political philosophy as we have tried to circumscribe it, has been cultivated since its beginnings almost without any interruption until a relatively short time ago. Today, political philosophy is in a state of decay and perhaps of putrefaction, if it has not vanished altogether. Not only is there complete disagreement regarding its subject matter, its methods, and its function; its very possibility in any form has become questionable. The only point regarding which academic teachers of political science still agree, concerns the usefulness of studying the history of political philosophy. As regards the philosophers, it is sufficient to contrast the work of the four greatest philosophers of the last forty years—Bergson, Whitehead, Husserl, and Heidegger—with the work of Hermann Cohen in order to see how rapidly and thoroughly political philosophy has become discredited. We may describe the present situation as follows. Originally political philosophy was identical with political science, and it was the all-embracing study of human affairs. Today, we find it cut into pieces which behave as if they were parts of a worm. In the first place, one has applied the distinction between philosophy and science to the study of human affairs, and accordingly one makes a distinction between a non-philosophical political science and a non-scientific political philosophy, a distinction which under present conditions takes away all dignity, all honesty from political philosophy. Furthermore, large segments of what formerly belonged to political philosophy or political science have become emancipated under the names of economics, sociology, and social psychology. The pitiable rump for which honest social scientists do not care is left as prey to philosophers of history and to people who amuse themselves more than others with professions of faith. We hardly exaggerate when we say that today political philosophy does not exist anymore, except as matter for burial, *i.e.*, for historical research, or else as a theme of weak and unconvincing protestations.

If we inquire into the reasons for this great change, we receive these answers: political philosophy is unscientific, or it is unhistorical, or it is both. Science and History, those two great powers of the modern world, have eventually succeeded in destroying the very possibility of political philosophy.

The rejection of political philosophy as unscientific is characteristic of present-day positivism. Positivism is no longer what it desired to be when Auguste Comte originated it. It still agrees with Comte by maintaining that modern science is the highest form of knowledge, precisely because it aims no longer, as theology and metaphysics did, at absolute knowledge of the Why, but only at relative knowledge of the How. But after having been modified by utilitarianism, evolutionism, and neo-Kantianism, it has abandoned completely Comte's hope that a social science modeled on modern natural science would be able to overcome the intellectual anarchy of modern society. In about the last decade of the nineteenth century, social science positivism reached its final form by realizing, or decreeing that there is a fundamental difference between facts and values, and that only factual judgments are within the competence of science: scientific social science is incompetent to pronounce value judgments, and must avoid value judgments altogether. As for the meaning of the term "value" in statements of this kind, we can hardly say more than that "values" mean both things preferred and principles of preference.

A discussion of the tenets of social science positivism is today indispensable for explaining the meaning, of political philosophy. We must reconsider especially the practical consequences of this positivism. Positivistic social science is "value-free" or "ethically neutral": it is neutral in the conflict between good and evil, however good and evil may be understood. This means that the ground which is common to all social scientists, the ground on which they carry on their investigations and discussions, can only be reached through a process of emancipation from moral judgments, or of abstracting from moral judgments: moral obtuseness is the necessary condition for scientific analysis. For to the extent to which we are not yet completely insensitive to moral distinctions, we are forced to make value judgments. The habit of looking at social or human phenomena without making value judgments has a corroding influence on any preferences. The more serious we are as social scientists, the more completely we develop within ourselves a state of indifference to any goal, or of aimlessness and drifting, a state which may be called nihilism. The social scientist is not immune to preferences; his activity is a constant fight against the preferences he has as a human being and a citizen and which threaten to overcome his scientific detachment. He derives the power to counteract these dangerous influences by his dedication to one and only one value—to truth. But according to his principles, truth is not a value which it is necessary to choose: one may reject it as well as choose it. The scientist as scientist must indeed have chosen it. But neither scientists nor science are simply necessary. Social science cannot pronounce on the question of whether social science itself is good. It is then compelled to teach that society can with equal right and with equal reason favor social science as well as suppress it as disturbing, subversive, corrosive, nihilistic. But strangely enough we find social scientists very anxious to "sell" social science, *i.e.*, to prove that social science is necessary. They will argue as follows. Regardless of what our preferences or ends may be, we wish to achieve our ends; to achieve our ends, we must know what means are conducive to our ends; but adequate knowledge of the means conducive to any social ends is the sole function of social science and only of social science; hence social science is necessary for any society or any social movement; social science is then simply necessary; it is a value from every point of view. But once we grant this we are seriously tempted to wonder if there are not a few other things which must be values from every point of view or for every thinking human being. To avoid this inconvenience the social scientist will scorn all considerations of public relations or of private advancement, and take refuge in the virtuous contention that he does not know, but merely believes that quest for truth is good: other men may believe with equal right that quest for truth is bad. But what does he mean by this contention? Either he makes a distinction between noble and ignoble objectives or he refuses to make such a distinction. If he makes a distinction between noble and ignoble objectives he will say there is a variety of noble objectives or of ideals, and that there is no ideal which is compatible with all other ideals: if one chooses truth as one's ideal, one necessarily rejects other ideals; this being the case, there cannot be a necessity, an evident necessity for noble men to choose truth in preference to other ideals. But as long as the social scientist speaks of ideals, and thus makes a distinction between noble and not noble objectives, or between idealistic integrity and petty egoism, he makes a value judgment which according to his fundamental contention is, as such, no longer necessary. He must then say that it is as legitimate to make the pursuit of safety, income, deference, one's sole aim in life, as it is to make the quest for truth one's chief aim. He thus lays himself open to the suspicion that his activity as a social scientist serves no other purpose than to increase his safety, his income, and his prestige, or that his competence as a social scientist is a skill which he is prepared to sell to the highest bidder. Honest citizens will begin to wonder whether such a man can be trusted, or whether he can be loyal, especially since he must maintain that it is as defensible to choose loyalty as one's value as it is to reject it. In a word, he will get entangled in the predicament which leads to the downfall of Thrasymachus and his taming by Socrates in the first book of Plato's *Republic*.

It goes without saying that while our social scientist may be confused, he is very far from being disloyal and from lacking integrity. His assertion that integrity and quest for truth are values which one can with equal right choose or reject is a mere movement of his lips and his tongue, to which nothing corresponds in his heart or mind. I have never met any scientific social scientist who, apart from being dedicated to truth and integrity, was not also whole-heartedly devoted to democracy. When he says that democracy is a value which is not evidently superior to the opposite value, he does not mean that he is impressed by the alternative which he rejects, or that his heart or his mind are torn between alternatives which in themselves are equally attractive. His "ethical neutrality" is so far from being nihilism or a road to nihilism that it is not more than an alibi for thoughtlessness and vulgarity: by saying that democracy and truth are values, he says in effect that one does not have to think about the reasons why these things are good, and that he may bow as well as anyone else to the values that are adopted and respected by his society. Social science positivism fosters not so much nihilism as conformism and philistinism.

It is not necessary to enter here and now into a discussion of the theoretical weaknesses of social science positivism. It suffices to allude to the considerations which speak decisively against this school.

1. It is impossible to study social phenomena, *i.e.*, all important social phenomena, without making value judgments. A man who sees no reason for not despising people whose horizon is limited to their consumption of food and their digestion may be a tolerable econometrist; he cannot say anything relevant about the character of human society. A man who refuses to distinguish between great statesmen, mediocrities, and insane imposters may be a good bibliographer; he cannot say anything relevant about politics and political history. A man who cannot distinguish between a profound religious thought and a languishing superstition may be

a good statistician; he cannot say anything relevant about the sociology of religion. Generally speaking, it is impossible to understand thought or action or work without evaluating it. If we are unable to evaluate adequately, as we very frequently are, we have not yet succeeded in understanding adequately. The value judgments which are forbidden to enter through the front door of political science, sociology or economics, enter these disciplines through the back door; they come from that annex of present day social science which is called psychopathology. Social scientists see themselves compelled to speak of unbalanced, neurotic, maladjusted people. But these value judgments are distinguished from those used by the great historians, not by greater clarity or certainty, but merely by their poverty: a slick operator is as well adjusted as, he may be better adjusted than, a good man or a good citizen. Finally, we must not overlook the invisible value judgments which are concealed from undiscerning eyes but nevertheless most effective in allegedly purely descriptive concepts. For example, when social scientists distinguish between democratic and authoritarian habits or types of human beings, what they call "authoritarian" is in all cases known to me a caricature of everything of which they, as good democrats of a certain kind, disapprove. Or when they speak of three principles of legitimacy, rational, traditional, and charismatic, their very expression "routinization of charisma" betrays a Protestant or liberal preference which no conservative Jew and no Catholic would accept: in the light of the notion of "routinization of charisma," the genesis of the Halakah out of Biblical prophecy on the one hand, and the genesis of the Catholic Church out of the New Testament teaching necessarily appear as cases of "routinization of charisma." If the objection should be made that value judgments are indeed inevitable in social science but have a merely conditional character, I would reply as follows: are the conditions in question not necessarily fulfilled when we are interested in social phenomena? Must the social scientist not necessarily make the assumption that a healthy social life in this world is good, just as medicine necessarily makes the assumption that health and a healthy long life are good? And also are not all factual assertions based on conditions, or assumptions, which however do not become questionable as long as we deal with facts *qua* facts (*e.g.*, that there are "facts," that events have causes)?

The impossibility of a "value-free" political science can be shown most simply as follows. Political science presupposes a distinction between political things and things which are not political; it presupposes therefore some answer to the question "what is political?" In order to be truly scientific, political science would have to raise this question and to answer it explicitly and adequately. But it is impossible to define the political, *i.e.,* that which is related in a relevant way to the *polis,* the "country" or the "state," without answering the question of what constitutes this kind of society. Now, a society cannot be defined without reference to its purpose. The most well known attempt to define "the state" without regard to its purpose, admittedly led to a definition which was derived from "the modern type of state" and which is fully applicable only to that type; it was an attempt to define the modern state without having first defined the state. But by defining the state, or rather civil society, with reference to its purpose, one admits a standard in the light of which one must judge political actions and institutions: the purpose of civil society necessarily functions as a standard for judging of civil societies.

2. The rejection of value judgments is based on the assumption that the conflicts between different values or value-systems are essentially insoluble for human reason. But this assumption, while generally taken to be sufficiently established, has never been proven. Its proof would require an effort of the magnitude of that which went into the conception and elaboration of the *Critique of Pure Reason;* it would require a comprehensive critique of evaluating reason. What we find in fact are sketchy observations which pretend to prove that this or that specific value conflict is insoluble. It is prudent to grant that there are value conflicts which cannot in fact be settled by human reason. But if we cannot decide which of two mountains whose peaks are hidden by clouds is higher than the other, cannot we decide that a mountain is higher than a molehill? If we cannot decide regarding a war between two neighboring nations, which have been fighting each other for centuries, whose nation's cause is more just, cannot we decide that Jezebel's action against Naboth was inexcusable? The greatest representative of social science positivism, Max Weber, has postulated the insolubility of all value conflicts, because his soul craved a universe, in which failure, that bastard of forceful sinning accompanied by still more forceful faith, instead of felicity and serenity, was to be the mark of human nobility. The belief that value judgments are not subject, in the last analysis, to rational control, encourages the inclination to make irresponsible assertions regarding right and wrong or good and bad. One evades serious discussion of serious issues by the simple device of passing them off as value problems. One even creates the impression that all important human conflicts are value conflicts, whereas, to say the least, many of these conflicts arise out of men's very agreement regarding values.

3. The belief that scientific knowledge, *i.e.,* the kind of knowledge possessed or aspired to by modern science, is the highest form of human knowledge, implies a depreciation of pre-scientific knowledge. If one takes into consideration the contrast between scientific knowledge of the

world and pre-scientific knowledge of the world, one realizes that positivism preserves in a scarcely disguised manner Descartes' universal doubt of pre-scientific knowledge and his radical break with it. It certainly distrusts pre-scientific knowledge which it likes to compare to folk-lore. This superstition fosters all sorts of sterile investigations or complicated idiocies. Things which every ten year old child of normal intelligence knows are regarded as being in need of scientific proof in order to become acceptable as facts. And this scientific proof which is not only not necessary, is not even possible. To illustrate this by the simplest example: all studies in social science presuppose that its devotees can tell human beings from other beings; this most fundamental knowledge was not acquired by them in classrooms; and this knowledge is not transformed by social science into scientific knowledge, but retains its initial status without any modification throughout. If this pre-scientific knowledge is not knowledge, all scientific studies which stand or fall with it, lack the character of knowledge. The preoccupation with scientific proof of things which everyone knows well enough, and better, without scientific proof, leads to the neglect of that thinking, or that reflection, which must precede all scientific studies if these studies are to be relevant. The scientific study of politics is often presented as ascending from the ascertainment of political "facts," *i.e.*, of what has happened hitherto in politics, to the formulation of "laws" whose knowledge would permit the prediction of future political events. This goal is taken as a matter of course without a previous investigation as to whether the subject matter with which political science deals, admits of adequate understanding in terms of "laws" or whether the universals through which political things can be understood as what they are, must not be conceived of in entirely different terms. Scientific concern with political facts, relations of political facts, recurrent relations of political facts, or laws of political behavior, requires isolation of the phenomena which it is studying. But if this isolation is not to lead to irrelevant or misleading results, one must see the phenomena in question within the whole to which they belong, and one must clarify that whole, *i.e.*, the whole political or politico-social order: *e.g.*, one cannot arrive at a kind of knowledge which deserves to be called scientific, of "group politics," if one does not reflect on what genus of political orders is presupposed if there is to be "group politics" at all, and what kind of political order is presupposed by the specific "group politics" which one is studying. But one cannot clarify the character of a specific democracy, or of democracy in general, without having a clear understanding of the alternatives to democracy. Scientific political scientists are inclined to leave it at the distinction between democracy and authoritarianism, *i.e.*, they absolutize the given political order by remaining within a horizon which is defined by the given political order and its opposite. The scientific approach tends to lead to the neglect of the primary or fundamental questions and therewith to thoughtless acceptance of received opinion. As regards these fundamental questions our friends of scientific exactness are strangely unexacting. To refer again to the most simple and at the same time decisive example, political science requires clarification of what distinguishes political things from things which are not political; it requires that the question be raised and answered "what is political?" This question cannot be dealt with scientifically but only dialectically. And dialectical treatment necessarily begins from pre-scientific knowledge and takes it most seriously. Pre-scientific knowledge, or "commmon sense" knowledge, is thought to be discredited by Copernicus and the succeeding natural science. But the fact that what we may call telescopic-microscopic knowledge is very fruitful in certain areas, does not entitle one to deny that there are things which can only be seen as what they are, if they are seen with the unarmed eye; or, more precisely, if they are seen in the perspective of the citizen, as distinguished from the perspective of the scientific observer. If one denies this, one will repeat the experience of Gulliver with the nurse in Brobdingnag and become entangled in the kind of research projects by which he was amazed in Laputa.

4. Positivism necessarily transforms itself into historicism. By virtue of its orientation by the model of natural science, social science is in danger of mistaking peculiarities of, say, mid-twentieth-century United States, or more generally of modern Western society, for the essential character of human society. To avoid this danger, it is compelled to engage in "cross-cultural research," in the study of other cultures, both present and past. But in making this effort, it misses the meaning of those other cultures, because it interprets them through a conceptual scheme which originates in modern Western society, which reflects that particular society, and which fits at best only that particular society. To avoid this danger, social science must attempt to understand those cultures as they understand or understood themselves: the understanding primarily required of the social scientist is historical understanding. Historical understanding becomes the basis of a truly empirical science of society. But if one considers the infinity of the task of historical understanding, one begins to wonder whether historical understanding does not take the place of the scientific study of society. Furthermore, social science is said to be a body of true propositions about social phenomena. The propositions are answers to questions. What valid answers—objectively valid answers—are, may be determined by the rules or principles of logic. But the questions depend on one's direction of interest, and hence on one's

values, *i.e.*, on subjective principles. Now it is the direction of interests, and not logic which supplies the fundamental concepts. It is therefore not possible to divorce from each other the subjective and objective elements of social science; the objective answers receive their meaning from the subjective questions. If one does not relapse into the decayed Platonism which is underlying the notion of timeless values, one must conceive of the values embodied in a given social science as dependent on the society to which the social science in question belongs, *i.e.*, on history. Not only is social science superseded by historical studies; social science itself proves to be "historical." Reflection on social science as a historical phenomenon leads to the relativization of social science and ultimately of modern science generally. As a consequence, modern science comes to be viewed as one historically relative way of understanding things which is not in principle superior to alternative ways of understanding.

It is only at this point that we come face to face with the serious antagonist of political philosophy: historicism. After having reached its full growth historicism is distinguished from positivism by the following characteristics. (1) It abandons the distinction between facts and values, because every understanding, however theoretical, implies specific evaluations. (2) It denies the authoritative character of modern science, which appears as only one among the many forms of man's intellectual orientation in the world. (3) It refuses to regard the historical process as fundamentally progressive, or, more generally stated, as reasonable. (4) It denies the relevance of the evolutionist thesis by contending that the evolution of man out of non-man cannot make intelligible man's humanity. Historicism rejects the question of the good society, that is to say, of *the* good society because of the essentially historical character of society and of human thought: there is no essential necessity for raising the question of the good society; this question is not in principle coeval with man; its very possibility is the outcome of a mysterious dispensation of fate. The crucial issue concerns the status of those permanent characteristics of humanity, such as the distinction between the noble and the base, which are admitted by the thoughtful historicists: can these permanencies be used as criteria for distinguishing between good and bad dispensations of fate? The historicist answers this question in the negative. He looks down on the permanencies in question because of their objective, common, superficial and rudimentary character: to become relevant, they would have to be completed, and their completion is no longer common but historical. It was the contempt for these permanencies which permitted the most radical historicist in 1933 to submit to, or rather to welcome, as a dispensation of fate, the verdict of the least wise and least moderate part of his nation while it was in its least wise and least moderate mood, and at the same time to speak of wisdom and moderation. The events of 1933 would rather seem to have proved, if such proof was necessary, that man cannot abandon the question of the good society, and that he cannot free himself from the responsibility for answering it by deferring to history or to any other power different from his own reason.

THE CLASSICAL SOLUTION

When we describe the political philosophy of Plato and of Aristotle as classical political philosophy, we imply that it is the classic form of political philosophy. The classic was once said to be characterized by noble simplicity and quiet grandeur. This suggestion guides us in the right direction. It is an attempt to articulate what was formerly also called the "natural" character of classical thought. "Natural" is here understood in contra-distinction to what is merely human, all too human. A man is said to be natural if he is guided by nature rather than by convention, or by inherited opinion, or by tradition, to say nothing of mere whims. Classical political philosophy is nontraditional, because it belongs to the fertile moment when all political traditions were shaken, and there was not yet in existence a tradition of political philosophy. In all later epochs, the philosophers' study of political things was mediated by a tradition of political philosophy which acted like a screen between the philosopher and political things, regardless of whether the individual philosopher cherished or rejected that tradition. From this it follows that the classical philosophers saw the political things with a freshness and directness which has never been equalled. They look at political things in the perspective of the enlightened citizen or statesman. They see things clearly which the enlightened citizens or statesmen do not see clearly, or do not see at all. There is no other reason for this than the fact that they look further afield in the same direction as the enlightened citizens or statesmen. They do not look at political things from the outside, as spectators of political life. They speak the language of the citizens or statesmen; they hardly use a single term which is not familiar to the market place. Hence their political philosophy is comprehensive; it is both political theory and political skill; it is as receptive to the legal and institutional aspects of political life, as it is to that which transcends the legal and institutional; it is equally free from the narrowness of the lawyer, the brutality of the technician, the vagaries of the visionary, and the baseness of the opportunist. It reproduces, and raises to its perfection, the magnanimous flexibility of the true statesman, who crushes the insolent and spares the vanquished. It is free from all fanaticism because it knows that evil cannot be eradicated and therefore that one's expectations from politics must be moderate. The spirit which animates it may be described as serenity or sublime sobriety.

Compared with classical political philosophy, all later political thought, whatever else its merits may be, and in particular modern political thought, has a derivative character. This means that in later times there has occurred an estrangement from the simple and primary issues. This has given to political philosophy the character of "abstractness," and has therefore engendered the view that the philosophic movement must be a movement, not from opinion to knowledge, not from the here and now to what is always and eternal, but from the abstract toward the concrete. It was thought that by virtue of this movement toward the concrete, recent philosophy had overcome the limitations not only of modern political philosophy, but of classical political philosophy as well. It was overlooked, however, that this change of orientation perpetuated the original defect of modern philosophy because it accepted abstractions as its starting point, and that the concrete at which one eventually arrived was not at all the truly concrete, but still an abstraction.

One example must suffice here. Today it is held in certain circles that the basic task of political or social science is to understand the most concrete human relationship, and that relationship is called the "I—Thou —We" relation. It is obvious that the "Thou" and the "We" are supplements to Descartes' "Ego"; the question is whether the fundamental inadequacy of Descartes' Ego can be disposed of by any supplements, and whether it is not necessary to return to a more fundamental beginning, or to the natural beginning. The phenomenon which is now called the I—Thou—We relation was known to the classics by the name of friendship. When speaking to a friend, I address him in the second person. But philosophic or scientific analysis is not speaking to a friend, i.e., to this individual here and now, but speaking to anyone concerned with such analysis. Such analysis cannot be meant to be a substitute for living together as friends; it can at best only point to such living-together or arouse a desire for it. When speaking about someone with whom I have a close relationship I call him my "friend." I do not call him "Thou." Adequately "speaking about" in analytical or objective speech must be grounded in and continue the manner of "speaking about" which is inherent in human life. By speaking of "the Thou" instead of "the friend," I am trying to preserve in objective speech what cannot be preserved in objective speech; I am trying to objectify something which is incapable of being objectified. I am trying to preserve in "speaking about" what can be actual only in "speaking to," i.e., I do injustice to the phenomena; I am untrue to the phenomena; I miss the concrete. While attempting to lay a foundation for genuine human communication, I preserve an incapacity for it.

The character of classical political philosophy appears with the greatest clarity from Plato's *Laws*, which is his political work *par excellence*. The *Laws* is a conversation, about law and political things in general, between an old Athenian stranger, an old Cretan, and an old Spartan. The conversation takes place on the island of Crete. At the beginning one receives the impression that the Athenian has come to Crete in order to study there the best laws. For if it is true that the good is identical with the ancestral, the best laws for a Greek would be the oldest Greek laws, and these are the Cretan laws. But the equation of the good with the ancestral is not tenable if the first ancestors were not gods, or sons of gods, or pupils of gods. Hence, the Cretans believed that their laws were originated by Zeus, who instructed his son Minos, the Cretan legislator. The *Laws* opens with an expression of this belief. It appears immediately afterward that this belief has no other ground, no better ground, than a saying of Homer—and the poets are of questionable veracity—as well as what the Cretans say, and the Cretans were famous for their lack of veracity. However this may be, very shortly after its beginning, the conversation shifts from the question of the origins of the Cretan laws and the Spartan laws to the question of their intrinsic worth. A code given by a god, Moy, a being of the superhuman excellence, must be unqualifiedly good. Very slowly, very circumspectly does the Athenian approach this grave question. To begin with, he limits his criticism of the principle underlying the Cretan and the Spartan codes by criticizing not these codes, but a poet, a man without authority and, in addition, an expatriate, who had praised the same principle. In the sequel, the philosopher attacks not yet the Cretan and the Spartan codes, but the interpretation of these codes which had been set forth by his two interlocutors. He does not begin to criticize these venerable codes explicitly until he has appealed to a presumed Cretan and Spartan law which permits such criticism under certain conditions—under conditions which are fulfilled, to some extent, in the present conversation. According to that law, all must say with one voice and with one mouth that all the laws of Crete, or of Sparta, are good because they are god-given, and no one is suffered to say something different; but an old citizen may utter a criticism of an allegedly divine law before a magistrate of his own age if no young men are present. By this time it has become clear to the reader that the Athenian has not come to Crete in order to study there the best laws, but rather to introduce into Crete new laws and institutions, truly good laws and institutions. These laws and institutions will prove to be, to a considerable extent, of Athenian origin. It seems that the Athenian, being the son of a highly civilized society, has embarked on the venture of civilizing a rather uncivilized society. Therefore he has to apprehend that his suggestions will be odious, not only as innovations, but above all as foreign, as Athenian; deep-seated, old animosities and suspicions will be aroused by his recommendations. He begins his explicit criticism with a remark about the probable connection between certain Cretan and Spartan institutions and the practice of homosexuality in these cities. The Spartan, rising in defense of his fatherland, does not, indeed, defend homosexuality, but, turning to the offensive, rebukes the Athenians for their excessive drinking. The Athenian is thus given a perfect excuse for recommending the introduction of the Athenian institution of banquets: he is compelled to defend that institution, and by defending it he acts the part, not of a civilizing philosopher who, being a philosopher, is a philanthropist, but of the patriot. He acts in a way which is perfectly understandable to his interlocutors and perfectly respectable in their opinion. He attempts to show that wine-drinking and even drunkenness, if it is practiced in banquets well presided over, is conducive to education in temperance or moderation. This speech about wine forms the bulk of the first two books of the *Laws*. Only after the speech about wine has been brought to its conclusion does the Athenian turn to the question of the beginning of political life, to a question which is the true beginning of his political theme. The speech about wine appears to be *the* introduction to political philosophy.

Why does *the* Platonic dialogue about politics and laws begin with such an extensive conversation about wine? What is the artistic or logographic necessity demanding this? The proper interlocutors in a conversation about laws are old citizens of communities famous for their laws, for their obedience and allegiance to their old laws. Such men understand best what living under laws, living in laws, means. They are the perfect incarnation of the spirit of laws: of lawfulness, of law-abidingness. However, their very virtue becomes a defect if there is no longer a question of preserving old laws, but of seeking the best laws or introducing new and better ones. Their habits and their competence make these men impervious to suggestions for improvement. The Athenian induces them to participate in a conversation about wine-drinking, about a pleasure that is forbidden to them by their old laws. The talk about wine-drinking is a kind of vicarious enjoyment of wine, especially since wine-drinking is a forbidden pleasure. Perhaps the talk reminds the two old interlocutors of secret and pleasurable transgressions of their own. The effect of the talk about wine is therefore similar to the effect of actual wine-drinking; it loosens their tongues; it makes them young; it makes them bold, daring, willing to innovate. They must not actually drink wine, since this would impair their judgment. They must drink wine, not in deed, but in speech.

This means, though, that wine-drinking educates to boldness, to cour-age, and not to moderation, and yet wine-drinking was said to be conducive to moderation. Let us therefore consider the other partner in the conversation, the Athenian philosopher. To doubt the sacredness of the ancestral means to appeal from the ancestral to the natural. It means to transcend all human traditions, nay, the whole dimension of the merely human. It means to learn to look down on the human as some-thing inferior, or, to leave the cave. But by leaving the cave one loses sight of the city, of the whole political sphere. If the philosopher is to give political guidance, he must return to the cave; from the light of the sun to the world of shadows; his perception must be dimmed; his mind must undergo an obfuscation. The vicarious enjoyment of wine through a conversation about wine, which enlarges the horizon of the law-bred old citizens, limits the horizon of the philosopher. But this obfuscation, this acceptance of the political perspective, this adoption of the language of political man, this achievement of harmony between the excellence of man and the excellence of the citizen, or between wisdom and law-abidingness, is, it seems, the most noble exercise of the virtue of moder-ation: wine-drinking educates to moderation. For moderation is not a virtue of thought: Plato likens philosophy to madness, the very opposite of sobriety or moderation; thought must be not moderate, but fearless, not to say shameless. But moderation is a virtue controlling the philosopher's speech.

We have suggested that the Athenian stranger had gone to Crete in order to civilize an uncivilized society, and that he had done this out of philanthropy. But does not philanthropy begin at home? Did he not have more pressing duties to perform at home? What kind of man is the Athenian stranger? The *Laws* begins with the word "God": it is the only Platonic dialogue which begins in that manner. There is one and only one Platonic dialogue which ends with the word "God": the *Apology of Soc-rates*. In the *Apology of Socrates* an old Athenian philosopher, Socrates, defends himself against the charge of impiety, of not believing that the gods worshipped by the city of Athens exist. It seems that there is a conflict between philosophy and accepting the gods of the city. In the *Laws* an old Athenian philosopher recommends a law about impiety which renders impossible the conflict between philosophy and the city, or which brings about harmony between philosophy and the city. The gods whose existence is to be admitted by every citizen of the city of the *Laws* are beings whose existence can be demonstrated. That old Athenian philosopher of the *Apology of Socrates* was condemned to death by the city of Athens. He was given an opportunity to escape from prison: he refused to avail himself of this opportunity. His refusal was not based on an appeal to a categorical imperative demanding passive obedience, without if's and but's. His refusal was based on a deliberation, on a prudential consideration of what was the right thing to do in the circumstances. One of the circumstances was Socrates' old age: we are forced to wonder how Socrates would have decided if he had been 30 or 40 years old instead of 70. Another circumstance was the unavailability of a proper place of exile: where should he flee? He seems to have a choice between law-abiding cities nearby, where his life would be unbearable since he would be known as a fugitive from justice, and a lawless country far away, where the prevailing lack of order would make his life miserable. The disjunction is obviously incomplete: there were law-abiding cities far away, for instance on Crete which is mentioned as a law-abiding place in the very deliberation in question. We are entitled to infer that if Socrates had fled, he would have gone to Crete. The *Laws* tells us what he would have done in Crete after his arrival: he would have brought the blessings of Athens, Athenian laws, Athenian institutions, banquets, and philosophy to Crete. (When Aristotle speaks about Plato's *Laws*, he takes it for granted that the chief character of the *Laws* is Socrates.) Escaping to Crete, living in Crete, was the alternative to dying in Athens. But Socrates chose to die in Athens. Socrates preferred to sacrifice his life in order to preserve philosophy in Athens rather than to preserve his life in order to introduce philosophy into Crete. If the danger to the future of philosophy in Athens had been less great, he might have chosen to flee to Crete. His choice was a political choice of the highest order. It did not consist in the simple subsumption of his case under a simple, universal, and unalterable rule.

But let us return after this long story to the beginning of Plato's *Laws*. If the originator of the Cretan laws, or any other laws, is not a god, the cause of laws must be human beings, the human legislator. There is a variety of types of human legislators: the legislator has a different character in a democracy, in an oligarchy, in a monarchy. The legislator is the governing body, and the character of the governing body depends on the whole social and political order, the *politeia*, the regime. The cause of the laws is the regime. Therefore the guiding theme of political philosophy is the regime rather than the laws. Regime becomes the guiding theme of political thought when the derivative or questionable character of laws has been realized. There are a number of biblical terms which can be properly translated by "law"; there is no biblical equivalent to "regime."

Regime is the order, the form, which gives society its character. Regime is therefore a specific manner of life. Regime is the form of life as living together, the manner of living of society and in society, since this manner depends decisively on the predominance of human beings of a certain type, on the manifest domination of society by human beings of a certain type. Regime means that whole, which we today are in the habit of viewing primarily in a fragmentized form; regime means simultaneously the form of life of a society, its style of life, its moral taste, form of society, form of state, form of government, spirit of laws. We may try to articulate the simple and unified thought, that expresses itself in the term *politeia,* as follows: life is activity which is directed toward some goal; social life is an activity which is directed toward such a goal as can be pursued only by society; but in order to pursue a specific goal, which is its comprehensive goal, society must be organized, ordered, constructed, constituted in a manner which is in accordance with that goal; this, however, means, that the men in authority must be attuned to that goal.

There is a variety of regimes. Each regime raises a claim, explicitly or implicitly, which extends beyond the boundaries of any given society. These claims conflict, therefore, with each other. There is a variety of conflicting regimes. Thus the regimes themselves, and not our preoccupation as mere bystanders, force us to wonder which of the given conflicting regimes is better, and ultimately, which regime is the best regime. Classical political philosophy is guided by the question of the best regime.

The actualization of the best regime depends on the coming together, on the coincidence of things, which have a natural tendency to move away from each other, *e.g.,* on the coincidence of philosophy and political power; its actualization depends, therefore, on chance. Human nature is enslaved in so many ways that it is almost a miracle if an individual achieves the highest good: what can one expect of society? The peculiar manner of being of the best regime—namely, its lacking actuality while being superior to all actual regimes—has its ultimate reason in the dual nature of man, in the fact that man is the in-between being existing between the life of brutes and that of the gods.

The practical meaning of the notion of the best regime appears most clearly, when one considers the ambiguity of the term "good citizen." Aristotle suggests two entirely different definitions of the good citizen. In his more popular *Constitution of Athens,* he suggests that the good citizen is a man who serves his country well, without any regard to the difference of regimes—who serves his country well with a fundamental indifference to the change of regimes. The good citizen, in a word, is the patriotic citizen, the man whose loyalty belongs first and last to his fatherland. In his less popular *Politics,* Aristotle says that there is not *the* good citizen without qualification. For what it means to be a good citizen depends entirely upon the regime. A good citizen in Hitler's Germany would be a bad citizen elsewhere. But whereas good citizenship is relative to the regime, good man does not have such a relativity. The meaning of good man is always and everywhere the same. The good man is identical with the good citizen only in one case—in the case of the best regime. For only in the best regime are the good of the regime and the good of the good man identical, that good being virtue. This amounts to saying that in his *Politics* Aristotle questions the proposition that patriotism is enough. From the point of view of the patriot, the fatherland is more important than any difference of regimes. From the point of view of the patriot, he who prefers any regime to the fatherland is a partisan, if not a traitor. Aristotle says in effect that the partisan sees deeper than the patriot but that only one kind of partisan is superior to the patriot; this is the partisan of virtue. One can express Aristotle's thought as follows: patriotism is not enough for the same reason for which the most doting mother is happier if her child is good than if he is bad. A mother loves her child because he is her own; she loves what is her own. But she also loves the good. All human love stands under the law to be both love of one's own and love of the good, and there is necessarily a tension between one's own and the good, a tension which may well lead to a break, be it only the breaking of a heart. The relationship between one's own and the good finds its political expression in the relationship between the fatherland and the regime. In the language of classical metaphysics, the fatherland or the nation is the matter whereas the regime is the form. The classics held the view that the form is higher in dignity than the matter. One may call this view "idealism." The practical meaning of this idealism is that the good is of higher dignity than one's own, or that the best regime is of higher consideration than the fatherland. The Jewish equivalent of this relation might be said to be the relation between the Torah and Israel.

Classical political philosophy is today exposed to two very common objections, the raising of which requires neither originality nor intelligence, nor even erudition. The objections are these: (1) classical political philosophy is anti-democratic and hence bad; (2) classical political philosophy is based on classical natural philosophy or on classical cosmology, and this basis has been proven to be untrue by the success of modern natural science.

To speak first of the classics' attitude toward democracy, the premises: "the classics are good" and "democracy is good" do not validate the conclusion "hence the classics were good democrats." It would be silly to deny that the classics rejected democracy as an inferior kind of regime. They were not blind to its advantages. The severest indictment of democracy that ever was written occurs in the eighth book of Plato's

Republic. But even there, and precisely there, Plato makes it clear—by coordinating his arrangement of regimes with Hesiod's arrangement of the ages of the world—that democracy is, in a very important respect, equal to the best regime which corresponds to Hesiod's golden age: since the principle of democracy is freedom, all human types can develop freely in a democracy, and hence in particular the best human type. It is true that Socrates was killed by a democracy; but he was killed when he was 70; he was permitted to live for 70 long years; in anti-democratic Sparta he would have been exposed as an infant and left to die. Yet Plato did not regard this consideration as decisive. For he was concerned not only with the possibility of philosophy, but likewise with a stable political order that would be congenial to moderate political courses; and such an order, he thought, depends on the predominance of old families. More generally, the classics rejected democracy because they thought that the aim of human life, and hence of social life, is not freedom but virtue. Freedom as a goal is ambiguous, because it is freedom for evil as well as for good. Virtue emerges normally only through education, that is to say, through the formation of character, through habituation, and this requires leisure on the part of both parents and children. But leisure in its turn requires some degree of wealth—more specifically a kind of wealth whose acquisition or administration is compatible with leisure. Now, as regards wealth, it so happens, as Aristotle observes, that there is always a minority of well-to-do people and a majority of the poor, and this strange coincidence will last forever because there is a kind of natural scarcity. "For the poor shall never cease out of the land." It is for this reason that democracy, or rule of the majority, is government by the uneducated. And no one in his senses would wish to live under such a government. This classical argument would not be stringent if men did not need education in order to acquire a firm adherence to virtue. It is no accident that it was Jean-Jacques Rousseau who taught that all knowledge which men need in order to live virtuously is supplied by the conscience, the preserve of the simple souls rather than of other men: man is sufficiently equipped by nature for the good life; man is by nature good. But the same Rousseau was compelled to develop a scheme of education which very few people could financially afford. On the whole the view has prevailed that democracy must become rule by the educated, and this goal will be achieved by universal education. But universal education presupposes that the economy of scarcity has given way to an economy of plenty, and the economy of plenty presupposes the emancipation of technology from moral and political control. The essential difference between our view and the classical view consists then, not in a difference regarding moral principle, not in a different understanding of justice: we, too, even the communists, with whom we co-exist, think that it is just to give equal things to equal people and unequal things to people of unequal merit. The difference between the classics and us with regard to democracy consists exclusively in a different estimate of the virtues of technology. But we are not entitled to say that the classical view has been refuted. Their implicit prophecy that the emancipation of technology, of the arts, from moral and political control would lead to disaster or to the dehumanization of man has not yet been refuted.

Nor can we say that democracy has found a solution to the problem of education. In the first place, what is today called education, very frequently does not mean education proper, *i.e.*, the formation of character, but rather instruction and training. Secondly, to the extent to which the formation of character is indeed intended, there exists a very dangerous tendency to identify the good man with the good sport, the cooperative fellow, the regular guy, *i.e.*, there is an over-emphasis on a certain part of social virtue and a corresponding neglect of those virtues which mature, if they do not flourish, in privacy, not to say in solitude. By educating people to cooperate with each other in a friendly spirit, one does not yet educate non-conformists, people who are prepared to stand alone, to fight alone, "rugged individualists." Democracy has not yet found a defence against the creeping conformism and the ever-increasing invasion of privacy which it fosters. Beings who look down on us from a star might find that the difference between democracy and communism is not quite as great as it appears to be when one considers exclusively the doubtless very important question of civil and political liberties, although only people of exceptional levity or irresponsibility say that the difference between communism and democracy is negligible in the last analysis. Now to the extent to which democracy is aware of these dangers, to the same extent it sees itself compelled to think of elevating its level and its possibilities by a return to the classics' notions of education: a kind of education which can never be thought of as mass-education, but only as higher and highest education of those who are by nature fit for it. It would be an understatement to call it royal education.

Yet granted that there are no valid moral or political objections to classical political philosophy—is that political philosophy not bound up with an antiquated cosmology? Does not the very question of the nature of man point to the question of the nature of the whole, and therewith to one or the other specific cosmology? Whatever the significance of modern natural science may be, it cannot affect our understanding of what is human in man. To understand man in the light of the whole means for modern natural science to understand man in the light of the sub-human. But in that light man as man is wholly unintelligible. Classical political philosophy viewed man in a different light. It was originated by Socrates, and Socrates was so far from being committed to a specific cosmology that his knowledge was knowledge of ignorance. Knowledge of ignorance is not ignorance; it is knowledge of the elusive character of the truth, of the whole. Socrates, then, viewed man in the light of the mysterious character of the whole. He held therefore that we are more familiar with the situation of man as man than with the ultimate causes of that situation. We may also say he viewed man in the light of the unchangeable ideas, *i.e.,* of the fundamental and permanent problems. For to articulate the situation of man means to articulate man's openness to the whole. This understanding of the situation of man which includes then the quest for cosmology rather than a solution to the cosmological problem, was the foundation of classical political philosophy.

To articulate the problem of cosmology means to answer the question of what philosophy is or what a philosopher is. Plato refrained from entrusting the thematic discussion of this question to Socrates. He entrusted it to a stranger from Elea. But even that stranger from Elea did not discuss explicitly what a philosopher is. He discussed explicitly two kinds of men which are easily mistaken for the philosopher, the sophist and the statesman. By understanding both sophistry (in its highest as well as in its lower meanings) and statesmanship, one will understand what philosophy is. Philosophy strives for knowledge of the whole. The whole is the totality of the parts. The whole eludes us, but we know parts: we possess partial knowledge of parts. The knowledge which we possess is characterized by a fundamental dualism which has never been overcome. At one pole we find knowledge of homogeneity: above all in arithmetic, but also in the other branches of mathematics, and derivatively in all productive arts or crafts. At the opposite pole we find knowledge of heterogeneity, and in particular of heterogeneous ends; the highest form of this kind of knowledge is the art of the statesman and of the educator. The latter kind of knowledge is superior to the former for this reason. As knowledge of the ends of human life, it is knowledge of what makes human life complete or whole; it is therefore knowledge of a whole. Knowledge of the ends of man implies knowledge of the human soul; and the human soul is the only part of the whole which is open to the whole and therefore more akin to the whole than anything else is. But this knowledge—the political art in the highest sense—is not knowledge of *the* whole. It seems that knowledge of the whole would have to combine somehow political knowledge in the highest sense with knowledge of homogeneity. And this combination is not at our disposal. Men are therefore constantly tempted to force the issue by imposing unity on the phenomena, by absolutizing either knowledge or homogeneity or knowledge of ends. Men are constantly attracted and deluded by two opposite charms: the charm of competence which is engendered by mathematics and everything akin to mathematics, and the charm of humble awe, which is engendered by meditation on the human soul and its experiences. Philosophy is characterized by the gentle, if firm, refusal to succumb to either charm. It is the highest form of the mating of courage and moderation. In spite of its highness or nobility, it could appear as Sisyphean or ugly, when one contrasts its achievement with its goal. Yet it is necessarily accompanied, sustained and elevated by *eros*. It is graced by nature's grace.

4

William A. Glaser

THE TYPES AND USES
OF POLITICAL THEORY*

William Glaser distinguishes "empirical" theories ("generalizations about observable reality") from "ethical" theories and "metaphysical" or "theological" theories, the latter categories comprising roughly what was earlier distinguished from the theoretical as being philosophical. He proceeds to develop the "various useful ways of studying political theory," contending that both "the study of past political theories and the creation of new theories can be valuable both in constructing scientific laws and in proposing public policy." He concludes in summary that although "the political theorist has contributed little to the techniques of scientific analysis," he can and should furnish factual hypotheses, ethical suggestions, and more adequate methodologies to the political scientist. Glaser warns that, "if the study of theory and the study of fact do not fertilize each other, both will be barren."

The word "theory" denotes an organized set of ideas about reality. "Empirical" theories are generalizations about observable reality. "Ethical" theories express some degree of preference or distaste about reality in accordance with certain a priori standards of evaluation; and some ethical theories state the ideal goals toward which reality ought to be

*Reprinted by permission of the author and publisher from *Social Research*, XXII (3: October, 1955), pp. 275–296.

changed. "Metaphysical" or "theological" theories are attempts by some writers to discover the ultimate nature of reality transcending the observable; and some of these theories are attempts to establish an ultimate justification for certain ethical convictions.

Every subject of human inquiry contains many theories of the foregoing types, as well as other kinds of knowledge. Thus the study of politics— like the fields of physics, linguistics, psychology, teacher training, and the like—includes a discussion of theories which are many in number and varied in character.

The study of theories in politics differs from such study in all other fields because it prevailingly uses an historical and descriptive approach. In the United States and abroad a card-carrying "political theorist" nearly always devotes his writing and teaching to the description of past and contemporary books written by other persons. By contrast, a "theorist" in the other social sciences, and in most other scholarly disciplines, creates original ideas himself and applies them to concrete contemporary problems in an explanatory or normative manner. In academic life the field of government devotes much of its curricula and personnel to studying the history of political theory, while other fields give the history of their theories little or no place in their university curricula and in their professional journals. In contrast to the specialized "historians of political theory," there are few or no historians of theory in such disciplines as biology, physics, and sociology.

Why should anyone theorize about politics? How useful is political theory as it is studied at present? Since these questions are rarely asked, they are rarely answered. Most universities require their graduate students to take courses in the history of political ideas without clearly specifying what these students are expected to learn. Most scholars in the field delve into the past because the material "interests" them, without bothering to wonder why this expenditure of time and paper is more worth while than work on other equally "interesting" subjects. The uneven quality of the work in political theory reflects the fact that most writers and lecturers have not clearly conceived what they are trying to achieve.

This situation should not exist. The study of past political theories and the creation of new theories can be valuable both in constructing scientific laws and in proposing public policy. The need is for political theorists to clarify what they are trying to do, and then to employ the methods necessary for fulfilling their objectives. I propose to discuss here the various useful ways of studying political theory, and to examine briefly the current state of the literature in each line of inquiry.

1 HISTORY: DESCRIPTIVE AND CRITICAL

Many scholars simply summarize the arguments of particular political philosophers and then generalize about the thought currents of particular periods. This is the usual treatment of the history of political thought in the literature and in university lectures. Occasionally a scholar may make an important contribution by discovering a neglected but important philosopher from the past, such as the modern "rediscoveries" of Giovanni Battista Vico and Johannes Althusius. Sometimes new research by a scholar can correct widely accepted errors in intellectual historiography, such as Carl Becker's reevaluation of the true character of eighteenth-century rationalist thought.[1] Some scholars have shed new light on certain periods in the history of political philosophy through patiently recording and generalizing about large quantities of detailed political writings by secondary leaders and publicists.[2] In recent decades intellectual historians have developed a new and valuable method of showing how a philosopher's ideas began and developed throughout his life.[3]

Descriptive history is important. An accurate knowledge of the past can be used for many of the purposes suggested in the remainder of this article. An historian of political thought who contributes something new in this area has produced a great achievement. But—few do. To discover an important but neglected thinker of the past is rare. To discover new data revolutionizing contemporary conceptions of past periods is almost equally rare. Not enough scholars undertake the arduous task of ploughing through the newspapers, magazines, diaries, official public statements, and other daily records of a period to produce detailed findings about the day-to-day patterns of thinking which characterized political actors. Instead, most contemporary historians of political thought simply repeat familiar material or produce "new" but unimportant minutiae about familiar subjects.

Perhaps historians of political ideas should broaden their role to become historians of political institutions too. Paradoxically, while university

[1]Carl Becker, *The Heavenly City of the Eighteenth-Century Philosophers* (New Haven, 1932).

[2]For example, Arthur M. Schlesinger, Jr., *The Age of Jackson* (Boston, 1945); Rollin G. Osterweis, *Romanticism and Nationalism in the Old South* (New Haven, 1949); William Holdsworth, *A History of English Law*, 1st and 3rd eds., 12 vols. (London, 1922–38); Louis Hartz, *Economic Policy and Democratic Thought: Pennsylvania, 1776–1860* (Cambridge, Mass., 1948); Alan P. Grimes, *The Political Liberalism of the New York Nation 1865–1932* (Chapel Hill, N. C., 1953).

[3]For example, Leo Strauss, *The Political Philosophy of Hobbes: Its Basis and Its Genesis* (Oxford, 1936); Sidney Hook, *From Hegel to Marx* (New York, 1936); Werner Jaeger, *Aristotle*, 2nd ed. (Oxford, 1948); Charles W. Hendel, *Jean-Jacques Rousseau —Moralist*, 2 vols. (London, 1934); Élie Halévy, *The Growth of Philosophic Radicalism* (London, 1928).

faculties and publishing outlets are saturated under the flood of historians of political ideas, there are no specialized historians of political institutions. As a rule this task is left to members of Departments of History, but usually their descriptions of past political institutions are part of an undifferentiated chronicle of all events, and also their categories of analysis usually differ from those used by political scientists. Most of the members of Departments of Government cannot perform this task adequately, because some are anti-historical while others are inept in historical method. Therefore the task of making methodologically valid and useful analyses of past political institutions may be left to the historians of political ideas or to a new breed of historians of political institutions. Such research can be used in contemporary political policymaking and in contemporary political science in many of the same ways as can the findings made by historians of political ideas.

Some historians of political philosophy try to go beyond conventional descriptions by critically evaluating the writings of great thinkers, particularly from the standpoint of logical consistency. Sabine, for example, in his classic book, repeatedly points out contradictions and dilemmas in the arguments of great philosophers, and Willmoore Kendall criticizes John Locke's philosophy for attempting to combine certain tacit assumptions and explicit arguments about such problems as majority rule, individual obedience, the moral justice of majority decisions, the characteristics of the typical citizen.[4] Kendall's critique is designed to help clarify the empirical and ethical assumptions and implications contained in any proposals for majoritarian democracy in the modern world. Hartz has recently analyzed the fundamental contradictions in the theories of writers who have attempted to fit certain ethical theories to American life. From these case studies he attempts to prove that neither Burkean conservatism, feudal conservatism, nor collectivist socialism can successfully become the basis for public policy in the United States.[5] Many writers have attacked the logic and epistemology of Marxism, and many others have similarly analyzed other past political theories.[6]

This approach is useful when it demonstrates which theories by past writers are logically sound, and which unsound. Ethical or empirical

[4]George H. Sabine, *A History of Political Theory*, 2nd ed. (New York, 1950); Willmoore Kendall, *John Locke and the Doctrine of Majority Rule* (Urbana, Illinois, 1941).

[5]Louis Hartz, *The Liberal Tradition in America* (New York, 1955); also various of his magazine articles, especially "The Reactionary Enlightenment: Southern Political Thought before the Civil War," in *Western Political Quarterly*, vol. 5 (March 1952) pp. 49–50.

[6]I think the best such critique of Marxism is Karl Federn, *The Materialist Conception of History* (London, 1939). Further works of this kind are cited in notes 23, 25, and 26.

theories that are logically valid may then be used as modern ethical guides or as scientific models, both of which I shall discuss in later sections. But unless the critical historian's evaluation of past writers is clearly directed at such an objective, I cannot see how his treatment serves any useful purpose. In practice, many such critical historians seem to have no clear goal in mind, aside from experiencing the exhilaration of "demolishing" the great minds of history. Another common error by these critics is their failure, in reevaluating the past philosopher's ideas, to use language which, from either an ethical or a scientific standpoint, is operationally relevant to modern events. As a result of this final defect, many such critics engage in an elaborate wordplay, in which they arbitrarily oppose their own cloudy words to the verbiage of the past philosophers whom they attack.[7]

2   SOCIOLOGY OF KNOWLEDGE

In their writings and lectures on the history of political ideas, some scholars use a "sociology of knowledge" approach. This may take various forms.

For example, the scholar may survey the entire social-political history of a period, summarize all of that period's political ideas, and state broad correlations between the two.[8] Or he may trace detailed relationships between a few selected ideas and the few relevant elements in the social and political environment.[9] Or the scholar may focus on a single philosopher and connect his ideas to the events of that time, showing precisely what practical experiences influenced the content of the man's thought.[10] Some scholars go even farther, by comparing similarities and differences in the ideas and social-political environments of different periods. Some of these historians describe the processes of historical change which occur

[7]For example, Leonard T. Hobhouse, *The Metaphysical Theory of the State* (London, 1918).

[8]For example, Werner Jaeger, *Paideia: The Ideals of Greek Culture*, 1st and 2nd eds., 3 vols. (New York, 1939–45); Carl J. Friedrich, *The Age of the Baroque 1610–1660* (New York, 1952).

[9]For example, Harold J. Laski, *The Rise of Liberalism* (New York, 1936); the writers cited in Ephraim Fischoff, "The Protestant Ethic and the Spirit of Capitalism —The History of a Controversy," in *Social Research*, vol. 11 (February 1944) pp. 53–77.

[10]For example, Noel G. Annan, *Leslie Stephen—His Thought and Character in Relation to His Time* (London, 1951); Bertram D. Wolfe, *Three Who Made a Revolution* (New York, 1948); Jacob P. Mayer, *Max Weber and German Politics* (London, 1944); Boris Nikolaievsky and Otto Mänchen-Helfen, *Karl Marx: Man and Fighter* (Philadelphia, 1936); Jeffrey Pulver, *Machiavelli—the Man, His Work, and His Times* (London, 1937).

in political ideas and in their accompanying social-political environments.[11]

The sociology-of-knowledge approach represents one of the great contributions that historians of political thought can make to the work of the political scientist. (Here and elsewhere in this paper I am distinguishing between the role of the political scientist and the role of the historian of political philosophy; the two roles involve different goals and different scholarly techniques.) But among the writers who have begun to employ the sociology of knowledge, only the surface has been scratched so far, and many writers use fuzzy language or weak logic when stating relationships between ideas and social-political phenomena.

The sociology-of-knowledge approach to past intellectual history cannot by itself produce scientific laws. This consequence follows from the fact that no scientist can prove conclusions on the basis of incomplete and unreliable records about events that he does not personally observe. Nevertheless there are two ways in which the sociology-of-knowledge technique in intellectual history can furnish valuable assistance to the political scientist when he constructs laws about the relationships between the content of thought and social-political phenomena. First, this approach can suggest hypotheses which the political scientist can verify in the current world. Second, this approach can furnish data which support or cast doubt upon the scientific laws that the political scientist independently derives from analysis of the current world.

3 CAUSAL INFERENCES

Some historians of political philosophy attempt to make causal inferences relating certain social-political phenomena and certain ideas. The scholar may cite the ideas either as the causes or as the effects of the social-political phenomena. He may designate one particular cause as exclusive, he may cite one particular cause as primary, or he may demonstrate the operation of many equally important causes. Such causal imputations go a step beyond the sociology of knowledge, which merely establishes correlations between the occurrence and specific content of ideas and social-political phenomena.

Some intellectual historians identify cause-effect relations at certain times and places. For example, Turner and his disciples have maintained that distinctive features of American political ideas and institutions have been due to the existence of the American frontier, and that foreign

[11]For example, Karl Mannheim, *Ideology and Utopia* (London, 1946) pp. 190–236. See also the many writers who correlate the rise of Liberal and Protestant ideas with the transition from feudal-agricultural to capitalist society.

political philosophies have differed because other countries lacked both the frontier way of life and its many social effects.[12] Other writers, also identifying fundamental differences between American and foreign political philosophies, attribute such differences to the fact that the United States alone has lacked a feudal heritage.[13] An example of the opposite type of causal inference (in which the ideas are causes and the events are effects) is the familiar argument that the adoption of Christianity caused the decline of Rome.[14] Similarly, many historians have traced the American Civil War primarily or wholly to ideological causes, such as rival feelings over slavery, rival feelings over democracy, sectional pride, and the like.[15]

Some intellectual historians try to go even farther and establish historical laws (apparently with predictive content) about recurring causal relationships between particular social-political phenomena and particular ideas. Such a writer may contend that ideas in general or particular ideas are the primary or exclusive causes of all or some social-political phenomena repeatedly throughout the past and future. Examples of this approach are the many past and present intellectual historians inspired by Hegel. On the other hand, another type of writer may assert historical laws in the opposite way—that is, he may contend that social-political phenomena in general or particular social-political phenomena cause all or some political ideas repeatedly throughout the past and future. Examples of this approach are the economic determinists.

Many intellectual historians have been tempted to offer the various causal explanations I have described in the foregoing paragraphs. But these writers' achievements—while often useful—fall far short of their objectives. The best of these writers can furnish exactly what the sociology-of-knowledge school can offer—that is, much data about the correlations between particular ideas and particular social-political phenomena. As I said in the previous section, the political scientist can use such

[12]Frederick Jackson Turner, *The Frontier in American History* (New York, 1920), especially chapters 1, 9, 11.

[13]For example, Louis Hartz's recent book (cited above, note 5); Raymond G. Gettell, *History of American Political Thought* (New York, 1928) chapter 1 passim; P. Kecskemeti, "Political Thought in America," in J. P. Mayer et al., *Political Thought—The European Tradition,* 2nd ed. (London, 1942) p. 424.

[14]For a survey of arguments and criticisms see Shelby T. McCloy, *Gibbon's Antagonism to Christianity* (Chapel Hill, N. C., 1933).

[15]For example, James Ford Rhodes, *Lectures on the American Civil War* (New York, 1913) Lecture I; Nathaniel W. Stephenson, *Abraham Lincoln and the Union* (New Haven, 1921), especially chapter 1; James G. Randall, *Lincoln—The Liberal Statesman* (New York, 1947) chapter 2; Avery Craven, *The Repressible Conflict 1830–1861* (Baton Rouge, La., 1939); J. H. Denison, *Emotional Currents in American History* (New York, 1932) chapters 4–5.

historical findings as evidence increasing or decreasing the probability of laws he has derived from his own contemporary research. Besides this, the intellectual historians who state causal inferences can offer to the political scientist certain hypotheses about the causal relationship between ideas and social-political phenomena; and the political scientist can then test these hypotheses in his investigation of the current world. Unfortunately, however, most of the causal historians fail to use scientifically operational language (a point to which I shall presently return), and therefore their suggestions about causal relations have rarely been subject to rigorous testing by political scientists.

Whether or not the intellectual historian uses valid logic and clear language, he cannot establish causation with a sufficiently high degree of probability. The reason, of course, is inherent in historiography. A causal inference can be firmly established only when the evidence is wholly reliable and plentiful. But the intellectual historian writes about events that he cannot observe, and he must depend almost wholly on written records, which are incomplete and biased.[16]

Consequently, while many historians of political thought claim to produce authoritative causal inferences, actually they can do no more than offer suggestive hypotheses.[17] Of course, this is valuable work, since the political scientist must depend on many outside sources for his hypotheses, and since historical perspective can often suggest important hypotheses that might not occur to persons immersed in current events. This is particularly true of hypotheses and laws at a high level of generality, for political scientists tend to concentrate on detailed relations among narrow classes of facts, and often only someone possessing historical perspective can suggest broader relations.

Even if the data did not prevent it, modern causal historians still could not establish reliable causal inferences, because of their defective methods. If any intellectual historian does wish to venture out on a limb by stating causal inferences, he is then playing the role of a full-fledged political scientist, and must be expected to observe all the canons of scientific method: accuracy in gathering facts, construction of operationally clear and useful concepts, valid logic in stating relationships, ade-

[16]For a discussion of this problem see Louis Gottschalk, *Understanding History* (New York, 1950) pp. 45–48, 118 ff., 211–212, 258.

[17]Even when such a hypothesis is proved after scientific investigation of the present, it is not a fully reliable explanation of the past events for which the historian first suggested it. The inadequacy of records about the past prevents us from knowing whether all the conditions in the current investigations also existed at the time of the past events. But the historian's causal explanation, when thus proved by the present, has a greater probability than when he first suggested it.

quate proof to achieve a significant degree of probability, and the like.[18] I have yet to find an intellectual historian making causal inferences who has fully absorbed the scientific habits of thinking that have become commonplace during the twentieth century in the physical sciences, and more recently in the social sciences. Thus the intellectual historians of this school fail to employ the method essential for the work they aim to perform. Instead, these writers often use vague language[19] or invalid logic, and often pass off intuitively derived hypotheses as adequately proved assertions.

In particular, these writers err in the logic of causality. On the one hand, as I have said earlier, some intellectual historians identify a single universal causal law recurring throughout history and in some way relating all political ideas to all social-political phenomena. But no one can prove that all events are reducible to any one exclusive or primary cause.[20] On the other hand, other intellectual historians may study intensively one or a very few events and then identify some kind of causal relationship between the ideas and social-political phenomena in those isolated situations. But this argument is fallacious, since definite causation cannot be discovered in a single event studied alone; it can be established only as a statement of probability holding for a class of recurring events.[21] When identifying the causes of a single situation the best the historian can do is to perform an imaginative experiment—that is, guess what might have occurred if certain supposed causes had differed.[22] But this speculation falls far short of reliable proof.

[18]In a later section I shall state some of the elements in scientific method at greater length. Certain principles of methodology in the natural and social sciences have become axiomatic in recent years, and have been elaborated in a flood of books and articles. In the social sciences two of the best sources are Felix Kaufmann, *Methodology of the Social Sciences* (New York, 1944); and Leon Festinger and Daniel Katz., eds., *Research Methods in the Behavioral Sciences* (New York, 1953).

[19]In Stephenson, for example (cited above, note 15), the following non-operational language is presented (p. 2) as the explanation of the American Civil War: "... *sectional consciousness,* with all its *emotional and psychological implications,* was the *fundamental impulse* of the stern events which occurred between 1850 and 1865" (italics added). For similar language and reasoning see Turner (cited above, note 12) p. 37.

[20]For criticisms of this "reductive fallacy" see Robert MacIver, *Social Causation* (Boston, 1942) pp. 113–120, 189–191.

[21]Causation is the relationship which the observer imputes to two phenomena that occur in temporal sequence. If the observer sees but one such event he cannot know whether the sequence is a coincidence or whether the two phenomena are significantly related. He can establish such a relationship only after he is sure that the two phenomena vary together, and that no other phenomena vary similarly. This can be established only after observing and comparing a number of analogous events.

[22]For descriptions of this procedure see MacIver (cited above, note 20) pp. 256–265; Ernest Greenwood, *Experimental Sociology* (New York, 1945), especially chapters 1, 4, 8–9; Gottschalk (cited above, note 16) pp. 242–243, 263.

The vague language and invalid logic of the causal writers lead to the temporary fads and frequent unresolvable scholarly feuds which have continually surrounded causal inferences in the history of political theory. Those who attribute all political ideas to economics have fought against those who attribute all social phenomena to ideas. Those who trace "liberalism" to "capitalism" have fought against those who trace "capitalism" to "liberalism." Those who attribute the American Civil War to ideas have fought against those who attribute the Civil War to other causes. And so on. Until the scholars of this school employ a valid and standardized methodology it will be impossible for the causal hypotheses of any one intellectual historian to be verified or disproved by other intellectual historians (who study the past) or by political scientists (who study the present).

In conclusion, the writers who employ causal inferences in the history of political theory can make certain valuable contributions to political science. First, like the sociology-of-knowledge school, they can furnish much evidence about correlations between ideas and social-political phenomena. Second, they can suggest causal hypotheses which political scientists can test. But the causal writers have not been able to establish the reliable causal relations that they seek. Partly this has been due to their defective methodology. But even with perfect techniques, they would be obstructed by our hopelessly limited knowledge of the past.

4 ETHICAL AND PROGRAMMATIC THEORY

The history of political theory can be a valuable source of ethical norms for the evaluation and reform of current events. Great thinkers of the past have often set forth the goals and implications of an ethical theory in a masterful manner, and their lessons can profitably be studied by modern citizens and by modern policymakers. (John Stuart Mill, for example, is now relegated to the museum of past political philosophers, but the depth, clarity, and cogency of his classic eulogy to liberty and democracy have never been exceeded by any writer since his day.) The historian of political philosophy can profitably select and adapt certain past ideas; and then he can analyze precisely how such normative ideas might prescribe what should and should not be done at present. Thus certain enduringly valid ethical norms from the past—after any necessary revision—would help modern men evaluate and solve their practical problems. In this area the historian of political theory would be helping the political policymaker rather than helping the political scientist.

Such a scholar need not summarize fully the past political philosopher's writings, since he would be drawing only certain essential lessons from that source. The scholar might even substantially reinterpret the past philosopher's ideas, if this proved a convenient way to point up his own ethical prescriptions for his current generation. Changes in current problems require changes in the lessons that scholars and policymakers may find in intellectual history. Historians and policymakers with different ethical preconceptions will derive different lessons from the same past philosophers, and they will choose different philosophers as their chief ethical models.

Some intellectual historians actually have attempted to show how the ideas of past writers contain suggestive implications for the present. For example, Richard Crossman demonstrates how Plato's political philosophy constitutes a standard for criticizing and solving the problems of modern democracy; and then he shows how certain fundamental weaknesses in Plato's elitist philosophy make it an inappropriate substitute for modern democracy. Crossman's book also contains a brief (unfortunately too brief) defence of modern democracy against this case example of elitist theory, and presents proposals for a reform of modern democracy to make it invulnerable to elitist attacks.[23] Russell Kirk traces the history of "the conservative idea" in England and America since Burke, and he concludes that it can still serve these two countries better than "liberalism" or "socialism."[24] Some modern scholars have examined how the political philosophy of Karl Marx can and cannot help contemporary men to understand, evaluate, and remedy their problems.[25] Various other scholars have treated other past political philosophers or past currents of thought in a similar fashion, whether by using these past ideas as models for contemporary reform, or by using certain past arguments as "straw men" for defending contemporary values and institutions, or by using these theories as "straw men" for defending the scholar's own norms.[26] Government leaders as well as scholars have often looked to past philosophers for inspiration.[27] Occasionally a scholar will attempt the even more

[23]Richard Crossman, *Plato Today* (New York, 1939).

[24]Russell Kirk, *The Conservative Mind* (Chicago, 1953).

[25]For example, G. D. H. Cole, *The Meaning of Marxism* (London, 1950); Rudolf Schlesinger, *Marx: His Time and Ours* (New York, 1950); Sidney Hook, *Reason, Social Myths, and Democracy* (New York, 1950) chapter 7; Henry Bamford Parkes, *Marxism: An Autopsy* (Boston, 1939).

[26]For example, Benedetto Croce, *What Is Living and What Is Dead of the Philosophy of Hegel* (New York, 1915); Carl J. Friedrich, *Inevitable Peace* (Cambridge, Mass., 1948); John H. Hallowell, *Main Currents in Modern Political Thought* (New York, 1950); David Spitz, *Patterns of Anti-Democratic Thought* (New York, 1949); James Burnham, *The Machiavellians* (New York, 1943); Karl R. Popper, *The Open Society and Its Enemies*, 2nd ed. (Princeton, 1950); Jacques Maritain's many books about St. Thomas, such as *Scholasticism and Politics* (New York, 1940).

[27]For example, the American Founding Fathers drew on the writings of the ancient Greek and Roman philosophers for lessons relevant to the problems of the 1780s. Im-

ambitious task of showing how the entire history of ideas contains lessons for modern men.[28]

Not enough of this type of work has been done by scholars. And much of the existing literature is too general. The scholar employing this approach usually summarizes the writings of past thinkers and then makes a few perfunctory statements that the ideas are useful or are not useful in the modern world. Often he fails to spell out precisely what ideas of the past philosopher do and do not help in evaluating current conditions; and the scholar almost always fails to describe the concrete results that would probably follow if the suggested ideas were adopted as the basis for practical policymaking (here his prediction would be a hypothesis subject to verification by the political scientist). In those rare instances where such writers do attempt to go this far, their argument is often marred by deficient logic. For example, they may claim that contemporary problems have been caused by rival ideologies, and that their favorite philosophies could cause satisfactory changes, but often these assertions omit certain essential requirements for establishing causal inferences.[29] When it is properly performed, however, the lessons-from-the-past technique is one of the most valuable uses for the history of political theory.

Some scholars of political theory do original normative theorizing themselves. They do not apply the arguments of past writers to current events, but originate their own recommendations for public policy. There are many such writers—some on university faculties, but most of them elsewhere in public life. The best of them—Reinhold Niebuhr, for example—combine clear ethical or theological premises, logic, and knowledge of the practical world, in order to produce a political philosophy which is insightful, internally consistent, and realistic. A scholar who aspires to such work needs a thorough grounding in contemporary ethics and theology, logical habits of thinking, and knowledge of the real world (both current events and the research findings of the social sciences).

---

manuel Kant's political philosophy recently infiltrated the State Department; see George V. Allen, "Perpetual Peace Through World-Wide Federation," in *Department of State Bulletin,* vol. 20 (19 June 1949) pp. 801–802. And, of course, American leaders continually cite the philosophy of Marx and Lenin as an example of what the United States should avoid.

[28]For example, Arnold J. Toynbee describes the different effects that different ideas have had throughout history, and then he concludes that particular Christian ideas can best prevent the modern West from repeating the mistakes of the past. See his *A Study of History,* 10 vols. (London, 1934–1954), and *Civilization on Trial* (New York, 1948) chapters 12–13.

[29]For a critique of such defects in Russell Kirk's book (cited above, note 24) see Gordon K. Lewis, "The Metaphysics of Conservatism," in *Western Political Quarterly,* vol. 6 (December 1953) pp. 734–737.

Since scholars are professional thinkers they should be expected to conform to such rigorous standards in their policy recommendations. But, like lesser mortals, most do not.[30]

5   MODEL CONSTRUCTION

Besides having all the aforementioned uses, political theory can become valuable as a source of conceptual frameworks, operational concepts, and logical relationships for the use of the political scientist. Realization that theoretical insights are indispensable to reliable understanding of the empirical world has become a commonplace principle of the modern philosophy of science—in both the natural sciences and the social sciences.[31] To create new analytical methods and testable hypotheses is the work of the imagination, and this accomplishment could be the theory-minded scholar's greatest contribution to the progress of political science. But nearly all American scholars specializing in political theory have specialized in the history of political thought or in political ethics, and few have contributed anything to the methodology and research of political science.

Where political theorists have contributed something is the formulation of "frames of reference" (or "conceptual frameworks") within which schools of political scientists have worked. A frame of reference is an overall viewpoint which determines how the political scientist selects and uses specific research techniques, and how he will perceive his data, and which suggests many hypotheses to him. A frame of reference constitutes the fundamental habits of thinking which the scientist carries into his research.[32] Some frames of reference that guide contemporary political scientists were either created or perfected by political theorists. For example, Bentley's picture of politics as a competition among pressure groups has been widely adopted by scientists seeking regularities in electoral behavior, in legislative voting, in administrative behavior, and

[30]See the criticisms in Donald W. Smithburg, "Political Theory and Public Administration," in *Journal of Politics*, vol. 13 (February 1951) pp. 62–66, and sources cited therein.

[31]This truism is stressed in almost every contemporary book on scientific method and the philosophy of science. See, for example, Philipp Frank, *Modern Science and Its Philosophy* (Cambridge, Mass., 1950) pp. 6–16, 26–45, 62–70, 146–155, 242–246, 291–297; Hans Reichenbach, *The Rise of Scientific Philosophy* (Berkeley, 1951) pp. 5–7, 17, 120–124, 255–275, 305–308; Robert K. Merton, *Social Theory and Social Structure* (Glencoe, Illinois, 1949) chapter 2; Felix Kaufmann (cited above, note 18) passim; William J. Goode and Paul K. Hatt, *Methods in Social Research* (New York, 1952) chapters 2, 5, passim.

[32]See Talcott Parsons, *The Structure of Social Action*, 2nd ed. (Glencoe, Illinois, 1949) pp. 28–30, 733–738.

the like.[33] Various writers have pictured international relations as a struggle for power among rival governments dedicated to satisfying domestic interests,[34] and many political scientists have employed this as their controlling assumption in their detailed analyses of foreign policymaking, in their studies of the work of international organizations, and in other such concerns. Many political theorists have suggested that the political process be viewed as some kind of equilibrium, and many scientists have used this model in research.[35]

The political theorist can also furnish concepts for scientific analysis. Every science requires clear and precisely defined concepts according to which the data can be identified and arranged in an intelligible, consistent, and manageable fashion.[36] There are many questions that must be satisfactorily answered before concepts can be scientifically useful, and the political theorist—who is a specialist in imaginative construction— could make a great contribution in solving them. For example, what is a "political party"; what are the characteristics that a group must have before it can be classified as a party; what are the criteria for differentiating among types of party? Or what is meant by the concept of "influence" or "power"; what are the behavioral characteristics that actors must reveal before the scientific observer can conclude that one actor is exercising influence over another; what are the criteria for designating different types of influence? Many other concepts can be exhaustively clarified and made scientifically operational in political science. Such work has become commonplace in physics, and occasionally it is performed in the other social sciences,[37] but it is still rare in political sci-

---

[33]Arthur F. Bentley, *The Process of Government* (Chicago, 1908).

[34]This "realistic" conception of international relations has been elaborated by many writers for decades. Two of the ablest recent exponents are Nicholas J. Spykman, *America's Strategy in World Politics* (New York, 1942), and Hans J. Morgenthau, *Politics Among Nations*, 2nd ed. (New York, 1954).

[35]For a summary of some of these equilibrium theories, and for citations of sources, see David Easton, *The Political System* (New York, 1953) chapter 11.

[36]For example, Percy W. Bridgman elaborates such a series of operational concepts in his own field in *The Logic of Modern Physics* (New York, 1927). For similar approaches to concept construction in the social sciences see T. D. Weldon, *The Vocabulary of Politics* (London, 1953); Otto Neurath, *Foundations of the Social Sciences* (Chicago, 1944) pp. 1–19; essays by S. S. Stevens, Gustav Bergmann, and Kenneth W. Spence in Melvin H. Marx, ed., *Psychological Theory* (New York, 1951) pp. 20–66; Goode and Hatt (cited above, note 31) chapter 5.

[37]For example, Talcott Parsons et al., *Toward a General Theory of Action* (Cambridge, Mass., 1951); Marion J. Levy, Jr., *The Structure of Society* (Princeton, 1952); A. L. Kroeber and Clyde Kluckhohn, *Culture—A Critical Review of Concepts and Definitions* (Cambridge, Mass., 1952); Raymond B. Cattell, "The Concept of Social Status," in Philip L. Harriman, ed., *Twentieth Century Psychology* (New York, 1946) pp. 128–145; S. Stansfield Sargent, "Conceptions of Role and Ego in Contemporary Psychology," in John H. Rohrer and Muzafer Sherif, eds., *Social Psychology at the Cross-*

ence—partly because political theorists have shown little interest in this area.[38] Instead, when political theorists do turn to the definition of concepts, they usually deal with words that stand at a very high level of generality (for example, they try to define "the state," "sovereignty," "law," "peace," "democracy," "freedom," "socialism," "progress"), and often such concepts cannot be used conveniently in empirical research.

The political theorist could also help the political scientist by suggesting how valid relationships may be stated when describing data. For example, from the recent literature in logic and in the philosophy of science, and also from his own original theorizing, the political theorist could inform the political scientist about the nature of causality, probability, predictability. He could prescribe (in the light of the modern philosophy of science) what would be the quantity and type of facts that must be found before a law concerning certain political phenomena might be stated at a particular degree of probability. Besides setting forth such abstract logical relationships the political theorist might also collaborate directly with the political scientist by showing how particular generalizations about certain designated political data might satisfy logical requirements and thereby become scientific laws. Thus if a political scientist were studying, say, the relationship between unemployment and voting behavior, the political theorist might suggest the type of proofs needed before a particular unemployment status might be designated as a significant cause of a particular voting pattern, and he might also specify the type of causal relationship that would hold in this case.

Besides clarifying existing logical relationships and constructing new statements for the use of political scientists, political theorists also should help to construct any new languages (if needed) for describing political relationships. In particular, many social scientists at present are wondering whether mathematics can help them express relationships more conveniently than words; and in the future, symbolic logic also might be widely used. Political theorists should help the political scientists think through the question of how (if at all) such special languages may fruitfully be employed in political science. Also, the theorists should

---

roads (New York, 1951) pp. 355–370; Lionel J. Nieman and James W. Hughes, "The Problem of the Concept of Role—A Re-Survey of the Literature," in Social Forces, vol. 30 (December 1951) pp. 141–149; Kurt Mayer, "The Theory of Social Classes," in Harvard Educational Review, vol. 23 (Summer 1953) pp. 149–167.

[38]Recently some belated stirrings have appeared. See, for example, Harold D. Lasswell and Abraham Kaplan, Power and Society (New Haven, 1950); Herbert A. Simon, "Notes on the Observation and Measurement of Political Power," in Journal of Politics, vol. 15 (November 1953) pp. 500–516; Quincy Wright, "The Nature of Conflict," in Western Political Quarterly, vol. 4 (June 1951) pp. 193–209.

collaborate with the mathematicians and logicians in adapting any existing models, and in inventing any new models that may be needed for analyzing and generalizing about politics. Unfortunately the specialized political theorists have contributed little either to the analysis of logical relationships or to the construction of efficient languages.

Not only can the political theorist construct new concepts and methodologies for use by the political scientist, but also he can perfect existing models by making constructive criticisms of past research. Here the political theorist would be seeking to improve the efficiency of techniques, and he would be seeking to improve the clarity with which research findings are expressed. He might also be able to establish the degree to which the research data support the research findings, and therefore the degree to which those findings may be considered to be scientific laws. (In his role of political theorist he can neither prove nor disprove the scientific laws emerging from the research. Empirical proof depends upon success in prediction. But the political theorist can judge the form in which findings are presented.) Such detailed constructive criticism of research has become common in the natural sciences, and is becoming common in the other social sciences,[39] but it is rare in political science.[40]

Obviously, in the various phases of model construction the political theorist cannot develop his ideas completely a priori. Frames of reference, analytical concepts, analytical relationships, and modes of expression all must be made operationally useful for research. Thus the political theorist must be acquainted with the literature of political science and must work closely with the political scientist, in order to understand the latter's general analytical problems and the particular empirical situation to be investigated. In many cases the roles of political theorist and political scientist may be combined in the same person.

In summary, the political theorist has contributed little to the techniques of scientific analysis. Probably the historian of political ideas can offer nothing, since the thinkers of the past used language and reasoning

[39]For example, Herbert Blumer, An Appraisal of Thomas and Znaniecki's "The Polish Peasant in Europe and America" (New York, 1939); Robert K. Merton and Paul F. Lazarsfeld, eds., Studies in the Scope and Method of "The American Soldier" (Glencoe, Illinois, 1950); Richard Christie and Marie Jahoda, eds., Studies in the Scope and Method of "The Authoritarian Personality" (Glencoe, Illinois, 1954); symposium on the Kinsey Reports, in Social Problems (April 1954).

[40]Some of these infrequent examples are the essays by Harold D. Lasswell (about James Bryce) and George E. G. Catlin (about Harold Gosnell) in Stuart A. Rice, ed., Methods in Social Science (Chicago, 1931) pp. 468–479, 697–706; Frederick Mosteller et al., The Pre-Election Polls of 1948 (New York, 1949); Ralph Gilbert Ross, "Elites and the Methodology of Politics," in Public Opinion Quarterly, vol. 16 (Spring 1952) pp. 27–32.

too different from the methods of modern political science. Among original political theorists of the present, the most important achievements have been the construction of some frames of reference within which many scientists work. But the political theorist has produced little in the other areas of model construction in political science—that is, in the invention and clarification of operational concepts, of logical relationships, of special languages, and of other political research techniques. In practice, scientific theorizing in these areas is done by the practicing political scientist himself, or is borrowed by him from the literature of other disciplines.[41] Or the research scientist may ignore the need for theory and consequently make many errors.[42]

CONCLUSION

If the study of theory and the study of fact do not fertilize each other, both will be barren. This axiom has held for every field of knowledge in which such separation has existed, and it has been true of the study of government until recently. Fortunately, changes are occurring, and political science may finally flower during the next few decades.

But at the present moment the gap between theory and fact in politics is only beginning to close. Most of the present literature, most of the present instruction of graduate students, and most of the research projects sponsored by learned societies in political science reflect the lazy habits of past years, in which theory and fact either were separated completely or were related in a logically invalid manner. Many (or perhaps most) academic Departments of Government are sharply divided among a distinct group of theorists who immerse themselves in the philo-

[41]Students of political behavior, for example, find little guidance in the literature of political theory, but rely on the theoretical insights and research methods developed by social psychologists. This can be seen readily throughout such books as that edited by Festinger and Katz (cited above, note 18). Nearly all books, articles, and doctoral dissertations about methodology in political science are so woefully superficial and erroneous that they offer no guidance to the political scientist. When political theorists do turn to the problems of political science, they usually spend most of their time in shallow and fruitless debates over the role of "values" in science.

[42]Such barefoot empiricism is common in political science. A scientist who lacks theoretical sophistication will create slipshod and untestable hypotheses, he will offer unproved conclusions as scientific laws, he will make erroneous predictions, he will be unable to recognize the literature that can and cannot guide his own work, and he will produce research projects that cannot be replicated and verified by other scientists. For evidence of such errors in one area of political science see Samuel J. Eldersveld, "Theory and Method in Voting Behavior Research," in *Journal of Politics*, vol. 13 (February 1951) pp. 70–87.

sophical literature of the past, a distinct group of fact-finding empiricists who spurn theorizing, and a distinct group of rule-of-thumb policy consultants. Most legislative committees and executive agencies get policy advice containing many words and hunches, but containing few adequately proved scientific facts and little subtle logic.

This situation has caused many evils in the literature and practice of politics. Theorizing without relevance to fact is a dilettantish hobby rather than a useful contribution; and fact-finding without theory produces a jumble that either is wholly useless or is used to justify defective empirical or ethical propositions. The past and present literature contains many such defects. Sometimes the divorce between theory and fact has led, on faculties, to silly and injurious factional feuds between the literary specialists and the "practical" men. In government itself the most damage has resulted. A random glance at the daily newspapers or at the *Department of State Bulletin* will readily show the superficial character of the thinking of American policymakers (of all parties and factions), a defect which for years has repeatedly prevented the United States from understanding and anticipating mortal problems.

Thus if American scholars, policymakers, and citizens are adequately to understand and reform their world, they must develop a proper relationship between theorizing and factual knowledge. Many of the problems now besetting the world arise from the fact that physicists and engineers know how to combine theory and fact more efficiently than do political scientists and political policymakers. In this paper I have shown the fruitful areas, and have cited some relevant books. The political theorist can furnish to the political scientist limited factual generalizations and hypotheses about the relationships between thought and action (Sections 2 and 3), and he can offer ethical suggestions to the policymaker and citizen in their attempts to solve modern problems (Section 4), though all these applications require a far more sophisticated method than the historians of political philosophy have used so far. Also, the political theorist can help the political scientist perfect his methods and hypotheses in many ways (Section 5), though in this vital area, specialists in political philosophy have contributed little.

In some cases the roles of political theorist, political scientist, and political policymaker may be combined through teamwork among men who are specialists in each. For example, a sophisticated government official could draw upon the insights contained in the writings and advice of specialists in political ethics and of specialists in political science. Or the roles could be combined in the same person. In recent years, for example, various individual writers have attempted to reformulate the fundamental premises and detailed implications of democratic theory in the light of political science's findings about human behavior.[43] But regardless of how it is done, political theory must be combined with policymaking and political science. The study and practice of government cannot afford a continued compartmentalization among them.

[43]For example, Reinhold Niebuhr, *The Children of Light and the Children of Darkness* (New York, 1944); Walter Lippmann, *Public Opinion* (New York, 1922); Bernard Berelson, "Democratic Theory and Public Opinion," in *Public Opinion Quarterly*, vol. 16 (Fall 1952) pp. 313–330.

Further Readings

Bluhm, William T., *Theories of the Political System: Classics of Political Thought and Modern Political Analysis* (Englewood Cliffs, N.J.: Prentice-Hall, Inc., 1965).

Charlesworth, James C., ed., *A Design for Political Science: Scope, Objectives, and Methods* (Philadelphia: The American Academy of Political and Social Science, December, 1966).

Deutsch, Karl W., and Leroy N. Rieselbach, "Recent Trends in Political Theory and Political Philosophy," *The Annals of the American Academy of Political and Social Science*, 360 (July, 1965), pp. 139–162.

Easton, David, "Problems of Method in American Political Science," *International Social Science Bulletin*, IV (1: 1952), pp. 107–124.

——, ed., *Varieties of Political Theory* (Englewood Cliffs, N.J.: Prentice-Hall, Inc., 1966).

Field, G. C., "What Is Political Theory?" *Proceedings of the Aristotelian Society* (London: Harrison and Sons, 1954), New Series LIV (1953–1954), pp. 145–166.

Friedrich, Carl J., *Man and His Government: An Empirical Theory of Politics* (New York: McGraw-Hill Book Company, Inc., 1963).

Gewirth, Alan, ed., *Political Philosophy* (New York: Macmillan, 1965), pp. 1–5.

Goldberg, Arthur, "Political Science as Science," *Yale Political Science Research Library Publication* No. 1 (Yale University Press, 1962).

Jouvenel, Bertrand de, "On the Nature of Political Science," *American Political Science Review*, LV (4: December, 1961), pp. 773–779.

Kaufman, Arnold S., "The Nature and Function of Political Theory," *Journal of Philosophy*, 51 (1: January 7, 1954), pp. 5–22.

McCloskey, H. J., "The Nature of Political Philosophy," *Ratio*, 6 (1: June, 1964), pp. 50–62.

Meehan, Eugene J., "The Structure of Political Thought," in Eugene J. Meehan, *Contemporary Political Thought: A Critical Study* (Homewood, Ill.: The Dorsey Press, 1967), pp. 1–48.

——, *The Theory and Method of Political Analysis* (Homewood, Ill.: The Dorsey Press, 1965).

Morgenthau, Hans J., *Dilemmas of Politics* (Chicago: University of Chicago Press, 1958), pp. 7–43.

Riemer, Neal, *The Revival of Democratic Theory* (New York: Appleton-Century-Crofts, 1962), pp. 1–51.

Rothman, Stanley, "The Revival of Classical Political Philosophy: A Critique," *American Political Science Review*, LVI (2: June, 1962), pp. 341–352.

Part II

METHODOLOGIES
IN POLITICAL THOUGHT

It will come as no surprise to students that disciplinarians incapable of agreement as to the nature of their subject matter are in disagreement as to methodology. Different conceptions of the nature of political thought obviously correlate with different methodological emphases. This point is demonstrated in the articles reproduced in this volume. Sabine's insistence, for example, that development of the historical setting of a theory is requisite to understanding the theory's emergence and essence ensures that his treatment of the subject matter will be largely historical. Other authors included in this volume consider the chronological approach unduly restrictive of their different logics.

It would be easy to dismiss the cleavage of opinion with Thoreau's observation that "if a man does not keep pace with his companions, perhaps it is because he hears a different drummer."[1] Acknowledgment

[1]Henry David Thoreau, *Walden and Other Writings of Henry David Thoreau* (New York: Modern Library, 1950), p. 290.

that different methodological assumptions and different judgments reasonably lead scholars to different results may be the best conclusion that political scientists can reach in the present state of the discipline, but it seems more appropriate to the scholarly enterprise to review the methodological emphases of the recent period in an attempt to perceive the trends of our discontents.

That many scholars are dissatisfied with the results of scholarship in political thought is the burden of this collection of essays. The historical, legalistic, institutional, ethical, and other methods of the nineteenth and early twentieth centuries did not afford knowledge of political thought convincing to those exposed to scientific methods. Critical of faith in conceptions, they might have said with C. J. Jung that "the arch sin of faith . . . was that it forestalled experience,"[2] except that they would have eschewed reliance upon such a word as sin. The age has been rife with charges and countercharges of inadequacy, with criticism and countercriticism. At least, none can say that it has been lacking in stimulation to search for better answers to the recurrent questions of politics. Professor Kress in one of the articles extends to "philosophy, literature, and politics" the range of our "search for viable entities or actors by means of which we may view and order our world": in these subject fields as in others, "modern men have sought a purchase upon their worlds—a point that would not crumble beneath their weight or rush away from them at the speed of light." In their search they have represented not only various closed systems and their viewpoints but also a struggle, as Marshall McLuhan puts it, "to discover how not to have a point of view, the method not of closure and perspective but of the open 'field' and the suspended judgment."[3]

That new ideas of proper methods did not replace old ones but came to a somewhat uncomfortable coexistence with them has prompted various reactions. Some say that the discipline is so unruly as to be nonexistent; their corrective proposal could be put in the uncongenial frame of a saying of the Middle Ages:

> The trees are old;
> We must fell the wood
> And plant new trees
> Where old trees stood.

More modest or more doubtful disciplinarians caution delay to permit careful distinction between what is outworn and what is merely

[2] C. J. Jung, *Memories, Dreams, Reflections* (Vintage edition: New York: Alfred A. Knopf, Inc. and Random House, Inc., 1965), p. 94.
[3] Marshall McLuhan, *The Gutenberg Galaxy* (Toronto: University of Toronto Press, 1962), p. 276.

well-worn. Other scholars look upon the unruliness as rich complexity and welcome each new suggestion as a further enrichment of the subject field. And, as in every profession, some profess from narrow and closed minds. Still other scholars weigh the new methods and the new knowledge derived from their application and find them wanting. The search for political knowledge continues unabated. Novitiate political thinkers confront a range of choice that is exceptional in a scholarly discipline. They enjoy, moreover, the prospect that much remains to be done.

Among the methodologies achieving prominence in political thought during the twentieth century, four have been selected for illustration of recent development: behavioralism, the analytic approach, functionalism, and existentialism. All result in part from some philosophical movement, but the analytic one more directly so than the others. Behavioralism has its roots in both positivism and pragmatism, emphasizing observation and verification and being strictly empirical. Functionalism is related to the teleological vitalistic tradition in philosophy in that it looks to the functioning organism as its model. The analytic approach was developed as his methodology in the later writings of Wittgenstein, who maintained that the study of language use reveals the meaning of philosophical terms. It is obvious that these three methodologies are not mutually exclusive. Thus these three basic methodologies in political thought reflect three outstanding modern philosophic-scientific movements (positivism, vitalism, and language analysis).

Existentialism is simultaneously a philosophical and a political conception because it emphasizes the committed person—commitment to both a personal and a social morality. Existentialists distinctively stress the free and individualistic man: each of us should strive to become an authentic individual in choosing what or who he is to be. In making his individual choices, he chooses also for mankind. His preference then becomes his guide to action in the ambiguous world about him. That this set of views has political significance is obvious; as the essay by Sartre shows, it sometimes seems preeminently *political* philosophy.

BEHAVIORAL METHODOLOGY

The history of political behavioralism is well summarized in the article by Dahl. What is political behavioralism? Some say that political behavioralism is only a mood or an attitude, others that it involves definite ideas, principles, and procedures.

David Easton characterizes behavioralism by a list of eight "assumptions and objectives," which he terms "the intellectual foundation stones on which this movement has been constructed": regularities, verification, techniques, quantification, values, systematization, pure science, and integration.[4] "This list," Easton says, "probably includes all the major tenets of the behavioral credo and represents the major differences between the behavioral and traditional modes of research."[5] Easton renders his list of assumptions and objectives meaningful by elaboration of each concept. Thus, regularities in political behavior can be ascertained and enable the student to construct generalizations or theories that can be used in both explanation and prediction. The generalizations must be subject to validation. Techniques for the study of political behavior should be subjected to continual review with an eye cocked to their refinement and validation. Quantification is essential to precision and should be used where possible and appropriate. Ethical values must be clearly distinguished so as not to be confused with empirical explanation. Theoretical understanding is merely preliminary to application in the scientific enterprise. A broadly integrative approach inclusive of knowledge from related social sciences is requisite for validity and generality in the research of political science. Easton acknowledges differences in emphasis among the foregoing assumptions and objectives in the views of political behavioralists but contends that these differences are submerged in the unity of the behavioralists', overweening objective: a "science of politics modeled after the methodological assumptions of the natural sciences."[6]

There is no doubt that behavioralism is influential. That behavioralism is most prominent among the new contenders is indicated not only by the number of books and treatises advocating it, but also by the number of political theorists espousing the doctrine.

Not only is there widespread advocacy of behavioralism but there is also much criticism of it. The criticisms are of two major types: the first relates to the adequacy of the basic principles of behavioral theory construction and verification procedures (which concerns items 1–4 and 6 on Easton's list); the second relates to matters of value and to the question of whether or not behavoiralism can adequately treat them. Criticisms of the former type are again twofold; one relating to theory construction, the other to verification procedures. Most behavioralists now realize that a theory based on pure empiricism (that is, without nonobservable statements) is sterile and that imaginative, nonempirical hypotheses are a necessity for an adequate theory. But nonempirical hypotheses involve statements not amenable to behavioral

[4]David Easton, *A Framework for Political Analysis* (Englewood Cliffs, N.J.: Prentice-Hall, Inc., 1965), pp. 6–7.

[5]David Easton, pp. 7–8.

[6]David Easton, p. 8.

study. If one resorts to such statements then one's behavioralism is not pure, that is, it needs criteria other than observation to determine the admissibility of such statements.

The second aspect of theory, the verification procedure (Easton's item 2), determines what statements may be made in relation to the political system. If the behavioralists accept this verification procedure, they encounter the fact that the doctrine that generalizations must be testable, in principle, by reference to relevant behavior has been rejected by philosophers.

The principle that generalizations must be testable originated with the Vienna logical positivists (Schlick, Ayer, and others) in the 1920s and has been much debated since its original formulation. It has been so heavily criticized that there are no present-day logical positivists in philosophy. Whereas logical positivism was the main Anglo-American philosophical movement in the 1930s, it has now been replaced by language analysis. Wittgenstein, the father of logical positivism, rejected his progeny; Ayer has changed to a position close to that of the ordinary language philosophers. There are many reasons why logical positivism was rejected:

1. No amount of empirical evidence could verify general statements as laws involving the words *all* or *none,* for it is impossible to know all cases.

2. If a statement is considered empirical, then its advocates must allow for the possibility of a meaningful statement that would be an exception.

3. If, on the other hand, the principle is considered analytic, its advocates face the problem that its opposite is not self-contradictory (a usual test for analytic statements).

4. Or if the political behavioralist contends that his principle is the rule of language for the use of the word *meaningful* that is implicit in ordinary discourse, it is a strong statement, for this principle rejects entire groups of statements, such as those in theology or ethics, which always have been accepted as meaningful. As the philosopher Urmson says, "It is hard to swallow the doctrine that one has always used the concept of 'sense' in such a way that 'this is good' is nonsense. . . . Whether the verification principle was in accord with ordinary usage seems then to be an empirical question easily decided in the negative."[7]

There are many prominent political behavioralists today—Dahl, Truman, Almond, Easton, and Eulau, among others. All seem to hold to

[7] J. O. Urmson, *Philosophical Analysis: Its Development between the Two Wars* (Oxford: Oxford University Press, 1956), p. 169.

some form of the verification principle. Dahl, Almond, and Easton speak for themselves in the essays that follow. Truman speaks of validation by "direct observation"; Eulau speaks of concern with "directly or indirectly observable political action." It would appear, in light of the philosophical criticisms, that the principle must be either significantly altered or abandoned altogether by the political behavioralists.

There are three basic criticisms of behavioralism concerning value issues. First, a behavioralist concerns himself with "political behavior," but what exactly is meant here by the term *political?* (This definitional problem has been considered earlier.) It is at least doubtful whether it is possible to define *political* without reference to the purpose(s) of the political group. The purposes of an anarchist and a collectivist are quite different. To state purposes is to state values. One might argue that politics can be defined in terms of what government officials *do*, but this definition is inadequate because, first, such officials might not be concerned about all the matters they should be and, second, there is the additional problem of determining who are government officials (whether for example, part-time advisers can be considered government officials).

The second critical point is that any behavioralist brings to his investigation certain motivations and basic conceptual frameworks—certain prescientific presuppositions that are value presuppositions. Two examples of such presuppositions are: the selection of topics for investigation and the formulation of one's concepts. Such selections and formulations cannot be derived through behavioral methods. Strauss says, moreover, that behavioralists are biased in favor of democracy. The presupposition of the value of behavioralism is a value judgment in itself. To such presuppositions it is necessary to add doubt as to whether a behavioralist can explain his own behavior as an observer.

Finally, behavioralism cannot tell us what our ultimate values ought to be. It can describe our values, but it cannot prescribe them. It might be able to tell us what we ought to do given certain circumstances and certain purposes, but it cannot establish scientifically one's ultimate purposes. This point is especially applicable in the area of public policy making. Determination of purposes requires ultimately moral decisions that are beyond the means of behavioralism.

Notwithstanding these criticisms, the behavioralist has made and still can make needed contributions. He can furnish valuable predictions about the likely and unlikely acts of men. He can make us aware of significant correlations. By his different emphases he may even produce bases that enable us to think in new categories. Is behavioralism then "the new departure in social research" its advocates claim it to be, or is it destined to become the dead horse that logical positivism has become in philosophy?

ANALYTIC POLITICAL METHODOLOGY

The origin of analytic political thought was the later philosophical writings (from 1930 on) of the Austrian philosopher Wittgenstein. As noted previously, Wittgenstein's earlier writings were the foundations of logical positivism. Hence one man played a major role in developing the philosophical grounds of two major political thought systems—behavioralism and the analytic school.

The dominant concern of Wittgenstein's analytic philosophy is ordinary language. He contends that philosophical problems and disputes are brought about by a lack of awareness of how we actually use language. The central task of philosophy, he feels, is to describe the use of words and expressions, to give a logical account of how certain common or technical terms work in their standard or nonstandard mode of employment. The word *logic* here does not refer to the orthodox formal logics (either deductive or inductive) but rather to the study of how certain key expressions like *know, cause, see, state, freedom* are standardly used. Hence philosophy, as Ryle says, can detect "the sources in linguistic idioms of recurrent misconstructions and absurd theories."[8]

Corollary to this thesis that the task of philosophy is elucidation of the use of certain key expressions is the view that philosophy yields no new knowledge of facts other than facts about the structure of language. Furthermore, analysis of language can yield neither prescriptions for action nor commendations of policies or institutions. Therefore such provision is not the task of the political philosopher, and political philosophy is a second-order activity. Its task is twofold: either it deals with the conceptual structure and methodology of political theory (which makes it a branch of the philosophy of science), or it deals with the language used in political thought. It can provide no ground for a stand on substantive matters. The best known political philosopher who followed Wittgenstein's thought was T. D. Weldon, whose *Vocabulary of Politics* is the classic of this tradition. In the selection included in this anthology Weldon says, "it is difficult to see how any political principle can significantly claim . . . non-contextual validity." This statement clearly exhibits the analysts' philosophy that meaning is a function of contextual use.

[8]G. Ryle, "Systematically Misleading Expressions," *Proceedings of the Aristotelian Society*, 32 (1931–1932), p. 170.

Weldon's view of political philosophy as conceptual clarification has been criticized on several points. Two of the main criticisms are:

1. Clarification of meaning is not enough. Clarification of a concept, such as that of a right, is merely a useful preliminary to the important questions of what and who possesses rights and how the rights are grounded.

2. Ideas themselves can be regulatory. Stanley Benn points out that "People who are politically active within a given system have an idea (or maybe a range of competing ideas) of what it is like and how it works, of the practices it sanctions and of those it could not tolerate. . . . And these ideas themselves regulate the behavior of individuals in their institutional roles."[9] Ideas are not simply something to be clarified; they can be regulatory in and of themselves.

THE METHODOLOGY OF FUNCTIONALISM

Functionalism is a method of explaining events or institutions by specifying what they do, that is, the function they perform, in a given complex. In political thought functionalism attempts to explain events in a political structure as it operates through time. It asserts that all political activities of a system function to maintain that political system.

Professors Flanigan and Fogelman in commentary upon functionalism in political science conceive three forms of functionalism: (1) an "eclectic functionalism," in which the concept of function is combined with other equally significant conceptions (such as structure, history, ideology) in a comprehensive analysis of political phenomena; (2) an "empirical functionalism" in which analysts focus upon the functions of a "limited range of phenomena"; and (3) a "structural functionalism" in which the attempt is to attain "a scientific theory of the political system."[10] Although there are differences in terminology and in approach among "structural functionalists," this third category, Flanigan and Fogelman think, can be characterized by "first, an emphasis on the whole system as the unit of analysis; second, postulation of particular functions as requisite to the maintenance of the whole system;

[9]Stanley I. Benn, "Political Philosophy, Nature of," *The Encyclopedia of Philosophy*, vol. 6 (New York: The Macmillan Company and the Free Press, 1967), p. 389.
[10]William Flanigan and Edwin Fogelman, "Functionalism in Political Science," in Don Martindale (ed.), *Functionalism in the Social Sciences: The Strength and Limits of Functionalism in Anthropology, Economics, Political Science, and Sociology* (Philadelphia: The American Academy of Political and Social Science, February, 1965), p. 111.

third, concern to demonstrate the functional interdependence of diverse structures within the whole system."[11]

Functionalism may be clarified by contrasting it in some aspects with behavioralism. As to the way each conceives of its "model"—its way of representing a complex of relationships—functionalism looks to a single system of interrelated elements akin to an organism, while behavioralism conceives a mechanistic model. Functionalism focuses on the unity and direction of the entire system, while behavioralism tends to concentrate on the precise determination of relationships between parts of the system. Functionalism starts with wholes having purposes; behavioralism with parts that combine into aggregates, although the latter still obey the laws of the parts. Both positions are attempts to construct general theories that can predict political events.

The functionalist concentrates upon purpose; the behavioralist studies behavior and avoids speculation as to the purpose that underlies that behavior. For the functionalist, purpose pertains to a unit; he must define the unit and determine the conditions for its persistence as well as its patterns of action. This unit can be either micro- or macrofunctional, that is, one can speak either of the United States Congress or of the entire political structure of the United States as functional units. The functionalist maintains that it is only in terms of these structured, bounded, persistent, and purposeful units that political groups can be understood.

There have been two usual criticisms of functional methodology:

1. Functionalism is implicitly conservative. The point here is that, as the approach emphasizes the conditions essential to stability and smooth functioning in the system, political justice may well be sacrificed by functionalists to these primary values.

2. Statements about function are nothing more than "cause and effect" statements. There is nothing unique about functions. Teleological statements cannot be translated into mechanistic statements.

Functionalists reply to the first criticism by pointing out that most functionalists are advocates of social change. They deem a stable but diseased society undesirable. Determination of the conditions for the persistence of disease may be viewed as requisite to consideration of a remedy. Therefore stability is not necessarily the primary value of functionalism. In regard to the second critical point, the functionalist claims that his approach enables the political scientist to predict the continuance of systems but such predictions are statements beyond single cause and effect relations.

[11]William Flanigan and Edwin Fogelman, p. 116.

EXISTENTIALISM AS A METHODOLOGY

Existentialism, along with analytic philosophy, is one of the two major movements in contemporary Western philosophy. It does not have the definite tenets of either behavioralism or analytic philosophy. It is very important for political philosophy, however, because most existentialists take strong political-philosophical positions in sharp contrast to both logical positivists and analytic philosophers. These two tend not to assert political philosophies.

The origins of existentialism are claimed for many philosophers: Plato, St. Augustine, and even St. Thomas. It is with Kierkegaard, however, that most writers note its origins. It is his emphasis on the *individual* that is the first hallmark of existentialism. Not only does Kierkegaard argue that "a crowd is the untruth," but also he champions, as Sartre says in the extract selected for this volume, "the cause of pure, unique subjectivity against the objective universality of essence. . . ." Thus the individual is centrally important to Kierkegaard. This view contrasts with Hegel's emphasis on groups (for example, nations). Truth is subjective rather than objective as Hegel maintained.

Perhaps more important, existentialism stresses the possibility of choice as the key factor of human nature. Man is free. He is condemned to be free because that is his condition in nature. Thus the famous existentialist dictum that "existence precedes essence" is a corollary of man's free condition. This freedom means, first, that man makes himself—he can become what he wishes to become; and, second, that by choosing for himself he chooses for all men (in this tenet the existentialists are Kantian); he is responsible for all men as he claims his position to be ideal for all.

For the purposes of political philosophy these doctrines, individualism and freedom, are the central existentialist tenets. And the consequences are both interesting and strange. Individualism and freedom of choice in political philosophy seem to imply subjectivity. The fact that existentialists have embraced Naziism (Heidegger), Liberalism (Jaspers), Communism (Sartre), and so on, bears out that there is no one particular political consequence following from the tenets of existentialism. Perhaps the only consequence is the existentialist stress on commitment, which could lead to irrational extremism. On the other hand, Sartre chastises Camus for his lack of political commitment. Perhaps ambiguity in application can be said to pertain to behavioralism, analytic philosophy, and functionalism as well? Again, one must ask if it is possible to be both an existentialist and a Marxist as in Sartre's case.

Concerning Camus, one must reflect on the two insoluble paradoxes he sees for those who argue for ethical consistency in political judgments. First, one must try to choose between nonviolence (and perhaps become a slave to the status quo) and violence (which conflicts with our commitments to institutions or rules such as "Thou shall not kill" and may involve killing of innocent bystanders). The second paradox is that all revolutions involve the choice between freedom and justice. Justice is usually chosen by revolutionaries at the expense of freedom. For example, revolutionists may choose to give up (temporarily they hope) such rights as free speech for economic justice. Anti-revolutionists often choose political freedom (free speech, free press, and so forth) at the expense of economic justice for all. Every political student must determine if these paradoxes are insoluble.

Many of the basic criticisms of existentialism have already been brought out. The question is whether any specific ethic and consequently political philosophy follows from this central tenet. It is difficult to explain the fact that Heidegger's Naziism, Sartre's Communism, and Jaspers' Liberalism arose out of the same type of philosophy.

Second, it is at least questionable whether its basic concepts are not so vague and its methods so objectionable that it fails as a philosophy. The existentialists characteristically express their philosophy in literary or artistic form in reflection of their view of life as inescapably ambiguous: "the existentialist believes that only the riches of the artistic consciousness can be adequate to the rich ambiguity of life itself."[12]

Third, man may not be as free as Sartre claims, for this freedom does not seem reconcilable with Marx's determinism. Which is dominant in Sartre—Existentialism or Marxism?

[12]Abraham Kaplan, *The New World of Philosophy* (New York: Random House, Inc., 1961), p. 117.

5

Andrew Hacker

CAPITAL
AND CARBUNCLES*

Andrew Hacker considers "the methodological trauma through which political science is now passing" with special reference to political thought. He contends that political thought is suffering not so much from a "decline into historicism" as from an "unquestioning reliance on the 'Great Books.'" This reliance has "served to thwart any significant expansion of the scope and function of political theory—in terms of value theory or any other kind." The "Great Books" have been taught "primarily . . . as history—more particularly, as history of ideas and historical biography—with often a smattering of logic added." Other methods of the political scientist are "painstakingly ignored."

Asserting that "Theory has the dual task of explaining behavior (causal theory) and adumbrating principles on how people ought to behave (ethical theory)," he examines the ways in which the Great Books have been approached and evaluates the relevance of these approaches to political science. He sees ten ways of reading the Great Books, ranging from that giving rise to the title of his article, "*Capital* and Carbuncles," to the "timeless." The first—to exemplify his treatment—is primarily biographical: "the fact that Marx had carbuncles made him vent all the more vitriol on the bourgeoisie in his *Capital*."

*Reprinted by permission of the author and publisher from *American Political Science Review*, XLVIII (3: September, 1954), pp. 775–786, where it was entitled *"Capital and Carbuncles: The 'Great Books' Reappraised."*

The last, or "timeless," approach is the proper one for political theorists in his view. The Great Books not only "can go far toward
explaining the political behavior of today" but also prescribe norms
"as worthy of attention . . . now as they ever were": they "faced up to
many important problems in ways which have never been bettered."
But the political theorist must recognize that his "job . . . is to explain
ideas, not to limit himself to knowing what a few historical writers
said about those ideas," and he must concern himself with ideas that
are relevant to the contemporary world. Political theory can be made
relevant to the rest of the social sciences "only . . . if much of the
excess historical, biographical, and logical baggage which surrounds
the 'Great Books' is ruthlessly thrown overboard."

Professor David Easton's widely discussed essay in academic psychoanalysis is indicative of the methodological trauma through which political
science is now passing. Of particular interest is his chapter on political
theory, which, according to his diagnosis, has suffered from a malady
known as "decline into historicism."[1] His specific point of criticism is that
the commentaries of Dunning, McIlwain, and Sabine have led students
away from serious study of value theory. This kind of attack, however,
does not get to the nub of the problem which surrounds political theory.
For while political scientists seem to feel that political theory should be
made the "heart" of their discipline,[2] they will also have to acknowledge
that the "heart" of political theory itself has been reading the "Great
Books." A far greater indictment than Easton's, then, is that it is an
unquestioning reliance on the "Great Books" which has served to thwart
any significant expansion of the scope and function of political theory—in
terms of value theory or any other kind. Students are told to read the
books with great care. But why they have to read them *at all* is a question
which has seldom been squarely confronted. Hence both undergraduates
and graduate students come away, perhaps somewhat pleased that they
can now quote a few choice axioms from Burke, but nonethemore edified
as to *how* the learned authors of yesteryear can aid them in understanding the science of politics.

The reason for this, as Easton has suggested and as I will make plain, is
that the "Great Books" are primarily taught as history—more particularly,

---

[1]David Easton, *The Political System* (New York, 1953), chap. 10.

[2]See Committee for the Advancement of Teaching, American Political Science Association, *Goals for Political Science* (New York, 1951), pp. 116–33. Citing "opinions
from the men and women who teach political science in the leading institutions of
higher education in the country," the Committee found that while in terms of actual
curricula political theory is not "the core of political science," at the same time there
was a "widespread feeling . . . that it should be made the heart of the subject" (p. 126).

as history of ideas and historical biography—with often a smattering of logic added. The student of politics, when he comes to study theory, is immediately given an historian's pair of shoes. Virtually all the methods which he learned as a political scientist are painstakingly ignored. It is not being deprecatory of the study of history to point out that it is something quite different from the study of politics. It would be a grave error to fail to see that a knowledge of history is vital for the political scientist. He cannot understand the American Senate of 1954 without knowing something of the War between the States; he cannot claim to know today's House of Commons without appreciating its Elizabethan counterpart. But history, when used by the student of politics, must, like Harold Laski's expert, be on tap and not on top. For this reason, then, the political scientist must always have before him the question, in paraphrase of Professor Lynd, "History for What?" For history is no more than a technique for the political scientist: it should be a handmaiden, as mathematics is to the physical sciences. A political scientist should be able to draw on historical evidence with as great facility as he utilizes public opinion polls and the files of the *Congressional Record.*

My contention here is that political science is a bona-fide member of the social science family. And, for this reason, it is contemporary. Economic and sociological theory deal solely with today's world. (Or they deal with generalizations which encompass all times and all places. But such theorizing must necessarily include the here and now of today's world.) It is only political theory which has failed to note its contemporaneity. Saddled, to a far greater extent than economics or sociology, with a shelf-full of "Great Books," the political theorist of today is content to discuss such topics as: "George Plekhanov and the 'Iskra' Period;" "Significance and Impact of Heinrich Treitschke;" "The Political Thought of L. T. Hobhouse;" and "Thomas Hobbes' Concept of Religion and the State's Relation to It." (These are four *of the first six* projects listed under Political Philosophy in the list of doctoral dissertations published, in the September, 1953, issue of the AMERICAN POLITICAL SCIENCE REVIEW.) As we are quite aware, Plekhanov, Treitschke, Hobhouse, and Hobbes are very much dead and buried. Yet political scientists continue to read them—and prescribe the reading of them to their students—in our own day. My concern, however, is not so much with the fact that Plekhanov, Treitschke, and writers like them form the corpus of political theory. Personally I desire to save the "Great Books" rather than bury them. And it is for that reason that I wish to examine the ways in which these books are approached, and evaluate the relevance that these approaches have for political science.

It may be well to admit here that I can do little more than assume that the function of political theory is to deal with the contemporary world (or, more grandiosely, with all periods in history, including the present). And I fear that this can be no more than an assumption about the character of political theory, which one either accepts or rejects prima facie. Theory has the dual task of explaining behavior (causal theory) and adumbrating principles on how people ought to behave (ethical theory). Hence, the burden must be shifted to the non-contemporaries. They must show how the study of history, or of the history of ideas, or of historical biography—in and of themselves—have a meaning for political science. The burden of justification, it seems to me, lies with those who would immerse themselves in history. They must show why political theory, unlike theory in the other social sciences, should be anything other than contemporary with regard to the problems that it sets for itself.

I have divided the prevalent ways of reading the "Great Books" into ten arbitrary (and occasionally overlapping) categories, designated as follows: (1) *Capital* and Carbuncles; (2) The Hero-Worshippers; (3) Intellectual Plagiarism; (4) Who-Said-It-First?; (5) The Mind-Readers; (6) The Camera-Eye; (7) Influencing the Intelligentsia; (8) Influencing the Masses; (9) The Logic Book;[3] and (10) Timeless. No brief rubric can tell the whole story and I have therefore attempted to capture the spirit of each approach. It is (10), and only (10), I will maintain, which is the appropriate way for students of political theory to approach the "Great Books."

1. *CAPITAL* AND CARBUNCLES

This first approach is primarily biographical. Here we are concerned to know how a particular book came to be written in a particular way. Thus the fact that Marx had carbuncles made him vent all the more vitriol on the bourgeoisie in his *Capital*. Or we are told that Rousseau's constricted bladder made him all the less coherent at the time he wrote the *Social Contract*. But there is more than this. If, we hear, there were vitiating circumstances surrounding the writing of a particular book, then a reading of *other*, and less well-known, books by the same author will show us his "real" outlook—and meaning. For example, Guglielmo Ferrero tells us that if we are to know the "real" Machiavelli, we must read his *Discourses*.

[3]The Logic-Book approach is not a victim of the historical bias to which I have been alluding. However, it is still non-political. Hence, even though logical analysis may be exonerated from the historical taint, it must nevertheless come under the axe because of its failure to pass the political test.

In fact, Ferrero tells us, even in *The Prince* there are only a few of the notorious "Machiavellian" strictures and these are

> not connected with each other nor with the rest of the argument, which could be either suppressed entirely without mutilating the work or rendered quite inoffensive by disguising their thought in less frank terminology. Anyone acquainted with the life and character of Machiavelli knows that these fragments of his thought, on which a whole theory of conduct has been erected, are nothing but bad-tempered explosions.[4]

Hence we must add to Marx's carbuncles and Rousseau's bladder, Machiavelli's bad temper. Once we know, and make allowance for, this character trait we can fully understand Machiavelli the Author. But if we follow this approach then we will concern ourselves not with the "whole theory of conduct" which grew out of Machiavelli's bad temper, but rather with the biography of a single man and perhaps the historical conditions which surrounded the writing of one of his books. The verdict here, then, must be that such a study is biography and history; but it is not politics.

2. THE HERO-WORSHIPPERS

"A hitherto undiscovered cache of the Harrington papers has been uncovered beneath the floor-boards of a remote Devonshire inn, and Professor Smith, a leading Harrington-scholar, has reported that he intends to spend the next five years studying and cataloging them." This quotation is wholly of my own making, but paraphrases of it are not hard to discover. The "Harrington-scholar" is concerned, and concerned only, with the life and works of Harrington *the man*. In (1) we saw how some people "interpreted" *Capital* in light of Marx's carbuncles. But the Hero-Worshippers are not only concerned with the significant books by a particular author; every single jotting that the man set down on paper is of crucial importance. Thus, for example, Mr. Pelczynski of Oxford, in the *Cambridge Journal*, elucidated Hegel's thoughts on the English Constitution: "In October 1831 *Die Preussische Staatszeitung* published an article entitled 'Ueber die englische Reformbill' by the Professor of Philosophy at the Royal University of Berlin, G. W. F. Hegel."[5] Mr. Pelczynski, how-

---

[4]Quoted in the bibliography of William Ebenstein's *Great Political Thinkers* (New York, 1951), p. 845. It should be said that Professor Ebenstein's short introductions in this book of readings are noteworthy examples of an attempt to show the relevance of the ideas contained in the "Great Books" to the problems of the contemporary world.

[5]Zbyszek Pelczynski, "Hegel on the English Constitution," *Cambridge Journal*, Vol. 5 (June, 1952), p. 519.

ever, is forced to confess that "On the whole. . . Hegel's account of the formal or legal side of the Constitution. . . contains nothing that can be called original or profound."[6] And he concludes: "And so he must join the large group of distinguished and learned foreigners who, while they said much about the English Constitution that was true and interesting, always managed in the end to misjudge it in some fundamental respect."[7] Now Mr. Pelczynski is a Hegel scholar. The rest of us remember Hegel because of such books as his *Philosophy of Right* or his *Philosophy of History*. But, for Mr. Pelcyznski, Hegel's article on the English Constitution is also of importance. However, most all of his remarks are either misunderstandings or commonplaces; there are at least a dozen better commentaries on the subject. Does the fact that *Hegel* made them make them any the less undistinguished? But the Hero-Worshipper must give the front rank to everything that his Hero wrote. By this token, if a Calhoun-scholar discovered a (thoroughly bad) picture by Calhoun, would he try to persuade the South Carolina Art Gallery to hang it?

We can see, then, that this approach must very definitely be classed as biography. It certainly is not politics.

3. INTELLECTUAL PLAGIARISM

Every author of a "Great Book," this approach postulates, is wittingly or unwittingly echoing the words of one of his predecessors. Marx's ideas are to be found in Babeuf, Ricardo, and Hodgskin. T. H. Green and Bosanquet (not so unwittingly) are based on Hegel. Even if an author does not give credit to his mentors, his plagiarisms can still be traced. One hears of the scholar who spent his life trying to reconstruct the exact contents of Rousseau's library, bibliography, and reading lists in order to discover which books might have influenced him. Along this line, the late Professor Laski once wrote:

> A careful comparison with Bodin has revealed to me that Montcretien, usually acclaimed as the founder of political economy, has, in fact, taken 300 pages wholesale from Bodin, merely inverting the order of Bodin's remarks. And in the books this unblushing plagiary is exhibited as supreme originality.[8]

Now one need not go so far as to accuse M. Montcretien of "unblushing" plagiarism. It may well be that he had just read so much of Bodin that he could not help but have his ideas in the forefront of his mind. When Mr.

[6]Pelczynski, p. 521.
[7]Pelczynski, p. 530.
[8]*The Holmes-Laski Letters*, ed. Mark Howe, 2 vols. (London, 1953), Vol. 2, p. 1098.

Plamenatz devotes a book to showing the dependence of the Utilitarians on Hobbes, he does not mean to say that Bentham consciously plagiarized Hobbes.[9] It is sufficient to note that the ideas of one man influenced another's writing. This approach seeks to find out the impact of writer on writer. It can depend on direct evidence, as a diary entry which might read, "Today read Locke and was much impressed;" or it can rest on mere deduction from similarity of words and phrases in the works of two men. But no matter whether we are charitable or otherwise, this method of study is concerned with either the history of ideas or the biographies of individual authors. It is not, however, concerned with politics.

4. WHO-SAID-IT-FIRST?

The previous approach was interested in the direct or indirect influence of one author upon another. Quite different are the searchers after the man who crossed the finish line first. Professor Friedrich writes of modern theorists:

> A review of their contributions to date to political theory reveals that most of what they have had to say has been a repetition of existing knowledge, developed in the course of the history of political thought.[10]

They usually frame such questions as: Who was the "father" of sociology? Who first spoke of sovereignty? or Who originated the notion of natural rights? The accepted procedure here is, for example, to take Comte, who is the "recognized" father of sociology, and show that Montesquieu emphasized sociological factors long before Comte was alive. Once Montesquieu begins to gain ground, then Hobbes or Machiavelli will be rushed in to take over the paternity. The difficulty with this approach is that the classicists are always ready at hand with Plato and Aristotle to show that they anticipated anything and everything that has since been said in political theory. For example, Professor Kecskemeti tells us:

> The idea of "policy science" is not a new one. . . . Its first, incomparable formulation is found in Plato's *Republic:* policy, the Platonic Socrates says, can be reasonable and sound only if it is based upon the fullness of scientific insight and knowledge.[11]

[9]John Plamenatz, *Mill's Utilitarianism, Reprinted with a Study of the English Utilitarians* (Oxford, 1949), pp. 16, 21, 116. For a splendid criticism of this Who-Influenced-Whom approach, see Arthur Child's review of Plamenatz's book in *Ethics,* Vol. 60 (April, 1950), p. 223.
[10]This statement was taken from notes for a paper which was delivered before the American Political Science Association in September, 1953, entitled "The Historical Approach to Political Thought: A Re-Evaluation." Professor Friedrich's argument is an authoritative counterweight to the viewpoint which I am suggesting in this article.
[11]"The Policy Sciences," *World Politics,* Vol. 4 (July, 1952), p. 520.

And they, by reason of seniority, crossed the finish-line long before anyone else. One effect here, of course, is to steal the thunder from modern theorists. If one postulates that there has been "nothing new" since Hobbes (that is, all the finish lines have already been crossed), then one need not bother to keep up to date on developments in the recent history of political thought. But no matter what the cause or consequences of such a study of the "Great Books," it is essentially subject-matter for the history of ideas and is not politics.

5. THE MIND-READERS

Most of us, it seems, do not know what the authors of the "Great Books" *really* meant. This is probably because we have not read those books closely enough or with enough care. Or it may be because we do not know a sufficient amount about the life of the author and about the historical surroundings. While the usual reason is that close attention has not been granted to the text, it is also occasionally said that we must know the contemporaneous definitions of words in order to understand the author's real intentions. Mr. C. H. Wilson gives us the sad tale of Bodin:

> By the majority perhaps of those in the succeeding centuries who were influenced by Bodin, his statement was read and received as a statement of absolute, unlimited sovereignty freeing the ruler, whether a person or a body of persons, from every restraint except that of his own sovereign will. Nothing was further from the author's real meaning. . . .[12]

Hence we see that not only modern students, but also "the majority . . . of those . . . who were influenced by Bodin" failed to capture his "real meaning." This is probably because, unlike Mr. Wilson, they read Bodin hastily and without appreciating the qualifications and nuances with which he surrounded his statements. What does not seem to trouble Mr. Wilson is that Bodin was influential simply *because he was misunderstood.* If people had known his "real meaning," as Mr. Wilson claims to, then they probably would not have paid any attention to him. In fact, the only reason that Mr. Wilson has even *heard* of Bodin—the only reason why his reputation has survived—is because people considered him as the author of a "statement of absolute, unlimited sovereignty." Without such an interpretation, however unjust to Bodin it may be, Bodin is historically meaningless. Perhaps, then, Mr. Wilson ought to join "the majority" and misread Bodin as well! But in any event the Mind-Reader approach is

[12]"Sovereign and Sovereignty," *Chambers Encyclopedia,* new edition (New York, 1951), Vol. 12, p. 775.

philosophical (insofar as it pays attention to the logic of a man's sentences), and historical and biographical. But it is not political.

6. THE CAMERA-EYE

The "Great Books" give us a good idea of what some thoughtful people had on their minds during a certain historical period. This is certainly true. One cannot deny that, at the time Rousseau's *Social Contract* appeared, a goodly number of people were thinking about social contracts. In this sense, then, we can see reflections of what was on men's minds. And we can read Burke on the French Revolution and Paine on the Rights of Man and see that different groups were thinking different things in the 1790s. Of course there were a lot of people who weren't thinking at all; or people who might have been thinking, but who couldn't read books. But the Camera-Eye can only focus on the literati. Hence while Locke's *Second Treatise* is useful for telling us what the American Founding Fathers had on their minds when they were thinking about politics, there is no book that will tell us what the illiterate Kikiyu in Kenya are thinking about today. In addition, "anticipatory" books, those which give vent to ideas prior to the time when they have become generally accepted, have a value insofar as they are the first to cross the finish-line. But they do not reflect the thought of the time in which they were written. Vico, for instance, was resurrected by Michelet long after he had passed away. The people of Vico's time had never heard of Vico; and he didn't give a Camera-Eye of his contemporaries' thinking anyway. But this is interesting to us only if we are concerned with the history of ideas. It is not any help with politics.

From another angle we can say that Tocqueville gives us a good historical picture of pre-Revolutionary France; or that Aristotle informs us of the constitutions of Ancient Greece. This, however, is cheating. If we want to know about France or Greece we ought to go about it the way historians do: through a careful study of manuscripts, records, eye-witness accounts, etc. The "Great Books" tell us little in the way of actual history. Burke's *French Revolution* is not an historical description of that event; it is a polemic telling us it ought never to have happened. There are not *two* histories: one for the political theorist, to be gained through the "Great Books", and another for the historian, to be gained through the traditional sources. There is only one history, and that is the historian's history. History via the "Great Books" is inaccurate, incomplete, and has such a strong bias as to be worthless. And anyhow this Camera-Eye value (or lack of value) in the "Great Books" is history and not politics.

7. INFLUENCING THE INTELLIGENTSIA

This approach is similar to (3). But (3) went down the historical scale; the fact that Montcretien "plagiarized" Bodin was of interest there. Here, however, we are interested in books because they influenced particular intellectuals in a later period. Theory, then, becomes the History of Political Books. Bosanquet, for example, captures our attention because we can see the influence of Hegel and T. H. Green on him. Of course Bosanquet didn't influence anyone himself. He wrote in Oxford and it is likely that no more than a small circle of dons read him at the time (and read him still). And Bosanquet seems in different ways, to have influenced Collingwood and A. D. Lindsay.[13] In this sort of study we are far removed from political events. We are not, as in (6), concerned to see what whole countries were thinking. It is merely that we set up a chain of book-writers and then do not have the heart to break it. Hence we can begin with Rousseau and move on up to Hegel (so far so good). If we say that Hegel influenced Marx, and Marx Lenin, then we are on the track of important political events. But if we say that Hegel influenced Green, and Green Bosanquet, and Bosanquet Lindsay, we are lost in the cloisters of Oxford's intelligentsia and far from anything in the world of political behavior. Hence we must conclude that this is the history of ideas that we are studying and not politics at all. And it can become the history of interesting, or logical, or worthwhile ideas—but they can well be ideas wholly divorced from any streams of action. Insofar as these ideas are worthwhile, the fact that they ever "influenced" any other writers is unimportant for our purposes. Hence, as we will see in (10), such books can be very useful in studying political theory. But this need not entail studying their historical pedigrees.

8. INFLUENCING THE MASSES

The title of this section is not wholly an accurate one. For here we are concerned to see how books influenced political events. A "Great Book" does not, however, have to be read by the masses in order to influence political movements. Hence we may speak, first, of books which had an impact on "thinking" people. In this vein we can see that Locke's *Second Treatise* and Montesquieu's *Spirit of the Laws* influenced Hamilton and

---

[13]For a careful study of the intellectual currents which influenced A. D. Lindsay, see Adam Ulam's *The Philosophical Foundations of English Socialism* (Cambridge, Mass., 1951), esp. chaps. 2, 5. But just who or what was influenced *by* Lindsay is something that Ulam never makes clear. Few will deny that Lindsay wrote intelligent and interesting books on democratic theory. But to say this is quite different from saying that he had a significant impact on English Socialism.

Madison. Thus we may say that Locke and Montesquieu had an impact, respectively, on the American Revolution and the American Constitution. But these authors were known only to the Founding Fathers; the rough farmers of the backwoods of Pennsylvania cannot be said to have been influenced directly by the "Great Books." On the other hand, books such as the *Communist Manifesto* and Rousseau's *Social Contract* were read by, and did influence, the masses directly. In this case the "Great Books" were really pamphlets and were read as polemical broadsides of their time. There is, of course, a middle ground between a book which influences a single influential man (as Pareto was said to have stirred Mussolini) and a book which sways millions (as the *Communist Manifesto* has). In fact most of the "Great Books" are in this in-between area. But it is important to know how much of a "best-seller" each one was.

Knowing *who* read a certain "Great Book" is vital because it ought to determine how *we* read it. There is no doubt that Madison read Locke very carefully; hence we ought to read him carefully as well. But the chances are that the pamphlet-type "Great Books" were read hastily and without too much attention to details. It would, therefore, be advisable for the student to read the *Communist Manifesto* on a crowded and noisy bus; that is probably the atmosphere in which most of the masses of mankind read it. But often we have to read a book in both ways. The *Federalist Papers*, for example, originally appeared as articles in New York newspapers. They were doubtless read by the electors of that State with the summary attention that we give to the Alsop brothers. On the other hand, the *Federalist* is important because Chief Justice Marshall relied heavily on it to form his judicial opinions. And it is certain that Marshall read the *Papers* with great care and close attention. So, depending on which particular group was influenced by it, we must be prepared to change our attitudes when we pick up a particular "Great Book." But no matter how a book influenced historical action, no matter whether it influenced the masses, the cultured few, or a single man, if we are concerned with its *influence* we are using it to study history. And history is not politics.

9. THE LOGIC-BOOK

Here we are bidden to take up a "Great Book" in one hand and an elementary logic-book in the other. We then search for (and are bound to find) tautologies, excluded middles, inconsistencies, and non-sequiturs galore. It matters not if the book was written as a tuppenny pamphlet (as were many of Paine's or Marx's works), if it was a magazine article for a middle-class audience (as was Mill's *On Liberty*), or if it was the studied product of Oxford professors (as were Green's and Bosanquet's books). Thus Mr. Toulmin tells us: "What makes the writings of Bentham, Hobbes, Hegel and Marx 'philosophical' in our sense is the logical characteristics of their statements, not the special purposes for which they make them.[14] Out of this conception of "political philosophy" can come a book by Mr. Weldon which shows us that Marxist foundations are "worthless," "metaphysical and empty."[15] Yet out of this "worthlessness" and "emptiness" came the Russian Revolution. If Czar Nicholas had distributed logic-books to the peasants would the revolution have been averted? But one wonders why Messrs. Toulmin and Weldon pick out *Marx* for their study. Why do they not tell us about the "logical characteristics" of the New York Telephone Directory? The answer is simple. Marx has a relation to practical political movements, and the Telephone Directory has not. But practical movements are not moved by logic. And if that is all that the logic-book people are telling us they are not telling us much. The quixotic element here is that *historical events* have made Bentham, Hobbes, Hegel, and Marx of interest to us. All four, in their own times and to this day, have influenced people. Indeed, as we saw in (5), that is *why* they have come to our notice. And "the logical characteristics" of the statements in these "Great Books" (or their lack of logic) were unimportant to the people who read them and were influenced by them. But if it is simply "logical characteristics" that are wanted, then Babeuf will do as well as Marx; Hooker as Locke; and the Voting Register of San Francisco as Bentham. In a word, these are logic-book exercises, or (in some people's eyes) philosophy, but it is not a study of politics.

10. TIMELESS

The "Great Books" are timeless for both causal and ethical theory. First, they can go far toward explaining the political behavior of today. They do this because of their universal application. Aristotle's comments on the role of the middle class, or the causes of revolution, can tell us much about those phenomena in our own society. St. Augustine's "original sin" is, many would maintain, still among us now and is the "cause" of the disruptions and maladjustments in politics. Rousseau's "general will" may have been a metaphor, but it alludes to a factor in social behavior which has still to be satisfactorily explained by modern verbiage. And certainly Machiavelli's strictures on what rulers actually do do are relevant at this

[14] *An Examination of the Place of Reason in Ethics* (Cambridge, Eng., 1950), p. 199.
[15] *The Vocabulary of Politics* (London, 1953), chap. 4.

moment. Second, various of the "Great Books" prescribe norms which are as worthy of attention—depending on your particular moral outlook—now as they ever were. Thus Tom Paine's "natural rights" of man can still ring a bell for many in 1954. John Stuart Mill on liberty may be listened to by some; and Burke on prescription is heeded by others. The *Federalist Papers* warn us (or those of us who care to be warned) of the undesirability of unchecked power; and Rousseau points up the virtues of equality if we care to listen. Many of these books, as I pointed out earlier, were pamphlets. But no small number of them can polemicize us today as well as they stirred their original readers. (We may recall that in the thirties the business organizations distributed a new edition of Herbert Spencer's *The Man v. The State.*)

But even here we must be wary of historical pitfalls. It should be borne in mind that if our political theory is to be contemporary, then only those books or parts of books which are *relevant* to the world today should be studied. Hence we can well ignore, on the descriptive side, Hegel on the absolute monarchy and Montesquieu on climatic forces in politics. The former deals with an institution which is no longer significant and the latter is too sketchy to have any descriptive value for us. On the ethical side it is hard to rule any "Great Book" out of court. For values are long-lived and are often applicable after the institutional arrangements which sired them have perished. Nevertheless one can doubt if there is much point in considering the desirability of St. Simon's kind of utopia. Utopias are excellent theory; but if they were designed as outgrowths of past societies, then it tends to be difficult to see them as catering to our present aspirations.

Nevertheless the "timelessness" of the "Great Books" must overcome still other hurdles before they can be accepted as sources for political theory. On the one hand, most of them are not as systematic or detailed as the treatises which appear today on the same general subjects (for example, Montesquieu on geographical factors). On the other hand, and this is really a truism, they do not contain applications which fit the theoretical problems of our own day. Hence one might suggest that if we are interested in conservatism we ought to read Mr. Russell Kirk's recent book, *The Conservative Mind*,[16] rather than Burke. For Kirk speaks, in

---

[16](Chicago, 1953). My sole criticism of this excellent analysis is that Kirk deals only with book-writing conservatives. This is well-and-good for the age when statesmen, for example, Burke, Adams, Calhoun, took time off to write theoretical tomes. But the more recent "conservative mind" is not to be discovered in the works of Babbitt, More, and Santayana. One must study the Supreme Court opinions of Justice Field, the speeches of Senator Taft, the pamphlets of the Liberty League, and the editorials of *Fortune* magazine. (Indeed, the reviews of Kirk's book in *Time* and *Fortune* are as revealing of the make-up of the contemporary "conservative mind" as is the book itself.)

his opening and closing chapters, of that political creed in 1953, and, as political theorists and moralists, that is what concerns us. Similarly Harold Laski's *Democracy in Crisis* (1932) might make Marxism more meaningful to us than the Master himself. And the same can be said for substituting R. H. Tawney for Tom Paine and James Burnham for Machiavelli. On the purely descriptive side it is possible that V. O. Key's or Earl Latham's detailed studies of parties and groups might be of more use than the vague references to "factions" in earlier works. In the same vein, "social class" has been explored more deeply and widely by modern sociologists than Aristotle ever managed to do. And to say that Plato first thought of "policy science" does not mean that we can get as much out of Socrates' mouth as we can out of Lerner and Lasswell's *The Policy Sciences.*

But despite the existence of these contemporary works in political theory it cannot be denied (and, indeed, this is the *raison d'être* of all I am saying) that the "Great Books" faced up to many important problems in ways which have never been bettered. I cannot think of any of Hume's successors who have discussed the notion of "consent" more adequately. Rousseau on "will" has been echoed but never expanded. And the "sin" expounded by the Church Fathers has never been explained away by modern psychologists. It is in these metaphorical or poetic moments that the "timelessness" of the "Great Books" comes to the fore. Both on descriptive and on moral grounds, especially the latter, they perform a function which cannot easily be belittled.

A further point must be made if we are to use the "Great Books" in our study of theory. This caveat may steal much of the ground from under those who explicate the "Great Books." But the dredging operation must be performed. This is that we should cease and desist from proving the "Great Books" *wrong.* It is well known that the cherished game of teachers is to debunk and disprove the ancient authors. Yet if we are to allow the "Great Books" admittance because they can explain political behavior in a valid way, then we should do it with a good grace. If particular books are not valid, then we should leave them outside the classroom and not give them entrance merely to castigate them for their "errors." I realize that it gives us a great feeling of exhilaration to show where "we know better" than Hobbes or Bentham or Lenin. But considering that the "Great Books" have been "great" just because many people have thought their arguments to be legitimate, it little behooves us—in our different surroundings—to spend our time parading the sins of our forefathers. I do not deny that, for example, we can better show Hume's "correct" idea of consent by contrasting it with Locke's "incorrect" idea (for, after all, Hume wrote as a critic of Locke). But it will be well to carry this constructive purpose in the front of our minds. My concern, then, is not with deifying the great authors; it is with the study of political theory. To devote a lecture to "Where Marx Went Wrong" is not much help unless it is by way of contrast to where someone else went right. Our concern should be not with Marx as an author, but with the *things* Marx was trying to theorize about. Our interest, as political theorists, is, for example, with the question of "social change" *per se;* it is *not* with Marx-on-social-change. And since theory is the search for "correct" answers, it should spend time disproving the "incorrect" answers in the "Great Books" only if it has a positive purpose in view.

The popularity of the historical-biographical-logical approach is not difficult to explain. If it is employed, then the political theorist need do no more than set his five-foot shelf of tomes by his armchair. That is his "data." All he need do is to read and re-read those few books. By way of "research," he can confine himself to libraries; his tasks will be such endeavors as discovering Machiavelli's bad temper, Hegel's views on the English Constitution, and Marx's debts to Hodgskin. If he is a logician he can sit in the fastness of his study and seek out tautologies in Mill or a seventh definition of "property" in Locke's *Second Treatise.* Or he can discover what Bodin "really meant" by unearthing some letters of his to a Swedish countess. And he can search for an obscure Swiss writer who anticipated Hobbes on sovereignty. But the great thing about all of this kind of study is that it hardly involves decamping from the texts themselves. The whole of theory, by these lights, is to be found in one place: all the "Great Books" can fit on one shelf. The overriding danger, of course, is that the venerable volumes become *ends in themselves.* One becomes concerned not with revolutions or liberty or parties, but merely with what Aristotle or Mill or Madison happened to say on those subjects. No doubt they said much of value. But the job of the political theorist is to explain ideas, not to limit himself to knowing what a few historical writers said *about* those ideas. In addition, the librarian's acquisition-policy for the five-foot shelf is often very indiscriminate. We find, alongside of the earth-shaking pamphlets of Marx and Rousseau, insignificant works by Vico and Bosanquet. Insignificant, that is, in the sense that if they had not been co-opted by the academics no one would ever have heard of them. I object to none of these co-options, however, if they explain political behavior adequately. But most of them do not. They are merely on the shelf because they are hoary-headed and no one has had the heart to evict them. Certainly a living author does not like to have his earlier books, if he has since found them inadequate, remaining in general use. Dead writers, I am sure, feel the same way.

My purpose here, as I said at the beginning, is to preserve the "Great Books" and not to demolish them. Many of them contain explanations and prescriptions which have great value for us now. And, if they are handled in the way that I suggest, they can still be used as the central theme of introductory study—and advanced research—in political theory. I have indicated that there are many "timeless" questions and answers which are better posed in the "Great Books" than in anything which has succeeded them. But the other social sciences, particularly social psychology and anthropology, are moving in on the province that should be political theory's. Professor Almond has pointed this out succinctly:

> The political scientist today has only one foot in the door of a house which he formerly occupied in secure tenure. Anthropology and social psychology . . . have moved rapidly on to a broad front attempting to provide answers to questions which the political scientist, operating with primitive theoretical and methodological tools, has given up asking.[17]

And it should be said that most of these "primitive theoretical tools" are what is found in the "Great Books." However, the difficulties that the political theorist encounters stem not from the fact that he is wedded to the "Great Books." It is because he is not willing to try to derive lessons for explaining the contemporary world *out of* those volumes. I have no doubt that the men who are engaged, for instance, in elucidating "misunderstood" adjectives on majority-rule in Locke are fully competent to discuss the problem of majority-rule *per se*. It is majority-rule and not John Locke that needs theoretical discussion. That is what political theorists should be doing.

Political theory must catch up with the rest of the social sciences. And this will only be done if much of the excess historical, biographical, and logical baggage which surrounds the "Great Books" is ruthlessly thrown overboard.

[17]"Anthropology, Political Behavior and International Relations," *World Politics*, Vol. 2 (Jan., 1950), pp. 277–284, at p. 282.

6

Robert A. Dahl

THE BEHAVIORAL APPROACH
IN POLITICAL SCIENCE*

Robert Dahl describes and evaluates what he terms the "behavioral approach." As Dahl puts it, the behavioral approach was the outgrowth of "dissatisfaction with the achievements of conventional political science, particularly through historical, philosophical, and the descriptive-institutional approaches" and of the "belief that additional methods and approaches either existed or could be developed that would help to provide political science with empirical propositions and theories of a systematic sort, tested by closer, more direct and more rigorously controlled observations of political events." Dahl thinks the protest movement has succeeded in "bringing political studies into closer affiliation with theories, methods, findings, and outlooks in modern psychology, sociology, anthropology and economics" but has shattered political science into five fragments in search of a unity: empirical political science, standards of evaluation, history, general theory, and speculation.

Dahl suggests that the behavioral approach is an attempt to make the empirical component of political science more scientific, that is, it "aims at *stating all the phenomena of government in terms of the observed and observable behavior of men*." It is the latter stress that

*Reprinted by permission of the author and publisher from *American Political Science Review*, LV (4: December, 1961), pp. 763–72, where it was entitled "The Behavioral Approach in Political Science: Epitaph for a Monument to a Successful Protest."

denotes behavioralism in political science, as in other areas of study. The emphasis of behavioralism is upon the "science" in "political science." Behavioralism calls for "closer attention to methodological niceties, to problems of observation and verification, to the task of giving operational meaning to political concepts, to quantification and testing, to eliminating unproductive intervening variables, to sources of data, hypotheses, and theory in the other social sciences" in search of "explanations of some important aspects of politics that are more thoroughly verified, less open to methodological objections, richer in implications for further explanation, and more useful in meeting the perennial problems of political life than the explanations they are intended to replace." Dahl is sufficiently confident of the merits of his behavioral approach to anticipate its disappearance as a distinctive outlook through gradual incorporation "into the main body of the discipline."

It should be recognized that there are degrees of behavioralism—weak to strong—depending upon whether emphasis is upon observational data or upon thought constructs. Although Dahl is eclectic in approach, he may be considered a strong behavioralist in the commitment he expresses in this article.

Perhaps the most striking characteristic of the "behavioral approach" in political science is the ambiguity of the term itself, and of its synonym "political behavior." The behavioral approach, in fact, is rather like the Loch Ness monster: one can say with considerable confidence what it is not, but it is difficult to say what it *is*. Judging from newspaper reports that appear from time to time, particularly just before the summer tourist season, I judge that the monster of Loch Ness is not Moby Dick, nor my daughter's goldfish that disappeared down the drain some ten years ago, nor even a misplaced American eight heading for the Henley Regatta. In the same spirit, I judge that the behavioral approach is not that of the speculative philosopher, the historian, the legalist, or the moralist. What, then, is it? Indeed, does it actually exist?

1

Although I do not profess to know of the full history of the behavioral approach, a little investigation reveals that confusing and even contradictory interpretations have marked its appearance from the beginning. The first sightings in the roily waters of political science of the phenomenon variously called political behavorial approach, or behavorial(ist) research, evidently occurred in the 1920s. The term "political behavior," it seems, was used by American political scientists from the First World War onward.[1] The honor of first adopting the term as a book title seems to belong, however, not to a political scientist but to the American journalist Frank Kent, who published a book in 1928 entitled *Political Behavior, The Heretofore Unwritten Laws, Customs, and Principles of Politics as Practised in the United States*.[2] To Kent, the study of political behavior meant the cynical "realism" of the tough-minded newspaperman who reports the way things "really" happen and not the way they're supposed to happen. This meaning, I may say, is often implied even today. However, Herbert Tingsten rescued the term for political science in 1937 by publishing his path-breaking *Political Behavior: Studies in Election Statistics*. Despite the fact that Tingsten was a Swede, and his work dealt with European elections, the term became increasingly identified with American political science.

The rapid flowering of the behavioral approach in the United States no doubt depended on the existence of some key attitudes and predispositions generated in the American culture—pragmatism, factmindedness, confidence in science, and the like.[3] But there were also at least six specific, interrelated, quite powerful stimuli.

One was Charles E. Merriam. In his presidential address to the American Political Science Association in 1925, Merriam said:

> Some day we may take another angle of approach *than the formal, as other sciences do*, and begin to look at *political behavior* as one of the essential objects of inquiry.[4]

During the next decade under Merriam's leadership at the University of Chicago, the Department of Political Science was the center of what would later have been called the behavioral approach. A number of the political scientists who subsequently were widely regarded as leaders in introducing that approach into American political science were faculty members or graduate students there: for example, Harold Lasswell as a faculty member and V. O. Key, Jr., David Truman, Herbert Simon, and Gabriel Almond, all graduate students in Merriam's department before the Second World War. Chicago was not the only place where the new

[1]David Easton, *The Political System* (1953), p. 203.

[2]Kent's earlier book, *The Great Game of Politics* (1924), made no pretence of being systematic and continued to be widely read by students of American politics, but within a few years *Political Behavior* fell into an obscurity from which it has never recovered.

[3]See Bernard Crick, *The American Science of Politics, Its Origins and Conditions* (London, 1959).

[4]"Progress in Political Research," *American Political Science Review*, Vol. 20 (February, 1926), p. 7, quoted in David B. Truman, "The Implications of Political Behavior Research," *Items* (Social Science Research Council, December, 1951), p. 37. Emphasis added.

mood of scientific empiricism was strong. At Cornell University, for example, G. E. G. Catlin was expounding similar views.[5] But the collective impact of "the Chicago school" as it was sometimes called, was greater than that of a single scholar.

A second force was the arrival in the United States in the 1930s of a considerable number of European scholars, particularly German refugees, who brought with them a sociological approach to politics that strongly reflected the specific influence of Max Weber and the general influence of European sociology. American political science had always been strongly influenced by Europeans. Not only have Americans often interpreted their own political institutions most clearly with the aid of sympathetic foreigners like de Tocqueville, Bryce, and Brogan, but American scholars have owed specific debts to European scholarship. The first American university chair in political science (actually in History and Political Science), established in 1858 at Columbia, was occupied by the liberal German refugee Francis Lieber. In the second half of the nineteenth century, many of the leading academic advocates of a "science of politics" sought to profit from the methods and teachings in some of the leading European universities.[6]

In the 1930s, there was once again an abrupt revival of European influences as the life of American universities was enriched by the great influx of refugee scholars.

A number of these scholars who came to occupy leading positions in departments of sociology and political science insisted on the relevance of sociological and even psychological theories for an understanding of politics. They drew attention to the importance of Marx, Durkheim, Freud, Pareto, Mosca, Weber, Michels and others. Although some of them might later reject the behavioral approach precisely because they felt it was too narrow, men like Franz Neumann, Sigmund Neumann, Paul Lazarsfeld, Hans Speier, Hans Gerth, Reinhard Bendix and many others exerted, both directly and indirectly, a profound influence on political research in the United States. Political sociology began to flourish. Political scientists discovered that their sociological colleagues were moving with speed and skill into areas they had long regarded as their own.

[5]See Catlin's *Science and Method of Politics* (1927). Another early example of the behavioral approach was Stuart Rice, *Quantitative Methods in Politics* (1928). Rice had received his Ph.D. at Columbia University.

[6]Bernard Crick, *op. cit.*, pp. 21–31. Crick notes that "The Fifth Volume of the Johns Hopkins University *Studies in Historical and Political Science* published a long study, edited by Andrew D. White, 'European Schools of History and Politics' (December, 1887). It reprinted his Johns Hopkins address on 'Education in Political Science' together with reports on 'what we can learn from' each major European country." Fn. 1, p. 27.

The Second World War also stimulated the development of the behavioral approach in the United States, for a great many American political scientists temporarily vacated their ivory towers and came to grips with day-to-day political and administrative realities in Washington and elsewhere: a whole generation of American political science later drew on these experiences. The confrontation of theory and reality provoked, in most of the men who performed their stint in Washington or elsewhere, a strong sense of the inadequacies of the conventional approaches of political science for describing reality, much less for predicting in any given situation what was likely to happen.

Possibly an even bigger impetus—not unrelated to the effects of the War—was provided by the Social Science Research Council, which has had an unostentatious but cumulatively enormous impact on American social science. A leading spirit in the Council for the past two decades has been a distinguished political scientist, E. Pendleton Herring. His own work before he assumed the presidency of the Council in 1948 reflected a concern for realism, for breaking the bonds of research confined entirely to the library, and for individual and group influences on politics and administration. In the mid-1940s Herring was instrumental in creating an SSRC committee on political behavior. The Annual Report of the SSRC for 1944-1945 indicated that the Council had reached a

> . . . decision to explore the feasibility of developing a new approach to *the study of political behavior*. Focused upon *the behavior of individuals* in political situations, this approach calls for examination of the political relationships of men—as citizens, administrators, and legislators—by disciplines which can throw light on the problems involved, with the object of *formulating and testing hypotheses*, concerning *uniformities of behavior* in different institutional settings. (Emphasis added.)

In 1945 the Council established a Committee on Political Behavior, with Herring as the chairman. The three other members[7] were also dissatisfied with the conventional methods and manners of the discipline, the new voting studies offered encouragement. For in spite of obvious defects, the voting studies seemed to provide ground for the hope that if political scientists could only master the tools employed in the other social sciences—survey methods and statistical analysis, for example—they might be able to go beyond plausible generalities and proceed to test hypotheses about how people in fact do behave in making political choices.

A sixth factor that needs to be mentioned is the influence of those uniquely American institutions, the great philanthropic foundations—

---

[7]Herbert Emmerich, Charles S. Hyneman, and V. O. Key, Jr.

especially Carnegie, Rockefeller, and more recently Ford—which because of their enormous financial contributions to scholarly research, and the inevitable selection among competing proposals that these entail, exert a considerable effect on the scholarly community. The relationship between foundation policy and current trends in academic research is too complex for facile generalities. Perhaps the simplest accurate statement is that the relationship is to a very high degree reciprocal: the staffs of the foundations are highly sensitive to the views of distinguished scholars, on whom they rely heavily for advice, and at the same time because even foundation resources are scarce, the policies of foundation staffs and trustees must inevitably encourage or facilitate some lines of research more than others. If the foundations had been hostile to the behavioral approach, there can be no doubt that it would have had very rough sledding indeed. For characteristically, behavioral research costs a good deal more than is needed by the single scholar in the library—and sometimes, as with the studies of voting in presidential elections, behavioral research is enormously expensive.

In the period after the Second World War, however, the foundations—reflecting important trends within the social sciences themselves, stimulated by the factors I have already mentioned—tended to view interdisciplinary and behavioral studies with sympathy. The Rockefeller Foundation, for example, had helped finance the pioneering panel study by Lazarsfeld, Berelson, and Gaudet of voting in the 1940 presidential election in Erie County, Ohio, and it has also, almost singlehandedly, financed the costly election studies of the Survey Research Center at the University of Michigan. In the newest and richest foundation, Ford, the short-lived Behavioral Sciences Program probably increased the use and acceptability of the notion of behavioral sciences as something both more behavioral and more scientific than the social sciences (I confess the distinction still remains cloudy to me despite the earnest attempts of a number of behavioral scientists to set me straight). The most durable offshoot of the Behavioral Sciences Program at Ford is the Center for Advanced Study in the Behavioral Sciences at Palo Alto. Although the Center has often construed its domain in most catholic fashion—the "fellows" in any given year may include mathematicians, philosophers, historians, or even a novelist—in its early years the political scientists who were fellows there tended to be discontented with traditional approaches, inclined toward a more rigorously empirical and scientific study of politics, and deeply interested in learning wherever possible from the other social sciences.

All these factors, and doubtless others, came to fruition in the decade of the 1950s. The behavioral approach grew from the deviant and unpopular views of a minor sect into a major influence. Many of the radicals of the 1930s (professionally speaking) had, within two decades, become established leaders in American political science.

Today, many American departments of political science (including my own) offer undergraduate or graduate courses in Political Behavior. Indeed, in at least one institution (the University of Michigan) Political Behavior is not only a course but a field of graduate study parallel with such conventional fields as political theory, public administration, and the like—and recently buttressed, I note enviously, with some fat fellowships.

The presidency of the American Political Science Association furnishes a convenient symbol of the change. From 1927, when [Charles] Merriam was elected president, until 1950, none of the presidents was prominently identified as an advocate of the behavioral approach. The election of Peter Odegard in 1950 might be regarded as the turning point. Since that time, the presidency has been occupied by one of Merriam's most brilliant and intellectually unconventional students, Harold Lasswell, and by three of the four members of the first SSRC Committee on Political Behavior.

Thus the revolutionary sectarians have found themselves, perhaps more rapidly than they thought possible, becoming members of the Establishment.

2

I have not, however, answered the nagging question I set out to answer, though perhaps I have furnished some materials from which an answer might be derived. What *is* the behavioral approach in political science?

Historically speaking, the behavioral approach was a protest movement within political science. Through usage by partisans, partly as an epithet, terms like political behavior and the behavioral approach came to be associated with a number of political scientists, mainly Americans, who shared a strong sense of dissatisfaction with the achievements of conventional political science, particularly through historical, philosophical, and the descriptive-institutional approaches, and a belief that additional methods and approaches either existed or could be developed that would help to provide political science with empirical propositions and theories of a systematic sort, tested by closer, more direct and more rigorously controlled observations of political events.

At a minimum, then, those who were sometimes called "Behaviorists" or "Behavioralists" shared a mood: a mood of skepticism about the current intellectual attainments of political science, a mood of sympathy toward "scientific" modes of investigation and analysis, a mood of optimism about the possibilties of improving the study of politics.

Was—or is—the behavioral approach ever anything more than this mood? Are there perhaps definite beliefs, assumptions, methods or topics that can be identified as constituting political behavior or the behavioral approach?

There are, so far as I can tell, three different answers to this question among those who employ the term carefully. The first answer is an unequivocal yes. Political behavior is said to refer to the study of *individuals* rather than larger political units. This emphasis is clear in the 1944–1945 SSRC report (which I quoted earlier) that foreshadowed the creation of the Political Behavior Committee. This was also how David Easton defined the term in his searching analysis and criticism of American political science published in 1953.[10] In this sense, Tingsten, Lasswell, and studies of voting behavior are prime examples of the behavioral approach.

The second answer is an unequivocal no. In his recent *Political Science: A Philosophical Analysis* (1960), Vernon Van Dyke remarks: "Though stipulative definitions of *political behavior* are sometimes advanced, as when a course or a book is given this title, none of them has gained general currency."[11] Probably the most eloquent and resounding "No!" was supplied three years ago by an editorial in *PROD*, a journal that some American political scientists—and many of its readers—probably regarded as the authentic spokesman for the newest currents among the *avant garde* of political behavior. As an alumnus both of Merriam's Chicago department and the SSRC Committee on Political Behavior, the editor of PROD, Alfred de Grazia, could be presumed to speak with authority. He denied that the term referred to a subject matter, an interdisciplinary focus, quantification, any specific effort at new methods, behaviorist psychology, "realism" as opposed to "idealism," empiricism in contrast with deductive systems, or voting behavior—or, in

---

[10]"To precisely what kind of research does the concept of political behavior refer? It is clear that this term indicates that the research worker wishes to look at participants in the political system as individuals who have the emotions, prejudices, and predispositions of human beings as we know them in our daily lives. . . . Behavioral research . . . has therefore sought to elevate the actual human being to the center of attention. Its premise is that the traditionalists have been reifying institutions, virtually looking at them as entities apart from their component individuals. . . . Research workers often use the terms . . . to indicate that they are studying the political process by looking at the relation of it to the motivations, personalities, or feelings of the participants as individual human beings." David Easton, *The Political System* (1953), pp. 201–205.

[11]As we shall see, Van Dyke distinguishes the term "behavioral approach" from "political behavior."

fact, to anything more than political science as something that some people might like it to be. He proposed that the term be dropped.[12]

The third view is perhaps no more than an elaboration of the mood I mentioned a moment ago. In this view the behavioral approach is an attempt to improve our understanding of politics by seeking to explain the empirical aspects of political life by means of methods, theories, and criteria of proof that are acceptable according to the canons, conventions, and assumptions of modern empirical science. In this sense, "a behavioral approach," as one writer recently observed, "is distinguished predominantly by the nature of the purpose it is designed to serve. The purpose is scientific. . . ."[13]

If we consider the behavioral approach in political science as simply an attempt to make the empirical component of the discipline more scientific, as that term is generally understood in the empirical sciences, much of the history that I have referred to falls into place. In a wise, judicious, and until very recently neglected essay entitled "The Implications of Political Behavior Research," David Truman, writing in 1951, set out the fruits of a seminar on political behavior research held at the University of Chicago in the summer of 1951. I think it is not misleading to say that the views Truman set forth in 1951 have been shared in the years since then by the members of the Committee on Political Behavior.

> Roughly defined, [he wrote] the term political behavior comprehends those actions and interactions of men and groups which are involved in the process of governing. . . . At the maximum this conception brings under the rubric of political behavior any human activities which can be said to be a part of governing.
>
> Properly speaking, political behavior is not a "field" of social science; it is not even a "field" of political science.
>
> . . . Political behavior is not and should not be a specialty, for it represents rather an orientation or a point of view which aims at *stating all the phenomena of government in terms of the observed and observable behavior of men.* To treat it as a "field" coordinate with (and presumably isolated from) public law, state and local government, international relations, and so on, would be to defeat the major aim. That aim includes an eventual reworking and extension of most of the conventional "fields" of political science. . . .
>
> The developments underlying the current interest in political behavior imply two basic requirments for adequate research. In the first place, research must be systematic. . . . This means that research must grow out of a precise statement of hypotheses and a rigorous ordering of evidence. . . . In the second place, research in political behavior must place primary emphasis

---

[12]"What Is Political Behavior?," *PROD*, July, 1958.
[13]"What Is Political Behavior?," *PROD*, July, 1958.

upon empirical methods. . . . Crude empiricism, unguided by adequate theory, is almost certain to be sterile. Equally fruitless is speculation which is not or cannot be put to empirical test.

>   . . . *The ultimate goal of the student of political behavior is the development of a science of the political process.* . . .[14]

Truman called attention to the advantages of drawing on the other social sciences and cautioned against indiscriminate borrowings. He argued that the "political behavior orientation . . . necessarily aims at being quantitative wherever possible. But . . . the student of political behavior . . . deals with the political institution and he is obliged to perform his task in *quantitative terms if he can and in qualitative terms if he must*." (Emphasis added). He agreed that "inquiry into how men *ought* to act is not a concern of research in political behavior" but insisted on the importance of studying values as "obviously important determinants of men's behavior."

> Moreover, in political behavior research, as in the natural sciences, the values of the investigator are important in the selection of the objects and lines of inquiry. . . . A major reason for any inquiry into political behavior is to discover uniformities, and through discovering them to be better able to indicate the consequences of such patterns and of public policy, existing or proposed, for the maintenance or development of a preferred system of political values.

Truman denied that "the political behavior orientation implies a rejection of historical knowledge. . . . Historical knowledge is likely to be an essential supplement to contemporary observation of political behavior." Finally, while suggesting that the conventional graduate training of political scientists needed to be supplemented and modified, Truman emphatically opposed the notion that the behavioral approach required "the elimination of . . . traditional training."

> Any new departure in an established discipline must build upon the accomplishments of the past. Although much of the existing literature of politics may be impressionistic, it is extensive and rich in insights. Without a command of the significant portions of that literature, behavioral research . . . is likely to be naive and unproductive. . . . Many attempts made by persons not familiar with the unsystematized facts [have been] substantively naive even when they may have been methodologically sound.

I have cited Truman's views at length for several reasons: because I wholeheartedly agree with them; because they were expressed a decade ago when the advocates of the behavioral approach were still searching for acceptance and self-definition; because they have been neglected;

[14] Social Science Research Council, *Items* (December, 1951), pp. 37–39. (Emphasis added.)

and because I believe that if the partisans and critics of "political behavior" and "the behavioral approach" had read them, understood them, and accepted them as a proper statement of objectives, much of the irrelevant, fruitless, and ill-informed debate over the behavioral approach over the past decade need never have occurred—or at any rate might have been conducted on a rather higher level of intellectual sophistication.

3

Thus the "behavioral approach" might better be called the "behavioral mood" or perhaps even the "scientific outlook."

Yet to explain the behavioral approach as nothing more or less than an emphasis on the term "science" in the phrase "political science" leaves unanswered whatever questions may be raised as to the present or potential achievements of this mood of protest, skepticism, reform, and optimism. Fortunately, there is an element of self-correction in intellectual life. The attempt to increase the scientific competence of political studies will inevitably be judged by results. And the judges of the next generation will share the skepticism of the past. If closer attention to methodological niceties, to problems of observation and verification, to the task of giving operational meaning to political concepts, to quantification and testing, to eliminating unproductive intervening variables, to sources of data, hypotheses, and theory in the other social sciences; if all of these activities do not yield explanations of some important aspects of politics that are more thoroughly verified, less open to methodological objections, richer in implications for further explanation, and more useful in meeting the perennial problems of political life than the explanations they are intended to replace; if, in short, the results of a scientific outlook do not measure up to the standards that serious students of politics have always attempted to apply, then we may confidently expect that the attempt to build an empirical science of politics will lose all the impetus in the next generation that it gained in the last.

The representatives of the "scientific outlook" are, it seems to me, right in saying that it is a little early to appraise the results. We shall need another generation of work before we can put the products of this new mood and outlook in political science in perspective. Nonetheless, I believe it may be useful to make a tentative if deliberately incomplete assessment.

The oldest and best example of the modern scientific outlook at work is to be found in studies of voting behavior using survey methods. These begin with *The People's Choice*,[15] a study of the 1940 presidential election first published in 1944, and end—for the moment at least—with the magnificent study of the 1956 election entitled *The American Voter*.[16] It is no exaggeration to say that in less than two decades this series of studies has significantly altered and greatly deepened our understanding of what in some ways is the most distinctive action for a citizen of a democracy—deciding how to vote, or indeed whether to vote at all, in a competitive national election. Each study has profited from the last; and as broadly trained political scientists have begun to work on these studies together with sociologists and social psychologists, the contributions of the studies to our understanding of politics—rather than of individual psychology—have greatly increased. On many topics where only a generation ago we had not much beyond impressionistic evidence, today we can speak with some confidence.

Although in a field as ambiguous and rich in contradictory hypotheses as political science, it is nearly always possible to regard a finding as merely confirming the obvious, in fact a number of the findings point in rather unexpected directions: for example, that "independent" voters tend to be less interested, involved, or informed than partisan voters;[17] that socio-economic "class" whether objectively or subjectively defined is not a factor of constant weight in American presidential elections but a variable subject to great swings; and that only a microscopic proportion of American voters can be said to bring any ideological perspectives, even loosely defined, to bear on their decisions. Where once one might have asserted these propositions or their contraries with equal plausibility, the evidence of the voting studies tends to pile up in a single direction. Moreover—and this is perhaps the most important point of all—these studies are cumulative. The early studies were highly incomplete and in many ways unsatisfactory. They were subject to a good deal of criticism, and properly so. Even the latest ones will not escape unharmed. Yet it seems to me there has been a steady and obvious improvement in quality, range, and depth.

[15]Paul F. Lazarsfeld, Bernard Berelson, and Hazel Gaudet, *The People's Choice* (New York, 1944).

[16]Angus Campbell, Philip Converse, Donald Stokes, and Warren Miller, *The American Voter* (New York, 1960), a study extended and refined by the same authors in "Stability and Change in 1960: A Reinstating Election," *American Political Science Review*, Vol. 55 (1961), pp. 269–280.

[17]A finding, incidentally, that may have to be revised in turn. A recent re-analysis of the data of the voting studies, completed after this paper was prepared, has turned up new evidence for the active, interested independent voter. William Flanigan, *Partisanship and Campaign Participation* (Ph.D. dissertation. Yale University Library, 1961).

The voting studies may have provided an indirect stimulus to the "scientific outlook" because of a psychological effect. It seems to be beyond much doubt that some political scientists, particularly younger ones, compared the yield produced by the methods used in the studies on voting with the normal yield of conventional methods and arrived at the inference—which is probably false—that the application of comparable new methods elsewhere could produce a comparable gain in results.

A closely related topic on which the scientific outlook, has, in my view, produced some useful and reliable results of great importance to an understanding of politics is in the general domain of political participation. A listing of some of the chapter headings in Robert E. Lane's *Political Life* (1959) indicates the sort of question on which our knowledge is very much better off than it was only a few years ago: "Who Takes Part in Elections and What Do They Do?," "Who Tries to Influence Public Officials and How Do They Do It?," "Political Discussion: Who Listens to What? Who Talks to Whom?," "Why Lower-Status People Participate Less than Upper-Status People," "The Way of the Ethnic in Politics," etc.

Since I am not responsible for a complete inventory, I shall limit myself to mentioning one more subject where the behavioral mood has clearly made itself felt. This is in understanding the psychological characteristics of *homo politicus:* attitudes, beliefs, predispositions, personality factors. The range of "behavioral" scholars and research in this area is very great, though the researchers and the research may not always bear the professional label "political science." A few scattered names, titles, and topics will indicate what I have in mind: Lasswell, the great American pioneer in this area; Cantril; Lane; McClosky; Adorno, *et al. The Authoritarian Personality;* Almond, *The Appeals of Communism;* Stouffer, *Communism, Conformity and Civil Liberties;* and Lipset, "Working Class Authoritarianism" in *Political Man.* The fact that these scholars bear various professional labels—sociologist, psychologist, political scientist—and that it is not easy to read from the professional or departmental label of the author to the character of the work itself may be regarded by some political scientists as an appalling sign of disintegration in the distinctive properties of political science, but it is also a sign of the extent to which a concern by "behavioral scientists" with similar problems now tends to transcend (though not to eliminate entirely) differences in professional origins.

4

What of the yield in other matters that have always been of concern to students of political life? There are a number of important aspects of political studies where the behavioral mood has had, is having, or probably soon will have an impact, but where we must reserve judgment for the time being simply because the results are too scanty.

A good example is the analysis of political *systems*. The most distinctive products of the behavioral mood so far have dealt with *individuals*— individuals who vote, participate in politics in other ways, or express certain attitudes or beliefs. But an individual is not a political system, and analysis of individual preferences cannot fully explain collective decisions, for in addition we need to understand the mechanisms by which individual decisions are aggregated and combined into collective decisions. We cannot move from a study of the attitudes of a random sample of American citizens to a reasonably full explanation of, say, presidential nominations or the persistent problems of policy coordination in the United States.

Yet one classic concern of students of politics has been the analysis of *systems* of individuals and groups. Although the impact of the scientific outlook on the study of political systems is still unclear, there are some interesting straws in the wind. In *Union Democracy*, Lipset, Trow and Coleman brought the behavioral mood and the intellectual resources of three highly trained social scientists to bear on the task of explaining how it is that a legitimate two-party system is maintained, as it is not in other American trade unions, in the International Typographers' Union. Recently a number of political scientists have followed sociologists into the study of local communities as systems of influence or decision-making.[18] Deutsch reflects the behavioral mood in his study of international political systems.[19] A number of other studies are in process that may help us formulate some new, or if not new then more persuasive, answers to some ancient questions.[20] But until more evidence is in, anyone who does not believe he knows *a priori* the outcome of this present expression of the scholar's age-old quest for knowledge will perhaps be pardoned if he reserves judgment and awaits the future with skepticism—mixed, depending on his prejudices, with hope or dread.

[18]See Janowitz, ed., *Community Political Systems* (1961); Edward Banfield, *Political Influence* (1961); and the English study by Birch and his colleagues at the University of Manchester, *Small Town Politics* (1959).

[19]For example, in his *Nationalism and Social Communication* (1953). See also his recent article with the economist Alexander Eckstein, "National Industrialization and the Declining Share of the International Economic Sector, 1890–1959," *World Politics* (January, 1961), pp. 267–299; and his "Social Mobilization and Political Development," *American Political Science Review*, Vol. 55 (September, 1961), pp. 493–514.

[20]For an interesting example of an application of the behavioral mood to comparative politics, see Stein Rokkan and Henry Valen, "Parties, Elections and Political Behavior in the Northern Countries: a Review of Recent Research," *Politische Forschung* (1960). Probably the most ambitious attempt to apply survey methods to comparative politics is represented by a study of political socialization and political values in five nations, conducted by Gabriel A. Almond; this study has not yet been completed.

5

Where will the behavioral mood, considered as a movement of protest, go from here? I think it will gradually disappear. By this I mean only that it will slowly decay as a distinctive mood and outlook. For it will become, and in fact already is becoming, incorporated into the main body of the discipline. The behavioral mood will not disappear, then, because it has failed. It will disappear rather because it has succeeded. As a separate, somewhat sectarian, slightly factional outlook it will be the first victim of its own triumph.

Lest I be misunderstood in what I am about to say, let me make clear that the present and probable future benefits of the behavioral revolt to political studies seem to me to outweigh by far any disadvantages. In retrospect, the "behavioral" revolt in political science was, if anything, excessively delayed. Moreover, had that revolt not taken place, political science would have become increasingly alienated, I believe, from the other social sciences. One consequence of the behavioral protest has been to restore some unity within the social sciences by bringing political studies into closer affiliation with theories, methods, findings, and outlooks in modern psychology, sociology, anthropology and economics.

But if the behavioral revolt in political science has helped to restore some unities, it has shattered others; and the fragments probably cannot ever again be united exactly along the old lines. There are, so to speak, five fragments in search of a unity. These are: empirical political science, standards of evaluation, history, general theory and speculation.

The empirical political scientist is concerned with what *is*, as he says, not with what *ought* to be. Hence he finds it difficult and uncongenial to assume the historic burden of the political philosopher who attempted to determine, prescribe, elaborate, and employ ethical standards—values, to use the fashionable term—in appraising political acts and political systems. The behaviorally minded student of politics is prepared to *describe* values as empirical data; but, *qua* "scientist" he seeks to avoid prescription or inquiry into the grounds on which judgments of value can properly be made. To whom, then, are we to turn for guidance on intricate questions of political appraisal and evaluation? Today, probably no single professional group is qualified to speak with wisdom on all important political alternatives.

It may be said that this is the task of the political philosopher. But the problem of the political philosopher who wishes to engage in political evaluation in a sophisticated way is rendered ever more formidable by the products of the behavioral mood. An act of political evaluation cannot be performed in a sterile medium free from contamination by brute facts.

Surely no one today, for example, can intelligently consider the relative merits of different political systems, or different arrangements within a particular political system, unless he knows what there is to be known about how these systems or arrangements work, what is required to make them work, and what effects they have on participants. No doubt the specialist who "knows the facts"—whether as physicist, physician, or political scientist—sometimes displays great naïveté on matters of policy. Still, the impatience of the empirical political scientist with the political philosopher who insists upon the importance of "values" arises in part from a feeling that the political philosopher who engages in political evaluation rarely completes all his homework. The topic of "consensus" as a condition for democracy is a case in point; when the political philosopher deals with this question, it seems to me that he typically makes a number of assumptions and assertions of an empirical sort without systematic attention to existing empirical data, or the possibility of gaining better empirical data.[21] Obviously some division of labor will always be necessary in a field as broad as the study of politics, but clearly the field needs more people who do not regard rapid shifts of mood—I mean from the behavioral to the philosophical—as a symptom of severe schizophrenia.

Second, in his concern for analyzing what *is*, the behavioral political scientist has found it difficult to make systematic use of what *has been:* that is, with history. In a trivial sense, of course, all knowledge of fact is historical, but I am speaking here of the history of the historian. Despite disclaimers and intentions to the contrary, there seems to me little room for doubt that the actual content of almost all the studies that reflect the behavioral mood is a-historical in character. Yet the scientific shortcomings of an a-historical theory in political science are manifest, and political scientists with "behavioral" predispositions are among the first to admit them. As the authors of *The American Voter* remark:

> In somewhat severe language, theory may be characterized as a generalized statement of the inter-relationships of a set of variables. In these terms, historical description may be said to be a statement of the values assumed by these variables through time. . . .

> If theory can guide historical descriptions, the historical context of most research on human behavior places clear limitations of the development of

---

[21]In 1942, in *The New Belief in the Common Man*, C. J. Friedrich challenged the prevailing generalizations about the need for consensus (chap. 5). However, his challenge seems to have met with little response until 1960, when Prothro and Grigg reported the results of an empirical study of consensus on "democratic" propositions in Ann Arbor, Michigan and Tallahassee, Florida. See their "Fundamental Principles of Democracy," *Journal of Politics* (May, 1960), pp. 276–294.

theory. In evolving and testing his theoretical hypotheses the social scientist usually must depend on what he is permitted to observe by the progress of history. . . . It is evident that *variables of great importance in human affairs may exhibit little or no change in a given historical period*. As a result, the investigator whose work falls in this period *may not see the significance of these variables* and may fail to incorporate them in his theoretical statements. And even if he does perceive their importance, the *absence of variation will prevent a proper test of hypotheses* that state the relation of these factors to other variables of his theory (pp. 8–10, emphasis added).

There are, I think, a number of nodes around which a unity between behavioral political studies and history may be expected to grow. Because it is unreasonable to suppose that anything like the whole field of history will lend itself successfully to the behavioral approach, both historians and political scientists might profitably look for targets-of-opportunity on which the weapons forged by modern social science can be brought to bear. In this respect the work of the American historian, Lee Benson, seems to me particularly promising. By the application of rather elementary methods, which the historian has not been prone to employ, including very simple statistical analysis, Benson has shown how the explanations of five eminent American historians of four different presidential elections are dubious, if not, in fact, downright absurd.[22] The sociologist, S. M. Lipset, has also contributed a new interpretation of the 1860 election, based upon his analysis of Southern voting patterns in the presidential election of that year and in referenda on secession a few months later.[23] Benson has also turned his attention both to Charles A. Beard's famous interpretation—which Beard called an economic interpretation—of the creation and adoption of the American Constitution, and to the latter-day critics of Beard's somewhat loosely stated theory; he demonstrates convincingly, at least to me, some of the gains that can arise from a greater methodological sophistication on matters of causation, correlation, and use of quantitative data than is customary among professional historians.[24]

In addition to these targets-of-opportunity that occur here and there in historical studies, a problem that obviously needs the joint attention of historian and "behavioral" political scientist is the matter of political change. To the extent that the political scientist is interested in gaining a

[22]The historians and the elections were: Arthur Schlesinger, Jr., on the election of 1824, Samuel E. Morison and Henry S. Commager on the election of 1860, Allan Nevins on the election of 1884, and William Diamond on the election of 1896. See his "Research Problems in American Political Historiography," in Komarovsky, ed., *Common Frontiers of the Social Sciences* (1957).

[23]"The Emergence of the One-Party South—the Election of 1860," in *Political Man* (1960).

[24]Lee Benson, *Turner and Beard, American Historical Writing Re-Considered* (1960).

better understanding of political change—as, say, in the developing countries, to cite an example of pressing importance—he will have to work with theories that can only be fully tested against historical data. Unfortunately, the a-theoretical or even anti-theoretical biases of many historians often make their works a storehouse of data so vast as to be almost unmanageable for the theorist. Rather than demand that every theorist should have to become his own historian, it may be more feasible to demand that more historians should become theorists, or at any rate familiar with the most relevant issues, problems, and methods of the modern social sciences.

I have already implied the third unity that needs to be established, namely a unity between empirical political studies and a concern for general theory. The scientific outlook in political science can easily produce a dangerous and dysfunctional humility: the humility of the social scientist who may be quite confident of his findings on small matters and dubious that he can have anything at all to say on larger questions. The danger, of course, is that the quest for empirical data can turn into an absorbing search for mere trivialities unless it is guided by some sense of the difference between an explanation that would not matter much even if could be shown to be valid by the most advanced methods now available, and one that would matter a great deal if it should turn out to be a little more or a little less plausible than before, even if it still remained in some considerable doubt. So far, I think, the impact of the scientific outlook has been to stimulate caution rather than boldness in searching for broad explanatory theories. The political scientist who mixes skepticism with methodological rigor is all too painfully aware of the inadequacies of any theory that goes much beyond the immediate data at hand. Yet it seems clear that unless the study of politics generates and is guided by broad, bold, even if highly vulnerable general theories, it is headed for the ultimate disaster of triviality.

Finally, I should like to suggest that empirical political science had better find a place for speculation. It is a grave though easy error for students of politics impressed by the achievements of the natural sciences to imitate all their methods save the most critical one: the use of the imagination. Problems of method and a proper concern for what would be regarded as an acceptable test of an empirical-hypothesis have quite properly moved out of the wings to a more central position on the great stage of political science. Yet surely it is imagination that has generally marked the intelligence of the great scientist, and speculation—oftentimes foolish speculation, it turned out later—has generally preceded great advances in scientific theory. It is only fair to add, however, that the speculation of a Galileo, a Kepler, a Newton, or an Einstein, was informed and controlled by a deep understanding of the hard empirical facts as they were known at the time: Kepler's speculations always had to confront the tables of Tycho Brahe.

There is every reason to think that unities can be forged anew. After all, as the names of Socrates, Aristotle, Machiavelli, Hobbes, and Tocqueville remind us, from time to time in the past the study of politics has been altered permanently, by a fresh infusion of the spirit of empirical inquiry—by, that is to say, the scientific outlook.

7

Christian Bay

A CRITICAL EVALUATION OF BEHAVIORAL LITERATURE*

Bay claims that in the attempt to achieve a science the tendency of behavioralists is to avoid politics. He argues that most current political behavioral work "fails to articulate its very real value biases. . . ." An adequate *political* theory, he maintains, is one that "deals with basic human needs" in contrast with the *pseudopolitics* that is concerned merely with alleviating personal neuroses and promoting private interests. Political research must concern itself with both *ought* and *is* problems. Bay further argues that many behavioralists (among whom are Dahl, V. O. Key, and Lipset) manifest in their writings tacit value assumptions. An example is the assumption that American democracy is the best government. Thus a basic dilemma confronts these behavioralists: how simultaneously to achieve value neutrality and to

*Reprinted by permission of the author and publisher from *American Political Science Review*, LIX (1: March, 1965), pp. 39–51, where it was entitled "Politics and Pseudopolitics: A Critical Evaluation of Some Behavioral Literature."

I am indebted to my friend Herbert H. Hyman, who has been generous with advice for improvements on an earlier draft. It should not be inferred that he is in agreement with opinions expressed in this paper, or that he might not once again find much to criticize in it. At a later stage I have received helpful suggestions also from Sidney Verba and Andrew Hacker—CHRISTIAN BAY.

support democracy. Pluralistic democracy in some countries often is a protective shield for the interests of the middle and upper classes. Furthermore, behavioralists often assume that stability is the most important social goal. Thus "current preoccupation with pseudo behavior carries conservative and anti-political implications. . . ." A final criticism is that, since political incentives can be developed only by "a gradual process of liberation from a preoccupation with personal . . . worries," we must create conditions conducive to that liberation. The pseudopolitics of behavioralism lacks the proper concern.

A curious state of affairs has developed within the academic discipline that bravely calls itself Political Science—the discipline that in a much-quoted phrase has been called "a device, invented by university teachers, for avoiding that dangerous subject politics, without achieving science."[1] A growing and now indeed a predominant proportion of leading American political scientists, the behavioralists, have become determined to achieve science. Yet in the process many of them remain open to the charge of strenuously avoiding that dangerous subject, politics.

Consider a recent essay on the behavioral persuasion in politics. The conclusion stresses the purpose of political inquiry: "The Goal is Man." There is to be a commitment to some humane purpose after all. But what kind of man? A democratic kind of man, a just man, or perhaps a power-seeking man? The answer follows: "These are philosophical questions better left to the philosophers."[2] Behavioral students of politics should, as scientists, engage in no value judgments concerning the kind of man or society their researches ought to serve. This is the general inference to be drawn, not only from this particular essay, but from much of the contemporary literature on political behavior.

As Heinz Eulau, the author, points out in the same essay, the area of behavioral political science includes a particular domain called policy science, in which empirical inquiry is geared to explicitly stated goal formulations; within *this* domain "political science, as all science, should be put in the service of whatever goals men pursue in politics." *Any* goals? Not quite; in this context Eulau points out that the choice of what goals to serve is a matter of personal ethics, and incidentally reminds us that behavioral research can be readily utilized also for purposes conflicting with the original ones. "In this sense, at least, science is value-free. I don't think the scientist can escape this dilemma of having his work

[1]Alfred Cobban, "The Decline of Political Theory," *Political Science Quarterly*, Vol. 48 (1953), p. 335.
[2]Heinz Eulau, *The Behavioral Persuasion in Politics* (New York, 1963), p. 133 and pp. 133–37.

misused without giving up his calling." And the author concludes with these words: "Only if he places himself at the service of those whose values he disagrees with does he commit intellectual treason."

In these pages I am concerned with sins less serious than intellectual treason; perhaps intellectual indolence is a more accurate term. My argument will be that much of the current work on political behavior generally fails to articulate its very real value biases, and that the political impact of this supposedly neutral literature is generally conservative and in a special sense anti-political. In conclusion I propose to develop a perspective on political inquiry that would relate it more meaningfully to problems of human needs and values; in that context I will suggest some important but neglected problems lending themselves to empirical research.

I am not about to argue that our investments in political behavior research have been too large; on the contrary, we need much more work in this area. But my principal concern is to argue for a more pressing need: an intellectually more defensible and a politically more responsible theoretical framework for guiding and interpreting our empirical work; a theory that would give more meaning to our research, even at the expense of reducing its conceptual and operational neatness.

1

It is necessary first to clarify some basic terms in which my concern is stated.

The prevailing concepts of "politics" in the literature under consideration are surely an important source of the difficulty. Definitions gravitate toward the most conspicuous *facts* and shy away from all reference to more norm-laden and less easily measurable aspects of social life. For the sake of brevity, let us consider only the most recent formulation by one of the unquestionably most influential political scientists of the present generation: "A political system is any persistent pattern of human relationships that involves, to a significant extent, power, rule, or authority."[3] My objection is not primarily to the extension of the reference of "political" to private as well as to public associations, and even to clans and families as well; rather, it is to the absence of any reference to a public purpose. Research work on power, rule, or authority can contribute significantly to our political knowledge, even if the data come from contexts not ordinarily thought of as political. But its significance must be gauged in relation to some criteria; until these are articulated and

[3]Robert Dahl, *Modern Political Analysis* (Englewood Cliffs, 1963), p. 6.

justified, or at any rate chosen, we can only intuit whether our researches on, say, power behavior are tackling significant or trivial issues.

"Politics" should refer to power, but the term should also refer to some conception of human welfare or the public good. The achievement of Plato and Aristotle is in part a result of their starting out by asking some of the right questions; above all, what is politics *for?* Their limitations were logical and methodological or, if you prefer, conceptual: they had not learned to distinguish between verifiable *descriptive* statements, statements of *normative* positions, and (empirically empty and normatively neutral) *analytical* statements, including definitions and other equations.

Once these distinctions had been developed, a process that began with David Hume, it became easy and fashionable to expose fallacies in Plato and Aristotle; but instead of attacking the ancient and perennial problems of politics with our new and sharper conceptual tools, recent generations of political scientists appear to have sought safety in seeking to exclude the normative realm altogether from the scope of their scientific inquiry. "Politics" has consequently been defined in a simple institutional or behavioral manner, unrelated to normative conceptions of any sort. Ironically, most modern behavioralists are back with the Greeks again in their assumption that political inquiry can be pursued by much the same methods as natural science inquiry; they have adjusted to David Hume and the modern logical positivists by the neat device of definitions that limit the scope of their inquiry to observable behavior.

This surely is a stance of premature closure. The alternative proposed here is to insist on the need for a political theory that deals with *basic human needs* as well as overt desires and other observable aspects of behavior. The task of improving concepts and methods toward establishing a stricter science of politics is formidable; but let us avoid establishing an orthodoxy that would have the whole profession contract for a faint-hearted purchase of rigor at the price of excluding much of the meat and spirit of politics.

As a modest and fragmentary beginning toward a more appropriate theory, let me suggest a distinction between "politics" and "pseudopolitics." I would define as *political* all activity aimed at improving or protecting conditions for the satisfaction of human needs and demands in a given society or community, according to some universalistic scheme of priorities, implicit or explicit.[4] *Pseudopolitical* in this paper refers to

---

[4] "Priorities" here refers to norms for guiding the choice among conflicting needs and demands. Political ideals and visions of the good life enter in here, and would do so even if our knowledge of needs and of human nature were as extensive as our knowledge of demands and of social determinants of "public opinion."

activity that resembles political activity but is exclusively concerned with either the alleviation of personal neuroses or with promoting private or private interest-group advantage, deterred by no articulate or disinterested conception of what would be just or fair to other groups.

Pseudopolitics is the counterfeit of politics. The relative prevalence of the counterfeit variety of democratic politics presumably depends on many ascertainable factors, including a society's degree of commercialization and the degree of socio-economic mobility (or the size of the stakes in the competitive struggle); on the other hand, the proportion of pseudopolitical activity would correlate negatively with the amount of psychological security, the amount of social welfare-type security, and the amount of political education effectively taught.

For present purposes it is not necessary to demonstrate in detail how the distinction between politics in the narrower sense and pseudopolitics can be made operationally useful. Suffice it to say that only a saint is pure from the taint of pseudopolitics and that hardly any pseudopolitician would be *wholly* without concern for the public welfare; mixed motives, in proportions varying from one person to the next and from one situation to the next, pervade all actions. It is a difficult but surely not an impossible task to develop indices for assessing the relative prevalence of political versus pseudopolitical incentives in voters and other political actors; the only essential prerequisite is to decide that the task must be tackled.

Without attempting to make this kind of distinction, untidy as it may at first appear to many a behavioralist, I don't see how we can begin to approach a condition of tidiness in our discussions of the *political significance* of research, or of the *political responsibility* of political scientists. But what should we mean by these two highly eulogistic terms; might we not be better advised to shun them altogether? The bulk of this paper seeks to demonstrate some sorry consequences of the latter course. We cannot avoid the realm of normative issues unless we really wish to disclaim all political significance for our work. Probably very few in our profession would adopt this position.

Although explicit cognizance of normative assumptions in his theoretical frame of reference is likely to entail some inconvenience for the researcher, he will by no means be blocked from continuing much of his present work. It should be clear that all competent research on pseudopolitical behavior illuminates political behavior as well, as the relative presence of one signals the relative absence of the other. In the real world the two aspects of behavior always coexist. My quarrel is not with research on pseudopolitics *per se*, but with the way findings are usually reported and interpreted. I object to the tendency in much of the behavior literature to deal with the pseudopolitical aspects of behavior almost exclusively, and to imply that the prevalence of pseudopolitics is and always will be the natural or even the desirable state of affairs in a democracy. Consequently, I object also to the absence of interest in research that could reveal some of the determinants of the relative prevalence of pseudopolitical behavior on our political arena, by which we might learn more about how we may advance toward a more strictly political consciousness, in the sense of concern for the public interest and for the future, in our population.

Now, how should we define political significance and political responsibility? In my conceptual world the two terms are tied together; I would judge degrees of political significance of research studies in the same way that I would judge degrees of political responsibility of political scientists (in the role of theorist-researcher, as distinct from the role of citizen). A research report is politically significant to the extent that it contributes to the kinds of knowledge most needed by politically responsible political scientists.

"Political responsibility" in this paper refers to the extent to which the social scientist observes the canons of rationality on two levels, which I shall call formal and substantive.[4a] Formal rationality refers to the familiar notion of clarifying the objectives first and then paying heed to the best available knowledge when seeking ways and means to implement them. Competent behavioral research in political science is highly rational in this formal sense; this is what the extensive work in theory and methodology is *for*.

The lack of political responsibility that I ascribe to much political behavior literature relates to the other level of rationality, the substantive level, which involves articulate attention to questions of fundamental commitment in social and political research literature. Problems of human welfare (including justice, liberty, security, and so forth), the objects of political research and of politics, can be adequately studied, and dealt with, only if their *ought*-side is investigated as carefully as their *is*-side. Ought-side inquiry must pertain to wants (or desires or, if insisted on, demands) as well as needs. Political communication must be analyzed carefully so that we may learn what aspects of *wants* are most salient and could be frustrated only at the cost of resentment, alienation, or upheaval. Yet, only analysis of data on wants in terms of a theory of *needs* will permit us to evaluate wants and aspects of wants with a view to longer-term consequences of their relative satisfaction or frustration.

[4a]Karl Mannheim employs a similar dichotomy of terms, though with different concepts, in his *Man and Society in an Age of Reconstruction* (New York, 1954), pp. 51–60.

There will be more to say about wants and needs in the concluding section. At this point it should only be added that the student of politics, once he has adopted a conception of human needs, should proceed from there to make explicit his inferences about political objectives and his choice of commitments with the utmost care. If this kind of inquiry is neglected, as it certainly is in the political science curricula in most of our universities, the danger is that the political scientist unwittingly becomes the tool of other people's commitments. And *theirs* may be even less responsibly arrived at; conceivably, the expertise of the political scientist may come to serve the irrational purposes of genteel bigotry in domestic policies or of paranoid jingoism and reckless gambling with our chances of survival in foreign policies. If advice-giving social scientists don't feel called on to invest their best intellectual energies in studying the ultimate ends of our national policies, it is unlikely that anyone else of influence will; most active politicians have, after all, more immediately pressing worries, and these are anyway the kinds of concerns they are best trained to handle.

Intellectual treason, to return to Eulau's phrase, is probably a remote hazard in our profession. For, rather than placing himself in the service "of those whose values he disagrees with," the political scientist usually will by natural, uninvestigated processes come to agree with the prevailing values of his profession, of the major foundations and of his government, at least on the more basic public policy objectives and assumptions. His training and career incentives focus on formal rationality. It is fortunate that many social scientists for other reasons tend to be humane and liberal individuals. We will be far better off, however, if we can make it respectable or even mandatory for many more of our researchers to be guided in their choice of theory and problems by their own articulated values, instead of acting willy-nilly on the supposedly neutral values impressed on them by the conventional wisdom of their profession.

2

In the contemporary political science literature it is by no means unusual to see the articulation of political norms begin and end with a commitment to "democracy" in some unspecified sense. Fifteen years ago a respected political scientist suggested a more critical orientation: "The democratic myth is that the people are inherently wise and just, and that they are the real rulers of the republic. These propositions do have meaning; but if they become, as they do even among scholars, matters of faith, then scientific progress has been sacrificed in the interest of a morally satisfying demagogy."[5] This advice has not been generally heeded. Even today many political scientists are writing as if democracy unquestionably is a good thing, from which unquestionably good things will flow, while at the same time they profess a disinterest in settling value issues. "The only cure for the ills of democracy is more democracy," is still the implicit slogan of quite a few social scientists, who seem unaware of even the *conceptual* difficulties involved in developing generally useful criteria, let alone a rationale, for "more democracy." To put it bluntly, it appears that a good number of otherwise able political scientists confuse a vaguely stated conventional "democratism"[6] with scientific objectivity.

That behavioral research not explicitly related to problems of democracy tends to be vague in its implications for normative democratic theory is perhaps to be expected. It is paradoxical that some of the leading behavioral writers *on democracy* continue to write as if they want to have it both ways: to be rigorously value-neutral and at the same time be impeccable champions of conventional pluralist democracy. To straddle on a sharp issue would not be comfortable; if we want to write as good democrats and as logical positivists, too, it is perhaps necessary to be obtuse on issues like "why democracy?" or "what is democracy for?" and, indeed, "what is democracy?"

For a first example, take the late V. O. Key's most recent book on *Public Opinion and American Democracy.*[7] Here we are presented with an admirably organized survey of what is now known of the characteristics of contemporary public opinion and of the extent of its bearing on American governmental decision processes. Yet for all these facts about public opinion, there is hardly a hint of their implications, in the author's judgment, for any of the relevant normative issues of democracy; what little is said on this score is uninformative indeed. For example, the point is made toward the end that political deviants "play a critical role in the preservation of the vitality of a democratic order as they urge alterations and modifications better to achieve the aspirations of men. Hence the fundamental significance of freedom of speech and agitation" (p. 555). There is no elaboration of this point, which one might take to be an important issue, considering the book's title and general subject. And there is no other discussion of what purpose all this political knowledge should serve. Is it the "preservation of the vitality of a democratic order"

---

[5] Gabriel A. Almond, *The American People and Foreign Policy* (New York, 1950), p. 4.

[6] The term is from Leo Strauss. See his "Epilogue" in Herbert J. Storing, ed., *Essays on the Scientific Study of Politics* (New York, 1962), p. 326.

[7] New York, 1961.

as far as we can articulate the criteria for the best possible government, or for trends in the best direction? What does "vitality" mean here, and what aspects of our democracy are most in need of it? Is free speech valuable solely as a means to this rather obscurely conceived end?

Or take the volume on *Voting*, by a team of top-notch political sociologists.[8] One of the book's two themes, we are told, is the social problem of how political preferences are formed, while the "confrontation of democratic theory with democratic practice is the second implied theme that runs throughout the book." There is much about certain kinds of practices, yes; but democratic theory is limited to a few examples of "impossible" demands of "traditional normative theory" on the role of the citizen: that he should be politically interested, knowledgeable and rational. These investigators find that most voters are indeed politically apathetic, ignorant and far from rational in their political behavior.

Given the second theme one might have expected the authors to raise some pertinent questions concerning the sense, if any, in which we nevertheless do have a democracy, or possibly the sense in which we nevertheless *ought* to be able to have a democracy, if what we have now does not fit this concept. Or perhaps an attempt toward reformulating democratic norms in better accord with political realities, if the term "democracy" should be saved for new uses.

Nothing of the sort happens. Instead, the authors make the happy discovery that the *system of democracy* that we have "does meet certain requirements for a going political organization"; indeed, as it is said just before, "it often works with distinction" (p. 312). What is good and bad about the system is left in the dark, as is the question of criteria for "distinction." Instead, we are given a list of dimensions of citizen behavior, and are told that the fact that individuals differ on these various dimensions (e.g., involvement–indifference) somehow is exactly what the modern democratic system requires. It all ends well, then; and in parting the authors leave us with this comforting if question-begging assurance: "Twentieth-century political theory—both analytic and *normative*—will arise *only* from hard and long observation of the actual world of politics, closely identified with the deeper problems of practical politics." (p. 323. Italics supplied.) *Only?*

Turn now to a widely and deservedly praised book with the promising title, *A Preface to Democratic Theory*. Robert Dahl explains his choice of title by asserting that "there is no democratic theory—only democratic theories. This fact suggests that we had better proceed by considering

[8]Bernard R. Berelson, Paul F. Lazarsfeld and William N. McPhee, *Voting: A Study of Opinion Formation in a Presidential Campaign* (Chicago, University of Chicago Press, 1954).

some representative theories in order to discover what kinds of problems they raise. . . ."[9] And in the landscape of behavioral literature this work does stand out as an impressive exercise in logical analysis. Excellent critical evaluations of the Madisonian and the populist-type democratic theories are offered; but subsequently Dahl changes his tack to what he calls (p. 63) the descriptive method: under "polyarchal democracy" he seeks to develop empirical criteria for a concept of democracy based on our knowledge of existing species. As we would expect of a competent behavioralist, the author develops some enlightening perspectives on how "the American hybrid" in fact appears to be functioning.

Penetrating as this account of the basic operating procedures of the American democracy is, the author's criteria for evaluating the result are surprisingly inarticulate and *ad hoc*. He will *not* try to determine whether it is a desirable system of government, he assures us toward the end of the book; and then proceeds to do just that, but vaguely:

> it appears to be a relatively efficient system for reinforcing agreement, encouraging moderation, and maintaining social peace in a restless and immoderate people operating a gigantic, powerful, diversified, and incredibly complex society. This is no negligible contribution, then, that Americans have made to the arts of government—and to that branch, which of all the arts of politics is the most difficult, the art of democratic government.

These are Dahl's parting words.

Having subjected the assumptions, hypotheses, implied definitions, and even the presumed value axioms of two theories of democracy to painstaking analysis, the author's ambition not to discuss the desirability of the American system of government would be difficult to understand for someone unacquainted with the currently prevailing fashions among behavioralists. To study the definitional characteristics of this hybrid species of government and of the genus, "polyarchal democracy," is a worthwhile endeavor, to be sure, but would in my opinion assume far greater significance if pursued within a framework of value assumptions, however tentatively presented, from which could be derived operational criteria for judging what aspects of a functioning democracy ought to be valued and strengthened, as against other aspects that should be deplored and, if possible, counteracted. Why does the author never say clearly whether in *his* view democracy is something to be valued in itself, and maximized (as he takes Madisonian theory to assert), or as valuable for some specified ends (for example, for maximizing political equality, after the fashion of populists)?

[9]Chicago, University of Chicago Press, 1956, p. 1.

In a Preface to democratic theory, and one which demonstrates a high order of rigor in analyzing other theories of democracy, the author's reluctance even to begin to develop operating criteria toward making meaningful the present system, or to provide pointers toward its more meaningful further development, is as astounding as it is disappointing. Reluctantly one concludes that Dahl in this particular context behaves like most political behavioralists: he feels he can permit himself to write normatively about political purposes, it would seem, only if they are stated in terms of "democracy" and are reasonably indeterminate, lest the suspicion should arise that he is pleading for some politically partisan position. Thus, a demeanor of scientific objectivity is maintained, and so is a persistently implied commitment to a certain political bias, which favors democracy roughly as it now exists in the West, or in this country.

3

Leo Strauss charges the behaviorists with a bias toward liberal democracy, and rightly so, in comparison to his position. Yet in some respects the bias of much behavioralist political literature is profoundly conservative, although this is a species of conservatism rather different from Strauss's. Philosophically speaking, this behaviorally oriented conservatism frequently includes an *anti-political* dimension which is not found in Strauss's work.[10] What is anti-political is the assumption, explicit or implicit, that politics, or at any rate American politics, is and must always remain primarily a system of rules for peaceful battles between competing private interests, and not an arena for the struggle toward a more humane and more rationally organized society.

Consider S. M. Lipset's recent suggestion that the age-old search for the good society can be terminated, for we have got it now. Democracy as we know it "is the good society itself in operation." Not that our democracy cannot still be improved upon, but roughly speaking, it appears, "the give-and-take of a free society's internal struggles" is the best that men can hope for. Our society is so good that Lipset welcomes, at least for the West, what he sees as a trend toward replacing political ideology with sociological analysis.[11]

[10]This is not to deny that the Straussian position is more authoritarian and far less respectful of the right to radical dissent, as is to be expected when a corner on objective truth is being claimed. See especially Leo Strauss, *What is Political Philosophy and Other Studies* (Glencoe, 1959), and his "Epilogue" in Herbert J. Storing, ed., *Essays on the Scientific Study of Politics*. See also Walter Berns, "The Behavioral Sciences and the Study of Political Things: The Case of Christian Bay's *The Structure of Freedom*," *American Political Science Review*, Vol. 55 (1961), pp. 550–559.

[11]Seymour Martin Lipset, *Political Man: The Social Bases of Politics* (Garden City, 1960), esp. pp. 403 and 415.

This is an extreme statement, although by a leading and deservedly famous political sociologist. We cannot saddle behavioralists in general with responsibility for such phrasing. But in substance, as we shall see, the same tendency toward affirming the *status quo* and, what is worse, toward disclaiming the importance and even the legitimacy of political ideology, and ideals, is discernible in other leading behaviorally oriented works as well.

Let us note incidentally that all the behavioral works referred to so far wind up affirming that American democracy on the whole works well, while failing to articulate the criteria on which this judgment is based.[12] In fairness it should be added that probably all these writers would make an exception for the place of the Negro and certain other underprivileged groups or categories for whom our democracy admittedly does not work so well; there are flaws, then, but fundamentally all is well or else will become well without any basic changes.

What is more troublesome than this somewhat conservative commitment to a somewhat liberal conception of democracy[13]—whether acknowledged or surreptitious—is the anti-political orientation referred to a moment ago; the failure to see politics as potentially, at least, an instrument of reason, legitimately dedicated to the improvement of social conditions.

Within a brief space that allows no extensive documentation perhaps the next best thing to do is to consider for a moment a recent example of a behavioralist approach in which, for a change, the underlying assumptions are spelled out with commendable clarity, and then let the reader judge to what extent other literature referred to above may not implicitly rest on similar starkly anti-political premises.

James M. Buchanan and Gordon Tullock have called their book *The Calculus of Consent*, with subtitle *Logical Foundations of Constitutional*

---

[12]An interesting attempt to evaluate the 1952 Presidential election in terms of five criteria of democratic consent (as opposed to non-rational responses to manipulated processes) is reported in Morris Janowitz and Dwaine Marvick, *Competitive Pressure and Democratic Consent* (Ann Arbor, Bureau of Government, University of Michigan, 1956). The five criteria are chosen somewhat haphazardly, but they are carefully and ingeniously operationalized and brought to bear on available data. The study shows what could just as well be done, in years to come, within a more carefully and systematically stated framework of political objectives and norms.

[13]Though perhaps paradoxical, the statement is not self-contradictory. A democracy that guarantees many liberties to people of most persuasions, and in theory to everybody, may well be considered a liberal democracy. Freedom of speech and related freedoms have a strong appeal to most intellectuals, many of whom may become staunch conservatives *because* they believe in preserving their liberal democracy. Some, indeed, will become fixated on the need for defense of the social order to the point of ignoring the plight of poverty-stricken fellow-citizens whose formal liberty may seem worthless to themselves.

Democracy.[14] The task set for the book, we are told in the Preface, is "to analyze the calculus of the rational individual when he is faced with questions of constitutional choice"; the authors, both of whom have most of their training in economics, intend to develop what they take to be the rationale for group action in the public sector in a free society—*i.e.*, for political action.

The authors take pains to assert the value-free nature of their approach to the science of politics. True, they choose to go along with "the Western philosophical tradition" in so far as they consider the human individual "the primary philosophical entity" (p. 11). From here on, supposedly, we are dealing with the political processes that flow from the desire of all individuals to try to maximize whatever they may value. "The grail-like search for some 'public interest' apart from, and independent of, the separate interests of the individual participants in social choice" (p. 12) is not the concern of *these* authors.

Only in one limited sense do the authors recognize a sort of collective interest in a free society: "it is rational to *have a constitution*" (p. 21), or a set of rules for deciding how decisions in the public sector are to be arrived at; *constitutional* issues are in principle to be settled by unanimity, while *operational* issues—all other political issues—must be settled according to constitutional provisions. The authors see no rationale for majoritarianism as a way of deciding, unless a constitution happens to require it in given contexts; consequently, constitutions can be changed only by unanimity, according to this "individualistic theory of political process," as one of the authors has lately named the theory.[15]

In his more recent statement, Buchanan recognizes as an "entirely reasonable interpretation" (p. 7) that this approach to political processes can be seen as a model for the defense of the *status quo*. His most important rejoinder is that "analysis must start from somewhere, and the existing set of rules and institutions is the only place from which it is possible to start" (p. 7).

The previously cited writings of leading behavioralists have been less explicit and also less bold in showing the way from assertedly value-free premises toward a conservative and in my sense anti-political orientation. Yet, in all the works given critical attention above, there are normative ambiguities wide enough to make room for a theory such as the one offered by Buchanan and Tullock. This is not to say that Eulau, Key, Berelson *et al.*, Dahl, or Lipset would concur with Buchanan and Tullock

[14]Ann Arbor, University of Michigan Press, 1962.

[15]James M. Buchanan, "An Individualistic Theory of Political Process." Paper prepared for delivery at the 1963 Annual Meeting of the American Political Science Association in Commodore Hotel, New York City.

in their normative position. But their approach to politics is philosophically similar in its emphasis on prevailing behavior patterns here and now as the thing to study and in its rejection of the legitimacy of normative positions as frameworks for research (except in a normatively *ad hoc* policy science context). Buchanan and Tullock have been able to explicate in considerable detail *one* rationale for an implicit stance that appears to be widely shared by students of politics today.

If a similar orientation were to be adopted in medical literature, its scope would in the main be confined to studying how patients choose to cope or at any rate do cope with their pathologies, while omitting or neglecting fundamental study of conditions for possible treatment and prevention.

4

Unlike other behavioral literature, modern works in comparative politics almost always focus on real political problems; when political institutions are compared cross-nationally or cross-culturally, pseudopolitical behavior can more readily be seen as dysfunctional in terms of some conception or other of the public good; usually such conceptions are couched in terms of "modernization" or "development," at least if comparisons are cross-cultural as well as cross-national. The point is that developmental perspectives and therefore political purposes are ever-present in this literature, even if they are not often well articulated. Yet, what is particularly impressive in some of this literature is its conceptual and theoretical scope, including the stress on psychological as well as social component explanations of political behavior, and on the need for integrating micro-analyses of personalities and small groups with macro-analyses of large collectivities.[16]

Concerned as the modern students of comparative politics have been with substantive problems, they have resisted temptations to pursue their inquiries according to immediately practical considerations such as the availability of operational indices and techniques of measurement.[17] On

[16]Some of the milestones in this literature are Gabriel A. Almond, "Comparative Political Systems," *Journal of Politics*, Vol. 18 (1956), pp. 391–409; Almond and James S. Coleman, eds., *The Politics of the Developing Areas* (Princeton, Princeton University Press, 1960); Almond and Sidney Verba, *The Civic Culture* (Princeton, Princeton University Press, 1963).

[17]For contrast, consider this statement on the ways of other behavioralists: "The focus of the political behaviorist, however, does not seem to be a result of the state of political theory. Elections have been intensively studied because they lend themselves to the methodology of empirical research into politics." Morris Janowitz, Deil Wright, and William Delany, *Public Administration and the Public—Perspectives Toward Government in a Metropolitan Community* (Ann Arbor, Bureau of Government, University of Michigan, 1958), p. 2.

the contrary, insistent efforts have been made to innovate concepts that would take account of variables which are not as yet accessible to observation and quantification—concepts such as political culture, political socialization, political identity, and political style, for example. The long-term strategy appears to be to start out with concepts broad enough to encompass all significant aspects of political reality, and then work toward parcelling out component concepts which come closer to corresponding to variables that can be observed, perhaps indirectly and by tentative indices at first. Thus the theoretical working hypotheses can gradually, it is hoped, be subjected to increasingly direct and stringent tests. This is a far cry from the piecemeal approach to political (or pseudopolitical) reality in many other works, which almost exclusively pays attention to disparate empirical relationships while neglecting to consider the possible systematic-theoretical reasons we might have for taking an interest in them.

There is also this to be said about the modern comparative politics literature, however, that its conceptual and theoretical innovations have as yet failed to make a significant dent in the same democratic myth that Almond himself—the leader in this field—has warned us against years ago (pp. 143–144). The dilemma already discussed, of desiring to support democracy and adopt a stance of value neutrality, too, has not as yet been satisfactorily resolved in this literature, either. And this failure is paradoxical in this particular context, in part because the ostensible chief concern is with "development" or "modernization" as the dependent variable, so that the question of development toward *what* immediately suggests itself. The failure is paradoxical also because these scholars have coined bold new concepts on the independent side of the ledger, and some have written extensively about concepts as far removed from realms of observation as "political culture" and "political identity."[18] Yet a concept such as "human need" has not been touched, and discussions of key terms like "political development" or "modernization" have been hampered, it would seem, by an unwillingness to question whether democratic ways or what kinds of democratic ways are most conducive to satisfying human needs.[19]

In the most extensive recent discussion of these concepts La Palombara begins well with a warning that what many scholars appear to have in

[18]See Almond and Verba, *The Civic Culture*, and Lucian W. Pye, *Politics, Personality, and Nation Building: Burma's Search for Identity* (New Haven, Yale University Press, 1962).
[19]Concepts of modernization or development are discussed by James S. Coleman in Almond and Coleman, eds., *The Politics of the Developing Areas*, pp. 532–536; by Lucian W. Pye, ed., *Communication and Political Development* (Princeton, Princeton University Press, 1963), pp. 14–20; and by Joseph La Palombara in his (ed.) *Bureaucracy and Political Development* (Princeton University Press, 1963), chaps. 1 and 2.

mind "when they speak of a modern or developed system is one that approximates the institutional and structural configuration that we associate with the Anglo-American (in any event, the Western) democratic systems" (p. 10). He calls this conceptualization culture-bound; yet in the same and the following chapter he goes to considerable lengths himself in arguing for the use of the same kinds of culture-bound criteria to evaluate development or modernity abroad. While he contributes a useful discussion of different dimensions along which political change can be measured, he never inquires whether in other countries there might be other criteria of development of equal or greater significance than his own essentially Anglo-Saxon criteria. "One of the great dilemmas of many of the developing countries," he writes, "is that they seem to want economic development more than freedom" (p. 41), and the last term he takes as a matter of course to refer to pluralist institutions. "Why should it not be possible to raise a belief in and desire for democracy to the same level?" (p. 58). And in conclusion La Palombara asserts that we Americans must expand our efforts to export not only technical know-how "but our political ideology and reasonable facsimiles of our political institutions and practices as well." Without such an effort, he adds, he is reasonably confident that "the probability of attaining democratic configuration in most of the newer states is very low indeed" (pp. 60–61).

The main difficulty with this reasoning is that men are motivated, also politically, by their immediate needs and wants, and not by foreign orthodoxies. La Palombara speculates "whether it would not be possible to manipulate demands so that goals of political development enjoy a status equal to that of economic change" (p. 30), and suggests the encouragement of private as against collectively oriented enterprise for this end. The answer is surely a flat no: it is *not* possible, in most countries in which most people are economically under-privileged, to create a broad popular interest in pluralist democratic institutions. "Acceptance of the norms of democracy requires a high level of sophistication and ego security," writes Lipset, on the basis of a variety of loosely connected empirical data.[20] An active concern for the public welfare presupposes a liberation both from anxiety neuroses and from realistic fears concerning one's own and one's family's physical sustenance, welfare and security. To put it more succinctly, needs for food and safety take precedence over political interest; no amount of political manipulation could be expected to alter such priorities.

To be sure, individuals can be lured into "the game of politics" as advantageous careers under the right circumstances; but is this the kind

[20]Lipset, *Political Man*, p. 115 and chap. 4.

of political development that the West should desire? If budding western-democracy-type pluralist institutions turn out to benefit only the middle and upper classes—as in many Latin American countries—then we should not be surprised if idealistic students and others with a passion for social justice, or for politics as distinct from pseudopolitics, may become disposed to reject the forms of pluralist democracy altogether.[21]

Nevertheless, the trend among political behavioralists, including students of comparative politics, appears to be toward a clean break not only with Plato's concern with justice as something above democracy, for the true philosopher; also, it seems that the classical conception of democracy as a system of rational deliberation for settling issues of justice and welfare is on its way out, *even as a political ideal.* Reference has been made to the *ad hoc* attempts of Berelson *et al.* to bring the norms of democracy in better accord with the facts of what I have termed pseudopolitical behavior. In *The Civic Culture* Almond and Verba present and discuss a variety of usefully differentiated survey data collected in five countries (United States, Britain, West Germany, Italy and Mexico). "What we have done in this book," they conclude, "is to spell out methodically the mixture of attitudes that support a democratic system. If it can create a more sober and informed appreciation of the nature and complexity of the problems of democratization, it will have served its purpose."[22] But what kind of democracy? The theoretical point of departure is neither in a conception of human needs nor in the classical theories of democracy, but in such literature as has been discussed above—notably Dahl's *Preface to Democratic Theory* and the last chapter in Berelson's *Voting.* In fact, Almond and Verba emphatically reject the classical "rationality-activist" ideal of democratic citizenship in favor of a more balanced "parochial-subject-participant" orientation; in a healthy, stable democracy as they conceive it (and American political culture comes close even though it does not quite embody this ideal), "the democratic citizen is called on to pursue contradictory goals; he must be active, yet passive; involved, yet not too involved; influential, yet deferential."[23]

Perhaps so, if the ultimate goal is democratic stability. And there is no denying, from my normative position, that democratic stability is valuable, and that many nations ought to have more of it. But is it the most important goal for political development; is it the goal that should serve as the basis for evaluating all other goals (whether wholly, in terms of

---

[21]Fidel Castro's wide following in Latin America can be plausibly explained in these terms.

[22]Almond and Verba, *The Civic Culture*, p. 505, and chap. 15.

[23]Bernard L. Berelson *et al.*, *Voting*, pp. 478–79 and 440–41.

instrumentality, or partially, in terms of compatibility)? Should we not instead hold, in Eulau's phrase, that "The Goal is Man?"

5

In the study of political behavior, "analysis must start from somewhere, and the existing set of rules and institutions is the only place from which it is possible to start," according to Buchanan. Students of comparative politics have nevertheless demonstrated the feasibility of analysing political developments in some countries in terms of valuable outcomes achieved in others.[24] It remains to be shown that political behavior and institutions can be analysed also in terms of normative assumptions to the effect that the purpose of politics is to meet human needs and facilitate human development.

Contrary to an apparently prevailing assumption among political behavioralists, psychological phenomena are just as *real* as economic and voting behavior phenomena, even though admittedly less accessible to observation and measurement. Some more of the same conceptual boldness displayed in the recent literature on comparative politics is required if political inquiry is to become related to important human wants and needs. For one thing, we need to distinguish more clearly between pseudopolitical and more strictly political behavior, if we want to learn how to encourage the latter at the expense of the former.[25]

A major conceptual and theoretical task is to develop a satisfactory theory of human needs and of the relationships between needs and *wants*—here referring to perceived or felt needs. Wants (or, synonymously, desires) and demands can be observed and measured by way of asking people or observing their behavior. Needs, on the other hand, can only be inferred from their hypothetical consequences for behavior or, more manifestly, from the actual consequences of their frustration. Whenever superficial wants are fulfilled but underlying needs remain frustrated, pathological behavior is likely to ensue.

Prior to the development of a viable theory of political development is at least a beginning toward a theory of individual human development. Such a beginning exists in psychological literature, but it has so far been inadequately drawn on by students of political behavior. Let me very

---

[24]See especially Robert E. Ward and Dankwart A. Rustow, *The Political Modernization of Japan and Turkey* (Princeton University Press, 1964).

[25]However, we should not assume without inquiry that *all* pseudopolitical behavior is dysfunctional for all high-priority human wants and needs; not, of course, that all varieties of political behavior are to be preferred to pseudopolitical self-seeking or neurotic striving.

briefly suggest the direction of this theorizing, and some of its implications for the study of political behavior.

Basic human needs are characteristics of the human organism, and they are presumably less subject to change than the social or even the physical conditions under which men live. Wants are sometimes mainfestations of real needs, but, as Plato and many other wise men since have insisted, we cannot always infer the existence of needs from wants. Wants are often artificially induced by outside manipulation, or they may be neurotically based desires whose satisfaction fails to satisfy needs, or both. Emphasis on a civic-culture type of democracy as the goal for political development may well perpetuate a state of affairs in which human needs as seen by the political-minded (in my strict sense of "political") will remain in the shadow of much-advertised human wants as promoted by pseudo-politicians and other enterprisers whose horizons do not extend beyond their own occupational or career interests and status anxieties.[26]

I say *may*, for I am raising a question rather than adopting a position. In order to investigate the relationship between needs and wants as they pertain to political functions we must start out with a tentative conception of priorities among human needs. The best available point of departure, in my opinion, is in A. H. Maslow's theory of a hierarchy of human needs; this theorizing ought to be drawn on until a more plausible and useful theory becomes available.

Maslow lists five categories of needs in the order of their assumed priority: (1) physical needs (air, water, food, and so forth); (2) safety needs (assurance of survival and of continuing satisfaction of basic needs); (3) needs to love and be loved; (4) need for esteem (by self and others); and (5) need for self-actualization and growth. This list presents a hierarchy, according to Maslow, in the sense that the "less prepotent needs are minimized, even forgotten or denied. But when a need is fairly well satisfied, the next prepotent ('higher') need emerges, in turn to dominate the conscious life and to serve as the center of organization of behavior, since gratified needs are not active motivators."[27] Note, however, that whenever in the course of a human life the "higher" needs have become activated, they are not necessarily extin-

---

[26]Joseph Tussman also stresses the danger of destroying the integrity of political communication when the modern bargaining approach to politics enters the "forum or tribunal" that a democratic electorate ought to constitute, according to classical theories of democracy. "We teach men to compete and bargain. Are we to be surprised, then, at the corruption of the tribunal into its marketplace parody?" *Obligation and the Body Politic* (New York, Oxford University Press, 1960), p. 109 and pp. 104–121.

[27]Abraham H. Maslow, "A Theory of Human Motivation," *Psychological Review*, Vol. 50 (1943), p. 394 and pp. 370–396. See also his *Motivation and Personality* (New York, 1954).

guished as a result of later deprivation of "lower" or more basic needs. For example, some individuals, provided they have once known physical safety, will unhesitatingly sacrifice all of it for love, or for standards of right conduct tied in with their self-esteem, etc.

In a recent volume, James C. Davies has suggested the utility of Maslow's theory as a generator of propositions regarding political behavior, and he illustrates the plausibility (without demonstrating the validity) of such propositions with a wealth of historical and contemporary political behavior data. For example, according to Davies's theorizing it is impractical to suggest with La Palombara, that it might be "possible to manipulate demands" in economically underdeveloped countries so that widespread loyalties to democratic institutions could emerge: "Long before there can be responsible or irresponsible popular government, long before the question of dictatorship or democracy can be taken up, the problem of survival must be solved so that a political community itself can develop, so that people can direct some of their attention to politics.[28] In another context he says, "Propaganda cannot paint a picture which conflicts with reality as it is seen by individuals in the light of their basic needs" (p. 134); the picture can be painted all right, but it will be a wasted effort. And Davies quotes Kwame Nkumrah, whose implicit rejoinder to La Palombara's argument is hard to improve on: "We cannot tell our peoples that material benefits in growth and modern progress are not for them. If we do, they will throw us out and seek other leaders who promise more. . . . We have to modernize. Either we shall do so with the interest and support of the West or we shall be compelled to turn elsewhere. This is not a warning or a threat, but a straight statement of political reality" (p. 135).

One shortcoming in Davies's as well as Maslow's work, in my judgment, is that both authors seek to relate events and behavior directly to the elusive concept of "need," without the use of an intermediate and more manageable concept such as "want." Both concepts are badly needed, and their interrelations and their application in hypotheses must be developed if we want to move toward a more adequate knowledge of political behavior. It must be granted that manifest wants are important aspects of our political reality, especially in democracies; what matters is that we also keep remembering, unlike many behavioralists, that there also are genuine needs to worry about, elusive though they may be to the researcher's conventional tools. The volume of competing loudspeakers, if I may use a metaphor, is in a pluralist democracy perhaps more likely to depend on the power of the purse than on the urgency of the need. Even

---

[28] *Human Nature in Politics* (New York, 1963), p. 28. Davies does not refer to La Palombara.

the most democratic governments are likely to come to a bad end—to say nothing of the individuals living under them—unless they learn to become at least as responsive to the basic needs of all their citizens as they are to the most insistent wants of the various articulate and influential interest groups and parties.

Most of Maslow's as well as Davies's discussion is highly speculative; only a beginning has been made. But their theory does lend itself to the production of testable hypotheses. For example, Almond's theory of political "input functions" (political socialization and recruitment; interest articulation; interest aggregation; political communication) and "output functions" (rule making; rule application; rule adjudication),[29] would seem to provide a fertile field for exploring what the participation in or other ego-involvement with each type of function can mean, in satisfying individual personality needs as well as wants. Moving in this direction we can perhaps get away from the customary *clichés* about the value of democracy, toward research-based knowledge on what (aspects of) democratic institutions have what kinds of value for human development.

I have argued elsewhere that the human goals of politics should be conceived in terms of maximizing individual freedom—psychological, social and potential.[30] Democracy and indeed every law and constitutional clause should be judged as a means to this end. A comprehensive treatment of norms of liberty with interrelationships and empirical consequences is necessary for this purpose, and so is a theory of human need such as Maslow's, which in effect predicts that with increasing satisfaction of sustenance and security needs men's tendency will be to become less anti-social, more capable of respecting and eventually perhaps insisting on respect for the basic needs and liberties of others.

The normative research[31] to be recommended can be done with far more precision than was attempted or achieved in the work on freedom just referred to. Perhaps philosophers working with political scientists can be expected to be active on this research frontier in future years. One

[29]See his introduction to Almond and Coleman, eds., *The Politics of the Developing Areas.*

[30]*The Structure of Freedom* (Stanford, Stanford University Press, 1958, and New York, 1965).

[31]The term "normative research" may be puzzling to some, who think of research exclusively as systematically re(peated) search for empirical data, in the real world or in contrived experimental worlds. And "research" has been one of the empirical social scientist's proud banners in his uphill fight against the sometime supremacy of armchair speculators. In our time a less parochial use of "research" is called for, as a way of recognizing the close interplay between the empirical, normative and logical aspects of inquiry that, as the present paper argues, is necessary for the further development of our knowledge of political as of other human behavior.

good example of normative research of this kind, even though its reference to empirical data is for purposes of normative interpretation only, is Naess's study of Gandhi's ethics of conflict resolution.[32]

The burden of this paper, then, is to plead for an expansion and a more systematic articulation of the psychological and the normative perspectives of political behavior research. I propose as a normative basis the proposition that politics exists for the purpose of progressively removing the most stultifying obstacles to a free human development, with priority for the worst obstacles, whether they hit many or few—in other words, with priority for those individuals who are most severely oppressed; as Harrington points out with respect to the poverty-stricken in the United States, they are also the least articulate, and the least likely to achieve redress by way of the ordinary democratic processes.[33] It is argued in this paper that the current preoccupation with pseudopolitical behavior carries conservative and anti-political implications, and that the best hope for a more politically useful reorientation of behavioral research—in addition to and beyond the comparative politics perspective—is to study how the various functions of government bear, and could bear, on the satisfaction of basic needs as well as conscious wants.

Among the questions to ask are these: What kinds of enduring satisfactions tend to be associated, for example, with particular participant and subject roles established by alternate forms of centralized or decentralized decision processes? Under what socio-cultural and socio-economic circumstances are majoritarian decision processes, of given types, likely to produce substantive satisfaction of the basic needs of, in Harrington's phrase, society's "rejects"?

As so often in our human condition, the dimensions of our ignorance appear to grow larger the closer we come to the most enduringly important issues of our social life. Much conceptual as well as basic psychological work remains to be done before our technical proficiency in the study of the relation of political forms to basic needs and to liberty can come to match the current work on analysis of voting patterns. But in this work political scientists should participate; our stakes in its progress are as high as anyone else's.

One particular type of research that should be pushed, as a much needed complement to the large supply of data on pseudopolitical behavior, is work that would focus on just how some citizens "graduate"

---

[32]Arne Naess, "A systematization of Gandhian ethics of conflict resolution," *Journal of Conflict Resolution*, Vol. 2 (1958), pp. 140–155, and also Johan Galtung and Arne Naess, *Gandhis politiske etikk* (Oslo, Tanum, 1955).

[33]Michael Harrington, *The Other America: Poverty in the United States* (Baltimore, Penguin Books, 1963; New York, 1962).

from the role of pseudopolitical actor to that of political actor. Or, more accurately—for surely there are more pseudopolitical actors in the older age groups, "hardened in the school of life"—how it is that some categories of individuals (or individuals in some categories of situations) manage to remain concerned with ideals and with politics, that is, with the welfare of their fellow men, all their lives.

A theory of human development is implied in the research approaches here recommended. It asserts that man is likely to become increasingly capable of being rational, or intellectual,[34] to the extent that he no longer needs the services of his beliefs and attitudes for the purpose of keeping his various anxieties in check. Deep-seated neurotic anxieties about one's worth as a human being predispose to right-wing or occasionally leftwing extremism, with glorification of ingroups or individuals, living or dead, along with hatreds against outgroups and deviants. Neurotic status anxieties predispose to eager adherence to whatever views appear expected in one's reference groups. Realistic fears about employment or future career prospects predispose against maintaining the luxury of political opinions at all, unless they are "safe." Only for individuals whose main anxiety problems have been faced and in some way resolved is it generally possible to think of and care about problems of politics in terms of standards of justice or the public interest, independently of personal worries.

The development of strictly political incentives in the individual, then, depends on a gradual process of liberation from a preoccupation with personal anxieties and worries. Stages in this process can be identified by research, although our concepts and instruments need some improvement before we can with confidence relate specific categories of political irrationality to (repressed or acknowledged) anxieties associated with specific levels in a hierarchy of human needs. Human nature being complex, so is the task of fully comprehending the dynamics of political behavior. My essential argument here is that we must face up to but not complacently accept, as the pseudopolitical outlook does, the fact that most of our citizens live too harassed lives or lack the education or opportunities for reflection to permit them the real satisfactions and the full dignity of democratic citizenship. We must pose the empirical problem of how the more stultifying pressures on adults and pre-adults can be reduced. A premature ruling out of the classic democratic citizenship ideal, with its stress on reason as a crucial factor in politics, would seem particularly inappropriate in our age of rapid technological change; never was the need for politics in the strict sense greater.

[34]See my "A Social Theory of Intellectual Development," in Nevitt Sanford, ed., *The American College* (New York, 1961), pp. 972–1005, esp. pp. 978 and 1000–1005.

It is conceivable that our prospects for developing much larger proportions of political-minded citizens will improve substantially if or when the "cybernetics revolution" does away with our omnipresent worries about making a living.[35] On the other hand, unless educational and cultural resources can be expanded as rapidly, so that more people may be enabled to base their sense of identity and self-esteem on their own attributes or ideals rather than on their occupational roles, status anxieties and despair about lack of purpose in life might remain at present levels, and become aggravated for some. But the over-all prospects surely would be brighter, to the extent that more of the principal *real* worries on which our current anxieties feed were removed.

In any event, let us not as political scientists rule out the possibility that a real *polity* may emerge eventually—a community of people capable of giving some of their energies to political as distinct from pseudopolitical reflection and activity. A less utopian first step that may be hoped for is that many more political scientists will adopt a more political (or a less pseudopolitical) perspective in their theorizing and research. As the horizons of behavior research expand to encompass latent need-behavior as well as manifest want-behavior, our political science will not only produce a new order of intellectual challenge; it may also become a potent instrument for promoting political development in the service of human development.

---

[35]W. H. Ferry and 25 associates have recently issued a statement that received front-page attention in the *New York Times* and other newspapers, under the title "The Triple Revolution: An Appraisal of the Major U. S. Crises and Proposals for Action" (Washington: Maurer, Fleischer, Zon and Associates, 1120 Connecticut Ave., 1964). Referring to the revolutions in cybernetics, in weaponry, and in human rights, but particularly to the first of the three, Ferry *et al.* argue that there "is an urgent need for a fundamental change in the mechanisms employed to insure consumer rights" (p. 9), now that the problem of production has been solved and the problem of full employment has become impossible to solve with our present system. "We urge, therefore, that society, through its appropriate legal and governmental institutions, undertake an unqualified commitment to provide every individual and every family with an adequate income as a matter of right. This undertaking we consider to be essential to the emerging economic, social, and political order in this country" (p. 16).

Further Readings

Bentley, Arthur F., *The Process of Government* (Evanston, Ill.: The Principia Press, Inc., 1935).

Berns, Walter, "The Behavioral Sciences and the Study of Political Things: The Case of Christian Bay's *The Structure of Freedom*," *American Political Science Review*, LV (3: September, 1961), pp. 550–559.

Butler, David E., *The Study of Political Behaviour* (London: Hutchinson, 1958).

Crick, Bernard R., *The American Science of Politics: Its Origins and Conditions* (Berkeley: University of California Press, 1959).

Eulau, Heinz, *The Behavioral Persuasion in Politics* (New York: Random House, 1963).

Gross, Bertram M., *The Legislative Struggle, A Study in Social Combat* (New York: McGraw-Hill Book Co., Inc., 1953).

Kaplan, Abraham, *The Conduct of Inquiry: Methodology for Behavioral Science* (San Francisco: Chandler Publishing Company, 1964).

Lasswell, Harold D., *The Political Writings of Harold D. Lasswell* (Glencoe, Illinois: The Free Press, 1951).

Schoeck, Helmut and James W. Wiggins, editors, *Scientism and Values* (Princeton, N. J.: D. Van Nostrand, 1960).

Schutz, Alfred, "Concept and Theory Formation in the Social Sciences," *Journal of Philosophy*, 51 (9: April 29, 1954), pp. 257–273.

Sibley, Mulford Q., "The Limitations of Behavioralism," in James C. Charlesworth, ed., *The Limits of Behavioralism in Political Science* (Philadelphia: The American Academy of Political and Social Science, October, 1962), pp. 68–93.

Storing, Herbert J., ed., *Essays on the Scientific Study of Politics* (New York: Holt, Rinehart and Winston, 1962).

Truman, David B., *The Governmental Process: Political Interests and Public Opinion* (New York: Alfred A. Knopf, 1962).

8

T. D. Weldon

ANALYTIC
POLITICAL PHILOSOPHY*

T. D. Weldon considers the logical status of political principles and
denies that they are self-evident truths or fundamental human rules
applicable in all places at all times. He contends that it is difficult to
see how any political principle can "significantly claim absolute or
non-contextual validity." *Political principles* seem to him more in the
nature of statements that are accepted within the state or political
party as beyond question, and for which no explanations are demanded. There is "nothing but a practical reason . . . for giving them the
high grade stop sign of 'self-evident' or 'intuitively obvious.' " It is
"dishonest" for a philosopher "to misstate the logical character of
such pronouncements and to claim special status for them."

Weldon represents the philosophical analytic approach to political
thought. Hence his approach is in sharp contrast to Dahl's behavioralism and the functionalism discussed by Runciman.

Weldon thinks political philosophers should neither pretend to
special competence nor expect special influence in political decision
making. Rather they should conceive their function as the exposure
and elucidation of "linguistic muddles": their proper task is to reveal
the "confusions which have occurred and are likely to recur in in-

*Reprinted by permission of the executor for T. D. Weldon from Peter
Laslett, ed., *Philosophy, Politics and Society* (New York: The Macmillan
Company, 1956), pp. 22–34, where it was entitled "Political Principles."

quiries into matter of fact because the structure and use of language
are what they are." They need feel no debasement of their activity
in abjuring claims to special knowledge of metaphysical truth on the
basis of intuition or revelation and restricting themselves to linguistic
analysis and clarification.

1

It is not the job of philosophy to provide new information about politics,
biology, physics or any other matter of fact. Philosophical problems are
entirely second order problems. They are problems, that is, which are
generated by the language in which facts are described and explained by
those whose function it is to construct and defend scientific, historical and
other types of theory.

This is not a revolutionary statement, indeed it is rather platitudinous.
As Professor Ryle puts it in his introduction to *The Concept of Mind,*
"The philosophical arguments which constitute this book are intended, not
to increase what we know about minds, but to rectify the logical geogra-
phy of the knowledge we already possess." The point, however, needs
constant repetition, since it is still widely believed that philosophers do,
or ought to do, something different from this. Political philosophers in
particular are thought to be concerned with the establishment and the
demolition of political principles, and it is therefore to be expected that
their conclusions will have a direct bearing on the decisions of politicians.
They should be qualified to give advice and helpful criticism on actual
plans for the framing of legislation, the reform of electoral systems, the
government of colonial empires and so on.

This is a strange view. Indeed, one has only to ask "What qualifications
have philosophers as a class for carrying out such a task?" to see that it is
a silly view. But philosophers themselves have encouraged it and it dies
hard.

But if philosophers are to make no claim to improve either the theories
or the methods of those who are engaged on scientific or political
activities, is there really anything left for them to do? Are they doomed to
technological unemployment? Some have feared that this might indeed
be the case. The development of knowledge during the past 400 years is
sometimes misrepresented as the gradual partitioning of the old philosophical empire among greedy physicists, biologists and psychologists,
and now the last fortress is threatened. The sociologists have laid siege to
Moral and Political Philosophy. This is an alarming picture, but fortunately it is based on a complete misunderstanding. No territory has been lost,
since none was ever held. What is true is that, especially in the seven-

teenth and eighteenth centuries, the same man often did two different jobs. Descartes and Leibniz were philosophers as well as physicists. But with the expansion of our knowledge this is no longer practicable and there is no good reason for rejecting the advantages derived from the division of labour in the making of theories any more than in the making of pins.

It is common knowledge that scientific experts such as Sir Arthur Eddington who talk profound sense within their own branch of knowledge, frequently lapse into pompous nonsense when they attempt to discourse on their own theorizing; when, that is to say, they turn from physics or biology to what is solemnly designated "The Relation of Science to Reality." Their first order talk is admirable, their second order talk is frequently pathetic. And why should it not be so? They are not expected to construct and repair for themselves all the complex apparatus they use in their laboratories.

The purpose of philosophy, then, is to expose and elucidate linguistic muddles; it has done its job when it has revealed the confusions which have occurred and are likely to recur in inquiries into matter of fact because the structure and use of language are what they are. This does not mean that either natural or technical ways of talking are inherently defective and in need of extensive reconstruction. Sometimes, indeed, they are more open to abuse than they need be, but there are usually compensating advantages to be gained from these defects. Any language is liable to lead to paradox and confusion unless it is studied and employed with reasonable care, but this is not an argument for mistrusting language. Motor cars and safety razors are not fool proof.

2

This prospectus for political philosophy has been widely criticized, both on the ground that the aim which it proposes is trivial and on the ground that it is subversive. To some extent these attacks cancel one another, but they are also in part complementary. I shall first consider very briefly the arguments by which they are separately supported and then go at greater length into the genuine discomfort from which, as it seems to me, they originate.

The argument from triviality is itself rather a trivial affair. Essentially it is that to restrict philosophy to the consideration and analysis of linguistic use is to debase the subject. It is comparable, as one critic has put it, to fiddling while Rome burns. This criticism, however, depends on a somewhat elementary misconception of what is at issue. Nobody has ever supposed that the study of French or English grammar is a substitute for philosophical inquiry; but no important philosopher has ever held that the logical grammar of scientific or natural discourse is unimportant. With what was Plato concerned in the *Theaetetus* and *Sophist*—or Kant in the *Critique of Pure Reason?* Indeed, it is senseless to attempt an inquiry into the use of any language without knowing what that use is, for second order talk presupposes at least competence to handle first order talk.

The idea that philosophical analysis is subversive or sceptical is no better founded. The purpose of philosophy, as already stated, is not to establish or to demolish physical, economic, political or any other principles. It is to clarify their meaning, or to examine their logical force.

These objections, then, fail, but that is by no means all that there is to be said about them. Both spring from a conviction, not always clearly expressed, that there is rather more in this process of analysis than is at first sight apparent. This suspicion is to some extent justified, for though second order talk is not directly concerned with the validity of the first order principles whose logical force it examines, it is a serious overstatement to say that the psychological attitude of those who adhere to such principles is quite unaffected by such examination. To say that political philosophy is concerned with linguistic analysis and with nothing else at least suggests that, since it has no aim except clarification, it can have no effect on actual political beliefs. And this is not true.

"Modern political philosophers do not preach," we say. "That was the heresy of the nineteenth century. We are plain, honest men who tidy up muddles and have no axe to grind." Up to a point this is perfectly correct, but the case is somewhat analogous to that of David Hume, from whom modern empiricism chiefly derives its inspiration. What Hume set out to do was not to make scientific or psychological discoveries, but to analyse such concepts as cause, identity, probability and so on. But in spite of the apparent innocence of this project, his philosophical conclusions gave rise to misgiving and indignation among those who claim special knowledge in virtue of intuition or revelation into theological and metaphysical truth.

In the same sort of way, talk about linguistic analysis and language games, though it is not revolutionary talk about facts (since it is not about facts) has a strongly deflating tendency from a psychological point of view. It inevitably (and quite rightly, in my opinion) deflates a great deal of talk which purports to be about facts, even though they are admittedly facts of a rather special and peculiar type.

As this is a mystifying pronouncement, I will try to elucidate it in the light of some political theorizing which was popular in the nineteenth and early twentieth centuries.

It was necessary for philosophers to make up their minds on the relation between what they claimed to be doing and the investigations of empirical scientists. They might have followed the path pointed out by

Hume, but for a number of reasons most of them did not do so. Instead of recognizing that philosophy was a second order study, they attempted to protect it from the "encroachments" of the scientists by maintaining that it was a first order study of an *a priori* or non-empirical kind. In pursuit of this aim they invented on the one hand a sort of para-science known as "The Theory of Knowledge" and a para-politics known by various names. "Political Philosophy," "Political Theory" and "Political Science" were all called into service, though this uncertainty in nomenclature itself suggested uncertainty as to the nature of the truths which were to be discovered.

The belief which supported the whole movement was that important discoveries might be made concerning both the 'laws' of nature and the rules of human behaviour by thinking alone. These truths were of such a kind that no evidence gained by observation and experiment could either confirm or refute them. In the philosophical language of the time, they were expressed in *synthetic a priori* propositions. What emerged from this belief was a highly sophisticated language game which teachers played regularly with their pupils and with one another. The purpose of playing the game in this country, as far as it was para-politics, was to give an *a priori* endorsement to the moral and political principles which the educational system inaugurated by Dr. Arnold impressed on the minds of those who were destined to be rulers. Controversies were little if at all concerned with those principles themselves. These were taken over with suitable adaptations from what was accepted as Christian ethics, and the primary aim of moral and political philosophy was to find their foundations. This mattered, or was thought to matter, because, as F. H. Bradley pointed out to Henry Sidgwick, if you chose the wrong foundations (e.g. Utilitarianism), you might find yourself committed to approving conduct which you knew to be wrong.

Hence it was common ground that one could prove the rightness of discipline, thrift, tolerance and other respectable virtues by non-empirical reasoning. It was unnecessary and indeed perilous to consult anthropologists, psychologists or economists on such matters. Philosophers were the only certified consultants, and they alone were qualified to expound the true basis of moral laws and, in the light of this exposition, to appraise political institutions. It is worth noticing that similar high-minded and high-handed proceedings were carried out by the para-scientists. H. W. B. Joseph proved that Einstein was talking nonsense and was neither surprised by nor suspicious of the simplicity of the argument by which he did the trick.

Now the obvious criticism of the whole of this philosophical procedure was that developed by the Viennese Circle in the nineteen-twenties. It was that, since the philosophers had avowedly excluded all factual inquiries from their field of study, their investigations were either linguistic or "metaphysical" and worthless. In the end, I think this criticism is justified, but the matter is not as simple as the early positivists supposed. As far as political philosophy is concerned, while it is true that this was generally regarded as an *a priori* inquiry, those who practised it certainly believed that they were somehow concerned with what goes on in human associations. They talked little about actual political institutions, but dealt with ghostly or abstract entities, the State, the Individual, Society, the General Will, the Common Good, and so on.

This raises an interesting question which is worth mentioning though I cannot go further into it here, namely, How were these fictitious entities of para-politics supposed to help?, What job were they supposed to do? The answer, I think, lies in a problem which underlies Locke's notion of abstract ideas. What was correctly noted in the seventeenth century and repeated and developed by Kant in the eighteenth century, was the real importance of blueprints, diagrams and models in engineering and other practical activities and their consequent perfectly legitimate force as explanatory techniques. The abstract ideas of political philosophy were supposed to have the same logical power. They had indeed no such power, but the reason why they had not deserves more attention than it has so far received.

But whatever is the answer here, it is certainly true that abstract entities like the State and the Individual are roughly treated by philosophical analysis. This, however, does not affect the issue as regards political principles since the political theories which postulate such entities, as we have seen, take political principles for granted and attempt to provide a philosophical foundation for them. It is a mistake, therefore, to suppose that criticism of a political theory commits us to a rejection of the principles which that theory claims to underwrite; but that this is so becomes clear only when some attention is given to the logical status of political principles themselves.

3

Generally speaking, to cite a principle is to put a stop to demands for reasons and explanation, but the closure is not always of universal application or completely efficacious. Two important truisms are involved here. The first is that demands for reasons and explanations have to stop somewhere; and the second, that no empirical explanation is ever complete.

This needs further explanation, but when it is understood, it is possible to see how it comes about that the application of analysis to political theories tends to give the impression of a confidence trick. It gives rise to the uneasy suspicion that, under the pretence of disposing of political ideologies, the philosopher is trying to recommend his own political principles for general consumption. Although, as will appear, this suspicion is not entirely without foundation, the proceeding is not a discreditable one.

There are plenty of English words and phrases which are commonly employed as explanation stoppers. Some of them, for instance, "intuition" and "revelation," suggest that the finality of the principle which is being cited is vouched for by a special method of understanding; others, like "self-evident," "indubitable," suggest a special kind of lucidity or intelligibility in what is asserted; others again, like "obviously" and "of course," are less specific and less restricted in their use. All, however, have a well recognized linguistic function akin to that performed by "Keep out" notices. They resemble "This part of the College is closed to visitors." Such notices are used arbitrarily. They register decisions, but not always decisions deliberately formulated by a governing body or other formally constituted authority. What is interesting and important about them from our point of view is that they are used with widely varying degrees of confidence and in more or less localized contexts.

This can best be elucidated by reference to the use of principles in the physical sciences, and it is convenient to consider these as they were in the Newtonian era. This avoids introducing modern complications and brings out the analogy (and the lack of it) with political principles which I shall consider later on.

It is self-evident (or apparent to intuition) that perceptual space has three and only three dimensions; and that perceptual time has one and only one dimension. What is the cash value of this principle? Shortly and dogmatically, it is equivalent to "I cannot envisage any state of affairs in which I should need more (or less) than 'above-below,' 'to the right of—to the left of,' 'in front of—behind,' 'before—after' in order to describe the spatio-temporal arrangement of what I observe. I cannot attach any definite meaning to the statement that cuttlefish or the inhabitants of Mars need more or get along with less."

Two points are to be noted here. It would be incorrect to say that the stop is final. I cannot say "I know for certain that statements like this are and always will be without significance for any intelligent being whatever"; but it is final in the sense that neither I nor, as far as I know, any other human being has any use for them now. This statement is quite unaffected by the technical terminology which modern physicists make use of for their own special purposes.

Hence, it is possible to be clear about the use of "self-evident principles" in this context. "Self-evident" means simply that there is no point (because no clearly assignable meaning) in demands for further explanation or elucidation here. "How do you know that space has three and only three dimensions?" is an empty question. It can be answered only by re-wording the statement (as I did). Otherwise one can say no more than "That is how things are." It is not indeed necessarily meaningless to say, "They might be otherwise," but to us at present it is in fact meaningless since we are quite unable to say how they might be otherwise. This being so it is reasonable to call "Space has three and only three dimensions" a linguistic convention, and it does no harm to say that such principles are expressed in *synthetic a priori* propositions provided we recognize that what is at issue is simply a decision that demands for further explanations are here out of place. There is, however, nothing ultimate or inviolable about such decisions. They can be revoked if circumstances alter. New facts such as those inquiries into extrasensory perception and para-normal psychology are said to reveal, may well lead to a revision of the self-evident principles which are at present generally accepted and which are implicit in our normal use of perception words and personal pronouns.

Few if any other principles of what may roughly be called Newtonian science have the same logical power as the spatio-temporal axiom. But there are others of a somewhat weaker type which are still powerful enough to make the use of "self-evident" and so forth, in connection with them intelligible. Take, for instance, the statement "Everything that happens has a cause." It is easy to see that this is a principle of a different order. It was an important part of Kant's aim in the *Analytic of Principles* to demonstrate that this difference, though real, was not fundamental; to show, in fact, that the principles of Newton were as ultimate (for human beings) as those of Euclid. But he was quite clear that proof was needed, and few philosophers would now hold that his attempt to provide it was successful. And this is hardly surprising since we handle without difficulty the concepts "luck," "chance" and "accident" in our ordinary discourse. It does not matter that they may ultimately be discarded as useless, that the language of a perfectly intelligent being might not include such words. We still have in our present state a significant employment for "It was a complete accident I met him yesterday."

It is, however, convenient for many purposes, notably for a great deal of scientific experimental procedure, to ignore this and to establish some sort of regularity principle such as the conservation of energy, which is treated as unquestionable in a wide but still restricted area of inquiry.

In addition to these types of principle there are others, e.g. the inverse square law, for which a much more restricted claim is made. They are not deemed to be "self-evident" or "a priori" at all, but still they are firmly established and are accepted without question. It is however, possible to see how things might be otherwise than as they are in these respects.

What this comes to is that for purposes of physical investigations, principles can be established, i.e. stop words and phrases can be used with a definite and statable force, either at the level of universal (so far as we know) human characteristics, built in physical limitations; or at the very much lower level of "We find it convenient for our purposes to accept this as a principle for the time being"; and there are intermediate stages between these.

4

How do political principles compare with those which I considered in the last section? It is at once clear that all political associations have principles. To put it differently, in any State and political party there are some statements which are generally accepted as being beyond question, and of which no explanations are to be demanded. Thus in a Communist State it is pointless to ask for reasons why the means of production should not be privately owned. The only answer which can be given is "Because profits involve the robbery (or exploitation) of man by man." It does not require a genius to see that "because" here is misleading. What is offered is not a reason but simply a restatement of the principle in question. The same may be said of "explanations" of the rejection of birth-control on principle in Roman Catholic States and of nationalization in the United States (because it restricts freedom of enterprise).

But these principles all seem to correspond to the least powerful level of physical principles. There is nothing but a practical reason (which may still be quite a good one) for giving them the high grade stop sign of "self-evident" or "intuitively obvious." Further reasons and explanations can be asked for, since things might be otherwise, though in a particular association at a particular point in time it may be useless and even perilous to ask for them.

Do any statements of political principles achieve a logically higher grade than this? I do not think that they do and I am not clear that it makes sense to say they ought to do so. Universality was indeed claimed for the Law of Nature (which is in effect a statement of political principles) but it is difficult to see how the claim might be substantiated. Some philosophers would certainly maintain that very general principles such as those enunciated by Kant or those embodied in the American Declaration of Independence have the logical force required; but the trouble here is that, as they stand, they are far too vague to qualify, and, if they are made precise, it can no longer be claimed with much plausibility that they are, or even might be, generally acceptable to all human beings. This, however, is a debatable point and I am not concerned to argue it here. My contention is simply that to assert any proposition as a principle is logically to put it outside discussion in some more or less precisely defined context. Hence it is difficult to see how any principle can significantly claim absolute or non-contextual validity. Furthermore, it appears that (1) political principles have a much more restricted context than some at any rate of the principles which are found in the physical sciences; (2) the adoption of any proposition as a political principle is a matter for decision. Such decision may be reached consciously and deliberately by a controlling authority, but this is by no means always the case.

Now this may easily be mistaken for a first order statement about political associations and as such it has a familiar ring. It may be thought simply to amount to the following:

1. any association possesses some principles (or rules of behaviour. The distinction is unimportant in the present context);

2. a significant change in the rules constitutes a revolution;

3. governing classes think poorly of revolutions;

4. governing classes sanctify what they deem to be the basic or important rules (or principles) by making inquiries into them or demands for explanations of them illegitimate.

This is roughly the Marxist account, and as a partial statement of what tends to happen it is moderately accurate. But my reason for introducing it here is to emphasize that it is irrelevant to the philosophical question in which I am interested. What I am asking is "Do associations have to have fundamental or basic principles about which no questions may be asked, and, if so, why?" Is this a logical "must"—part of the meaning of the word "association," or is it just an empirical fact about associations which may or might be otherwise?

It is safe to say, dogmatically, that the second of these answers is correct. It is indeed part of the meaning of "association" that there should always be some rules; but there might (logically) be an association in which all the rules were open to question all the time, in which, that is, no propositions had the status of principles. There is, however, an excellent reason why no actual association should be like that, for it is a psychological truism that every man, since life is short, and he has to act in order to stay alive, normally desists from demands for explanations fairly quickly. To appreciate the desirability of doing so is part of the process called "growing up."

A similar point to this, which may help to explain what I have in mind, has been emphasized in epistemological discussions in recent years. "The cat is on the mat" and "There is a bottle of beer in the cupboard" are basic in the sense that they call for no explanation or inquiry at common-sense level (explanation stops there): but they can be questioned (since no empirical explanation is final) and are in fact challenged by opticians, physiologists and logicians, from different points of view. It is indeed a commonplace that the same table looks different to different people at the same time and to the same person at different times. This can be simply explained when we take into account the relevant conditions (light, perspective, positions of observers and so on). Certainly such differences should not lead us to suppose either that there is really no table there or that no statement made about the table by any observer is ever true. All that is involved is the unmysterious fact that everybody sees things from his own point of view. This, however, is itself a "self-evident" epistemological principle. I cannot give any precise meaning to "I might feel your toothache."

So, epistemologically considered, is "Everyone has his own sentiments, adopts his own attitudes, formulates his own value judgments, decides on his own political principles." These ways of speaking differ only idiomatically. I do not mean that anyone sits down, excogitates propositions like "The private ownership of the means of production is intolerable" and then decides that this proposition is "self-evident," "a revealed truth" or some equivalent phrase. There are all sorts of explanations, historical, psychoanalytical, historical, etc., of the fact that this particular individual attaches "Keep off" notices, or confers immunity from further inquiry on one set of propositions rather than another. All that matters politically is that he does confer it, and confers it where he does. He may or may not have good and statable reasons for conferring it, but these justify and do not entail the conferring.

It is therefore not at all a surprising truth that groups of people who live together tend to confer this status on the same sets of propositions. Recalcitrants either conceal their preferences or end by being forced to be free in Wormwood Scrubbs or Broadmoor. It is also unsurprising that psychological stops are frequently, but not always, accompanied by linguistic stops. It is pointless in this country to ask whether freedom is a good thing. The linguistic job of the "revelation" and "intuition" family of words is largely to bring about this agreement.

I hope that this examination disposes of the point at issue, namely "Does linguistic analysis of political 'principles' beg an important question?" More specifically, "Does it aim at selling a favoured ideology under the pretence of being down to earth and anti-ideological?" The answer is "No, except in an accidental and perfectly blameless way."

Everyone can decide what are his own political principles. This really says no more than "All men are human." And it is no part of the job of philosophy to criticize language in the sense of recommending an ideally antiseptic language which can give rise to no confusions and create no paradoxes. Russell, indeed, has yearned for this, but it is still not a sensible aim. The job is to reveal the confusions and misunderstandings which may follow from the careless or uncriticized use of language as it is. Philosophically in the context in which I am now talking, it is to show that there is nothing logically disreputable about my own or anyone else's political intuitions, revelations, value judgments or whatever else you prefer to call them. Any particular set of them may be (and should be) criticized on non-philosophical grounds. They may be, and often are, of shady origin, lead to unforeseen and undesired consequences, be internally incoherent, be accepted without argument and under threats from a self-styled arbiter of faith and morals, and so on. But what I am interested in here is solely their logical function as stop signs.

If this point is agreed, I see no reason why a philosopher or a clergyman or a communist should not advocate his own views. And there is in particular no reason why anyone who is engaged in second order talk about politics should not use his own first order principles as examples. He naturally feels more comfortable with them than he does with those of other people. Certainly in choosing these as examples he is not performing as a philosopher, but he is not acting as a crook either.

What is dishonest is to misstate the logical character of such pronouncements and to claim special status for them; that is, to pretend that they are like the highest grade of physical principles when they are in fact like the lowest. Some writers even claim that political principles are, in some unexplained sense, logically superior even to *synthetic a priori* statements about perceptual space. I do not pretend to know what this means.

Such irresponsible up-grading inevitably leads to trouble in talk about "Fundamental human rights"—but even this kind of talk is innocuous when the logical grammar of it is understood. Such understanding, however, is unlikely to be popular with contemporary "dealers in magic and spells."

5

The points to which I wish to direct attention in this paper may be summarized as follows:

1. To claim for a statement that it asserts a political principle is to claim for it exemption from questioning in a particular context. Linguisti-

cally such claims are often made by employing such words as "intuition," "self-evident," "obviously," etc. These function as stop signs, in the same sort of way as "Keep off the grass" notices.

2. Such notices do not have to be set up anywhere in particular, indeed, they do not (logically) have to be used at all. But there are overwhelming practical reasons for using them and, in any actual society, for having a wide measure of agreement as to their location.

3. Anyone who is occupied with second order or philosophical talk about political institutions tends to use his own principles as instances.

4. This practice may encourage the reader to suppose that these principles are being recommended for more general adoption. So they are. But this recommendation has nothing to do with the author's activity as a philosopher. For this purpose any set of principles would do equally well.

5. Nevertheless, the importance of such second order talk should not be underrated. It is inevitably much resented by those who claim that their private principles are not simply the product of human decisions but have some logically superior status.

6. It is a philosophical obligation on those who make such a claim to explain clearly what this superior status is or might be.

9

Joseph Margolis

DIFFICULTIES IN ANALYTIC POLITICAL PHILOSOPHY*

Professor Margolis claims that T. D. Weldon's *Vocabulary of Politics* (the classical book in analytical political philosophy) is valuable "precisely from its failings." Margolis argues that Weldon's crucial distinction between *puzzles* ("capable of being so formulated that propositions offered in solution may be tested as correct or incorrect"), *problems* (not "so formulable"), and *difficulties* (which "stand only for complications, tensions, conflicts actually experienced or encountered") is inadequate. Margolis shows not only that these distinctions do not distinguish, but also that they do not take into account necessary moral, legal, and politically traditional considerations.

Weldon, in the tradition of analytic philosophy, looks toward ordinary usage for his definitions. But this approach unfortunately becomes a *rule* on meaningfulness of words in ordinary usage. Margolis argues that this is especially true when terms of appraisal are used.

Margolis' final point is that Weldon does not question the adequacy of his own criteria (that is, how "usable" they are) for judging "the 'goodness' and 'badness' of such institutions as 'the British legal system.'" It is the fundamental unexamined question existing for Weldon.

*Reprinted by permission of the author and publisher from *American Political Science Review*, LII (4: December, 1958), pp. 1113–1117, where it was entitled "Difficulties in T. D. Weldon's Political Philosophy."

T. D. Weldon's *The Vocabulary of Politics*[1] is one of those unusually useful books whose contribution derives precisely from its failings. This sort of merit, as a matter of fact, is particularly noticeable in a number of books written in the current philosophical vogue of the ordinary language school. It is a quality very much to be prized, because it serves to fix unmistakably clear-cut doctrines as plausible and attractive, but inadequate or mistaken, alternative solutions for certain persistent philosophical problems. To say this is to say that such doctrines enjoy very much the same sort of status that many of the contributions of classical philosophy possess.

I shall confine my discussion of the weaknesses of Weldon's account to those matters that belong to the very dim region in which political and legal and moral philosophy merge. It is here that Weldon's clarity is at its best and, therefore, on the thesis proposed, that the inadequacy of his own view is most illuminating.

1

Weldon invites us[2] to distinguish between "puzzles," "problems," and "difficulties." The distinctions are important because, as he sees it, determining political policies has to do primarily with resolving difficulties (p. 75), and the confusing of difficulties with either problems or puzzles leads to what he is pleased to label an "intellectualist fallacy," the sort of thing that is exhibited in the liquidation of the kulaks for the sake of eliminating would-be obstructions to Soviet social engineering (p. 82). His tactic here, as throughout the volume, is to elucidate ordinary usage; in this respect, his distinctions seem rather reasonable. But what Weldon fails to notice, an oversight that costs him much of the force of his analysis and exhibits, by the way, the inadequacy of defining philosophy as the mere elucidation of ordinary meanings, are the implications of treating puzzles, problems, and difficulties as sub-species of a common genus. Let me list some of his clarifying statements:

> A puzzle is deliberately made up and there is usually one way and only one way in which it can be solved correctly (p. 75). Puzzles are fabricated and have correct answers; difficulties occur and have to be surmounted. They do not have answers right or wrong, for they are not that sort of thing (p. 76). [problems] are not set by anybody, but they have answers (p. 80).

There are superficial resemblances that have undoubtedly encouraged Weldon to compare these notions. But the fundamental difference be-

[1]Penguin Books, 1953.
[2]Chap. 3, sect. 7.

tween puzzles and problems, on the one hand, and difficulties, on the other, seems (from the above quotations) to lie in this: the former are capable of being so formulated that propositions offered in solution may be tested as correct or incorrect; the latter are not to be viewed as so formulable. This at least is the sense of Weldon's first remarks about difficulties. He is, however, interested in turning our attention to the "menace" of over-zealous economic planning, social engineering, and the like. And we see from his account in this context that he has inadvertently shifted the meaning of "difficulty." He observes:

> If theoretical puzzle-solving fails to deal with difficulties because of refractory human behaviour there is always a temptation to do what the engineer does to the scenery rather than to admit that the puzzle-solving was *inappropriate* or was on the *wrong lines*. If the Jews or the kulaks are or appear to be the obstacle, one can liquidate them in the hope that when they are out of the way the theory will work after all (p. 82).

There is no question that, here, Weldon means to say that proposed solutions for given difficulties may be incorrect (I have italicized the relevant words). In what sense, therefore, are difficulties to be distinguished from puzzles and problems?

The answer, inaccessible to Weldon for a number of reasons, betrays the fact that his humane instincts have outrun the prejudice of his philosophical system. If we allow "difficulties" to stand only for complications, tensions, conflicts actually experienced or encountered, we cannot be said to solve difficulties (in the sense of the other terms) for the trivial reason that a difficulty is *not yet* formulated as a problem and only problems can be solved. Either we *have* a difficultly or we *do not have it;* either we *solve* a problem or we *do not solve* it. If problems and puzzles are sub-species of the genus, questions, difficulties (on this view) are not. But then, why is not the formulation of a difficulty merely a problem? If it is merely a problem (or a puzzle), reference to the corresponding difficulty is merely a way of drawing attention to the poignancy of human decision-making; it has no theoretical importance. If, on the other hand, the formulation is different from a problem (or a puzzle), Weldon has failed to provide us with an adequate table of the types of question-answer relations for the very issues he himself raises.

I submit that if we press Weldon's reasons for demurring against such resolutions of difficulties as are illustrated by the liquidation of the kulaks or the Jews, we shall find that the following objections are intended: (a) the problems that are the alleged statements of the difficulties encountered are not "well-formulated"; or (b) even if the problems are "well-formulated," the solutions are "inadmissible," "inappropriate," "improper," "wrong." I do not think that these objections are really distinct. In their most important usage, they refer to moral, or legal, or politically traditional considerations that impose palpable limits on the formulation of an admissible political problem or its solution. We must be honest here. It is surely possible to formulate a problem of socializing farms, corresponding to some vague "difficulty," whose successful solution does entail the liquidation of the kulaks. What we really mean to say is that we cannot endorse a political problem as a legitimate problem if it goes counter to the sense of the restrictions mentioned, nor can we endorse a ventured solution for a political problem if it suffers from the same failing. That is, if we wish to identify, on the illustrations afforded, a set of questions corresponding to difficulties and distinct from problems and puzzles, we shall find the likeliest candidate in questions about the *status* of formulated problems and puzzles and the *status* of their successful solutions. Given any difficulty, which is really a vaguely defined sense of dislocation, tension, conflict, we can formulate a problem which imputes to it (but surely does not discover in it—this being a question-begging maneuver) a goal for the energies enmeshed and we can set about solving that problem. *Given* the bare problem, we can judge the correctness of any solution that would attempt to meet it; but we mean to ask as well, in the context of political activity, whether we *ought* to accept such a problem for our immediate energies or, accepting it, whether we *ought* to admit any merely successful solution to be a legitimate solution. This is obviously the point of Weldon's unwillingness to accept the gross tactics of liquidation and at least a part of the meaning of the misleading label, "intellectualist fallacy." What we might mean by "ought" and "status" and "legitimate" must as yet remain vague because Weldon fails altogether to broach here, in an open way, the relevant questions. It is enough to see that the third sort of question identified as difficulty is addressed, in a challenging way, to matters of appraisal. What we require, if the solving (rather than the resolving) of difficulties is to be treated as a sub-species of the genus, questions (that includes puzzles and problems as well), is a determinate procedure for appraising in a relevant way both problems and their solutions.

2

Several independent, but not unrelated, ambiguities about the technique of elucidating ordinary usage appear in Weldon's analysis of political terms. He says that to define, in the sense of "to give the ordinary use of . . . ," is "to give instances of sentences in which the relevant word is used and thereby clear up its logical function." (p. 23) This seems straightforward enough. But we soon discover that Weldon means not merely to *elucidate,* in the sense of "give the ordinary use of . . . ," but also to *rule* on the admissibility or meaningfulness of the ordinary uses of words. Thus he says:

> Consider . . . the words "ghost" and "devil." They resemble "phlogiston" and "ether" in that some of their uses have now disappeared. We no longer employ them as our ancestors did because we have discovered other and more satisfactory methods for explaining the occurrence of diseases, floods, neurotic affections, and hallucinations. But they are not dead in the sense in which "phlogiston" and "ether" are dead, since some people still claim to have a use for them. It is therefore important to notice what can profitably be asked about them, and this is not "Do ghosts or devils exist?" but "What are, or are alleged to be, the phenomena which we need 'ghost' and 'devil' to describe or explain, and which we cannot satisfactorily describe or explain without them or their synonyms?" (p. 25).

Surely, Weldon is right in advancing, as a philosophical concern, the question of the cogency or defensibility of any ordinary use of words; in fact, the elucidation of words could reduce otherwise to a mere study of the frequency of ordinary usage. But the way in which he has reformulated the questions concerning ghosts and devils would allow us, in principle, to recover even "dead" words like "phlogiston," should a telling problem force us in the future to speculate in this direction. The mere decay of use is not philosophically significant, however suggestive, just as the mere vigor of continuing use lacks any philosophical force. The study of ordinary usage may well be a pre-condition for philosophical analysis; it is not a substitute for it.

3

I come now, by this roundabout route, to another, more profound ambiguity that directly affects the analysis of political terms. On the issue of ruling among uses, Weldon offers the following:

> Verbal usage is stable because the *objects* and *situations* with which people are confronted and which they need to *describe, discuss,* and *alter,* are also fairly stable . . . there is no single test which will decide whether a word like "State" is being correctly used, and the same is true of "justice," "temperance," and the rest. The position is rather that at any given time there is a number of tests, and it is not necessary that all of them should be passed. . . . Thus a particular piece of legislation may be *correctly* described as "just" in that it places financial burdens on those who are best able to carry them, but unjust in that it penalizes those who have in the past been provident and thrifty as compared with those who have been careless and extravagant. (p. 29)

I have italicized the significant words. Ruling among the ordinary uses of words, without intending to establish unique meanings, is relatively easy when the words are to be applied to palpable and experienceable "objects and situations." The word "State" presents no theoretical complications beyond those that attend the use of the word "wristwatch." Even if, as he says, it is not necessary that all the tests of correct usage apply in any case, it would seem that Weldon supposes that the tests are substantially of the same sort, a measure of convenience in referring to actual "objects and situations." Now, he mentions (in the quotation above) words like "temperance" and "justice" in the company of "State," though it is clear that one cannot rule on their use in the same way as on the use of "State" and "wristwatch." There are simply no "fairly stable . . . objects and situations" to point to when one refers to justice or temperance, "and the rest." What one intends ordinarily in using such terms is an appraisal, and not a description, of "fairly stable . . . objects and situations." Appraisal concerns an ordering of preference or value-status among "objects and situations" that occur or exist and not a description of what merely does occur or exist. If we construe them in this way, the ordinary use of appraisal-words would seem to be of quite doubtful value on the sort of rule that would be called into play in adjudicating among the uses of "ghost," "phlogiston," "State," and "wristwatch." Or, if one insisted that appraisal-words are to correspond with actual appraisal-activities, either we should have no basis for distinguishing between appraisal and description or we should have no way of distinguishing between ruling among the uses of appraisal-words and merely persuading others to persist in, or change, their habits of appraisal. In a fairly obvious sense, there are no appraisals to discover; we make appraisals. But the things to be appraised are truly discovered. Hence, the rules by which we might judge the "correctness" of appraisal-terms would differ seriously and fundamentally from the rules applied to description-terms. Weldon does not enter into the matter here.

4

Weldon's therapeutic intentions extend, again by way of a revealing oversight, to the problem of political standards and measurement. Ostensibly, he wishes to expose "the illusion of absolute standards" in politics for what it is, an illusion.[3] But in drawing a parallel between the problems of measurement in physics, say, and politics, Weldon has carelessly treated the two as basically similar. Now, there are, to be sure, areas of similarity; political measurement need not reject the advantages of whatever discipline in measurement the physical sciences have man-

---

[3]Chap. 1, sect. 3.

aged to develop. But the question remains whether or not *kinds* of measurements are called for in politics for which there are no suitable parallels in the physical sciences. If such differences arise, then the philosophical grounds for the cogency of measurement in politics and in the physical sciences will also differ. Grossly stated, in the physical sciences we are interested in measuring-rods that give us apparently consistent readings in repeated measurement and that give us readings translatable into those of other independently applied and apparently also consistent measuring-rods. If we say that A is taller than B, presumably any suitable measuring-rod will record what we ordinarily mean by "taller than" and the findings of one rod will be translatable into the findings of another. "Taller than" is a relation that can be discovered by inspection; it is not an appraisal-relation, in the sense in which "appraisal" has already been employed. This is why translation is possible. But if I ask whether one State is more just or liberal than another, I cannot translate the findings on the basis of one political measuring-rod into those formed from another. Moreover, we expect this sort of conflict in politics and we do not expect it in physics. The order of height can be discovered, however conventional the units by which we express it; the order of justice cannot be discovered but is created only by our mode of appraisal. Or, we may say, given a criterion of justice, we may discover the measure of justice of particular things; but we cannot appeal back to the actual justice, the discoverable property logically prior to our stipulated criterion, by which to correct discrepancies in measurement due to the use of our criterion—as we can in comparing heights. We can only appeal back to the discoverable and describable properties that we have *independently* decided to appraise in a certain way.

The point of this quarrel leads us back to the issue at stake in the previous three objections. The criteria for judging the adequacy of standards in the physical sciences have to do typically with the reliability of findings on the procedures recommended. It makes no difference what properties are to be measured, because the properties are fundamentally discoverable; the only considerations are *procedural*. But in political disputes, though the reliability of measurement is also at stake, we find that it is precisely the choice of standards of appraisal that receives the greatest attention and is open to the greatest dispute; that is, the questions have to do with what we *stipulate* as the criterion of appraisal itself. Now, although Weldon is absolutely right in exposing "the illusion of real essences,"[4] the question suggests itself whether there may be grounds, resembling the grounds for judging the adequacy of physical

[4]Chap. 1, sect. 2.

standards of measurement, for judging the cogency of the criteria that we stipulate for political appraisal. The question may at least be formulated, though Weldon does not address himself to it here in any way.

5

Weldon does, later, speak of the logical status of appraisals and, in particular, of political appraisals. But, again, his own discussion inadvertently identifies the unsolved problems. Suppose, he asks, we make such a statement as "X is important" (p. 155; the words "good," "right," "better," "free," and the like may be treated much as "important"), what do we mean to say? Consider his answer:

> Three points deserve attention. (1) Such phrases always refer to a person or a group of people. (2) They assume some context. (3) They are "more or less," not "either . . . or," phrases. A typical complete question is "How important is it to you that you should go to London tomorrow?" and a proper answer is "It is fairly important. I have an appointment with my dentist and he is going away for his holiday on the day after to-morrow; but it is not vital." (p. 155)

I believe Weldon's point (2) holds a decisive clue; (3) merely refers to the problem of vagueness, and (1) sets reasonable, but very gross, limits to the use of the term (and similar terms). The logical condition for appraising something antecedently describable is to place it in an appropriate context. To do so is to provide for "relevant reasons though not deductive proofs for the correctness" of our decision (p. 156). This seems eminently fair. Of course, if we ask why our reasons are relevant, in what sense do they support the appraisal, we must let the cat out of the bag. Because, if we stipulate a goal for decisions in a given context, if we inspect the context to "see" what it is we want to achieve, we can appraise the decisions accordingly; but Weldon himself has freely acknowledged, and quite properly, that

> there is *no comparable method* of confirming "Parliamentary Government is a good political institution." We do not know how to complete "The aim of political institutions is to . . ." in the same way as we can complete "The aim of doctors is to . . ." or "The aim of fullbacks is to . . ." (pp. 161–162; italics mine).

This is really an extremely neat restatement of the problem of Plato's *Republic,* the distinction between royal art and such arts as medicine and pilotship; but it is not a solution. In contexts relevant to the first sort of art, we dispute about the goals themselves (preempting attention directed to disputes about mere means); in those of the second sort, the goals are more or less apparent and agreed upon, so we dispute chiefly about the adequacy of means. Problems of the first sort may, of course, always intrude upon those of the second. The question then is, are there any plausible grounds for weighing the cogency of proposed goals offered as a basis for appraisal? From a logical point of view, Weldon's example about the dental appointment may be formulated thus: "*If* . . . dental appointment, then . . . to London is important," where the dental appointment fixes the goal in the context. But in political appraisal what we seem to be involved in may be formulated thus: "*Since* . . . is a political goal that is good, . . . ought to be done," where the goodness of the goal depends on an antecedent criterion of the properties candidate goals would have to exhibit to qualify as good goals. In the first case, *given* a criterion of appraisal, say, facilitation of a certain end, we can appraise candidate decisions. In the second case, we wish to go beyond mere appraisals of the first sort and appraise instead the very criteria of appraisal. We are not in any vicious circle here because the grounds for the "goodness" of an action are logically distinct from the grounds for the "goodness" of a rule for determining good actions. It may suffice to note here that Chapter 7 of Book I of the *Nicomachean Ethics* is occupied with this matter precisely. Weldon does not pursue it.

6

I should like to expose one final, complex ambiguity in Weldon's discussion. Toward the end of this book, he announces: "Now it is clear that 'Is the British legal system a good institution?,' 'Is it superior to that of the USSR?' are not philosophical questions." (p. 175) That he does not mean to say that these are meaningless questions is clear from the remarks that immediately follow as well as from his earlier dicta that "appraisals are empirical judgements made by individuals" and that "it is an abuse of language to say that appraisals are simply statements of baseless prejudices." (p. 170) Let me add a further admission that concedes at a stroke much of what has already been demonstrated:

> It is not the case that political institutions can always or usually be completely appraised in the language of means and ends. This, however, does not make them exceptional since the same characteristic is found in esthetic creation. (p. 170)

Now, if we understand the notion of appraisal with all of the difficulties disclosed, we must see that appraisals are empirical only in the sense what they appraise are empirically describable. We must decide how to appraise things, especially where they cannot "be completely appraised in the language of means and ends," where we cannot pretend merely to "discover" the appropriate goal in the context of our activities. But if this is so, why are our appraisals not "baseless prejudices?"

To see how completely Weldon's analysis fails at this point, we need only examine the following, addressed to our question, and, interestingly enough, expressed in a way that recalls C. L. Stevenson's distinction between disagreements in belief and disagreements in attitude:

> But what is to be done when disagreements occur? Fortunately we are not destitute of resources. I can draw your attention to points *you may have missed,* and we can both study the works of professionals and improve our *knowledge* of the actual situation by the *ordinary methods* of research. Certainly there are *limits* to this process, but it is *not nearly as* barren or unprofitable as it is often supposed to be. (pp. 170–171; italics mine)

The "limits," obviously, are precisely those that distinguish between description and appraisal. On this basis, again as in Stevenson's account, there is no procedural way to distinguish between merely *persuading* another to make certain preferences and *confirming* an appraisal as such. We may ask again why our appraisals are not "baseless prejudices."

Weldon himself offers a very interesting list of "tests" failing which "any set of institutions . . . is *prima facie* a bad one. . . ." (p. 176), presumably in the troublesome sense that is analogous to esthetic appraisal. He hedges considerably about these tests (p. 176) and in a way that is highly ambiguous:

> . . . this is my personal view, or *prejudice* if that word is preferred. It has *nothing philosophical* about it and may be rejected by anyone who *disapproves* of it. I suggest, however, that anyone who does reject it should offer an alternative and *at least equally usable* set of tests (p. 176; italics mine).

We seem to be invited to conclude that, although appraisals are not "baseless prejudices," the criteria of appraisal are. It is also not clear whether when someone "disapproves" of our criteria, he is merely expressing his prejudice or has "relevant reasons" for disapproving. The whole discussion is disingenuously complicated by Weldon's insistence on a deliberate, but unexplained, play on Mill's notorious use of the word "desirable." In any case, the term "usable" would appear to invite us to consider initial philosophical grounds for the cogency of candidate criteria; but if this is so (note the phrase "at least equally usable"), Weldon's own "prejudice" does have philosophical implications. To return then to the first remark with which I began this objection, even if the "goodness" of "the British legal system" is not itself a philosophical question, the "goodness" of Weldon's criteria for judging (in part) the "goodness" and "badness" of such institutions as "the British legal system" is indeed a philosophical question.

It is the question that we have tracked through Weldon's entire text and found unexamined. And it is, in fact, one of the most crucial questions that moral, legal, and political philosophy have yet to address themselves to in a convincing and fruitful way.

Further Readings

Benn, Stanley I., and R. S. Peters, *Social Principles and the Democratic State* (London: George Allen & Unwin, Ltd., 1959).

Field, G. C., "What is Political Theory?" *Proceedings of the Aristotelian Society* (London: Harrison & Sons, 1954), New Series LIV (1953–1954), pp. 145–166.

Flew, A. G. N., ed., *Essays on Logic and Language* (Oxford, England: Blackwell, 1951; New York: Philosophical Library, 1951), esp. pp. 8–9.

——, ed., *Logic and Language (Second Series)* (Oxford, England: Blackwell, 1953), esp. pp. 4–9.

Kaplan, Abraham, "Analytic Philosophy," in Abraham Kaplan, *The New World of Philosophy* (New York: Random House, 1961), pp. 53–96.

Laslett, Peter, ed., *Philosophy, Politics and Society* (New York: The Macmillan Company, 1956).

—— and W. G. Runciman, eds., *Philosophy, Politics and Society (Second Series)* (New York: Barnes and Noble, Inc., 1962).

Macdonald, Margaret, "The Language of Political Theory," in A. G. N. Flew, ed., *Essays on Logic and Language* (Oxford, England: Blackwell, 1951; New York: Philosophical Library, 1951), pp. 167–186.

McCloskey, H. J., "The Nature of Political Philosophy," *Ratio,* VI (1: June, 1964), pp. 50–62.

Rees, J. C., "The Limitations of Political Theory," *Political Studies,* II (3: October, 1954), pp. 242–257.

Weldon, T. D., *The Vocabulary of Politics* (London: Penguin Books, 1953), esp. chaps. 1 and 2.

10

W. G. Runciman

FUNCTIONALISM AS A METHOD IN POLITICAL THOUGHT*

The element "common to the functionalist approach in all its forms" is that one asks "in studying a given social or political system not how a pattern of behaviour may have originated so much as what part it plays in maintaining the system as a whole." W. G. Runciman assesses the scope of the functionalist approach in political science, which he considers the only serious candidate for the status of a general theory of society, and finds that "functionalism, like even the most scientific Marxism, turns out in several ways to look more like a philosophy of politics than the general sociological theory which its supporters claim it to be." From treatment of the merits and limitations of the functionalist approach Runciman moves to consideration of other methods available to the "sociologist of politics." Although he finds the empirical methods "have greatly advanced the search for better explanations of political behaviour," he sees in each method significant limitations. He concludes that "even the most successful of formal analogues, or quantitative techniques, or comparative case-studies, or general explanatory theories cannot provide a solution by itself to the questions which philosophers of politics have raised since the time of Plato and Aristotle." The answer to their questions "depends ultimately on a

*Reprinted by permission of the author and publisher from *Social Science and Political Theory* (Cambridge, England: At the University Press, 1963), pp. 109–134, 191–193, where it was entitled "Methods, Models and Theories."

philosophical view of the world and of the human beings who live in it." But to argue for any answer to such questions will require "the maximum possible reference to our knowledge, whether formal or empirical," about how politics do work or, might be made to work. "The attempt to reduce all political philosophy to political science is foredoomed to failure; but the philosopher of politics must be as aware as the political scientist that any attempt to enlarge the scope or application of political science is an attempt worth making."

Even if it is a mistake to look for general theories of society, and even if all theories in the social sciences are bound to be subject to limitations from which the natural sciences are exempt, it is still worth asking how far any particular social science may have progressed in the direction of a full-fledged theory. In political science, there is in fact one and only one serious candidate for such a theory—using theory in its non-prescriptive sense—apart from Marxism. Not even its strongest partisans would yet argue that it has produced a set of propositions about political behaviour comparable in scope or force to those of Marxism. But they would, despite this concession, claim that an alternative set of general propositions can be formulated which provide a better explanation of the known facts of political behaviour than Marxism has done. This alternative approach to Marxism is the functionalist approach, which I have already referred to. I am only really concerned with its application to specifically political systems of institutions and behaviour. But it shares with Marxism the important characteristic of setting out to provide an explanation of all social processes; and before, therefore, considering its relevance to the theorist (in either the prescriptive or the non-prescriptive sense) of politics, we shall have to make some brief assessment of this general claim. In doing so, moreover, we shall find that functionalism, like even the most scientific Marxism, turns out in several ways to look more like a philosophy of politics than the general sociological theory which its supporters claim it to be.

Functionalism, as I remarked . . . , came into the social sciences from biology; and in some ways this is less of a novelty than it might seem, because organic analogies and modes of reasoning about the body politic and its members are of very ancient origin. But the main impact of what is now meant by functionalism on the social sciences may be fairly dated from 1922, when there appeared the two classics of functionalism, Malinowski's *Argonauts of the Western Pacific* and Radcliffe-Brown's *Andaman Islanders*. There are a number of differences between Malinowski and Radcliffe-Brown, as between many other subsequent functionalists, so that to lump them together involves something of an oversimplification. Both, however, exemplify what is common to the functionalist approach in all its forms, which is to ask in studying a given social or political system not how a pattern of behaviour may have originated so much as what part it plays in maintaining the system as a whole. This represented at the time a salutary shift of emphasis. It was a useful departure from the sort of conjectural evolutionary history which had been the previous anthropological fashion, and it was a good antidote against any implicit disdain for the habits of undeveloped or "primitive" peoples. Obviously, it is more sensible when studying a polygamous society to look for the way in which polygamy helps to keep the society going than to treat it as a retrograde stage in the "normal" evolution towards Christian monogamy. But functionalism, however useful as a shift of emphasis, has as a theory of social processes been subjected to some damaging logical criticisms.

Two often-quoted passages from Malinowski and Radcliffe-Brown may be cited as illustrations of classic—or, one should perhaps say, old-fashioned—functionalism. First, Malinowski: "In every type of civilisation, every custom, material object, idea and belief fulfils some vital function, has some task to accomplish, represents an indispensable part within a working whole."[1] This assertion, though it carries the useful implication that nothing in any society should be taken for granted, is nevertheless either quite obviously false or else true only by definition. As Radcliffe-Brown himself points out in one essay, it is unlikely that the taboo against spilling salt in our own society has any social function[2]; and if Malinowski means that everything accomplishes some task simply by virtue of existing as it is and not otherwise, then this is merely a trivial assertion to the effect that everything in a society must be just as it is for the total society to be just as it is.

Radcliffe-Brown's own formulation, however, is not very much less open to objection. He does not maintain that every teaspoon or neurosis in a given civilization is essential to it. But he claims that "the function of any recurrent activity, such as the punishment of a crime or a funeral ceremony, is the part it plays in the social life as a whole and therefore the contribution it makes to the maintenance of the structural continuity."[3] This is, perhaps, at first sight more plausible (or less trivial); but there is, as Radcliffe-Brown's critics have rightly detected,[4] a crucial flaw in the "therefore." Radcliffe-Brown's assertion is just as much as Malinowski's either an obvious falsehood or else an unhelpful tautology. To say that it

---

[1]This quotation is taken from Malinowski's article "Anthropology" in the *Encyclopaedia Britannica* (1926), Suppl. vol. 1, p. 132.

[2]A. R. Radcliffe-Brown, *Structure and Function in Primitive Society* (1952), p. 145.

[3]See A. R. Radcliffe-Brown, *Structure and Function in Primitive Society*, p. 180.

[4]See George C. Homans, *The Human Group* (1950), p. 271; Homans and David M. Schneider, *Marriage, Authority and Final Causes* (1955), p. 16.

follows from the fact that a recurrent activity plays a part in the social life as a whole that it therefore helps to maintain the structural continuity, is only true if any recurrent activity is by definition part of the continuity to which it must contribute by its mere occurrence. It should be made clear that these two statements are of a much less subtle version of functionalism than any of its advocates would nowadays put forward. But the difficulties which the two statements clearly involve persist even in more sophisticated versions of functionalism, and are enough to prevent functionalism from ever becoming an explanatory theory of social processes.

The central difficulty is this: it is mistaken to suppose that a behaviour-pattern which is shown to have an important effect on the total social structure has thereby been explained. As Durkheim pointed out a good many years before Malinowski, to show how something is useful is not to explain how it originated or why it is what it is.[5] It may do so in the case where conscious purposes are at work, for here (and here only) an occurrence or a pattern of behavior may be explained by reference to its results. But to explain something as a result of the intentions of given persons does not necessarily require the notion of functionalism. Biologists may, on occasion, speak in such phrases as plants having roots "in order to" extract nourishment from the soil. But the phrase is not intended to imply a conscious purpose, but simply observed results (unless, of course, it is God's purpose which is in the speaker's mind). Functionalist terms may also be used (as is done by Malinowski) for determinism by needs, as in the statement that getting food is a functional prerequisite for the continuing existence of any human society. But this is very obviously trivial; and though it may become interesting when a pattern of behaviour is seen as deriving from the need to acquire food or to limit its consumption, this once again does not have to be deduced from a functionalist theory. That an institution may survive its original purpose because it comes to satisfy some other need is a phenomenon familiar to any historian. But it is a phenomenon which can be as well or better explained in historical terms than teleological ones. Similarly, it may be interesting to suggest that because of a universal need among mankind for some form of organized religion the messianic appeal of Marxism may be better understood. But this does not enable us to deduce the actual spread of Marxism from a functionalist theory whereby the messianic urges of mankind must somehow or other be fulfilled.

A number of other accusations have been levelled against functionalism, notably that it is incapable of accounting for historical change. But this is secondary to the main issue, quite apart from the fact that

---

[5]Durkheim, *The Rules of Sociological Method* (ed. Catlin), p. 90.

self-styled functionalists have often claimed to explain specific historical changes. The prior question is whether functionalism can provide an explanatory theory at all, and on this the central point is a very simple one: any meaningful statement in terms of "function" can without loss of meaning to be translated into an "if . . . then" statement of cause and effect. It can be shown that in the case of all self-regulating systems where functionalist language is most often and appropriately used, such statements can be effectively formalized.[6] This does not mean, however, that the use of functionalist terminology, even where most appropriate, subsumes the causal proposition concerned under a general explanatory theory. It may help the investigator in his search for one; but this is hardly the same thing.

It has, in fact, been argued that this help to the investigator should be seen as the sole usefulness of functionalist language: it directs him to particular statements of cause and effect about "self-regulation" or "adaptation" or "universal prerequisites" which he might otherwise be less likely to discern.[7] It has also been suggested that functionalist analysis is in fact synonymous with sociological analysis in general, and that we should therefore be well advised to stop talking about "functionalism" altogether.[8] However, the proponents of functionalism still champion it as a distinctive approach which can lead to, although it may not yet constitute, an explanatory theory of some or even all social processes. Before, therefore, considering this claim as it applies in particular to politics, it is worth asking whether there are any particular kinds of statement of sociological cause and effect for which functionalist terminology may be both heuristically useful and logically defensible. The view which I want to suggest is that there are two and only two types of such statements.

The first type is where the analogy from biology is in fact appropriate— that is to say, where it is possible to specify the extreme permissible limits of certain variables such that where these limits are exceeded the system breaks down. Perhaps the most familiar example is the temperature of the human body and the homeostatic mechanisms which exist "for the purpose of"—that is, with the effect of—maintaining it within the acceptable limits. The difficulty when this notion is applied to social, economic or political systems rather than to biological ones is that it becomes much more difficult to define in advance the acceptable limits; but a functional-

[6]See Ernest Nagel, *Logic Without Metaphysics* (1956), part 1, chapter 10, "A Formalization of Functionalism."

[7]Carl G. Hempel, "The Logic of Functional Analysis" in L. Gross (ed.), *Symposium on Sociological Theory* (1959), pp. 301–302.

[8]Kingsley Davis, "The Myth of Functional Analysis in Sociology and Anthropology," *Amer. Sociol. Rev.*, xxiv (1959), pp. 757–772.

ist analysis can still be made logically unexceptionable. The language and procedures of cybernetics are likely to be useful for this purpose. When a system has been defined as a set of variables, then a subset of the possible values of these variables can be designated as constituting the range of acceptable states. In the case of an economic system, the acceptable states might be any subset of possibilities which excluded those involved in the definition of "slump." In the case of a political system, they might be any subset which excluded those involved in the definition of "anarchy" or "civil war." But however they are defined (and their good or bad definition is a separate, though difficult, issue) it becomes possible to ask what aspects of the system's state or behaviour may be regarded as "functional." This is the same, in other words, as asking what serves to keep the essential variables of the system within their predefined acceptable limits. This still does not amount to an explanation, let alone a theory, of the behaviour involved. But it makes it possible to isolate those particular relations or suggested relations of cause and effect which, if the functionalist approach has the merits which are claimed for it, are most likely to lead the investigator to such an explanation on the lines of "functional interdependence," "reciprocal causality," "dynamic equilibrium" and so on.

The second type of statement where functionalist terminology may be useful and where it may be employed without logical disaster is a statement which is, in fact, about purposes. I do not mean by this only individual intentions, as in such cases as "Hitler wanted the war," but cases where it is possible to speak unambiguously about the "goals" of a system as such. This is perfectly possible, but only provided that we can avoid the two chief dangers which occur in practice. Both of these arise from the fact that the concept of "goal" presupposes the notion of "purpose." The first is the difficulty to which, as I have mentioned, any full-scale functional theory is liable, namely that purposes cannot properly be spoken of when only observed results are meant. The second is that even where purposes are not being confused with results, it must be possible to specify the particular persons whose specific purposes are meant. The first of these points is obvious enough: when, for instance, a well-known anthropological textbook speaks of distinguishing an "ulterior" purpose construed by the observer from the "proximate" purpose of the actors whom he observes,[9] it would clearly be less misleading to speak of results or, perhaps, utility than of "ulterior purposes"; similarly, Lévi-Strauss has been quite rightly criticized for making human intelligence his efficient cause when he argues that tribesmen adopt their rules

[9] S. F. Nadel, *Foundations of Social Anthropology* (1951), p. 368.

governing exchanges of women between kin-groups literally "in order to" preserve and increase the solidarity of their societies by means of such exchanges.[10] The second difficulty, however, may be harder to deal with, and deserves separate comment.

We are certainly not required to limit the notion of purpose to single, conscious intentions implemented by individual persons. It is, for instance, perfectly legitimate to speak of the explanatory validity of a learning model, or of a "purposeful" machine such as a torpedo with a target-seeking mechanism. But an adequate explanation of observed behaviour in terms of goals must involve not only a description of the mechanism by which a goal is pursued but also an ascertained purpose on the part of a designated person or set of persons. This applies directly in the case of any social system. We must be able to specify the values of the "state coordinates" of the system which constitute the purpose of designated members (present or past) of that system. If we cannot, then the concept of "goal-attainment" can have no value either for the explanation of particular findings or for the formulation of some more general theory. Moreover, we must know in advance what sort of evidence would entitle us to reject an assertion of the form "the goal of system S is X," for only with this can we assign an unambiguous meaning to assertions of the form "A is functional for S" in this second sense.

Sometimes this is straightforward enough. For example, the main organizational objectives of bureaucratic agencies can in general be clearly defined,[11] or it can be legitimately asserted that "the goal of any specific industry is to add value to its typical products."[12] But when we try to consider a total society, as opposed to a definable political, economic or familial system (or set of variables), it becomes immediately clear that there are unlikely to be any such readily definable objectives. Do we mean by the goals of a total society the purposes of its effective rulers, or the wishes of the majority of its members, or the principles written into its constitution by its founders? Professor Talcott Parsons, whose contention it is that goal-attainment is a "functional prerequisite" of all social systems, never seems to consider this problem. One of many historical examples would be France between the revolution of 1848 and the *coup d'état* of Louis Napoleon in 1851. It is difficult to see by what criteria it could be established what the "societal goals" of France as such were during this period, or, indeed, whether France had any "societal goals" at all. But the only alternative to this, on the basis of Parsons's

[10]Homans and Schneider, *Marriage, Authority, and Final Causes*, on Claude Lévi-Strauss, *Les Structures Elémentaires de la Parenté* (1949).
[11]P. M. Blau, *The Dynamics of Bureaucracy* (1955), p. 8.
[12]Neil J. Smelser, *Social Change in the Industrial Revolution* (1959), p. 22.

assertion, is to say that during this period France was not a social system at all for precisely this reason. In this case, however, it becomes clear that the claim that goal-attainment is a functional prerequisite for all social systems is neither a theory nor even an empirical generalization but a tautology.

We can, however, without tumbling into such pitfalls as these, make functionalist statements about causes and effects related either to the predefined acceptable states of the system concerned or to the designated purposes of persons whom it is plausible in some sense to identify with the system. In both cases, a sense can be given to the adaptation or adjustment of the system which the observed patterns of behaviour are presumed by functionalists to help to bring about. In neither case, moreover, need such notions presuppose a value-judgement in the way that many of the opponents of functionalism have been apt to argue and even some of its champions to concede. Nadel, for example, goes so far as to allow that "If we do not employ the function concept we cannot speak of adjustment; yet if we employ it, we must be prepared to judge by ultimate values."[13] This, as I hope the foregoing discussion has made clear, need not be so, provided that we are careful about defining our terms. Two senses can be given to "functional," "adjustment" and similar terms where no question of "ultimate values" is involved. It is a question only of concern with particular types of statement of cause and effect, or, more precisely, with the question whether a given pattern of behaviour tends to produce a result tending to cause the system to change in a predefined direction. Whether this is useful or not will be a further question.

It can be strongly argued that the functionalist approach has in fact proved useful, if only in directing the observer's attention to the possibilities of a particular type of cause and effect which may help to explain what puzzles him. A good example from political behaviour may be taken from the work of Professor Merton, whose essay on "Manifest and Latent Functions" remains one of the clearest and most useful discussions by a sympathetic critic. Merton shows how the phenomenon of American boss-politics may be readily understood by seeing it as satisfying needs generated by the American social structure which are not otherwise met. In Merton's own words, "The functional deficiencies of the official structure generate an alternative (unofficial) structure to fulfil existing needs somewhat more effectively. Whatever its specific historical origins, the machine persists as an apparatus for satisfying otherwise unfulfilled needs of diverse groups in the population."[14] Machine-politics arise, on Merton's

---

[13]Nadel, *Foundations of Social Anthropology*, p. 378.
[14]R. K. Merton, *Social Theory and Social Structure* (rev. edn., 1957), p. 73.

analysis, because there are large sub-groups within the American population for whose needs the existing legal and political institutions are
inadequate. On top of this, the American ethic of competitive success
imposes on all members of American society a compulsion towards a type
of goal which minority ethnic groups are in practice denied many of the
means to achieve. The result is Tammany Hall. That this line of argument, which I have briefly summarized, serves to account for much of the
pattern of big-city politics in the United States would, as far as I know, be
generally agreed by all those who have studied it. Accordingly, Merton's
discussion may be claimed as a good example of how the functionalist
presupposition of needs being consciously or unconsciously met helps us
to understand a particular structure of institutions and behaviour. But it
remains necessary to stress that a complete explanation cannot be given
except in historical terms. It is not a case of deducing American politics
from a general law about the fulfilment of political needs, but a case of
the sort of general notion of psychological cause and effect which all
historical explanations must at some point rest on. Merton's analysis is
social and political history, not codified science. To see the inadequacy
of an attempt to interpret findings about political behaviour in terms of a
would-be general functionalist theory it is worth turning to Parsons's
discussion of the findings of the American voting studies.

In an essay entitled "*Voting* and the Equilibrium of the American
Political System," Parsons takes the findings of the second of the Lazarsfeld studies and argues that they support his general functionalist-type
theory. But how the findings either confirm his general theory or are
explained by it is very far from clear. At one point Parsons states only
that they fit "with a more general conceptual scheme," but a few lines
later he is claiming that they fit closely with deductions from "highly
general theory." On the other hand, a footnote allows that this is "very
different from deducing the *specific* findings of the empirical research. Of
course this has not been done."[15] It is difficult, in all this, to make out
just what Parsons is claiming for his "theory." There is the confusion
between a theory and a conceptual scheme, or between classification and
analysis, . . . which Parson's critics have detected throughout his work.
But in any case, even if we should be prepared to concede that Parsons
is putting forward what can in some sense be properly designated a
theory, it is not a theory amenable to adequate validation or falsification.
At one point, Parsons does seem to be aware of this, for he assigns to his
schema only a heuristic value, and says that "By applying the model to

[15]Talcott Parsons, "*Voting* and the Equilibrium of the American Political System,"
in E. Burdick and A. J. Brodbeck (eds.), *American Voting Behavior* (1959), p. 115
and n. 48.

the general structure it was possible to identify four main areas in which to look for mechanisms relevant to these functional requirements."[16] But if this is what Parsons is really saying, it only defers the problems of explanation one step further. Even the heuristic value of the conceptual scheme is not justified until a testable, non-tautologous assertion of "if . . . then" form has been put forward which (as in Merton's case) can explain, at least in part, the behaviour under discussion. The findings of *Voting* may well constitute evidence for such an assertion as "American politics follow a relatively stable pattern," and this is an assertion which Parsons might wish to maintain to be true. But no redescription of the findings in terms of "integration" or "pattern-maintenance" can properly answer the question "why?".

This brings us to the basic issue. The presupposition that social systems, of whatever kind, have a built-in tendency to equilibrium is as undemonstrable, and therefore as incapable of providing satisfactory explanations, as the assumptions underlying Marxism. Functionalism, as a theory, is not a set of causal laws but an interpretation which places a prior emphasis and value on the normative elements of social systems, just as Marxism places a prior emphasis and value on the essential conflicts which it points to in such systems. The point has been simply made against Parsons by David Lockwood in a discussion of Parsons's book *The Social System*: "Why," asks Lockwood, "has Parsons given conceptual priority to the normative structuring of action?"[17] And the answer, of course, is that Parsons wishes to make an assumption which precedes and cannot be deduced from the analysis of the social relations which he describes. Parsons cannot prove that the factors in society which make for agreement and harmony are fundamentally more important than those making for disagreement and conflict. Just as we saw in the case of Marx, such assumptions can never be proved, but only, like all philosophical standpoints, well or badly defended. It is not a case of rival systems of laws, like Ptolemaic astronomy versus Copernican, but of rival interpretations of human actions.

Functionalism can, indeed, be interpreted as a conscious alternative to Marxism. Some of its critics have even wanted to interpret it as a political ideology conditioned by the structure of American capitalism. But leaving aside the separate issue of its historical origins, it is interesting to notice just how far functionalism provides a sort of mirror-image of

[16]Parsons, "*Voting* and the Equilibrium of the American Political System," p. 114.
[17]David Lockwood, "Some Remarks on 'The Social System'," *Brit. J. Sociol.*, VII (1956), p. 136. Parsons is, in fact, quite explicit about his assumption that "the stabilization of the processes of mutual interaction within complementary roles is a fundamental tendency of interaction," but seems not to realize how far the question is begged by the use of "fundamental."

Marxism. In both cases, the crux of interpretation rests on assumptions which cannot be strictly proved from the evidence of historical fact; but each theory claims to offer a better interpretation of all the known facts than can the other. "Look," says the Marxist, "don't you see that there is a fundamental conflict between the classes? This is the basic fact of politics, resulting from the iron laws of economic determinism." "Look," says the functionalist, "don't you see that there is a fundamental harmony in the role-structure of society? This is the basic fact of politics, resulting from the way in which patterns of behavior emerge in response to the needs felt by all human societies." Neither claim is wholly absurd, but nor is it wholly demonstrable. Moreover, both sides claim to be able to incorporate precisely the evidence most relied upon by the other. "Apparent identity of interest," says the Marxist, "is merely a distortion in the ideological superstructure produced by the economic base." "Conflict," says the functionalist, "is really functional, for by releasing or resolving tensions it enables a society better to adjust." There is no evidence which both sides could agree on as constituting a definitive test of their rival views. If they are to persuade each other, they must persuade each other on philosophical grounds to adopt an alternative view of the world.

The fact remains, however, that some form of functionalism is the only current alternative to Marxism as the basis for some kind of general theory in political science. We have already seen . . . the danger involved in attempting a functionalist definition of the State; . . . this chapter has suggested grounds for scepticism about the capacity of functionalism to provide full explanations of political or other social behaviour. But its usefulness must be assessed by the value of the explanatory propositions to which it guides the investigator of a particular problem. It may, if nothing else, provide a framework for the comparative discussion of different political systems, for which the vocabulary of traditional political theory is no longer adequate. It may direct attention to causes and effects which would otherwise pass unnoticed. It may even help in clarifying some of the problems of traditional political theory, such as the "collective purpose" or "general will" of society as expounded by some of the idealist philosophers.[18] It is only as a would-be general theory that it becomes more likely to be misleading than helpful, and to by-pass the search for the rigorous and testable statements of cause and effect out of which a political science

---

[18]This use of the term "function" is demonstrated in S. I. Benn and R. S. Peters, *Social Principles and the Democratic State* (1959), p. 240. The sense which is given to the general will by interpreting it as a functional concept is not, of course, the only possible one, but it does, as Benn and Peters show, make better sense of Bosanquet's version. The distinction between a person's "actual" and "real" will in Bosanquet's sense is then that between his personal objectives and the institutional duties deriving from his role in the total system of functionally related roles and institutions which constitute a society.

is to be constructed. The fact is that the empirical methods, rather than the deductive theories, of political science have since Marx and Weber been more productive of such statements. These methods have not, perhaps, produced quite so close an approximation to natural science as some of their practitioners have claimed. But there can be little doubt that they have greatly advanced the search for better explanations of political behaviour, and a brief discussion of their scientific status is in order at this point.

I do not mean to try to summarize, or even to mention, all the methods which are available to the sociologist of politics. Different methods, whether anthropological, historical or statistical, are appropriate to different problems and they must be judged, like functionalist or other theories, by the value of the explanatory propositions to which they lead. But the more recent of them are on the whole the more statistical and those for which the most "scientific" claims are apt to be made. With their help, questions of an unaccustomed precision can be answered which may lead to the far more accurate detection of correlations between social phenomena than it had previously been possible to envisage. The question, therefore, is whether they can make possible the sort of statements of correlation which have, at their most successful, yielded the laws of natural science. The danger here is not so much the simple danger of mistaking correlation for causation, for this is no less possible in the natural sciences. The danger is rather that of supposing that all the precautions of natural sciences can be so reproduced that we may ultimately be led to laws of political behaviour strictly analogous to the laws which govern the behaviour of such natural phenomena as gases or electric currents. . . .

The concluding moral remains the same as in all these essays. Even the most successful of formal analogues, or quantitative techniques, or comparative case-studies, or general explanatory theories cannot provide a solution by itself to the questions which philosophers of politics have raised since the time of Plato and Aristotle. How and why the will of the people should be given expression, under what conditions the citizen should or should not obey the State, what are the necessary and sufficient conditions of the just society, are questions whose answer depends ultimately on a philosophical view of the world and of the human beings who live in it. But to argue for any one of the conflicting views which can be held will require the maximum possible reference to our knowledge, whether formal or empirical, about how politics do (or, more important, might under different conditions) work. The attempt to reduce all political philosophy to political science is foredoomed to failure; but the philosopher of politics must be as aware as the political scientist that any attempt to enlarge the scope or application of political science is an attempt worth making.

11

David Easton

SYSTEMS ANALYSIS: AN EXAMPLE OF FUNCTIONALISM*

David Easton in this extract draws a model of *"the life processes of political systems*—those fundamental functions without which no system could endure—together with the typical modes of response through which systems manage to sustain them." Easton perceives the political system as only one system among many: it is marked off from its various environments—physical, biological, and so forth—in that it is the combination of "interactions through which values are authoritatively allocated for a society." The environments feed "inputs" into the system that are then processed through the interrelated functions of the system into "outputs." Easton conceives a "feedback loop" as a part of the system that enables it to "take advantage of what has been happening by trying to adjust its future behavior." The proof of the system's adaptive success is its persistence. The system is, in short, "a continuous and interlinked flow of behavior," allocating decisions so as to induce most members of the society to accept the allocation as binding. Actors appear in Easton's account but always in relation to one of the functions in the interrelationship that is the system. Easton's systemic model obviously is an application of functionalism.

*Reprinted by permission of the author and publisher from David Easton, ed., *Varieties of Political Theory* (Englewood Cliffs, N. J.: Prentice-Hall, Inc., 1966), pp. 143–154, where it was entitled "Categories for the Systems Analysis of Politics."

The question that gives coherence and purpose to a rigorous analysis of political life as a system of behavior is: How do political systems manage to persist in a world of both stability and change? Ultimately, the search for an answer will reveal what we may call *the life processes of political systems*—those fundamental functions without which no system could endure—together with the typical modes of response through which systems manage to sustain them. The analysis of these processes, and of the nature and conditions of the responses, I posit as a central problem of political theory.[1]

POLITICAL LIFE AS AN OPEN
AND ADAPTIVE SYSTEM

Although I shall end by arguing that it is useful to interpret political life as a complex set of processes through which certain kinds of inputs are converted into the type of outputs we may call authoritative policies, decisions, and implementing actions, it is useful at the outset to take a somewhat simpler approach. We may begin by viewing political life as a system of behavior imbedded in an environment to the influences of which the political system itself is exposed and in turn reacts. Several vital considerations are implicit in this interpretation, and it is essential that we become aware of them.

First, such a point of departure for theoretical analysis assumes, without further inquiry, that political interactions in a society constitute a *system* of behavior. This proposition is deceptive in its simplicity. The truth is that if the idea *system* is used with the rigor it permits and with all its currently inherent implications, it provides a starting point that is already heavily freighted with consequences for a whole pattern of analysis.

Second, to the degree that we are successful in analytically isolating political life as a system, it is clear that that system cannot usefully be interpreted as existing in a void. It must be seen as surrounded by

---

[1]This essay is a slightly revised version of Chapter Two of my book, *A Systems Analysis of Political Life* (New York: John Wiley & Sons, Inc., 1965). It is reprinted here with permission of the publishers. In effect this essay summarizes my book, *A Framework for Political Analysis* (Englewood Cliffs, N. J.: Prentice-Hall, Inc., 1965) and points forward to the more detailed elaboration of my views now to be found in *A Systems Analysis of Political Life*. The value of its presence here is not only that it offers an overview of the analytic structure developed in both of these volumes, but also that it represents strategy toward a general theory substantially different from the strategies presented in the other essays in this book.

physical, biological, social, and psychological *environments*. Here again, the empirical transparency of the statement ought not to distract us from its crucial theoretical significance. If we were to neglect what seems so obvious once it is asserted, it would be impossible to lay the groundwork for an analysis of how political systems manage to persist in a world of stability or change.

This brings us to a third point. What makes the identification of the environments useful and necessary is the further presupposition that political life forms an *open* system. By its very nature as a social system that has been analytically separated from other social systems, such a system must be interpreted as lying exposed to influences deriving from the other systems in which it is embedded. From them flows a constant stream of events and influences that shape the conditions under which the members of the system must act.

Finally, the fact that some systems do survive, whatever the buffets received from their environments, awakens us to the fact that they must have the capacity to *respond* to disturbances and thereby to adapt to the conditions under which they find themselves. Once we are willing to assume that political systems may be adaptive, and need not just react passively to their environmental influences, we shall be able to cut a new path through the complexities of theoretical analysis.

In a political system's internal organization, a critical property that it shares with all other social systems is an extraordinarily variable capacity to respond to the conditions under which it functions. Indeed, political systems accumulate large repertoires of mechanisms by which they may try to cope with their environments. Through these mechanisms, they may regulate their own behavior, transform their internal structure, and even go so far as to remodel their fundamental goals. Few types of systems, other than social systems, have this potentiality. In practice, students of political life cannot help but take this into account; no analysis could even begin to appeal to common sense if it did not do so. Nevertheless, this potentiality is seldom built into a theoretical structure as a central component; certainly its implications for the internal behavior of political systems have never been set forth and explored.[2]

[2]K. W. Deutsch, in *The Nerves of Government* (New York: Free Press of Glencoe, Inc., 1963), has considered the consequences of the response capacity of political systems in international affairs, although in very general terms. Some work has also been done for formal organizations. See J. W. Forrester, *Industrial Dynamics* (New York: MIT Press and John Wiley & Sons, Inc., 1961); and W. R. Dill, "The Impact of Environment on Organizational Development," in S. Mailick and E. H. Van Ness, *Concepts and Issues in Administrative Behavior* (Englewood Cliffs, N. J.: Prentice-Hall, Inc., 1962), pp. 94–109.

EQUILIBRIUM ANALYSIS AND ITS SHORTCOMINGS

It is a major shortcoming of the one form of inquiry latent but prevalent in political research—equilibrium analysis—that it neglects such variable capacities of systems to cope with environmental influences. Although the equilibrium approach is seldom explicitly elaborated, it has permeated a good part of political research, especially group politics[3] and international relations. Of necessity, an analysis that conceives of a political system as seeking to maintain a state of equilibrium must assume the presence of environmental influences. It is these that displace the power relationships in a political system from their presumed stable state. It is then customary to analyze the system, if only implicitly, in terms of a tendency to return to a presumed pre-existing point of stability. If the system should fail to do so, it would be interpreted as moving on to a new state of equilibrium; and then this would need to be identified and described. A careful scrutiny of the language used reveals that *equilibrium* and *stability* are usually assumed to mean the same thing.[4]

Numerous conceptual and empirical difficulties stand in the way of an effective use of the equilibrium idea for the analysis of political life.[5] Among these difficulties, there are two that are particularly relevant for present purposes.

In the first place, the equilibrium approach leaves the impression that the members of a system have only one basic goal as they seek to cope with change or disturbances: namely, to re-establish the old point of equilibrium or to move on to some new one. This is usually phrased, at least implicitly, as the search for stability, as though stability were sought above all else. In the second place, little if any attention is explicitly given to formulating the problems relating to the path that the system takes in seeking to return to its presumed old point of equilibrium or to attain a new one. It is as though the pathways taken to manage the displacements were an incidental . . . theoretical consideration.

But it is impossible to understand the processes underlying the capacity of some kind of political life to sustain itself in a society if either the objectives or the form of the responses are taken for granted. A system may well have other goals than that of reaching one or another point of

[3]See David Easton, *The Political System* (New York: Alfred A. Knopf, Inc., 1953), Chapter Eleven.

[4]In "Limits of the Equilibrium Model in Social Research," *Behavioral Science*, I (1956), pp. 96–104, I discuss difficulties created by the fact that social scientists typically fail to distinguish between stability and equilibrium. We often assume that a state of equilibrium must always refer to a stable condition, but in fact there are at least two other kinds of equilibria: neutral and unstable.

[5]Easton, "Limits of the Equilibrium Model."

equilibrium. Even though the idea of a state of equilibrium were to be used only as a theoretical norm that is never achieved,[6] such a conception would offer a less useful theoretical approximation of reality than one that takes into account other possibilities. We would find it more helpful to devise a conceptual approach that recognized that members in a system may at times wish to take positive actions to destroy a previous equilibrium or even to achieve some new point of continuing disequilibrium. This is typically the case when the authorities seek to keep themselves in power by fostering internal turmoil or external dangers.

Furthermore, with respect to these variable goals, it is a primary characteristic of all systems that they are able to adopt a wide range of actions of a positive, constructive, and innovative sort for warding off or absorbing any forces of displacement. A system need not react to a disturbance just by oscillating in the neighborhood of a prior point of equilibrium or by shifting to a new one. It may cope with the disturbance by seeking to change its environment so that the exchanges between its environment and itself are no longer stressful; it may seek to insulate itself against any further influences from the environment; or the members of the system may even fundamentally transform their own relationships and modify their own goals and practices so as to improve their chances of handling the inputs from the environment. In these and other ways, a system has the capacity for creative and constructive regulation of disturbances.

It is clear that the adoption of equilibrium analysis, however latent it may be, obscures the presence of system goals that cannot be described as a state of equilibrium. It also virtually conceals the existence of varying pathways for attaining these alternative ends. For any social system, including a political one, adaptation represents more than simple adjustment to the events in its life. It is made up of efforts—limited only by the variety of human skills, resources, and ingenuity—to control, modify, or fundamentally change either the environment or the system itself, or both together. In the outcome, the system may succeed in fending off or incorporating successfully any influences stressful for it.

MINIMAL CONCEPTS FOR A SYSTEMS ANALYSIS

A systems analysis promises a more expansive, inclusive, and flexible theoretical structure than is available even in a thoroughly self-conscious and well-developed equilibrium approach. To do so successfully, however, a systems analysis must establish its own theoretical imperatives. At

[6] J. A. Schumpeter, *Business Cycles* (New York: McGraw-Hill Book Company, 1939), especially in Chapter Two, discusses the idea of equilibrium as a theoretical norm.

the outset, we may define a *system* as any set of variables regardless of the degree of interrelationship among them. The reason for preferring this definition is that it frees us from the need to argue about whether or not a political system is really a system. The only question of importance about a set selected as a system to be analyzed is whether this set constitutes an interesting system. Does it help us to understand and explain some aspect of human behavior of concern to us?

As I have argued in *The Political System,* a *political* system can be designated as those interactions through which values are authoritatively allocated for a society; this is what distinguishes a political system from other systems in its environment. This environment itself may be divided into two parts: the intrasocietal and the extrasocietal. The first consists of those systems in the same society as the political system which are not political systems due to our definition of the nature of political interactions. Intrasocietal systems include such sets of behavior, attitudes, and ideas as the economy, culture, social structure, and personalities; they are functional segments of the society of which the political system is itself a component. In a given society, the systems other than the political system are the source of many influences that create and shape the conditions under which the political system itself must operate. In a world of newly emerging political systems, we do not need to pause to illustrate the impact that a changing economy, culture, or social structure may have upon political life.

The second part of the environment, the extrasocietal, includes all those systems that lie outside the given society itself. They are functional components of an international society, a suprasystem of which any single society is part. The international cultural system is an example of an extrasocietal system.

Taken together, these two classes of systems—the intra- and extra-societal—which we conceive to lie outside a political system, comprise the *total environment* of a political system.[7] From these sources arise influences that are of consequence for possible stress on the political system. *Disturbances* is a concept that we may use to refer to those influences from the total environment of a system that act upon the system, and thereby change it. Not all disturbances need strain the system: Some may be favorable to the persistence of the system; others may be entirely neutral with regard to stress. But many can be expected to contribute to stress.

When may we say that *stress* occurs? This question involves us in a

[7]The total environment is presented in Table 1, Chapter Five, of *A Framework for Political Analysis.* That volume also includes a full discussion of the various components of the environment.

rather complex idea, one that embodies several subsidiary notions. All political systems as such are distinguished by the fact that if we are to be able to describe them as persisting, we must attribute to them the successful fulfillment of two functions. They must be able to allocate values for a society, and they must manage to induce most members to accept these allocations as binding, at least for most of the time. These two properties distinguish political systems from other kinds of social systems.

Hence, these two distinctive properties—the allocations of values for a society and the relative frequency of compliance with them—are the *essential variables* of political life. But for their presence, we would not be able to say that a society has any political life. And we may here take it for granted that no society could exist without some kind of political system; elsewhere I have sought to demonstrate this in detail.[8]

One of the important reasons for identifying these essential variables is that they give us a way of establishing when and how the disturbances acting upon a system threaten to cause it stress. We can say that stress occurs when there is a danger that the essential variables will be pushed beyond what we may designate as their *critical range*. What this means is that something may be happening in the environment—the system suffers total defeat at the hands of an enemy, or a severe economic crisis arouses widespread disorganization in and disaffection from the system. Let us assume that, as a result, either the authorities are consistently unable to make decisions, or the decisions they do make are no longer regularly accepted as binding. Under these conditions, authoritative allocations of values are no longer possible, and the society collapses for want of a system of behavior to fulfill one of its vital functions.

Here we cannot help but accept the interpretation that the political system had come under stress, so severe that any and every possibility for the persistence of a system for that society had disappeared. But frequently the disruption of a political system is not that complete; even though stress is present, the system continues to persist in some form. Severe as a crisis may be, it still may be possible for the authorities to be able to make some kinds of decisions and to get them accepted with at least minimal frequency, so that some of the problems typically subjected to political settlements can be handled.

In other words, it is not always a matter of whether or not the essential variables are operating. It is possible that they may only be somewhat displaced, as when the authorities are partially unable to make decisions

---

[8]In David Easton, *A Theoretical Approach to Authority*, Office of Naval Research, Technical Report No. 17 (Stanford, California: Department of Economics, 1955).

or to get them accepted with complete regularity. Under these circumstances, the essential variables remain within some normal range of operation; they may be under stress, but not to a sufficient degree to displace them beyond a determinable critical point. As long as the system keeps its essential variables operating within their critical range, some kind of system can be said to persist.

As we have seen, every system has the capacity to cope with stress on its essential variables. Not that systems always do so; a system may collapse precisely because it has failed to take measures appropriate for handling the impending stress. But it is the existence of the capacity to respond to stress that is of paramount importance. The kind of response (if any) actually undertaken will help us to evaluate the probability that the system will be able to ward off the stress. Raising the question of the nature of the response to stress points up the special objectives and merit of a systems analysis of political life. It is especially suited for interpreting the behavior of the members in a system in the light of the consequences this behavior has for alleviating or aggravating stress upon the essential variables.

THE LINKAGE VARIABLES BETWEEN SYSTEMS

But a fundamental problem remains: How do the potentially stressful conditions from the environment communicate themselves to a political system? After all, common sense tells us that there is an enormous variety of environmental influences at work on a system. Do we have to treat each change in the environment as a separate and unique disturbance, the specific effects of which have to be independently worked out?

If this were indeed the case, the problems of systematic analysis would be virtually insurmountable. But if we can devise a way for generalizing our method for handling the impact of the environment on the system, there would be some hope of reducing the enormous variety of influences into a manageable number of indicators. This is precisely what I seek to do through the use of the concepts of *inputs* and *outputs*.

How are we to describe these inputs and outputs? Because of the analytic distinction that I have been making between a political system and its parametric or environmental systems, it is useful to interpret the influences associated with the behavior of persons in the environment as *exchanges* or *transactions* that can cross the boundaries of the political system. *Exchanges* will be used when we wish to refer to the mutuality of the relationships between the political system and the other systems in the environment. *Transactions* will be used when we wish to emphasize the movement of an effect in one direction, from an environmental system to the political system, or the reverse, without being concerned at the time about the reactive behavior of the other system.

Up to this point, there is little to dispute. If systems were not in some way coupled together, all analytically identifiable aspects of behavior in society would be independent of each other, a patently unlikely condition. What makes the fact of this coupling more than a mere truism, however, is the proposal of a way to trace out the complex exchanges so that we can readily reduce their immense variety to theoretically and empirically manageable proportions.

To accomplish this, I have proposed that we condense the major and significant environmental influences into a few indicators. Through the examination of these we should be able to appraise and follow through the potential impact of environmental events on the system. With this objective in mind, I have designated the effects that are transmitted across the boundary of a system toward some other system as the outputs of the first system and hence, symmetrically, as the inputs of the second system. A transaction or an exchange between systems will therefore be viewed as a linkage between them in the form of an input-output relationship.

DEMANDS AND SUPPORTS AS INPUT INDICATORS

The value of inputs as a concept is that through their use we shall find it possible to capture the effect of the vast variety of events and conditions in the environment as they pertain to the persistence of a political system. Without using the concept of inputs, it would be difficult to delineate the precise operational way in which the behavior in the various sectors of society affects what happens in the political sphere. Inputs will serve as *summary variables* that concentrate and mirror everything in the environment that is relevant to political stress. Thereby the concept of inputs serves as a powerful analytic tool.

The extent to which inputs can be used as summary variables will depend, however, upon how we define them. We might conceive of them in their broadest sense. In that case, we would interpret them as including any event external to the system that alters, modifies, or affects the system in any way.[9] But if we used the concept in so broad a fashion, we would never be able to exhaust the list of inputs acting upon a system. Virtually every parametric event and condition would have some signifi-

---

[9] I am confining my remarks here to external sources of inputs. For the possibility of inputs deriving from internal sources and therefore constituting "withinputs," see *A Framework for Political Analysis*, Chapter Seven.

cance for the operations of a political system at the focus of attention; a concept so inclusive that it does not help us to organize and simplify reality would defeat its own purposes.

But as I have already intimated, we can greatly simplify the task of analyzing the impact of the environment if we restrict our attention to certain kinds of inputs that can be used as indicators to sum up the most important effects, in terms of their contributions to stress, that cross the boundary from the parametric to the political systems. In this way, we could free ourselves from the need to deal with and trace out separately the consequences of each type of environmental event.

As the theoretical tool for this purpose, it is helpful to view the major environmental influences as focusing in two major inputs: *demands* and *support*. Through them, a wide range of activities in the environment can be channeled, mirrored, summarized, and brought to bear upon political life. Hence, they are key indicators of the way in which environmental influences and conditions modify and shape the operations of the political system. If we wish, we may say that it is through fluctuations in the inputs of demands and support that we shall find the effects of the environmental systems transmitted to the political system.

OUTPUTS AND FEEDBACK

In a comparable way, the idea of *outputs* helps us to organize the consequences flowing from the behavior of the members of the system rather than from actions in the environment. Our primary concern is, to be sure, with the functioning of the political system. For understanding political phenomena, we would have no need to be concerned with the consequences in and of themselves that political actions have for the environmental systems. This is a problem that can be better handled by theories dealing with the operations of the economy, culture, or any of the other parametric systems.

But the activities of the members of the system may well have some importance for their own subsequent actions or conditions. To the extent that this is so, we cannot entirely neglect those actions that do flow out of a system into its environment. As in the case of inputs, however, there is an immense amount of activity that takes place within a political system. How are we to isolate the portion relevant to an understanding of the way in which systems manage to persist?

A useful way of simplifying and organizing our perceptions of the behavior of the members of the system (as reflected in their demands and support) is to do so in terms of the effects these inputs have on what we may call the *political outputs*. These are the decisions and actions of the authorities. Not that the complex political processes internal to a system that have been the subject of inquiry for so many decades in political science will be considered in any way irrelevant. Who controls whom in the various decision-making processes will continue to be a vital concern, since the pattern of power relationships helps to determine the nature of the outputs. But the formulation of a conceptual structure for this aspect of a political system would draw us onto a different level of analysis. Here, I am only seeking economical ways of summarizing—not of investigating—the outcomes of these internal political processes, which can, I suggest, be usefully conceptualized as the outputs of the authorities. Through them, we are able to trace out the consequences of behavior within a political system for its environment.

Outputs not only help to influence events in the broader society of which the system is a part, but also, in doing so, they help to determine each succeeding round of inputs that finds its way into the political system. There is a *feedback loop*, the identification of which helps us to explain the processes through which the system may cope with stress. Through it, the system may take advantage of what has been happening by trying to adjust its future behavior.

When we speak of the system as acting, however, we must be careful not to reify the system itself. We must bear in mind that all systems, to make collective action possible, have those who usually speak in the name or on behalf of the system. We may designate these as the *authorities*. If actions are to be taken to satisfy demands or create conditions that will do so, information must be fed back, at least to these authorities, about the effects of each round of outputs. Without information-feedback about what is happening in the system, the authorities would have to operate in the dark.

If we take as our analytic point of departure the capacity of a system to persist, and if we view as one of the possible and important sources of stress a possible drop in support below some specifiable minimum, we can appreciate the importance of information-feedback to the authorities. The authorities need not necessarily seek to bolster the input of support for themselves or for the system as a whole. But if they should wish to do so—and their own survival may well force them to do so—information about the effects of each round of outputs and about the changing conditions under which the members find themselves is essential. It enables them to take whatever action they feel is necessary to keep support at some minimal level.

For this reason, a model of this kind suggests that exploration of the operations of the feedback processes is of vital significance. Anything that serves to delay, distort, or sever the flow of information to the authorities interferes with their capacity to take action, if so desired, to keep support at a level high enough to ensure the persistence of the system.

The feedback loop itself has a number of parts worthy of detailed investigation. It consists of the production of outputs by the authorities, a response by the members of the society to these ouputs, the communication of information about this response to the authorities, and finally, possible succeeding actions by the authorities. Thereby, a new round of outputs, response, information-feedback, and reaction by the authorities is set in motion, forming a seamless web of activities. What happens in this feedback thus has a profound influence on the capacity of a system to cope with stress and persist.

A FLOW MODEL OF THE POLITICAL SYSTEM

It is clear from what has been said that this mode of analysis enables and indeed compels us to analyze a political system in dynamic terms. Not only do we see that a political system gets something done through its outputs, but we are also sensitized to the fact that what the system does may influence each successive stage of behavior. We appreciate the urgent need to interpret political processes as a continuous and inter-linked flow of behavior.

If we were to be content with what is basically a static picture of a political system, we might be inclined to stop at this point. Indeed, most political research today does just this. It is concerned with exploring all those intricate subsidiary processes through which decisions are made and put into effect. Therefore, insofar as we were concerned with how influence is used in formulating and putting into effect various kinds of policies or decisions, the model to this point would be an adequate if minimal first approximation.

But the critical problem confronting political theory is not just to develop a conceptual apparatus for understanding the factors that contribute to the kinds of decisions a system makes—that is, to formulate a theory of political allocations. As I have indicated, theory needs to find out how any kind of system manages to persist long enough to continue to make such decisions, and how it deals with the stress to which it may be subjected at any time. For this reason we cannot accept outputs as the terminus of either the political processes or our interest in them. Thus it is important to note, as part of this model, that the outputs of the conversion process characteristically feed back upon the system and thereby shape its subsequent behavior. It is this feature, together with the capacity of a system to take constructive actions, that enables a system to try to adapt or to cope with possible stress.

Thus, a systems analysis of political life rests on the idea of a system imbedded in an environment and subject to possible environmental influences that threaten to drive the essential variables of the system beyond their critical range. Such an analysis suggests that, to persist, the system must be capable of responding with measures that alleviate that stress. The actions of the authorities are particularly critical in this respect. But if they are to be able to respond, they must be in a position to obtain information about what is happening so that they may react insofar as they desire, or are compelled, to do so. With information, they may be able to maintain a minimal level of support for the system.

A systems analysis poses certain major questions, answers to which would help to flesh out the skeletal outline presented here: What precisely is the nature of the influences acting upon a political system? How are they communicated to a system? In what ways, if any, have systems typically sought to cope with such stress? What kinds of feedback processes must exist in any system if it is to acquire and exploit the potential for acting so as to ameliorate these conditions of stress? How do different types of systems—modern or developing, democratic or authoritarian—differ with regard to their types of inputs, outputs, and internal conversion and feedback processes? What effects do these differences have upon the capacity of the system to persist in the face of stress?

The task of theory construction is not of course to give substantive answers to these questions initially. Rather, it is both to formulate the appropriate questions and to devise appropriate ways for seeking answers.[10]

[10] I have addressed myself to these objectives in *A Framework for Political Analysis* and *A Systems Analysis of Political Life*.

12

Paul F. Kress

A CRITIQUE
OF EASTON'S
SYSTEMS ANALYSIS*

Paul Kress' commentary upon David Easton's systems theory indicates
some of the problems, presuppositions, and consequences of the theory.
He reviews developments in twentieth-century literature and painting
and analogizes the "loss of the self" therein and Easton's systems analysis. He holds systems analysis to be Easton's "weapon against two
ghosts he helped instal in the house of political science . . . the boundary and the units problems. . . . system is Easton's answer to the
former and 'interaction' his solution to the latter." He notes "the dilemma and the paradox of much of modern social theory: it reveres 'facts'
(data), but it must look elsewhere for their meaning or significance,
and it finds nothing in nature or experience that provides the latter."
He describes Easton's theory as an " 'empty vision' of politics," using
the phrase "empty vision" to summarize his "arguments concerning the
theory's lack of substance, the artificial nature of system and member,
the replacement of the actor by the container, and the disappearance
of boundaries as limits of possibility." It indicates also his agreement with Marshall McLuhan's observation that "today our science
and method strive not towards a point of view but to discover how

*Reprinted by permission of the author and publisher from *Ethics*, LXXVII
(1: October, 1966), pp. 1–13, where it was entitled "Self, System, and Significance: Reflections on Professor Easton's Political Science."

not to have a point of view, the method not of closure, and perspective but of the open 'field' and the suspended judgment," and with Hannah Arendt's contention that what distinguishes modern science and history is their joint implication "that we think and consider everything in terms of processes and are not concerned with single entities or individual occurrences and their special separate causes." Although dubious about "the ultimate value of Easton's recommendations," Kress maintains that we should remain "open to the possibility that systems theory of this sort may someday prove capable of ordering political inquiry in a satisfying manner." He poses questions that must be answered before we can decide that systems theory can so order political inquiry.

. . . for a self is the thing the world is least apt to inquire about, and the thing of all things the most dangerous for a man to let people notice he has it. The greatest danger, that of losing one's own self, may pass off as quietly as if it were nothing; every other loss, that of an arm, a leg, five dollars, a wife, etc., is sure to be noticed.—SOREN KIERKEGAARD, *The Sickness unto Death.*

Art and science are both universal in scope in that there is no subject that is unfit for the probing insight of the artist, nor is there anything unsuitable for the scientist to examine.—HAROLD G. CASSIDY, *The Sciences and the Arts.*

This is an exploratory essay—exploratory in two senses.[1] It is an attempt, first, to examine a contemporary work of political theory through an analogy and, second, to employ that analogy to raise questions about the theory. This paper originated in my reading of recent essays by David Easton and C. P. Snow,[2] who, despite the generous latitude afforded contemporary essays in political theory, might seem rather strange bedfellows. I will, therefore, briefly indicate the nature of my interest in these essays and then proceed to a full discussion of the theme.

Easton's volume is a summary statement of long-term concerns with applications of "systems theory" to the study of politics. It was preceded by his 1953 effort, *The Political System,*[3] and stands as an extended preface to his more detailed *A Systems Analysis of Political Life.*[4] As Easton indicates, these books illustrate his sustained interest and partici-

[1]This paper incorporates research conducted in 1962–1963 under a grant from the Political Theory Committee of the Social Science Research Council.
[2]David Easton, *A Framework for Political Analysis* (Englewood Cliffs, N. J.: Prentice-Hall, Inc., 1965); C. P. Snow, "Science, Politics, and the Novelist," *Kenyon Review,* XXIII (Winter, 1961), pp. 1–17.
[3]David Easton, *The Political System* (New York: Alfred A. Knopf, Inc., 1953).
[4]David Easton, *A Systems Analysis of Political Life* (New York: John Wiley & Sons, 1965).

pation in the University of Chicago's Committee on Behavioral Sciences and its successor, the incongruously named Mental Health Research Institute of the University of Michigan. We are entitled, then, to regard this output as a major contribution of a mature and respected political scientist.

Professor Easton's systems analysis belongs to that genre we call "formal" theory. Part of the burden of succeeding pages will be the elaboration of my meaning of "formal," but for the moment let me designate it as "the use of abstract categories in the ordering of data." This definition stresses the communications aspect of theory, that is, the manner in which completed research is reported to the larger community. If I understand him, Easton would not be satisfied with this description of his efforts; systems analysis is for him not simply a distinct language, or methodology, but a "conceptual framework" capable of directing research and sustaining "secondary concepts" which will some-day constitute "a full fledged set of interrelated categories."[5] I happen to agree with Easton on this point—any significant set of methodological principles contains or presupposes judgments about the world in which it is to operate and may not be fully understood or adequately defended by considering its narrowest dictates. Easton himself affirms the utility of metaphor in theory construction and describes his essay as an attempt "to sketch a map of the new terrain, showing its outer limits and the contours of the major formations."[6] I feel justified, therefore, in treating his essay as the promulgation of a mataphor, a total approach, a vision of the political universe.

Easton's work belongs to an interesting line of descent in American political and sociological theory. Within the confines of this paper I can but briefly indicate a major concern of this tradition, namely, its dissatis-faction with such central disciplinary concepts as state, society, law, and government.[7] The idea of system, as an ordering concept, is a surrogate for these and comparable terms. Systems analysis is Easton's weapon against two ghosts he helped instal in the house of political science—we know them as the boundary and the units problems. I will discuss these problems at some length below, but for the moment it will suffice to say that system is Easton's answer to the former and "interaction" his solution to the latter.

C. P. Snow's essay is, in a different but analogous manner, concerned

---

[5] Easton, *Framework*, p. 135.
[6] Easton, *Framework*, p. 2.
[7] I have elsewhere undertaken a fuller exploration of these diverse themes; see my "The Idea of Process in American Political and Social Science" (unpublished Ph.D. dissertation, University of California, Berkeley, 1964).

with boundary and units problems. He argues, in essence, that the novel of sensibility (personal experience, interior monologue, stream of consciousness) is incapable of exploring or portraying the large themes of our time, for example, science and politics. To write significantly and truthfully about politics, continues Snow, one must express a sense of structure external to the actor; certainly so, if we think of politics as the power relations of men in society. This means that the novelist must encounter the problems of "large scale architecture." The novel's range must not be limited: "By range . . . I mean a specific kind of psychological depth as well as social extension."[8] In the great panoramic canvasses of Tolstoy, Dostoevsky, Proust, and Dickens, Snow finds what he calls "causal psychological insight" and "introspective insight"; we learn not only what happened but why. "This causal insight, in both Tolstoy and Dostoevsky, though in different fashions, makes for a complex and enriching interaction between their individual personages and their immense social range."[9]

Snow does not exorcise ghosts, but he does expose flesh and blood villainy in the person of the introspective, psychological novelist. This artist has become so preoccupied with the analysis and exposition of his thoughts and sensations that he fails not only to communicate the contours of an external structure but also necessary introspective insight into self. This must seem an odd conclusion, for an avowed purpose of many stream-of-consciousness writers was to render reality *wie es eigentlich gewesen*, that is, memories, impressions, sensations, etc., without the mediating and disrupting entry of conceptual thought. Surely this must yield psychological depth whatever its other shortcomings? But this is not necessarily or uniformly the case. Ironically, the stream-of-consciousness technique often fails to provide introspective insight precisely because it consists in passing thoughts without a self to appraise or even "contain" the thoughts. Our insight is limited to a jumble of events and sensations flowing into, around, and through one another in time and space. But this is to anticipate my argument. The central point here is to recognize that Snow, just as Easton, stands in juxtaposition to a tradition, and, while their postures toward their respective predecessors appear to differ, the similarity of concern is striking. Easton proposes the political system as an ordering concept to lend coherence to a discipline badly disorganized by hyperfactualism and bitterly divided about its nature and goals. Snow, reflecting upon literary currents of the century, laments the inability of

[8] Snow, "Science, Politics, and the Novelist," p. 8.
[9] Snow, "Science, Politics, and the Novelist," p. 6. It is intresting to note that Max Weber turned increasingly to Tolstoy for insight into the impact of large-scale social developments (advent of rational thought and organization) on individual lives. See Max Weber, *The Rational and Social Foundations of Music*, ed. Don Martindale and Johannes Riedel (Carbondale: Southern Illinois University Press, 1958), p. xxi.

the novel of sensibility to significantly portray self and society. With apologies for the violence I am doing the art of literature and the craft of criticism, Snow is raising our very own social science ghosts, unit and boundary.

Easton approvingly notes the suggestion that metaphor is justifiable as a device for moving from the known to the unknown. In the remainder of this paper I propose to construct an analogy between the "loss of the self" as a phenomenon of twentieth-century literature and painting and the type of systems analysis proposed by Easton. This effort will, I hope, enable me to pose some questions about the possibilities and consequences of adopting political systems analysis. The major premise of this enterprise is that political science and literature are on some level comparable—at least in that they are two symbol systems, each possessing some coherent arrangement of internal characteristics, and consequently certain possibilities and limitations. As Murray Edelman has said: "We may be able to learn something about expressive political symbols from aesthetic theory, for an art form consists of condensation symbols. Its function, like that of the abstract political symbols discussed here, is to serve as a vehicle for expression, both for the artist and for the audience, rather than as an instrument for changing the world."[10]

The phrase "stream of consciousness" is itself a metaphor; to my knowledge it was first employed by William James in the 1890 edition of Principles of Psychology, wherein he referred to "the passing thought that seems to be the thinker." James used the phrase in the course of a philosophical and psychological investigation, but it is important to recall that the stream of consciousness or interior monologue emerged, almost coincidentally, as a narrative technique.[11] Many critics consider Édouard Dujardin's Les lauriers sont coupés, published in 1887, as the earliest example of the genre. Erich Kahler discerns the origins of that movement called the "new sensibility" (preoccupation with introspection and the minutiae of experience) in the late eighteenth century. He shows how the process began with the discovery of a detached spectator within the mind, a "second and coldest consciousness, a consciousness on another,

---

[10]Murray Edelman, The Symbolic Uses of Politics (Urbana: University of Illinois Press, 1964), p. 11; see also Ernst Cassirer, The Philosophy of Symbolic Forms (3 vols.; New Haven, Conn.: Yale University Press, 1953, 1955, 1957).

[11]See also Robert Humphrey, The Stream of Consciousness in the Modern Novel ("Perspectives in Criticism," No. 3 [Berkeley: University of California Press, 1958]), for an indication of the diverse meanings given these terms. Interior monologue is sometimes viewed as an extension of stream of consciousness, sometimes as an alternative device, and sometimes they are considered synonymous. The comment of René Wellek and Austin Warren, that "there is little that seems scientific or even 'realistic' about the device," appears to me to miss the point. See their Theory of Literature (New York: Harcourt, Brace & World, 1956), p. 81.

even more detached plane, a consciousness beyond individual conscious-ness, as it were."[12] This is the beginning of the process. Speaking of the later development of stream of consciousness and related devices, Kahler remarks: "These new techniques effected something most important: They have broken through the bottom of consciousness—on which the psyche had hitherto rested with confidence—and have likewise cracked the supposed solid foundation of chronological time."[13]

An obvious parallel to developments within nineteenth- and twentieth-century literature is the "gradual disintegration of the concrete object" in the painting of Monet, Cézanne, van Gogh, the cubists, and Picasso.[14] Wylie Sypher, in an essay appropriately entitled *The Loss of the Self in Modern Literature and Art*, points to the work of Jean Dubuffet which achieves the "zero degree of painting" where identity is annihilated.[15] Everett Knight describes cubism as the attempt to paint what the artist *sees*, not what he knows. "From my window I can see a stretch of a lawn in the distance, it appears to be a green wall; I can also see a tower and the cloud appears to be pressing in upon it from all sides. Why should I not paint the lawn as jutting into some white fluffy solid?"[16] Kahler's remark about the futurist movement of the early twentieth century, the precursor of Dadaism and surrealism, is appropriate: "They wanted to smash not only the institutions, but also all their forms of expression, the artistic structures, the linguistic syntax."[17] The violence suggested by these words was necessary because the revolutionists were demanding the annihilation of a ruling paradigm of artistic vision. The existing symbol system no longer served to illuminate but rather to conceal the reality of experience.

The dissolution of the self did not occur immediately but progressed through more radical stages until it reached the limits of what Kahler calls the "existential experience." Antoine Roquentin, the protagonist of Sartre's *Nausea*, is the paradigm case of this experience. Roquentin first experiences a loss of coherence in his awareness of objects, actions, and perceptions; temporarity too, seems to dissolve. Ultimately, "the thinking, perceiving ego merges with the phenomenal mass of external existence. It is a mystical union, but by no means a mystical act. It is rather the

---

[12]Erich Kahler, *The Tower and the Abyss* (New York: George Braziller, Inc., 1957), p. 89.

[13]Kahler, *The Tower and the Abyss*, p. 167.

[14]Kahler, *The Tower and the Abyss*, p. 153.

[15]Wylie Sypher, *The Loss of Self in Modern Literature and Art* (New York: Random House, 1964), esp. chap. vi.

[16]Everett Knight, *The Objective Society* (New York: George Braziller, Inc., 1959), p. 43.

[17]Kahler, *The Tower and the Abyss*, p. 147.

opposite: a mystical giving in, a mystical breakdown."[18] Roquentin then experiences a companion symptom, the deep sense of disgust, literally of nausea.

Certain rough epistemological and perceptual parallels should now be apparent. The self, as coherent unit within the external, environmental system, is found unsatisfactory. It becomes increasingly difficult to draw boundaries that can withstand the test of introspection, and man's very self becomes remote, without location. Of equal and perhaps greater interest is the manner in which this discovery assumes value dimensions. Kahler notes Clarissa Dalloway's remark about the extreme danger of living even one day and sees in it the anxiety that accompanies "this feeling of the boundlessness of experience." Critics of both Left and Right political persuasion have been sensitive to these value implications. Ortega's judgment was intended to characterize modern music, painting, and literature when he remarked: "Wherever we look we see the same thing: flight from the human person."[19] The Marxist critic Ernst Fischer declares: "The fragmentation of man and his world has found expression again and again in works of our period. There is no unity left, no wholeness."[20] To the men of the Left, this fragmentation is often seen as the promised stage of human alienation under capitalism. Georg Lukács, perhaps the foremost aesthetician of philosophical Marxism, presents such an analysis of contemporary realism. "Attenuation of reality and dissolution of personality are thus interdependent: the stronger the one, the stronger the other. Underlying both is the *lack of a consistent view of human nature*. Man is reduced to a sequence of unrelated experiential fragments; he is as inexplicable to others as to himself" (italics mine).[21]

When Kahler speaks of the condition of the "man without values" he is referrring to the devaluing of *valuing activity itself*. Robert Musil's *Man without Qualities*, written in the second decade of our century, was surely an anticipation of Kahler's diagnosis. We have no difficulty in understanding Musil's observation that "these days one never sees oneself whole and one never moves as a whole," nor are we deaf to the cry of Ulrich, Musil's protagonist, that the center of gravity lies not in the individual but in the relations among things.[22] We have, in short, no

[18]Kahler, *The Tower and the Abyss*, pp. 181–82.
[19]José Ortega y Gasset, *The Dehumanization of Art and Other Writings on Art and Culture* (Garden City, N. Y.: Doubleday & Co., 1960), p. 30.
[20]Ernst Fischer, *The Necessity of Art: The Marxist Approach* (Baltimore: Penguin Books, Inc., 1964), p. 72. See his remark about the concluding dialogue of Dashiell Hammett's classic *Maltese Falcon*, "Man is nothing. Success is all."
[21]Georg Lukács, *The Meaning of Contemporary Realism* (London: Merlin Press, 1963), p. 26.
[22]Quoted in Sypher, *The Loss of the Self*, p. 123.

vision of an inner or essential man to sustain either our expectations or our values.

It would be a mistake, I think, to dismiss these warnings from the artistic community as a romantic rejection of modernity. One need not be a literary critic or intellectual historian to understand that the universe of communication we call "art" both creates and reflects a level of reality in human experience, nor may that level be regarded as isolated from the province of politics and science. Consider this perceptive passage: "The distinctive characteristics of the realistic novel of the era between the two great wars . . . multipersonal representation of consciousness, time strata, disintegration of the continuity of external events, shifting of the narrative viewpoint . . . seem to us indicative of a striving for certain objectives, of certain tendencies and needs on the part of both authors and public.[23] Perhaps the history of western Europe in this century, its "imagination of disaster" in Henry James' lively phrase, is a vindication of Karl Mannheim's thesis—that it is during periods of disintegration that the subtle and innermost connections of the social fabric become visible.

But the case for the relevance of the literary analogy to social science need not rest on these grounds alone; indeed, the convergence of themes is probably much broader. Sypher has suggested a relationship between the loss of identity in art and literature and the elimination of simple location from modern physics. In both realms it would seem that the desire to attain a strict observational truth, an "objectivity" of description, has resulted in the escape of identity into the flux. "A certain paradox is implicit in the new science, in anti-painting, in the anti-novel: we find the self by losing the self in things; or, vice versa, we lose the self by finding the self in things. We recover the meaning of things by surrendering to them without supposing we can know them through our own clear ideas of them."[24] Floyd Matson is but a recent commentator on the fact that the uncertainty relation that obtains at the microbehavioral level makes the physicist "participant observer rather than detached spectator,"[25] and Heisenberg himself spoke of the inadequacy of dualisms that divide subject from object, inner from outer worlds. A. N. Whitehead found the problem of identity so vexing that he began to question the law of identity itself. Nor are these isolated reactions to the "crisis" in modern physics. In 1933, C. Delisle Burns wrote: "In philosophy, the theories of

[23]Erich Auerbach, Mimesis: The Representation of Reality in Western Literature (Garden City, N. Y.: Doubleday & Co., 1957), p. 483. Two recent and interesting attempts to relate literary themes to their wider social and intellectual contexts are: Césare Graña, Bohemian vs. Bourgeoisie (New York: Basic Books, Inc., 1964), and Leo Lowenthal, Literature and the Image of Man (Boston: Beacon Press, Inc., 1957).
[24]Sypher, The Loss of the Self, p. 123.
[25]Floyd Matson, The Broken Image (New York: George Braziller, Inc., 1964), p. 145.

Whitehead and Alexander in England, of Husserl and Hartmann in Germany and of Bergson in France have 'placed' the *nisus* or the process of things at the very heart of the explanation of experience."[26]

Perhaps the most recognizable echo of these larger themes to social scientists is the transactional schema recommended by Arthur Bentley and John Dewey. Beginning in 1926, when he sought accommodation for social scientific inquiry within the framework of relativity theory, Bentley stressed what he called "observational coherence." Essentially, this meant that the investigator must frame new categories, such as "behavioral space-time," to surmount the obstacles of Euclidean space and common-sense temporality. This effort required him to suspect, and frequently to reject, "mere" appearance: for example, we might describe a conversation situation, *not* as "Smith-speaking-'sounds'-across-space-to-Jones on the terrace at 4:00 P.M.," but as a full speaking-hearing transaction with infinitely extendable antecedents and consequences in both space and time.[27] Bentley's teaching has been largely misunderstood by political scientists, but Easton is an exception. Indeed, Bentley's legacy is a part of the very complex tradition that lies behind *A Framework for Political Analysis*. Whatever the positive accomplishments of transactional analysis may be, its critical message is reasonably clear: the new social science was to be a vision of a process universe, sensitive to the dynamics of behavior, wedded to hard fact, alert to the infinite interconnectedness of the social, and happily free of "mentalisms," sterile formalism, false entities.

Ironically, for men so wary of metaphysics, transactionalists found themselves in a dilemma familiar to some Hegelians; having postulated the "interconnectedness of everything," how were they to restore being to a universe of becoming, or, in the more earthy language of social science, how were they to make their "cuts"? The very richness and multiplicity of the world that their shining tools uncovered was to overwhelm them. David Easton has worried about this problem more persistently than any contemporary political scientist and has invested more than a decade of concern with the difficulties of setting the boundaries of the discipline, developing common units of investigation, and laying the foundation for cumulative, systematic theory. I would like to turn now to examine his discussion of political systems in the light of my prior remarks.

There are two ways we might conceive of a system, according to

[26]C. Delisle Burns, *The Horizon of Experience* (London: George Allen & Unwin, 1933), p. 41.

[27]Generally, see Arthur F. Bentley, *Behavior, Knowledge, Fact* (Bloomington, Ind.: Principia Press, Inc., 1935); John Dewey and Arthur Bentley, *Knowing and the Known* (Boston: Beacon Press, Inc., 1949); and Kress, "The Idea of Process in American Political and Social Science."

Easton; we may search for interactions that seem to "naturally cohere," or we may say that "any aggregate of interactions that we choose to identify may be said to form a system." Our choice, he continues, "is solely a matter of conceptual or theoretical convenience."[28] Easton advances three arguments against the first conception. Designation of a system as "natural" is provisonal in that we must shortly proceed to test the coherence of the constituent interactions. If, in fact, we find coherence, we face the boundary problem—as Easton puts it, at what point do attenuated relationships cease being a system and become a random collection or "heap"? Should the boundary difficulty be overcome, it remains to explain or understand, not simply to note, covariance. Frank adoption of the view that all systems are "constructed" would simplify if not eliminate these difficulties, but Easton takes the argument a step further. Whether systems exist in nature or only in the mind is *"operationally* a pointless and needless dichotomy"; later we are told that "all systems of behavior are analytic."[29] The supporting argument urges that systems are abstractions, isolating and simplifying portions of reality, and in this sense, systems may be composed of any elements we choose.

Despite their analytic character, systems can be empirical. This seems to mean that we must employ at least two languages: a conceptual and an object language.[30] But does this mean that the conceptual language expressing the interrelationships constituting the system can be thought of as true or false, or do those terms apply only to the object language that expresses states of affairs? This query raises what is perhaps the central difficulty with Easton's argument, for at times he seems to suggest that the conceptual language can somehow be checked against the object language. "Through experience, insight, and wisdom it has become apparent that, given the kind of questions to which answers are being sought, the observer will probably not be able to resolve them without considering a specified set of variables. It is likely that these will fall somewhere within a range of phenomena with respect to the relevance of which most students of political life would agree. These comprise a natural system in the sense that they appear to cohere significantly. Without them it does not appear likely, on *a priori* grounds, that an adequate explanation of the major aspects of political phenomena could be obtained."[31]

Thus some interrelationships in nature appear to cluster or cohere,

---

[28]Easton, *Framework,* p. 27.

[29]Easton, *Framework,* pp. 30, 44.

[30]I am indebted to Richard C. Snyder for this suggestive dichotomy. Compare Talcott Parsons' use of "analytic" and "concrete" in *The Structure of Social Action* (Glencoe, Ill.: Free Press, 1949), chap. i.

[31]Easton, *Framework,* p. 33.

but Easton is reluctant to consider truth relevant to the conceptual language. "Concepts are neither true nor false; they are only more or less useful."[32] The question, of course, is: useful for what? A little earlier, he suggests that, instead of describing apparently cohesive variables as real, true, or "given in nature," we call them "interesting" as opposed to trivial. But, again, how do we justify our judgment? Is one system interesting because it is useful or productive, because it conforms to the expectations of the scientific community, or because it satisfies our aesthetic sensibilities? I have no particular quarrel with these or other possible answers, but whatever justification is offered it is difficult to see how we can avoid reference to a substantive vision of a political realm. Easton holds that our criteria of relevance are not and cannot be entirely arbitrary or capricious, but he states this less as a faith in an informing and sustaining vision than as a welcome safeguard against the possible absurdities of imagination. This may be a difference in emphasis (though an important one), but the point I wish to urge is this: if it appears that we must eventually refer to our experience, historical concerns, or our colleagues for both an orientation and justification for research, what have we gained by severing the conceptual language from any concern with naturally occurring systems? Is there not instead the risk that we will blunt our sensitivity to the source and subject of our entire enterprise? Admittedly, the task of identifying and setting out the boundaries of naturally occurring political systems is arduous and perhaps unending, but we may surely wonder if an ambiguous convenience is sufficient justification for laying difficulties aside.

But it is in his discussion of the system's components that the significance of Easton's theory emerges most clearly. The units of a system, just as its boundaries, are analytic. If the external dimensions are not given by nature, we can expect no greater generosity in the case of the elements. "A system composed of interacting human beings, palpable, visible and whole, certainly does not stretch the imagination. Yet, strangely enough, in this commonsense interpretation lurk unusual ambiguities that are not easily ignored or glossed over."[33] If, for example, phenomenal man with his location in Euclidean space is taken as unit of analysis, we must seek to distinguish his political actions from the totality of activities and processes in which he is imbedded. Phenomenal man as unit fails to exclude; as Henry Kariel has said, there is always an impinging environment. Conversely, as Bentley saw, phenomenal man as unit cannot express the full range of political activity.

Easton's alternative is not unfamiliar; he urges adoption of *interaction*

[32]Easton, *Framework,* p. 33.
[33]Easton, *Framework,* pp. 35–36.

as the unit of analysis. The question of what constitutes a politically relevant interaction remains, but Easton offers his earlier formula (the authoritative allocation of values for a society) as at least a working hypothesis. As a container for these political interactions he proposes the term "member": "By this I shall mean the most general role of a person in a given society with respect to political life."[34] Easton offers this statement of the theory: "A political system, therefore, will be identified as a set of interactions, abstracted from the totality of social behavior, through which values are authoritatively allocated for a society. Persons who are in the process of engaging in such interactions, that is, who are acting in political roles, will be referred to as the members of the system."[35] Stark and hard as this formulation appears, it has interesting and important corollaries. Easton rejects the belief that either systems or acting units are given in nature; we see our commonsense notions of political institutions expand and dissolve within his analytic grasp, just as phenomenal man reduces himself to interactions. We are left with two constructed or analytic elements: the total system and the reconstituted unit, which, if not a stream of consciousness, is certainly a passage of events. In the late nineteenth century, Wilhelm Dilthey could write that one difference between the natural and social sciences was that the units of the latter were given in experience (man) and had been known for twenty-odd centuries, while the units of the former (molecules) were conceptual entities physicists had only recently learned to create. Easton is clearly telling us that Dilthey was mistaken.

I have already indicated some of my misgivings about solving theoretical problems by giving ourselves to the idea of analytic systems, but I do not wish to press these here. Instead, I would like to return to the literary analogy and consider the consequences for political theory should we decide to make Easton's commitment, that is, what vision of politics will be left to us? The following quotation from Hans Meyerhoff will be helpful and merits quotation at length:

> Thus it is commonly believed that the "stream of consciousness" technique in modern fiction shows the total disintegration of the traditional conception of selfhood. This is true in the obvious sense that the notion of the self as a solid, substantial entity has become quite untenable. Moreover, this method breaks up, separates, and analyzes contents of the conscious and unconscious life of man not previously treated so articulately; and the prevalance of this

[34] Easton, *Framework*, p. 57. In thus proposing tthe reintroduction of an entity such as "member," Easton stops short of Bentley's radical statement of transactional analysis, which would not have entertained such a lapse into object language except with the most strenuous reservations.

[35] Easton, *Framework*, p. 57.

technique in modern literature reflects the increasing fragmentization of the self in the modern world. But the technique is also a subtle and ingenious way of conveying a sense of continuity and unity of the self *despite* the increased fragmentization of time and experience; for the scattered fragments of free association make "sense" only if we presuppose that they belong to the same person. In this respect, the literary portrait outlines within the aesthetic context, a concept of the self which is difficult to justify in any other language; and the technique of free association may actually serve the function of reconstructing, rather than destroying, a sense of personal identity.[36]

If we follow Meyerhoff and consider Easton's systems analysis within an "aesthetic context" we may then ask: "Does it constitute a reconstruction of experience, and if so, what is its substance, and what are its consequences?"

The central problem is that of establishing identity. There are, I think, two ways to view identity which correspond to Easton's dichotomy of natural and analytic systems. An identified unit may be considered a "container," a conventional basket we use to collect and transport our materials and activities; alternatively we may think of it as an actor. The history of Western political thought displays great variation in the identification of political actors, and each nomination has carried with it a unique sense of what is politically relevant knowledge. If for Plato the state was man writ large, we may come to gain knowledge of politics by inquiring into the nature of man. This kind of knowledge is irrelevant at best if we believe the state to be an instrument of oppression and class to be the vehicle on which history moves. The notion of politics as education may be central to Aristotle but preposterous to Lenin, and so on. Whatever these differences, and they are difficult to exaggerate, the conviction that there were, in nature, identifiable political actors was not shaken until our century.

These actors were, of course, abstractions from an experienced totality, and they were also aesthetic reconstructions of reality; what, then, distinguishes them from Easton's system and member? I think it is that Easton is proposing a container, not an actor—he has dissolved the traditional actor in the acid of interaction but has not attempted an aesthetic reconstruction. In the end, Easton offers us a behavioral complement to Musil's man without qualities—a politics without substance. But, it may be asked, what of this? What if contextual man has replaced essential man? Are we not, as Easton claims, freed from a host of conceptual difficulties and enabled to get on with the business of build-

[36]Hans Meyerhoff, *Time in Literature* (Berkeley: University of California Press, 1955), pp. 38–39.

ing systematic theory? The answer, of course, is affirmative, provided we admit two important qualifications. The first is obvious. We do not learn how to walk erect by electing to crawl on all fours no matter what other advantages the latter strategy may possess. To opt for the latter is rather to suggest that the game has been played by the wrong rules and that we should revise our ideas about the game we ought to be playing. This suggests the second qualification. If we are comparing games, and not alternative strategies within the same game, we will want to know what kinds of activities, that is, moves and plays, are possible; what kinds of skills are required; how the score is kept; and, perhaps most important of all, what constitutes winning, or even playing well. An examination of alternative games is clearly beyond the scope of this paper, but an illustration might clarify what I have in mind.

At least since the time of Antigone, men have been aware of a tragic dimension to politics; political tragedy conforms to the general structural demands of the genre. Cassirer has observed that man's discovery of the self, as an entity separable and separated from the *Umwelt*, was a tragic isolation;[37] the tragic vision itself involves what Jaspers, among others, has called a "boundary situation." "Man at the limits of his sovereignty—Job on the ash-heap, Prometheus on the crag, Oedipus in his moment of self-discovery, Lear in the heath, Ahab on his lonely quarter-deck. Here, with all the protective covering stripped off, the hero faces as if no man had ever faced it before the existential question—Job's question, 'What is man?' or Lear's 'Is man no more than this?' "[38] Whether we think of tragedy in politics as defeat by an overwhelming challenge, as man's failure to attain his full stature, or as destruction visited by a malignant or indifferent destiny, the form demands that the actor be set off from the environment. It is as the actor has an identity, and a character or nature, that he can approach or transcend his limitations. Paul Tillich put it this way: "The human boundary situation is encountered when human possibility reaches its limit, when human existence is confronted by an ultimate threat."[39] Even to assert with Protagoras that "man is the measure of all things" is to suggest that man has an identifiable and enduring dimensionality.

To Easton's political science, such considerations are encumbrances,

[37] Ernst Cassirer, *An Essay on Man* (Garden City, N. Y.: Doubleday & Co., 1953) and *The Logic of the Humanities* (New Haven, Conn.: Yale University Press, 1961).

[38] Richard B. Sewall, *The Vision of Tragedy* (New Haven, Conn.: Yale University Press, 1962), p. 5.

[39] Paul Tillich, *The Protestant Era* (Chicago: University of Chicago Press, 1948), quoted in Sewall, *The Vision of Tragedy*, p. 151. Sewall finds similar formulations in Jaspers, Kierkegaard, Ralph Harper, and Erich Frank.

not sources of insight. When the units of political analysis are arbitrarily "frozen" interactions or members, what can "causal psychological insight" possibly mean?[40] It seems strange that a theory so respectful of "fact" should be so lacking in substance, but this is a consequence of a fundamental shift in the epistemic perspective of modern empirical theory. This shift has been described by Hannah Arendt as the search for an Archimedean point from which to initiate inquiry. It is surely relevant to our inquiry that Descartes's introspective odyssey begins modern epistemology. The method of systematic doubt, as Arendt shows, was to "transfer" the Archimedean point ("a point outside the earth from which to unhinge the world") from the transcendent universe to the individual consciousness.[41] One consequence of this reorientation was to sunder experience from reality; experience became suspect, perception lost its claim to prima facie validity. All such claims were brought before the tribunal of the clear and distinct idea—the ancestor of contemporary courts of mathematics.

But, despite these consequences, the Cartesian *self* remained intact. It is in Ernest Gellner's interesting phrase a "Pure Visitor" to the universe, an intellect untainted by the virus of man's appearance, protected always by the vaccine of unrelenting doubt.[42] It was left to Hume and his analytic progeny to demonstrate that the traveler might journey the interior distance forever without encountering a self; the mind as it constituted a bounded self or system, was threatened with dissolution into its elements—the passage of discrete states of consciousness. This "atomization" of the Pure Visitor would suggest that there can be knowledge or knowing without a knower—a possibility noted by Nietzsche in *The Will to Power*.

The shock of discovery that individual consciousness could not provide the unassailable bastion Descartes had sought disturbs us today. We can see in the eighteenth century's versions of human progress, and the historical dramas of Hegel and Comte, attempts to reestablish Archimedean perspectives beyond the individual. "Men could become history-

---

[40]Here I pass over the profound problem of the concept-data relationship. For an astute discussion of this difficulty in the work of Max Weber and Talcott Parsons, see John Gunnell, "Time and the Concept of Development" (unpublished manuscript, Graduate School of Public Affairs, Albany, N. Y., 1965).

[41]See her discussion, *The Human Condition* (Garden City, N. Y.: Doubleday & Co., 1959), pp. 249–62.

[42]Ernest Gellner, *Thought and Change* (Chicago: University of Chicago Press, 1965). "But within the flux and uncertainties, the rivalries and oppositions and complexities of *this* world, where is one to seek the firm base, the premiss on which one can rest, the criterion to which one may apply?" (p. 30).

intoxicated, as Spinoza had been God-intoxicated."[43] I have already reviewed Kahler's discussion of the internal dissolution of the self, but it should at least be mentioned that a second phase of his diagnosis identifies a "split from without." By this he means to indicate the absorption of ethnic communities by the state; the extreme stage of this process is the familiar portrait of alienated man and political monolith.[44]

I can but suggest the relevance of these larger themes to our central concern. The attempt to fix the Archimedean point appears in another guise as the search for viable entities or actors by means of which we may view and order our world. In philosophy, literature, and politics, modern men have sought a purchase upon their worlds—a point that would not crumble beneath their weight or rush away from them at the speed of light. This is the dilemma and the paradox of much of modern social theory: it reveres "facts" (data), but it must look elsewhere for their meaning or significance, and it finds nothing in nature or experience that provides the latter.

I have described this attitude as it appears in the study of politics as the doubt that identifiable and significant political actors exist. Easton's "analytic" solution to the boundary problem in both systems and units is a gesture of despair and a suggestion that we have been playing the wrong game, or at least that we have misunderstood its operation. The very language of his essay, words such as "boundary," "input," and "output," suggests a passion for the undistinguished. It is, for him, a virtue that "inputs" may as easily denote caloric intake or message units as constituency demands. This desire for a neutral language complements what I began in this essay by calling the "formal" character of Easton's theory. I will now go beyond this description and remark that the theory might best be described as an "empty vision" of politics.[45] By the phrase "empty vision" I wish to summarize my arguments concerning the theory's lack of substance, the artificial nature of system and member, the replacement of the actor by the container, and the disappearance of boundaries as limits of possibility. I wish it also to indicate my agreement with Marshall McLuhan's observation that "today our science and method strive not

[43]Gellner, Thought and Change, p. 31. On this view, Comte's evolutionism and Hegel's dialectic are both examples of the totality perspective. For contrasting interpretations, see Friedrich Hayek, The Counterrevolution of Science (Glencoe, Ill.: Free Press, 1952); Herbert Marcuse, Reason and Revolution (Boston: Beacon Press, Inc., 1960); and Albert Salomon, The Tyranny of Progress (New York: Noonday Press, Inc., 1955).

[44]See William Kornhauser's discussion of the aristocratic and democratic critics of mass society, The Politics of Mass Society (Glencoe, Ill.: Free Press, 1959).

[45]I first heard this paradoxical phrase used by Norman Jacobson. It seems to me to describe brilliantly political systems theory, and I believe my use here is consistent with his.

towards a point of view but to discover how not to have a point of view, the method not of closure and perspective but of the open 'field' and the suspended judgment,"[46] and with Hannah Arendt's suggestion that the distinctive aspect of modern science and history is their joint implication, "that we think and consider everything in terms of processes and are not concerned with single entities or individual occurrences and their special separate causes."[47]

Though my doubts about the ultimate value of Easton's recommendations are apparent, I want to emphasize that my primary concern has been to explore the gross contours of his theory through the prism of other disciplines. His essay is silent on a number of questions that are usually considered central to any theoretical enterprise. It is important to know what "explanation" would mean in his universe, or how we might go about evaluating alternative conceptions of systems and members, and especially how knowledge of interaction patterns is different from knowledge of entities. It would, at the very least, be instructive to discover if and how Snow's large-scale architecture and causal psychological insight could find expression in Easton's political system.

Easton apparently does not regard consideration of questions of this kind as essential to the elaboration of his framework. Despite these omissions, which in my view weaken his proposal, I think we should welcome this essay. We should also remain open to the possibility that systems theory of this sort may someday prove capable of ordering political inquiry in a satisfying manner. But to decide this we need to know more about the nature of the theoretical universe than is offered.[48] What are the rules of the game? What kinds of problems, values, and knowledge can it express, and which does it favor? We need, in short, to understand it as a universe of discourse as well as a program of inquiry.

[46]Marshall McLuhan, *The Gutenberg Galaxy* (Toronto: University of Toronto Press, 1962), p. 276.

[47]Hannah Arendt, *Between Past and Future: Six Exercises in Political Thought* (New York: Viking Press, 1961), p. 61.

[48]See Thomas Kuhn's discussion of scientific paradigms (*The Structure of Scientific Revolutions* [Chicago: University of Chicago Press, 1962]). Easton's essay must, I think, be considered the proposing of a paradigm, and thus as "extraordinary" science.

Further Reading

Agger, Robert E., Daniel Goldrich, and Bert E. Swanson, *The Rulers and the Ruled: Political Power and Impotence in American Communities* (New York: John Wiley & Sons, Inc., 1964).

Almond, Gabriel A., "A Functional Approach to Comparative Politics," in Gabriel A. Almond and James S. Coleman, eds., *The Politics of the Developing Areas* (Princeton, N. J.: Princeton University Press, 1960), pp. 3–66.

Barber, Bernard, "Structural-Functional Analysis: Some Problems and Misunderstandings," *American Sociological Review*, XXI (2: April, 1956), pp. 129–135.

Braithwaite, Richard Bevan, *Scientific Explanation; A Study of the Function of Theory, Probability and Law in Science* (Cambridge, England: The University Press, 1953), pp. 319–341.

Easton, David, *A Framework for Political Analysis* (Englewood Cliffs, N. J.: Prentice-Hall, Inc., 1965).

———, *A Systems Analysis of Political Life* (New York: John Wiley & Sons, Inc., 1965).

———, "An Approach to the Analysis of Political Systems," *World Politics*, IX (3: April, 1957), pp. 383–400.

———, *The Political System; An Inquiry into the State of Political Science* (New York: Alfred A. Knopf, 1953).

Emmet, Dorothy M., *Function, Purpose and Powers; Some Concepts in the Study of Individuals and Societies* (London: Macmillan; New York: St. Martin's Press, 1958).

Hempel, Carl G., "The Logic of Functional Analysis," in Llewellyn Gross, ed., *Symposium on Sociological Theory* (Evanston, Illinois: Row, Peterson and Co., 1959), pp. 271–307.

Kaplan, Morton A., *System and Process in International Politics* (New York: John Wiley & Sons, Inc., 1957).

Levy, Jr., Marion J., "Some Aspects of 'Structural-Functional' Analysis and Political Science," in Roland Young, ed., *Approaches to the Study of Politics* (Evanston, Illinois: Northwestern University Press, 1958), pp. 52–66.

Lowi, Theodore, "Toward Functionalism in Political Science: The Case of Innovation in Party Systems," *American Political Science Review*, LVII (3: September, 1963), pp. 570–583.

Martindale, Don, ed., *Functionalism in the Social Sciences: The Strength and Limits of Functionalism in Anthropology, Economics, Political Science and Sociology* (Philadelphia: The American Academy of Political and Social Science, February, 1965).

Meehan, Eugene J., "Functionalism," in Eugene J. Meehan, *Contemporary Political Thought: A Critical Study* (Homewood, Illinois: The Dorsey Press, 1967), pp. 111–189.

Merton, Robert K., *Social Theory and Social Structure* (revised and enlarged edition; Glencoe, Illinois: Free Press, 1957).

Nadel, S. F., "Function and Pattern," *The Foundations of Social Anthropology* (Glencoe, Illinois: Free Press, 1951), pp. 367–408.

Nagel, Ernest, "A Formalization of Functionalism," *Logic Without Metaphysics, and Other Essays in the Philosophy of Science* (Glencoe, Illinois: The Free Press, 1956), pp. 247–283.

Wiseman, Herbert V., *Political Systems: Some Sociological Approaches* (London: Routledge and Kegan Paul, 1966).

13

Jean-Paul Sartre

MARXISM
AND EXISTENTIALISM[*]

Existentialism emphasizes the individual and his free choice. Marxism stresses the unified group and determining forces. The questions arise, how then can Sartre join commitments to both Marxism and existentialism? Which does he sacrifice to the other? In this famous 1957 tract he argues that although existentialism is "a parasitic system," it has the task of curing the lethargy of contemporary Marxism.

Sartre claims that philosophy is "born from the movement of society . . . [which] acts upon the future . . . [as] a social and political weapon." He argues that there have been three main creative philosophical periods, represented by Descartes, Kant and Hegel, and Marx, and that one must not try to project such philosophies beyond the historical moment they express. They are too close to their eras.

He also maintains that today existentialism is a "parasitic system" arising from Kierkegaard's reaction to Hegel. Claiming that Hegel hems man in by concepts, Kierkegaard criticizes Hegel for his failure to stress the subjective *existing* man. Marx criticizes Hegel for thinking that a "dialectical sleight of hand can make alienation" come from contemplation of the world. Alienation comes, rather, from concrete involvement in the world, says Sartre. Thus he thinks Marx right and Kierkegaard wrong, for the latter fails to see "the concrete man in his objective existence."

[*]Reprinted by permission of the publisher from *Search for a Method*, trans. H. Barnes (New York: Alfred A. Knopf, 1963), pp. 3–34, 174–181.

Sartre unreservedly supports Marx's materialism, that is, his view that "the mode of production of material life generally dominates the development of social, political, and intellectual life." Marxism, which he considers still in its infancy, like existentialism sees all movement as dialectical. When Marxism takes on a thoroughly man-as-agent dimension, "existentialism will no longer have any reason for being." Marxism must incorporate man into its system, for otherwise it "will degenerate into a non-human anthropology. . . ." Marxism must reject its traditional dogmatic metaphysics and incorporate existentialism at its bases.

Philosophy appears to some people as a homogeneous milieu: there thoughts are born and die, there systems are built, and there, in turn, they collapse. Others take *Philosophy* for a specific attitude which we can freely adopt at will. Still others see it as a determined segment of culture. In our view *Philosophy* does not exist. In whatever form we consider it, this shadow of science, this Gray Eminence of humanity, is only a hypostatized abstraction. Actually, there are *philosophies*. Or rather—for you would never at the same time find more than *one* living philosophy— under certain well-defined circumstances *a* philosophy is developed for the purpose of giving expression to the general movement of the society. So long as a philosophy is alive, it serves as a cultural milieu for its contemporaries. This disconcerting object presents itself *at the same time* under profoundly distinct aspects, the unification of which it is continually effecting.

A philosophy is first of all a particular way in which the "rising" class becomes conscious of itself.[1] This consciousness may be clear or confused, indirect or direct. At the time of the *noblesse de robe*[2] and of mercantile capitalism, a bourgeoisie of lawyers, merchants, and bankers gained a certain self-awareness through Cartesianism; a century and a half later, in the primitive stage of industrialization, a bourgeoisie of manufacturers, engineers, and scientists dimly discovered itself in the image of universal man which Kantianism offered to it.

[1]If I do not mention here the *person* who is objectified and revealed in his work, it is because the philosophy of a period extends far beyond the philosopher who first gave it shape—no matter how great he may be. But conversely we shall see that the study of particular doctrines is inseparable from a real investigation of philosophies. Cartesianism illuminates the period and *situates* Descartes within the totalitarian development of analytical reason; in these terms, Descartes, taken as a person and as a philosopher, clarifies the historical (hence the particular) meaning of the new rationality up to the middle of the eighteenth century.

[2]*Noblesse de robe* was originally the designation given in France to those members of the bourgeoisie who were awarded titles of nobility in recognition of outstanding achievement or services to the State. Later it was used more loosely to refer to any "new" nobility. H. B.

But if it is to be truly philosophical, this mirror must be presented as the totalization of contemporary Knowledge. The philosopher effects the unification of everything that is known, following certain guiding schemata which express the attitudes and techniques of the rising class regarding its own period and the world. Later, when the details of this Knowledge have been, one by one, challenged and destroyed by the advance of learning, the over-all concept will still remain as an undifferentiated content. These achievements of knowing, after having been first bound together by principles, will in turn—crushed and almost undecipherable— bind together the principles. Reduced to its simplest expression, the philosophical object will remain in "the objective mind" in the form of a regulative Idea, pointing to an infinite task. Thus, in France one speaks of "the Kantian Idea" or in Germany of "Fichte's *Weltanschauung*." This is because a philosophy, when it is at the height of its power, is never presented as something inert, as the passive, already terminated unity of Knowledge. Born from the movement of society, it is itself a movement and acts upon the future. This concrete totalization is at the same time the abstract project of pursuing the unification up to its final limits. In this sense philosophy is characterized as a method of investigation and explication. The confidence which it has in itself and in its future development merely reproduces the certitudes of the class which supports it. Every philosophy is practical, even the one which at first appears to be the most contemplative. Its method is a social and political weapon. The analytical, critical rationalism of the great Cartesians has survived them; born from conflict, it looked back to clarify the conflict. At the time when the bourgeoisie sought to undermine the institutions of the Ancien Régime, it attacked the outworn significations which tried to justify them.[3] Later it gave service to liberalism, and it provided a doctrine for procedures that attempted to realize the "atomization" of the Proletariat.

Thus a philosophy remains efficacious so long as the *praxis*[4] which has engendered it, which supports it, and which is clarified by it, is still alive. But it is transformed, it loses its uniqueness, it is stripped of its original, dated content to the extent that it gradually impregnates the masses so as to become in and through them a collective instrument of emancipation. In this way Cartesianism, in the eighteenth century, appears under two

---

[3]In the case of Cartesianism, the action of "philosophy" remains negative; it clears the ground, it destroys, and it enables men, across the infinite complexities and particularisms of the feudal system, to catch a glimpse of the abstract universality of bourgeois property. But under different circumstances, when the social struggle itself assumes other forms, the theory's contribution can be positive.

[4]The Greek word *praxis* means "deed" or "action." As Sartre uses it, *praxis* refers to any purposeful human activity. It is closely allied to the existential project which Sartre made so important a part of his philosophy in *Being and Nothingness*. H. B.

indissoluble and complementary aspects. On the one hand, as the Idea of reason, as an analytical method, it inspires Holbach, Helvetius, Diderot, even Rousseau; it is Cartesianism which we find at the source of anti-religious pamphlets as well as of mechanistic materialism. On the other hand, it passes into anonymity and conditions the attitudes of the Third Estate. In each case universal, analytical Reason vanishes and reappears in the form of "spontaneity." This means that the immediate response of the oppressed to oppression will be *critical*. The abstract revolt precedes the French Revolution and armed insurrection by some years. But the directed violence of weapons will overthrow privileges which have already been dissolved in Reason. Things go so far that the philosophical mind crosses the boundaries of the bourgeoisie and infiltrates the ranks of the populace. This is the moment at which the French bourgeoisie claims that it is a universal class; the infiltrations of its philosophy will permit it to mask the struggles which are beginning to split the Third Estate and will allow it to find a language and common gestures for all revolutionary classes.

If philosophy is to be simultaneously a totalization of knowledge, a method, a regulative Idea, an offensive weapon, and a community of language, if this "vision of the world" is also an instrument which ferments rotten societies, if this particular conception of a man or of a group of men becomes the culture and sometimes the nature of a whole class—then it is very clear that the periods of philosophical creation are rare. Between the seventeenth century and the twentieth, I see three such periods, which I would designate by the names of the men who dominated them: there is the "moment" of Descartes and Locke, that of Kant and Hegel, finally that of Marx. These three philosophies become, each in its turn, the humus of every particular thought and the horizon of all culture; there is no going beyond them so long as man has not gone beyond the historical moment which they express. I have often remarked on the fact that an "anti-Marxist" argument is only the apparent rejuvenation of a pre-Marxist idea. A so-called "going beyond" Marxism will be at worst only a return to pre-Marxism; at best, only the rediscovery of a thought already contained in the philosophy which one believes he has gone beyond. As for "revisionism," this is either a truism or an absurdity. There is no need to readapt a living philosophy to the course of the world; it adapts itself by means of thousands of new efforts, thousands of particular pursuits, for the philosophy is one with the movement of society. Despite their good intentions, those very people who believe themselves to be the most faithful spokesmen for their predecessors transform the thoughts which they want simply to repeat; methods are modified because they are applied to new objects. If this movement on the part of the philosophy no longer exists, one of two things is true: either the philosophy is dead or it is going through a "crisis." In the first case there is no question of revising, but of razing a rotten building; in the second case the "philosophical crisis" is the particular expression of a social crisis, and its immobility is conditioned by the contradictions which split the society. A so-called "revision," performed by "experts," would be, therefore, only an idealist mystification without real significance. It is the very movement of History, the struggle of men on all planes and on all levels of human activity, which will set free captive thought and permit it to attain its full development.

Those intellectuals who come after the great flowering and who undertake to set the systems in order or to use the new methods to conquer territory not yet fully explored, those who provide practical applications for the theory and employ it as a tool to destroy and to construct—they should not be called philosophers. They cultivate the domain, they take an inventory, they erect certain structures there, they may even bring about certain internal changes; but they still get their nourishment from the living thought of the great dead. They are borne along by the crowd on the march, and it is the crowd which constitutes their cultural milieu and their future, which determines the field of their investigations, and even of their "creation." These *relative* men I propose to call "ideologists."[5] And since I am to speak of existentialism, let it be understood that I take it to be an "ideology." It is a parasitical system living on the margin of Knowledge, which at first it opposed but into which today it seeks to be integrated. If we are to understand its present ambitions and its function we must go back to the time of Kierkegaard.

The most ample philosophical totalization is Hegelianism. Here Knowledge is raised to its most eminent dignity. It is not limited to viewing Being from the outside; it incorporates Being and dissolves it in itself. Mind objectifies itself, alienates itself, and recovers itself—without ceasing; it realizes itself through its own history. Man externalizes himself, he loses himself in things; but every alienation is surmounted by the absolute Knowledge of the philosopher. Thus those cleavages, those contradictions which cause our unhappiness are moments which are posited in order that they may be surpassed. We are not only *knowers;* in the triumph of intellectual self-consciousness, we appear as the *known.* Knowledge pierces us through and through; it situates us before dissolving us. We are integrated alive in the supreme totalization. Thus the pure, lived aspect of a tragic experience, a suffering unto death, is absorbed by the system as

---

[5]Sartre's word is *idéologues.* I translate it "ideologists" after the analogy of words such as *philologue* (English "philologist"). H. B.

a relatively abstract determination which must be mediated, as a passage toward the Absolute, the only genuine concrete.[6]

Compared with Hegel, Kierkegaard scarcely seems to count. He is certainly not a philosopher; moreover, he himself refused this title. In fact, he is a Christian who is not willing to let himself be enclosed in the system and who, against Hegel's "intellectualism," asserts unrelentingly the irreducibility and the specificity of what is lived. There is no doubt, as Jean Wahl has remarked, that a Hegelian would have assimilated this romantic and obstinate consciousness to the "unhappy consciousness," a moment which had already been surpassed and known in its essential characteristics. But it is precisely this objective knowledge which Kierkegaard challenges. For him the surpassing of the unhappy consciousness remains purely verbal. The *existing* man cannot be assimilated by a system of ideas. Whatever one may say or think about suffering, it escapes knowledge to the extent that it is suffered in itself, for itself, and to the degree that knowledge remains powerless to transform it. "The philosopher constructs a palace of ideas and lives in a hovel." Of course, it is religion which Kierkegaard wants to defend. Hegel was not willing for Christianity to be "surpassed," but for this very reason he made it the highest moment of human existence. Kierkegaard, on the contrary, insists on the transcendence of the Divine; between man and God he puts an infinite distance. The existence of the Omnipotent cannot be the object of

[6]It is entirely possible, of course, to draw Hegel over to the side of existentialism, and Hyppolite endeavored to do so, not without success, in his *Studies in Marx and Hegel*. Was it not Hegel who first pointed out that "the appearance as such is a reality"? And is not his panlogicism complemented by a pantragicism? Can we not with good reason say that for Hegel "existences are enmeshed in the history which they make and which, as a concrete universality, is what judges and transcends them"? One can do this easily, but that is not the question. What Kierkegaard opposes in Hegel is the fact that for Hegel the tragedy of a particular life is always surpassed. The lived fades away into knowledge. Hegel talks to us about the slave and his fear of death. But the fear which was *felt* becomes the simple object of knowing, and the moment of a transformation which is itself surpassed. In Kierkegaard's view it is of no importance that Hegel speaks of "freedom to die" or that he correctly describes certain aspects of faith. What Kierkegaard complains of in Hegelianism is that it neglects the *unsurpassable opaqueness* of the lived experience. The disagreement is not only and not primarily at the level of concepts but rather has to do with the critique of knowledge and the delimitation of its scope. For example, it is perfectly correct to point out that Hegel is profoundly aware of the unity of life and consciousness and of the opposition between them. But it is also true that these are already recognized as incomplete *from the point of view of* the totality. Or, to use for the moment the terms of modern semeiology—for Hegel, the *Signifying* (at any moment of history) is the movement of Mind (which will be constituted as the signifying-signified and the signified-signifying; that is, as absolute-subject); the *Signified* is the living man and his objectification. For Kierkegaard, man is the Signifying; he himself produces the significations, and no signification points to him from outside (Abraham does not know whether he is Abraham); man is never the *signified* (not even by God).

an objective knowledge; it becomes the aim of a subjective faith. And this faith, in turn, with its strength and its spontaneous affirmation, will never be reduced to a moment which can be surpassed and classified, to a knowing. Thus Kierkegaard is led to champion the cause of pure, unique subjectivity against the objective universality of essence, the narrow, passionate intransigence of the immediate life against the tranquil mediation of all reality, faith, which stubbornly asserts itself, against scientific evidence—*despite* the scandal. He looks everywhere for weapons to aid him in escaping from the terrible "mediation"; he discovers within himself oppositions, indecisions, equivocations which cannot be surpassed: paradoxes, ambiguities, discontinuities, dilemmas, etc. In all these inward conflicts, Hegel would doubtless see only contradictions in formation or in process of development—but this is exactly what Kierkegaard reproaches him for: even before becoming aware of them, the philosopher of Jena would have decided to consider them truncated ideas. In fact, the *subjective* life, just insofar as it is lived, can never be made the object of a knowledge. On principle it escapes knowing, and the relation of the believer to transcendence can only be conceived of in the form of a *going beyond*. This inwardness, which in its narrowness and its infinite depth claims to affirm itself against all philosophy, this subjectivity rediscovered beyond language as the personal adventure of each man in the face of others and of God—this is what Kierkegaard called *existence*.

We see that Kierkegaard is inseparable from Hegel, and that this vehement negation of every system can arise only within a cultural field entirely dominated by Hegelianism. The Dane feels himself hemmed in by concepts, by History, he fights for his life; it is the reaction of Christian romanticism against the rationalist humanization of faith. It would be too easy to reject this work as simply subjectivism; what we ought rather to point out, in placing it back within the framework of its period, is that Kierkegaard has as much right on his side as Hegel has on his. Hegel is right: unlike the Danish ideologist, who obstinately fixed his stand on poor, frozen paradoxes ultimately referring to an empty subjectivity, the philosopher of Jena aims through his concepts at the veritable concrete; for him, mediation is always presented as an enrichment. Kierkegaard is right: grief, need, passion, the pain of men, are brute realities which can be neither surpassed nor changed by knowledge. To be sure, Kierkegaard's religious subjectivism can with good reason be taken as the very peak of idealism; but in relation to Hegel, he marks a progress toward realism, since he insists above all on the *primacy* of the specifically real over thought, that the real cannot be reduced to thought. There are today some psychologists and psychiatrists[7] who consider certain

---

[7] See Lagache: *Le Travail du deuil* (*The Work of Mourning*).

evolutions of our inward life to be the result of a work which it performs upon itself. In this sense Kierkegaardian *existence* is the *work* of our inner life—resistances overcome and perpetually reborn, efforts perpetually renewed, despairs surmounted, provisional failures and precarious victories—and this work is directly opposed to intellectual knowing. Kierkegaard was perhaps the first to point out, against Hegel and thanks to him, the incommensurability of the real and knowledge. This incommensurability may be the origin of a conservative irrationalism; it is even one of the ways in which we may understand this ideologist's writings. But it can be seen also as the death of absolute idealism; ideas do not change men. Knowing the cause of a passion is not enough to overcome it; one must live it, one must oppose other passions to it, one must combat it tenaciously, in short one must "work oneself over."

It is striking that Marxism addresses the same reproach to Hegel though from quite another point of view. For Marx, indeed, Hegel has confused objectification, the simple externalization of man in the universe, with the alienation which turns his externalization back against man. Taken by itself—Marx emphasizes this again and again —objectification would be an opening out; it would allow man, who produces and reproduces his life without ceasing and who transforms himself by changing nature, to "contemplate himself in a world which he has created." No dialectical sleight of hand can make alienation come out of it; this is why what is involved here is not a mere play of concepts but real History. "In the social production of their existence, men enter into relations which are determined, necessary, independent of their will; these relations of production correspond to a given stage of development of their material productive forces. The totality of these relations of production constitutes the real foundation upon which a legal and political superstructure arises and to which definite forms of social consciousness correspond."[8]

Now, in the present phase of our history, productive forces have entered into conflict with relations of production. Creative work is alienated; man does not recognize himself in his own product, and his exhausting labor appears to him as a hostile force. Since alienation comes about as the result of this conflict, it is a historical reality and completely irreducible to an idea. If men are to free themselves from it, and if their work is to become the pure objectification of themselves, it is not enough that "consciousness think itself"; there must be *material* work and revolutionary *praxis*. When Marx writes: "Just as we do not judge an individual

---

[8]Sartre has not given the source for this important quotation. It comes from Marx's *"Preface* to Contribution to a Critique of Political Economy." I am indebted for the discovery to Erich Fromm, who quotes the passage in *Marx's Concept of Man* (New York: Frederick Ungar; 1961), p. 17. H. B.

by his own idea of himself, so we cannot judge a . . . period of revolutionary upheaval by its own self-consciousness," he is indicating the priority
of action (work and social *praxis*) over *knowledge* as well as their heterogeneity. He too asserts that the human fact is irreducible to knowing,
that it must *be lived* and *produced;* but he is not going to confuse it with
the empty subjectivity of a puritanical and mystified petite bourgeoisie.
He makes of it the immediate theme of the philosophical totalization, and
it is the concrete man whom he puts at the center of his research, that
man who is defined simultaneously by his needs, by the material conditions of his existence, and by the nature of his work—that is, by his
struggle against things and against men.

Thus Marx, rather than Kierkegaard or Hegel, is right, since he asserts
with Kierkegaard the specificity of human *existence* and, along with
Hegel, takes the concrete man in his objective reality. Under these
circumstances, it would seem natural if existentialism, this idealist protest
against idealism, had lost all usefulness and had not survived the decline
of Hegelianism.

In fact, existentialism suffered an eclipse. In the general struggle which
bourgeois thought leads against Marxist dialectic, it gets its support from
the post-Kantians, from Kant himself, and from Descartes; it never thinks
of addressing itself to Kierkegaard. The Dane will reappear at the
beginning of the twentieth century when people will take it into their
heads to fight against Marxism by opposing to it pluralisms, ambiguities,
paradoxes; that is, his revival dates back to the moment when for the first
time bourgeois thought was reduced to being on the defensive. Between
the two World Wars the appearance of a German existentialism certainly
corresponds—at least in the work of Jaspers[9]—to a surreptitious wish to
resuscitate the transcendent. Already—as Jean Wahl has pointed out—one
could wonder if Kierkegaard did not lure his readers into the depths of
subjectivity for the sole purpose of making them discover there the
unhappiness of man without God. This trap would be quite in keeping
with the "great solitary" who denied communication between human
beings and who saw no way to influence his fellow man except by
"indirect action."

Jaspers himself put his cards on the table. He has done nothing except
to comment upon his master; his originality consists especially in putting
certain themes into relief and in hiding others. The transcendent, for
example, appears at first to be absent from his thought, which in fact is
haunted by it. We are taught to catch a presentiment of the transcendent
in our failures; it is their profound meaning. This idea is already found in

[9]The case of Heidegger is too complex for me to discuss here.

Kierkegaard, but it is less emphasized since this Christian thinks and lives within the compass of a revealed religion. Jaspers, mute on Revelation, leads us back—through discontinuity, pluralism, and impotence—to the pure, formal subjectivity which is discovered and which discovers transcendence through its defeats. Success, indeed, as an *objectification*, would enable the person to inscribe himself in things and finally would compel him to surpass himself. The meditation on failure is perfectly suited to a bourgeoisie which is partially deChristianized but which regrets its past faith because it has lost confidence in its rationalist, positivist ideology. Kierkegaard already considered that every victory is suspect because it turns man away from himself. Kafka took up this Christian theme again in his *Journal*. And one can find a certain truth in the idea, since in a world of alienation the individual conqueror does not recognize himself in his victory and becomes its slave. But what is important to Jaspers is to derive from all this a subjective pessimism, which ultimately emerges as a theological optimism that dares not speak its name. The transcendent, indeed, remains veiled; it is attested only by its absence. One will never go beyond pessimism; one will have a presentiment of reconciliation while remaining at the level of an insurmountable contradiction and a total cleavage. This condemnation of dialectic is aimed no longer at Hegel, but at Marx. It is no longer the refusal of *Knowledge*, but the refusal of *praxis*. Kierkegaard was unwilling to play the role of a concept in the Hegelian system; Jaspers refuses to cooperate *as an individual* with the history which Marxists are making. Kierkegaard realized some progress over Hegel by affirming the *reality* of the lived; Jaspers regresses in the historical movement, for he flees from the real movement of *praxis* and takes refuge in an abstract subjectivity, whose sole aim is to achieve a certain inward *quality*.[10] This ideology of withdrawal expressed quite well only yesterday the attitude of a certain Germany fixed on its two defeats and that of a certain European bourgeoisie which wants to justify its privileges by an aristocracy of the soul, to find refuge from its objectivity in an exquisite subjectivity, and to let itself be fascinated by an ineffable present so as not to see its future. Philosophically this soft, devious thought is only a survival; it holds no great interest. But it is one more existentialism which has developed at the margin of Marxism and not against it. It is Marx with whom we claim kinship, and Marx of whom I wish to speak now.

By its *actual* presence, a philosophy transforms the structures of Knowledge, stimulates ideas; even when it defines the practical perspec-

---

[10]Jaspers gives the name "existence" to this quality which is at once immanent (since it extends throughout our lived subjectivity) and transcendent (since it remains beyond our reach).

tives of an exploited class, it polarizes the culture of the ruling classes and changes it. Marx wrote that the ideas of the dominant class are the dominant ideas. He is *absolutely* right. In 1925, when I was twenty years old, there was no chair of Marxism at the University, and Communist students were very careful not to appeal to Marxism or even to mention it in their examinations; had they done so, they would have failed. The horror of dialectic was such that Hegel himself was unknown to us. Of course, they allowed us to read Marx; they even advised us to read him; one had to know him "in order to refute him." But without the Hegelian tradition, without Marxist teachers, without any planned program of study, without the instruments of thought, our generation, like the preceding ones and like that which followed, was wholly ignorant of historical materialism.[11] On the other hand, they taught us Aristotelian and mathematical logic in great detail. It was at about this time that I read *Capital* and *German Ideology*. I found everything perfectly clear, and I really understood absolutely nothing. To understand is to change, to go beyond oneself. This reading did not change me. By contrast, what did begin to change me was the *reality* of Marxism, the heavy presence on my horizon of the masses of workers, an enormous, somber body which *lived* Marxism, which *practiced* it, and which at a distance exercised an irresistible attraction on petit bourgeois intellectuals. When we read this philosophy in books, it enjoyed no privilege in our eyes. A priest, who has just written a voluminous and very interesting work on Marx, calmly states in the opening pages: "It is possible to study [his] thought just as securely as one studies that of any other philosopher or any other sociologist."[12] That was exactly what we believed. So long as this thought appeared to us through written words, we remained "objective." We said to ourselves: "Here are the conceptions of a German intellectual who lived in London in the middle of the last century." But when it was presented as a real determination of the Proletariat and as the profound meaning of its acts—for itself and in itself—then Marxism attracted us irresistibly without our knowing it, and it put all our acquired culture out of shape. I repeat, it was not the idea which unsettled us; nor was it the condition of the worker, which we knew abstractly but which we had not experienced. No, it was the two joined together. It was—as we would have said then in our idealist jargon even as we were breaking with idealism—the Proletariat as the incarnation and vehicle of an idea. And I believe that we must here complete Marx's statement: When the rising

[11]This explains why intellectual Marxists of my age (whether Communists or not) are such poor dialecticians; they have returned, without knowing it, to mechanistic materialism.

[12]Calvez: *La Pensée de Karl Marx* (Le Seuil).

class becomes conscious of itself, this self-consciousness acts at a distance upon intellectuals and makes the ideas in their head disintegrate. We rejected the official idealism in the name of "the tragic sense of life."[13] This Proletariat, far off, invisible, inaccessible, but conscious and acting, furnished the proof—obscurely for most of us—that not *all* conflicts had been resolved. We had been brought up in bourgeois humanism, and this optimistic humanism was shattered when we vaguely perceived around our town the immense crowd of "sub-men conscious of their subhumanity." But we sensed this shattering in a way that was still idealist and individualist.

At about that time, the writers whom we loved explained to us that existence is a *scandal*. What interested us, however, was real men with their labors and their troubles. We cried out for a philosophy which would account for everything, and we did not perceive that it existed already and that it was precisely this philosophy which provoked in us this demand. At that time one book enjoyed a great success among us—Jean Wahl's *Toward the Concrete*. Yet we were disappointed by this "toward." The total concrete was what we wanted to leave behind us; the absolute concrete was what we wanted to achieve. Still the work pleased us, for it embarrassed idealism by discovering in the universe paradoxes, ambiguities, conflicts, still unresolved. We learned to turn pluralism (that concept of the Right) against the optimistic, monistic idealism of our professors—in the name of a Leftist thought which was still ignorant of itself. Enthusiastically we adopted all those doctrines which divided men into watertight groups. "Petit bourgeois" democrats, we rejected racism, but we liked to think that "primitive mentality," the universe of the child and the madman, remained entirely impenetrable to us. Under the influence of war and the Russian Revolution, we offered violence—only theoretically, of course—in opposition to the sweet dreams of our professors. It was a wretched violence (insults, brawls, suicides, murders, irreparable catastrophes) which risked leading us to fascism; but in our eyes it had the advantage of highlighting the contradictions of reality. Thus Marxism as "a philosophy which had become the world" wrenched us away from the defunct culture of a bourgeoisie which was barely subsisting on its past. We plunged blindly down the dangerous path of a pluralist realism concerned with man and things in their "concrete" existence. Yet we remained within the compass of "dominating ideas." Although we wanted to know man in his real life, we did not as yet have the idea of considering him first a worker who produces the conditions of his life. For a long time we confused the *total* and the *individual*.

[13]This phrase was made popular by the Spanish philosopher Miguel de Unamuno. Of course, this tragic sense had nothing in common with the true conflicts of our period.

Pluralism, which had served us so well against M. Brunschvieg's idealism, prevented us from understanding the dialectical totalization. It pleased us to decry essences and artificially isolated types rather than to reconstitute the synthetic movement of a truth that had "become." Political events led us to employ the schema of the "class struggle" as a sort of grid, more convenient than veridical; but it took the whole bloody history of this half century to make us grasp the reality of the class struggle and to situate us in a split society. It was the war which shattered the worn structures of our thought—War, Occupation, Resistance, the years which followed. We wanted to fight at the side of the working class; we finally understood that the concrete is history and dialectical action. We had repudiated pluralist realism only to have found it again among the fascists, and we discovered the world.

Why then has "existentialism" preserved its autonomy? Why has it not simply dissolved in Marxism?

Lukacs believed that he had answered this question in a small book called *Existentialism and Marxism*. According to him, bourgeois intellectuals have been forced "to abandon the method of idealism while safeguarding its results and its foundations; hence the historical necessity of a 'third path' (between materialism and idealism) in actuality and in the bourgeois consciousness during the imperialistic period." I shall show later the havoc which this wish to conceptualize a priori has wrought at the center of Marxism. Here let us simply observe that Lukacs fails absolutely to account for the principal fact: we were convinced *at one and the same time* that historical materialism furnished the only valid interpretation of history and that existentialism remained the only concrete approach to reality. I do not pretend to deny the contradictions in this attitude. I simply assert that Lukacs does not even suspect it. Many intellectuals, many students, have lived and still live with the tension of this double demand. How does this come about? It is due to a circumstance which Lukacs knew perfectly well but which he could not at that time even mention: Marxism, after drawing us to it as the moon draws the tides, after transforming all our ideas, after liquidating the categories of our bourgeois thought, abruptly left us stranded. It did not satisfy our need to understand. In the particular situation in which we were placed, it no longer had anything new to teach us, because it had come to a stop.

Marxism stopped. Precisely because this philosophy wants to change the world, because its aim is "philosophy-becoming-the-world," because it is and wants to be *practical*, there arose within it a veritable schism which rejected theory on one side and *praxis* on the other. From the moment the USSR, encircled and alone, undertook its gigantic effort at industrialization, Marxism found itself unable to bear the shock of these new struggles, the practical necessities and the mistakes which are always inseparable from them. At this period of withdrawal (for the USSR) and of ebb tide (for the revolutionary proletariats), the ideology itself was subordinated to a double need: security (that is, unity) and the construction of socialism *inside* the USSR. Concrete thought must be born from *praxis* and must turn back upon it in order to clarify it, not by chance and without rules, but—as in all sciences and all techniques—in conformity with principles. Now the Party leaders, bent on pushing the integration of the group to the limit, feared that the free process of truth, with all the discussions and all the conflicts which it involves, would break the unity of combat; they reserved for themselves the right to define the line and to interpret the event. In addition, out of fear that the experience might not provide its own clarities, that it might put into question certain of their guiding ideas and might contribute to "weakening the ideological struggle," they put the doctrine out of reach. The separation of theory and practice resulted in transforming the latter into an empiricism without principles; the former into a pure, fixed knowledge. On the other hand, the economic planning imposed by a bureaucracy unwilling to recognize its mistakes became thereby a violence done to reality. And since the future production of a nation was determined in offices, often outside its own territory, this violence had as its counterpart an absolute idealism. Men and things had to yield to ideas—a priori; experience, when it did not verify the predictions, could only be wrong. Budapest's subway was real in Rakosi's head. If Budapest's subsoil did not allow him to construct the subway, this was because the subsoil was counter-revolutionary. Marxism, as a philosophical interpretation of man and of history, necessarily had to reflect the preconceptions of the planned economy.

This fixed image of idealism and of violence did idealistic violence to facts. For years the Marxist intellectual believed that he served his party by violating experience, by overlooking embarrassing details, by grossly simplifying the data, and above all, by conceptualizing the event *before* having studied it. And I do not mean to speak only of Communists, but of all the others—fellow travelers, Trotskyites, and Trotsky sympathizers—for they have been *created* by their sympathy for the Communist Party or by their opposition to it. On November 4, 1956, at the time of the second Soviet intervention in Hungary, each group already had its mind made up before it possessed any information on the situation. It had decided in advance whether it was witnessing an act of aggression on the part of the Russian bureaucracy against the democracy of Workers' Committees, with a revolt of the masses against the bureaucratic system, or with a counter-revolutionary attempt which Soviet moderation had known how to check. Later there was news, a great deal of news; but I have not heard it said that even one Marxist changed his opinion.

Among the interpretations which I have just mentioned, there is one which shows the method in all its nakedness, that which reduces the facts in Hungary to a "Soviet act of aggression against the democracy of Workers' Committees."[14] It is obvious that the Workers' Committees are a democratic institution; one can even maintain that they bear within them the future of the socialist society. But this does not alter the fact that they did not exist in Hungary at the time of the first Soviet intervention; and their appearance during the Insurrection was much too brief and too troubled for us to be able to speak of an organized democracy. No matter. There were Workers' Committees; a Soviet intervention took place. Starting from there, Marxist idealism proceeds to two simultaneous operations: conceptualization and passage to the limit. They push the empirical notion to the perfection of the type, the germ to its total development. At the same time they reject the equivocal givens of experience; these could only lead one astray. We will find ourselves then in the presence of a typical contradiction between two Platonic ideas: on the one side, the wavering policy of the USSR gave way to the rigorous and predictable action of that entity, "the Soviet Bureaucracy"; on the other side, the Workers' Committees disappeared before that other entity, "the direct Democracy." I shall call these two objects "general particularities"; they are made to pass for particular, historical realities when we ought not to see in them anything more than the purely formal unity of abstract, universal relations. The process of making them into fetishes will be complete when each one is endowed with real powers: the Democracy of Workers' Committees holds within itself the absolute negation of the Bureaucracy, which reacts by crushing its adversary.

Now there can be no doubt that the fruitfulness of living Marxism stemmed in part from its way of approaching experience. Marx was convinced that facts are never isolated appearances, that if they come into being together, it is always within the higher unity of a whole, that they are bound to each other by internal relations, and that the presence of one profoundly modifies the nature of the other. Consequently, Marx approached the study of the revolution of February 1848 or Louis Napoleon Bonaparte's *coup d'état* with a synthetic intent; he saw in these events totalities produced and at the same time split apart by their internal contradictions. Of course, the physicist's hypothesis, before it has been confirmed by experimentation, is also an interpretation of experience; it rejects empiricism simply because it is mute. But the constitutive schema of this hypothesis is universalizing, not totalizing. It determines a

[14]Maintained by former Trotskyites.

relation, a function, and not a concrete totality. The Marxist approaches the historical process with 'universalizing and totalizing schemata. Naturally the totalization was not made by chance. The theory had determined the choice of perspective and the order of the conditioning factors; it studied each particular process within the framework of a general system in evolution. But in no case, in Marx's own work, does this putting in perspective claim to prevent or to render useless the appreciation of the process as a *unique* totality. When, for example, he studies the brief and tragic history of the Republic of 1848, he does not limit himself—as would be done today—to stating that the republican petite bourgeoisie betrayed its ally, the Proletariat. On the contrary, he tries to account for this tragedy in its detail and in the aggregate. If he subordinates anecdotal facts to the totality (of a movement, of an attitude), he also seeks to discover the totality by means of the facts. In other words, he gives to each event, in addition to its particular signification, the role of being revealing. Since the ruling principle of the inquiry is the search for the synthetic ensemble, each fact, once established, is questioned and interpreted as part of a whole. It is on the basis of *the fact*, through the study of its lacks and its "oversignifications," that one determines, by virtue of a hypothesis, the totality at the heart of which the fact will recover its truth. Thus living Marxism is heuristic; its principles and its prior knowledge appear as regulative in relation to its concrete research. In the work of Marx we never find entities. Totalities (e.g., "the petite bourgeoisie" of the *18 Brumaire*) are living; they furnish their own definitions within the framework of the research.[15] Otherwise we could

---

[15]The concept of "the petite bourgeoisie" exists in Marxist philosophy, of course, well before the study of Louis Napoleon's *coup d'état*. But this is because the petite bourgeoisie itself had already existed as a class for a long time. What is important is the fact that it evolves with history and that in 1848 it presents unique characteristics which the concept cannot derive from itself. We will see that Marx goes back to the general traits which defined it as a class and at the same time—in those terms and in the light of experience—he determines the specific traits which determined it as a unique reality in 1848. To take another example, see how he tries in 1853, in a series of articles (*The British Rule in India*), to portray the peculiar quality of Hindustan. Maximilien Rubel in his excellent book quotes this curious passage (so shocking to our contemporary Marxists). "This strange combination of Italy and Ireland, of a world of pleasure and a world of suffering, is anticipated in the old religious traditions of Hindustan, in that religion of sensual exuberance and savage asceticism. . . ." (Rubel: *Karl Marx*, p. 302. The quotation from Marx appeared June 25, 1853, under the title *On India*.) Certainly we can find behind these words the true concepts and method: the social structure and the geographical aspect—that is what recalls Italy; English colonization—that is what recalls Ireland; etc. No matter. He gives a *reality* to these words—pleasure, suffering, sensual exuberance, and savage asceticism. Better yet, he shows the actual situation of Hindustan "anticipated" (*before the English*) by its old religious traditions. Whether Hindustan is actually this or something else matters little to us; what counts here is the synthetic view which *gives life* to the objects of the analysis.

not understand the importance which Marxists attach (even today) to "the analysis" of a situation. It goes without saying that this analysis is not enough and that it is but the first moment in an effort at synthetic reconstruction. But it is apparent also that the analysis is indispensable to the later reconstruction of the total structures.

Marxist voluntarism, which likes to speak of analysis, has reduced this operation to a simple ceremony. There is no longer any question of studying facts within the general perspective of Marxism so as to enrich our understanding and to clarify action. Analysis consists solely in getting rid of detail, in forcing the signification of certain events, in denaturing facts or even in inventing a nature for them in order to discover it later underneath them, as their substance, as unchangeable, fetishized "synthetic notions." The open concepts of Marxism have closed in. They are no longer *keys,* interpretive schemata; they are posited for themselves as an already totalized knowledge. To use Kantian terms—Marxism makes out of these particularized, fetishized types, constitutive concepts of experience. The real content of these typical concepts is always *past Knowledge;* but today's Marxist makes of it an eternal knowledge. His sole concern, at the moment of analysis, will be to "place" these entities. The more he is convinced that they represent truth a priori, the less fussy he will be about proof. The Kerstein Amendment, the appeals of Radio Free Europe, rumors—these are sufficient for the French Communists to "place" the entity "world imperialism" at the origin of the events in Hungary. The totalizing investigation has given way to a Scholasticism of the totality. The heuristic principle—"to search for the whole in its parts"—has become the terrorist practice[16] of "liquidating the particularity." It is not by chance that Lukacs—Lukacs who so often violates history—has found in 1956 the best definition of this frozen Marxism. Twenty years of practice give him all the authority necessary to call this pseudophilosophy *a voluntarist idealism.*

Today social and historical experience falls outside of Knowledge. Bourgeois concepts just manage to revive and quickly break down; those which survive lack any foundation. The real attainments of American Sociology cannot hide its theoretic uncertainty. Psychoanalysis, after a spectacular beginning, has stood still. It knows a great many details, but it lacks any firm foundation. Marxism possesses theoretical bases, it embraces all human activity; but it no longer *knows* anything. Its concepts are *dictates;* its goal is no longer to increase what it knows but to be itself constituted a priori as an absolute Knowledge. In view of this twofold ignorance, existentialism has been able to return and to maintain

[16]At one time this intellectual terror corresponded to "the physical liquidation" of particular people.

itself because it reaffirmed the reality of men as Kierkegaard asserted his own reality against Hegel. However, the Dane rejected the Hegelian conception of man and of the real. Existentialism and Marxism, on the contrary, aim at the same object; but Marxism has reabsorbed man into the idea, and existentialism seeks him everywhere *where he is*, at his work, in his home, in the street. We certainly do not claim—as Kierkegaard did— that this real man is unknowable. We say only that he is not known. If for the time being he escapes Knowledge, it is because the only concepts at our disposal for understanding him are borrowed either from the idealism of the Right or from the idealism of the Left. We are careful not to confuse these two idealisms: the former merits its name by the *content* of its concepts, and the latter by the *use* which today it makes of its concepts. It is true also that among the masses Marxist *practice* does not reflect, or only slightly reflects, the sclerosis of its theory. But it is precisely the conflict between revolutionary action and the Scholastic justification of this action which prevents Communist man—in socialist countries as in bourgeois countries—from achieving any clear self-consciousness. One of the most striking characteristics of our time is the fact that history is made without self-awareness. No doubt someone will say this has always been the case; and this was true up until the second half of the last century—that is, until Marx. But what has made the force and richness of Marxism is the fact that it has been the most radical attempt to clarify the historical process in its totality. For the last twenty years, on the contrary, its shadow has obscured history; this is because it has ceased to live *with history* and because it attempts, through a bureaucratic conservatism, to reduce change to identity.[17]

[17]I have already expressed my opinion on the Hungarian tragedy, and I shall not discuss the matter again. From the point of view of what concerns us here, it matters little a priori that the Communist commentators believed that they had to justify the Soviet intervention. What is really heart-breaking is the fact that their "analyses" totally suppressed the originality of the Hungarian fact. Yet there is no doubt that an insurrection at Budapest a dozen years after the war, less than five years after the death of Stalin, must present very particular characteristics. What do our "schematizers" do? They lay stress on the faults of the Party but without defining them. These indeterminate faults assume an abstract and eternal character which wrenches them from the historical context so as to make of them a universal entity; it is "human error." The writers indicate the presence of reactionary elements, but without showing their Hungarian *reality*. Suddenly these reactionaries pass over into eternal Reaction; they are brothers of the counter-revolutionaries of 1793, and their only distinctive trait is the will to injure. Finally, those commentators present world imperialism as an inexhaustible, formless force, whose essence does not vary regardless of its point of application. They construct an interpretation which serves as a skeleton key to everything—out of three ingredients: errors, the local-reaction-which-profits-from-popular-discontent, and the exploitation-of-this-situation-by-world-imperialism. This interpretation can be applied as well or as badly to all insurrections, including the disturbances in Vendée or at Lyon in 1793, by merely putting "aristocracy" in place of "imperialism." In short, nothing new has happened. That is what had to be demonstrated.

Yet we must be clear about all this. This sclerosis does not correspond to a normal aging. It is produced by a world-wide combination of circumstances of a particular type. Far from being exhausted, Marxism is still very young, almost in its infancy; it has scarcely begun to develop. It remains, therefore, the philosophy of our time. We cannot go beyond it because we have not gone beyond the circumstances which engendered it. Our thoughts, whatever they may be, can be formed only upon this humus; they must be contained within the framework which it furnishes for them or be lost in the void or retrogress. Existentialism, like Marxism, addresses itself to experience in order to discover there concrete syntheses; it can conceive of these syntheses only within a moving, dialectical totalization which is nothing else but history or—from the strictly cultural point of view which we have adopted here—"philosophy-becoming-the-world." For us, truth is something which becomes, it *has* and *will have* become. It is a totalization which is forever being totalized. Particular facts do not signify anything; they are neither true nor false so long as they are not related, through the mediation of various partial totalities, to the totalization in process.

Let us go further. We agree with Garaudy when he writes (*Humanité*, May 17, 1955): "Marxism forms today the system of coordinates which alone permits it to situate and to define a thought in any domain whatsoever—from political economy to physics, from history to ethics." And we should agree all the more readily if he had extended his statement (but this was not his subject) to the actions of individuals and masses, to specific works, to modes of life, to labor, to feelings, to the particular evolution of an institution or a character. To go further, we are also in full agreement with Engels when he wrote in that letter which furnished Plekhanov the occasion for a famous attack against Bernstein: "There does not exist, as one would like to imagine now and then, simply for convenience, any effect produced automatically by the economic situation. On the contrary, it is men themselves who make their history, but within a given environment which conditions them and on the basis of real, prior conditions among which economic conditions—no matter how much influenced they may be by other political and ideological conditions—are nevertheless, in the final analysis, the determining conditions, constituting from one end to the other the guiding thread which alone puts us in a position to understand." It is already evident that we do not conceive of economic conditions as the simple, static structure of an unchangeable society; it is the contradictions within them which form the driving force of history. It is amusing that Lukacs, in the work which I have already quoted, believed he was distinguishing himself from us by recalling that Marxist definition of materialism: "the primacy of existence over consciousness"—whereas existentialism, as its name sufficiently indicates, makes of this primacy the object of its fundamental affirmation.[18]

[18]The *methodological* principle which holds that certitude begins with reflection in no way contradicts the *anthropological* principle which defines the concrete person by his materiality. For us, reflection is not reduced to the simple immanence of idealist subjectivism; it is a point of departure only if it throws us back immediately among things and men, in the world. The only theory of knowledge which can be valid today is one which is founded on that truth of microphysics: the experimenter is a part of the experimental system. This is the only position which allows us to get rid of all idealist illusion, the only one which shows the real man in the midst of the real world. But this realism necessarily implies a reflective point of departure; that is, the *revelation* of a situation is effected in and through the *praxis* which changes it. We do not hold that this first act of becoming conscious of the situation is the originating source of an action; we see in it a necessary moment of the action itself—the action, *in the course of its accomplishment,* provides its own clarification. That does not prevent this clarification from appearing in and by means of the attainment of awareness on the part of the agents; and this in turn necessarily implies that one must develop a theory of consciousness. Yet in the theory of knowledge continues to be the weak point in Marxism. When Marx writes: "The materialist conception of the world signifies simply the conception of nature as it is without any foreign addition," he makes himself into an *objective observation* and claims to contemplate nature as it is absolutely. Having stripped away all subjectivity and having assimilated himself into pure objective truth, he walks in a world of objects inhabited by object-men. By contrast, when Lenin speaks of our consciousness, he writes: "Consciousness is only the reflection of being, at best an approximately accurate reflection"; and by a single stroke he removes from himself the right to write what he is writing. In both cases it is a matter of suppressing subjectivity: with Marx, we are placed beyond it; with Lenin, on this side of it.

These two positions contradict each other. How can the "approximately accurate reflection" become the source of *materialistic rationalism?* The game is played on two levels: there is in Marxism a constituting consciousness which asserts a priori the rationality of the world (and which, consequently, falls into idealism); this constituting consciousness determines the constituted consciousness of particular men as a simple reflection (which ends up in a skeptical idealism). Both of these conceptions amount to breaking man's real relation with history, since in the first, knowing is pure theory, a non-situated observing, and in the second, it is a simple passivity. In the latter there is no longer any experimenting, there is only a skeptical empiricism; man vanishes and Hume's challenge is not taken up. In the former the experimenter transcends the experimental system. And let no one try to tie one to the other by a "dialectical theory of the reflection"; the two concepts are essentially *anti-dialectical.* When knowing is made apodictic, and when it is constituted against all possible questioning without ever defining its scope or its rights, then it is cut off from the world and becomes a formal system. When it is reduced to a pure psycho-physiological determination, it loses its primary quality, which is its relation to the object, in order to become itself a pure object of knowing. No mediation can link Marxism as a declaration of principles and apodictic truths to psycho-physiological reflection (or "dialectic"). These two conceptions of knowing (dogmatism and the knowing-dyad) are both of them *pre-Marxist.* In the movement of Marxist "analyses" and especially in the process of totalization, just as in Marx's remarks on the *practical* aspect of truth and on the general relations of theory and *praxis,* it would be easy to discover the rudiments of a *realistic* epistemology which has never been developed. But what we can and ought to construct on the basis of these scattered observations is a theory which *situates* knowing *in the world* (as the theory of the reflection attempts awkwardly to do) and which determines it in its *negativity* (that negativity which Stalinist

To be still more explicit, we support unreservedly that formulation in *Capital* by which Marx means to define his "materialism": "The mode of production of material life generally dominates the development of social, political, and intellectual life." We cannot conceive of this conditioning in any form except that of a dialectical movement (contradictions, surpassing, totalizations). M. Rubel criticizes me for not making any allusion to this "Marxist materialism" in the article I wrote in 1946, "Materialism and Revolution."[19] But he himself supplies the reason for this omission. "It is true that this author is directing his comments at Engels rather than at Marx." Yes, and even more at contemporary French Marxists. But Marx's statement seems to me to point to a factual evidence which we cannot go beyond *so long as* the transformations of social relations and technical progress have not freed man from the yoke of scarcity. We are all acquainted with the passage in which Marx alludes to that far-off time: "This reign of freedom does not begin in fact until the time when the work imposed by necessity and external finality shall cease; it is found, therefore, beyond the sphere of material production proper" (*Capital*, III, p. 873). As soon as there will exist *for everyone* a margin of *real* freedom beyond the production of life, Marxism will have lived out its span; a philosophy of freedom will take its place. But we have no means, no intellectual instrument, no concrete experience which allows us to conceive of this freedom or of this philosophy. . . .

These considerations enable us to understand why we can at the same

---

dogmatism pushes to the absolute and which it transforms into a negation). Only then will it be understood that knowing is not a knowing of ideas but a practical knowing of *things;* then it will be possible to suppress the *reflection* as a useless and misleading intermediary. Then we will be able to account for the thought which is lost and alienated in the course of action so that it may be rediscovered by and in the action itself. But what are we to call this situated negativity, as a moment of *praxis* and as a pure relation to things themselves, if not exactly "consciousness"?

There are two ways to fall into idealism: The one consists of dissolving the real in subjectivity, the other in denying all real subjectivity in the interests of objectivity. The truth is that subjectivity is neither everything nor nothing; it represents a moment in the objective process (that in which externality is internalized), and this moment is perpetually eliminated only to be perpetually reborn. Now, each of these ephemeral moments—which rise up in the course of human history and which are never either the first or the last—is lived as a *point of departure* by the subject of history. "Class-consciousness" is not the simple lived contradiction which objectively characterizes the class considered; it is that contradiction already surpassed by *praxis* and thereby preserved and denied all at once. But it is precisely this revealing negativity, this distance within immediate proximity, which simultaneously constitutes what existentialism calls "consciousness of the object" and "non-thetic self-consciousness."

[19]"Matérialisme et révolution," *Les Temps modernes*, Vol. I, Nos. 9 and 10 (June–July 1946). The article has been translated into English by Annette Michelson and is included in Jean-Paul Sartre's *Literary and Philosophical Essays* (New York: Criterion Books; 1955). H.B.

time declare that we are in profound agreement with Marxist philosophy and yet for the present maintain the autonomy of the existential ideology. There is no doubt, indeed, that Marxism appears today to be the only possible anthropology which can be at once historical and structural. It is the only one which at the same time takes man in his totality—that is, in terms of the materiality of his condition. Nobody can propose to it another point of departure, for this would be to offer to it *another man* as the object of its study. It is *inside* the movement of Marxist thought that we discover a flaw of such a sort that despite itself Marxism tends to eliminate the questioner from his investigation and to make of the questioned the object of an absolute Knowledge. The very notions which Marxist research employs to describe our historical society—exploitation, alienation, fetishizing, reification, etc.—are precisely those which most immediately refer to existential structures. The very notion of *praxis* and that of dialectic—inseparably bound together—are contradictory to the intellectualist idea of a knowledge. And to come to the most important point, *labor*, as man's reproduction of his life, can hold no meaning if its fundamental structure is not to pro-ject. In view of this default—which pertains to the historical development and not to the actual principles of the doctrine—existentialism, at the heart of Marxism and taking the same givens, the same Knowledge, as its point of departure, must attempt in its turn—at least as an experiment—the dialectical interpretation of History. It puts nothing in question except a mechanistic determinism which is not exactly Marxist and which has been introduced from the outside into this total philosophy. Existentialism, too, wants to situate man in his class and in the conflicts which oppose him to other classes, starting with the mode and the relations of production. But it can approach this "situation" in terms of *existence*—that is, of comprehension. It makes itself the questioned and the question as questioner; it does not, as Kierkegaard did apropos of Hegel, set the irrational singularity of the individual in opposition to universal Knowledge. But into this very Knowledge and into the universality of concepts, it wants to reintroduce the unsurpassable singularity of the human adventure.

Thus the comprehension of existence is presented as the human foundation of Marxist anthropology. Nevertheless, we must beware here of a confusion heavy with consequences. In fact, in the order of Knowledge, what we know concerning the principle or the foundations of a scientific structure, even when it has come—as is ordinarily the case—later than the empirical determinations, is set forth first; and one deduces from it the determinations of Knowledge in the same way that one constructs a building after having secured its foundations. But this is because the foundation is itself a knowing; and if one can deduce from it certain propositions already guaranteed by experience, this is because one has induced it in terms of them as the most general hypothesis. In contrast, the foundation of Marxism, as a historical, structural anthropology, is man himself inasmuch as human existence and the comprehension of the human are inseparable. Historically Marxist Knowledge produces its foundation at a certain moment of its development, and this foundation is presented in a disguised form. It does not appear as the practical foundations of the theory, but as that which, on principle, pushes forward all theoretical knowing. Thus the singularity of existence is presented in Kierkegaard as that which on principle is kept outside the Hegelian system (that is, outside total Knowledge), as that which can in no way be *thought* but only *lived* in the act of faith. The dialectical procedure to reintegrate existence (which is never *known*) as a foundation at the heart of Knowledge could not be attempted then, since neither of the current attitudes—an idealist Knowledge, a spiritual existence—could lay claim to concrete actualization. These two terms outlined abstractly the future contradiction. And the development of anthropological knowing could not lead then to the synthesis of these formal positions: the movement of ideas—as the movement of society—had first to produce Marxism as the only possible form of a really concrete Knowledge. And as we indicated at the beginning, Marx's own Marxism, while indicating the dialectical opposition between knowing and being, contained implicitly the demand for an existential foundation for the theory. Furthermore, in order for notions like reification and alienation to assume their full meaning, it would have been necessary for the questioner and the questioned to be made one. What must be the nature of human relations in order for these relations to be capable of appearing in certain definite societies as the relations of things to each other? If the reification of human relations is possible, it is because these relations, even if reified, are fundamentally distinct from the relations of things. What kind of practical organism is this which reproduces its life by its work so that its work and ultimately its very reality are alienated; that is, so that they, *as others*, turn back upon him and determine him? But before Marxism, itself a product of the social conflict, could turn to these problems, it had to assume fully its role as a practical philosophy—that is, as a theory clarifying social and political *praxis*. The result is a profound *lack* within contemporary Marxism; the use of the notions mentioned earlier—and many others—refers to a comprehension of human reality which is missing. And this lack is not—as some Marxists declare today—a localized void, a hole in the construction of Knowledge. It is inapprehensible and yet everywhere present; it is a general anemia.

Doubtless this *practical* anemia becomes an anemia in the Marxist man—that is, in us, men of the twentieth century, inasmuch as the insurpassable framework of Knowledge is Marxism; and inasmuch as this Marxism clarifies our individual and collective *praxis*, it therefore determines us in our existence. About 1949 numerous posters covered the walls in Warsaw: "Tuberculosis slows down production." They were put there as the result of some decision on the part of the government, and this decision originated in a very good intention. But their content shows more clearly than anything else the extent to which man has been eliminated from an anthropology which wants to be pure knowledge. Tuberculosis is an object of a practical Knowledge: the physician learns to know it in order to cure it; the Party determines its importance in Poland by statistics. Other mathematical calculations connecting these with production statistics (quantitative variations in production for each industrial group in proportion to the number of cases of tuberculosis) will suffice to obtain a law of the type $y = f(x)$, in which tuberculosis plays the role of independent variable. But this law, the same one which could be read on the propaganda posters, reveals a new and double alienation by totally eliminating the tubercular man, by refusing to him even the elementary role of *mediator* between the disease and the number of manufactured products. In a socialist society, at a certain moment in its development, the worker is alienated from his production; in the theoretical-practical order, the human foundation of anthropology is submerged in Knowledge.

It is precisely this expulsion of man, his exclusion from Marxist Knowledge, which resulted in the renascence of existentialist thought outside the historical totalization of Knowledge. Human science is frozen in the non-human, and human-reality seeks to understand itself outside of science. But this time the opposition comes from those who directly demand their synthetic transcendence. Marxism will degenerate into a non-human anthropology if it does not reintegrate man into itself as its foundation. But this comprehension, which is nothing other than existence itself, is disclosed at the same time by the historical movement of Marxism, by the concepts which indirectly clarify it (alienation, etc.), and by the new alienations which give birth to the contradictions of socialist society and which reveal to it its abandonment; that is, the incommensurability of existence and practical Knowledge. The movement can *think* itself only in Marxist terms and can *comprehend* itself only as an alienated existence, as a human-reality made into a thing. The moment which will surpass this opposition must reintegrate comprehension into Knowledge as its non-theoretical foundation.

In other words, the foundation of anthropology is man himself, not as the object of practical Knowledge, but as a practical organism producing

Knowledge as a moment of its *praxis*. And the reintegration of man as a concrete existence into the core of anthropology, as its constant support, appears necessarily as a stage in the process of philosophy's "becoming-the-world." In this sense the foundation of anthropology cannot precede it (neither historically nor logically). If *existence*, in its free comprehension of itself, preceded the awareness of alienation or of exploitation, it would be necessary to suppose that the free development of the practical organism historically preceded its present fall and captivity. (And if this were established, the historical precedence would scarcely advance us in our comprehension, since the retrospective study of vanished societies is made today with the enlightenment furnished by techniques for reconstruction and by means of the alienations which enchain us.) Or, if one insisted on a logical priority, it would be necessary to suppose that the freedom of the project could be recovered in its full reality *underneath* the alienations of our society and that one could move dialectically from the concrete existence which understands its freedom to the various alterations which distort it in present society. This hypothesis is absurd. To be sure, man can be enslaved only if he is free. But for the historical man who *knows* himself and *comprehends* himself, this practical freedom is grasped only as the permanent, concrete condition of his servitude; that is, across that servitude and by means of it as that which makes it possible, as its foundation. Thus Marxist Knowledge bears on the alienated man; but if it doesn't want to make a fetish of its knowing and to dissolve man in the process of knowing his alienations, then it is not enough to describe the working of capital or the system of colonization. It is necessary that the questioner understand how the questioned—that is, himself—*exists his alienation*, how he surpasses it and is alienated in this very surpassing. It is necessary that his very thought should at every instant surpass the intimate contradiction which unites the comprehension of man-as-agent with the knowing of man-as-object and that it forge new concepts, new determinations of Knowledge which emerge from the existential comprehension and which regulate the movement of their contents by its dialectical procedure. Yet this comprehension—as a living movement of the practical organism—can take place only within a concrete situation, insofar as theoretical Knowledge illuminates and interprets this situation.

Thus the autonomy of existential studies results necessarily from the negative qualities of Marxists (and not from Marxism itself). So long as the doctrine does not recognize its anemia, so long as it founds its Knowledge upon a dogmatic metaphysics (a dialectic of Nature) instead of seeking its support in the comprehension of the living man, so long as it rejects as irrational those ideologies which wish, as Marx did, to separate being from Knowledge and, in anthropology, to found the knowing of man on human existence, existentialism will follow its own path of study. This means that it will attempt to clarify the givens of Marxist Knowledge by indirect knowing (that is, as we have seen, by words which regressively denote existential structures), and to engender within the framework of Marxism a veritable *comprehensive knowing* which will rediscover man in the social world and which will follow him in his *praxis* —or, if you prefer, in the project which throws him toward the social possibles in terms of a defined situation. Existentialism will appear therefore as a fragment of the system, which has fallen outside of Knowledge. From the day that Marxist thought will have taken on the human dimension (that is, the existential project) as the foundation of anthropological Knowledge, existentialism will no longer have any reason for being. Absorbed, surpassed and conserved by the totalizing movement of philosophy, it will cease to be a particular inquiry and will become the foundation of all inquiry. The comments which we have made in the course of the present essay are directed—to the modest limit of our capabilities—toward hastening the moment of that dissolution.

14

Thomas L. Thorson

THE POLITICAL PHILOSOPHY OF CAMUS*

Professor Thorson responds to those who claim that political philosophy is dead with the assertion that it "will never die for the simple reason that it is far too important for men in society." He acknowledges, however, that it has been "quieted by modern methodological proscriptions." It is, he asserts, "for just this reason that political philosophy appears in places which by former standards seem odd." One of the "odd" places was in the work of Albert Camus.

Camus fashioned a political philosophy different from that of Sartre. Although he did not like to be referred to as an existentialist because he didn't wish to be associated with the militant atheism of Sartre and because he rejected Sartre's existentialist doctrine that existence precedes essence, he is an existentialist in that "his philosophical point of departure is the fact of individual personal existence."

Perhaps the most important fact about the modern world is the "death of God." The traditional theological and philosophical standards "which gave meaning to the world and to the life of man are no longer intellectually available. . . ." Finding no meaning, man encounters "the absurd." The absurd is the meaninglessness of reality. Camus perceives three ways of dealing with the absurd: suicide, hope, or living with it. Only life makes possible the "encounter between human inquiry and

*Reprinted by permission of the author and publisher from *Ethics*, LXXIV (4: July, 1964), pp. 281–291, where it was entitled "Albert Camus and the Rights of Man."

the silence of the universe," and hence Camus affirms the value of human life.

Politically, Camus' fundamental point is that everything is not permitted—that the absurd carries limits wihin itself. There must be a limit to the revolutionist's actions: he cannot kill in the name of life. A "perverted revolt" in the name of socialism has become "socialism of the gallows." There must be limits. Thus Camus moves from absurdist reasoning to an individual ethic and from an individual ethic to a social one. Also, as he puts it, "if I judge that a thing is true, I must preserve it." Camus' commitment is evident.

My purpose in this paper is, first, to make the beginnings of a case for the inclusion in the tradition of Western political philosophy of the French Nobel Laureate, Albert Camus. It is, second, to explore and to evaluate those aspects of Camus's thought which seem to me relevant to the continuing problems of political philosophy.

The moment that one raises the name of a man known primarily as a novelist and playwright in the context of political philosophy he gives a kind of prima facie validity to a pair of charges frequently invoked against political philosophy in the twentieth century. Partly because these charges seem to me to be in an important sense superficial, and partly because an examination of them will help to delineate the framework of the analysis that I shall attempt to present, we shall do well to pause for a moment to look into them.

The first of these allegations is that contemporary students of political philosophy spend their time discovering or "rediscovering some deservedly obscure text";[1] and the second, the oft-repeated claim that political philosophy is dead.[2] These charges are, of course, closely related: One looks, it is suggested, under every rock for a snippet of yet-unanalyzed political philosophy, or what, by some stretch of the imagination, can be classed as political philosophy, because political philosophy as a "going concern" no longer exists. To put it more pointedly, is not a discussion of Camus, a man whom very few would think of as a political philosopher and who certainly did not so present himself, a rather pathetic grasping

---

[1]Robert A. Dahl, "Political Theory: Truth and Consequences," *World Politics*, XI (October, 1958), p. 89.

[2]See Dahl, "Political Theory: Truth and Consequences," and Morton White, *Religion Politics and the Higher Learning* (Cambridge, Mass.: Harvard University Press, 1959), p. vii. Similar thoughts are expressed by Arnold Brecht, *Political Theory: The Foundations of Twentieth-Century Political Thought* (Princeton, N. J.: Princeton University Press, 1959), and even by Leo Strauss, *What Is Political Philosophy? and Other Studies* (Glencoe, Ill.: Free Press, 1959).

at straws by someone who will not admit defeat even though it stares him in the face? It is superfluous, I suppose, to answer that I do not think so.

The claim that political philosophy is dead is in many ways a superficial one because it hinges upon a particular, and, I would argue, an excessively narrow conception of what political philosophy is. If one insists that political philosophy *must* consist of a set of political prescriptions which are rooted in and inferred from an elaborate and general philosophical apparatus of a metaphysical and/or ontological sort, then, of course, contemporary political philosophy which is not for the most part a resuscitation of the classics is hard to find. In short, if Plato and Hegel are the paradigms, then political philosophy (since 1900 or so) *is* dead. A man must on this analysis be a philosopher first (in the sense of logical priority) in order to be a political philosopher at all.

This definition is, however, an anachronous one; it demands of the political thinker a style of argument which is no longer intellectually available. I would argue instead for what might be called a functional definition of political philosophy. Political philosophy is always a set of recommendations about how men should engage in politics.[3] Men have always and will always have questions concerning the proper way to organize politically and the criteria of proper decision in a political context. Whoever undertakes to answer such questions by a careful and yet general analysis of their meaning and the consequences of deciding them one way or another is a political philosopher.

The political philosopher is very often less an observer of the political process than a special kind of participant in it.[4] All men who are engaged in politics, whether as leaders or as followers, have as their prime problems matters of choice, matters of value. The political philosopher is a member of society who allocates his resources and his energies toward the articulation of answers to these questions of choice and value. In short, he tries to help people who have choices to make to make them intelligently. The political scientist, who by his own definition is the dispassionate observer of the political process, speaks primarily to other political scientists. The political philosopher, on the other hand, speaks only incidentally to political scientists and, for that matter, only incidentally to other political philosophers; he speaks primarily to human beings. Modern professional criticism of political writing inclines to use the fact that an author states preferences as a reason for the most severe condemnation. It is, however, grossly unfair to so condemn a man who intends to

---

[3]See my *The Logic of Democracy* (New York: Holt, Rinehart & Winston, 1962), pp. 67–86.

[4]See the illuminating essay by Leo Strauss, "On Classical Political Philosophy," in *What Is Political Philosophy?*

state preferences; it is only fair if the support which he offers is inadequate.

Political philosophy will never die for the simple reason that it is far too important for men in society. It has, to be sure, been quieted by modern methodological proscriptions, and it is for just this reason that political philosophy appears in places which by former standards seem odd. There is little in twentieth-century political literature which those (and this includes opponents of political philosophy as well as supporters) who adhere to a classical conception would recognize as political philosophy. This is because the old mode of argument no longer convinces either the would-be political philosopher himself or his intended audience. The intellectual world in general has changed, and it would be foolishness not to suppose that political philosophy has (and should have) also changed. Leo Strauss gets at this point quite sharply (although, perhaps, unintentionally) in the following introductory passage in his *Natural Right and History:*

> The issue of natural rights presents itself today as a matter of party allegiance. Looking around us, we see two hostile camps, heavily fortified and strictly guarded. One is occupied by the liberals of various descriptions, the other by the Catholic and non-Catholic disciples of Thomas Aquinas. But both armies and, in addition, those who prefer to sit on the fences or hide their heads in the sand are, to heap metaphor on metaphor, in the same boat. They are all modern men. We are all in the grip of the same difficulty. Natural right in its classic form is connected with a teleological view of the universe. All natural beings have a natural end, natural destiny, which determines what kind of operation is good for them. In the case of man, reason is required for discerning these operations; reason determines what is by nature right with ultimate regard to man's natural end. The teleological view of the universe, of which the teleological view of man forms a part, would seem to have been destroyed by modern natural science. From the point of view of Aristotle—and who could dare to claim to be a better judge in this matter than Aristotle?—the issue between the mechanical and the teleological conception of the universe is decided by the manner in which the problem of the heavens, the heavenly bodies, and their motion is solved. Now in this respect, which from Aristotle's own point of view was the decisive one, the issue seems to have been decided in favor of the nonteleological conception of the universe. Two opposite conclusions could be drawn from this momentous decision. According to one, the nonteleological conception of the universe must be followed up by a nonteleological conception of human life. But this "naturalistic" solution is exposed to grave difficulties; it seems to be impossible to give an adequate account of human ends by conceiving of them merely as posited by desires or impulses. Therefore, the alternative solution has prevailed. This means that people were forced to accept a fundamental, typically modern, dualism of a nonteleological natural science and a teleological science of man. This is the position which the modern followers of Thomas Aquinas, among others, are forced to take, a position

which presupposes a break with the comprehensive view of Aristotle as well as that of Thomas Aquinas himself. The fundamental dilemma, in whose grip we are, is caused by the victory of modern natural science. An adequate solution to the problem of natural right cannot be found before this basic problem has been solved.[5]

If the world could still reasonably be conceived in terms of the comprehensive teleological view[6] of Aristotle or St. Thomas, modern man could without difficulty write political philosophy on the Aristotelian model. As Strauss suggests, however, such political philosophy is only possible as a consequence of a considerable act of will. Modern man, with, of course, some notable exceptions, is unwilling to ignore the character of the natural world or unwilling to accept the radical separation, characteristic of contemporary Aristotelians, of it from the human world. Thus, for post-positivist, post-existentialist modern man political philosophy poses a new problem, a problem which may legitimately be met by an unusual mode of discourse.

Albert Camus is modern man par excellence. For him political philosophy was no mere academic exercise. He was drawn to its problems, as were the classics, by the political turmoil and crisis of his times. Like Plato, his major task as an intellectual became the search for reasons which would support the restoration of order and justice. In many ways, however, Camus's task was a more difficult one, for he was faced to a degree that Plato was not with the persuasive negations contained in the philosophy of his immediate predecessors. Where Plato had the sophists, Camus had the romantics, the atheistic existentialists, the Hegelians, the Marxists, the surrealists, the positivists, and nihilists of all varieties.

There is no point in attempting to deny that Camus's fundamental approach to the world was that of the artist. Aesthetics posed a continuing problem for him from his earliest essays composed in his early twenties to his final works. He repeatedly denied that he was a philosopher, but this, I think it is clear, meant that he did not see himself primarily as a metaphysician. In somewhat the same way Wittgenstein would surely have denied being a philosopher had the category been defined exclusively in terms of the work of a Thomas Aquinas or a Hegel. Camus made no attempt to write his own *Being and Nothingness* and he

[5]Chicago: University of Chicago Press, 1953, pp. 7–8.
[6]For a good discussion of modern physics and Aristotelian teleological physics see F. S. C. Northrop in Werner Heisenberg, *Physics and Philosophy* (New York: Harper & Bros., 1958), pp. 1–26. For an illuminating commentary on the teleological view of nature see Stephen Toulmin, *Foresight and Imagination: An Enquiry into the Aims of Science* (Bloomington: Indiana University Press, 1961), pp. 62–82.

surely harbored no desire to do so. Camus himself was, I think, caught in the difficulties of definition which we discussed earlier. To a Frenchman, even more than to an American or an Englishman, philosophy means metaphysics and ontology.

Even though all of this is true, Camus's art, his numerous essays, and what may reasonably be called his treatises can only be understood in terms of an overriding concern which is distinctly philosophical. "The important thing," says Camus in the introductory pages of *The Rebel*, is "the world being what it is, to know how to live in it." Camus's thought began on the theme of the encounter between man and the universe, but the theme soon became the encounter between man and state. His search was for a permanent standard of value, for a place to stand when viewing and interacting with the natural and political universe.

Albert Camus was born in Mondovi, Algeria, on November 7, 1913. His father was a French agricultural worker who was killed in World War I. His mother was of Spanish origin. Camus did graduate work in philosophy at the University of Algiers. His financial situation during his student days was a difficult one—he worked at various times as a meteorologist, an auto supply salesman, for the *Préfecture*, and for a shipbroker's concern. His degree of *études supérieures* was awarded after completion of a thesis relating Christianity and Hellenism. He was in his early years an enthusiastic athlete, excelling particularly in swimming, but his athletic activities were curtailed and his doctoral studies terminated by tuberculosis which for a time put him close to death.

Camus exhibited an early interest in the theater; he organized a theater group as a student at Algiers and like Molière acted, directed, and wrote for it. Some years later Camus traveled as a vagabond throughout Italy, Spain, and Czechoslovakia. His earliest meditative essays reflect his early travels. He became a journalist in Algiers and, after 1939, in Paris where he ultimately joined the *Résistance*. He published anonymous essays and editorials and finally became editor-in-chief of the newspaper *Combat*, a position he held until 1945; after which he continued to publish editorials. His first, and most famous, novel, *The Stranger*, appeared in 1942, although it had been written some years earlier in Algiers. *The Myth of Sisyphus*, his first extensive philosophical essay, was published in 1943, and his widely acclaimed plays *The Misunderstanding* and *Caligula* appeared shortly after. In 1947 came *The Plague*, a novel which established Camus as perhaps *the* dominant figure in postwar French letters. He published a large number of articles and editorials in the years following the war, and in 1951 the work which marks him most clearly as a political philosopher, the lengthy essay *The*

Rebel, appeared. His final major novel, *The Fall,* came in 1956. In 1957 Albert Camus was awarded the Nobel Prize for Literature, and on January 4, 1960, he was killed in an automobile accident.

This brief summary marks out the high points of a remarkable life, but it gives no answer to the question, "Was it the life of a political philosopher?" For this we shall have to look with care into Camus's work itself.

Examining Camus as a philosopher raises the perhaps unimportant, but nonetheless unavoidable, question, "Was he an existentialist?" The question is interesting, because while Camus is quite frequently classed, particularly by American and British critics, as an existentialist, he himself repeatedly denied any such association. The problem, of course, is peculiarly difficult because no one is quite sure what an existentialist is. The dimensions of the category vary, depending on who is doing the categorizing, all the way from the most broad, which is likely to include Socrates and Jesus, to the very narrow self-definitions of certain recent writers who are inclined to include only themselves. Camus apparently objected to his own inclusion primarily on two grounds.[7] He did not want to associate himself with the militant atheism of Sartre and he could not accept the traditional existentialist doctrine that existence precedes essence. Camus ultimately comes to stand upon an implicit, if not quite explicit, conception of a universal human nature; thus, arguing, even if not in the classical sense, that essence precedes existence.

It is, however, quite certain that Camus deals centrally with problems defined by existentialism from a perspective very much like that of existentialist philosophers from Kierkegaard to Sartre. His philosophical point of departure is the fact of individual, personal existence. For Camus the brute fact for every man is that he exists and the world exists, and any sort of philosophizing which attempts to explain this fact away or to minimize its importance is either destructive or irrelevant to the human situation. A corollary of great significance is that Camus brings no analytical presupposition of a rigid distinction between reason and emotion to philosophical problems. It is this aspect of his thought, and of existentialist thought generally, which is most bothersome to Anglo-American readers.[8] When Camus makes what he describes as a logical move, it is often not merely logical in an Anglo-American sense, but emotional (again in an Anglo-American sense) as well. A logical conclusion usually involves a commitment as well, and what a British moral philosopher of linguistic bent might regard as a "reasonable commitment" is for Camus a matter of logic. If this is puzzling, as it may very well be, it

[7] Henri Peyre, "Camus the Pagan" in Germaine Bree (ed.), *Camus: A Collection of Critical Essays* (Englewood Cliffs, N. J.: Prentice-Hall, Inc., 1962), pp. 65–70.

[8] See for example, A. J. Ayer, "Novelist-Philosophers," *Horizon,* March, 1946.

hopefully will become more clear as we proceed. There is little connection between Camus's notion of "truth" of "significance" and the verifiability theory of meaning.

Thus, while Camus's thought exhibits significant differences from what may be called the conventional existentialist position, he is nonetheless very much in the tradition of Kierkegaard, Nietzsche, Heidegger, and Sartre. If a label is demanded, I would suggest "post-existentialist," for in many ways the whole purpose of Camus's investigations is to create a new and positive moral position by solving the existentialist dilemma.

One further introductory question needs to be considered: what is the relationship between Camus's explicitly philosophical essays and his novels and plays? There are three possible positions. The first is that there is no connection at all, or at least no significant connection. Camus was a writer; he wrote novels, plays, articles, editorials, and essays. He was a man of diverse interests and diverse talents, and the only thing which connects his diverse production is that it happened to be written by the same man. No commentator that I have read explicitly takes this view, although it is surely not prima facie an unreasonable one. Because Camus's reputation is primarily literary, most of the work done on him (and there is a great deal) is by literary critics or academic teachers of French literature. They are inclined to abstract his plays and novels from his other work and, thus, to take implicitly an interpretative position quite like the one just described. My own judgment is that such a view is inadequate, and I shall try to support it in a moment. One fact, I think, is most important in this connection: Camus was trained as a philosopher; most of his interpreters were not.

The second position is that Camus's essays are important, but only in a secondary way, that is, his essays are mere explications of his novels and plays. Such a view, when it is advanced, is generally directed at *The Myth of Sisyphus*, and, indeed, it is only in this connection that it makes any sense at all.[9] *The Myth*, it is suggested, is simply an expository formulation of the themes advanced in *The Stranger*, that is, both concern what Camus called "the absurd." Even if this were the whole truth, which I think it is not, no similar account could sensibly be given for *The Rebel*. *The Rebel* is certainly related to the novel, *The Plague*, and the plays, *The State of Siege* and *The Just Assassins*, but if anything the literary works are dramatic explications of the philosophical work.

This brings us to the third position—that Camus's philosophical concerns and therefore his philosophical essays are primary—which seems to me most accurate. In what is in many ways the best full-length critical

[9]Jean-Paul Sartre, "An Explication of *The Stranger*," in Bree (ed.), *Camus: A Collection of Critical Essays*, pp. 108–121.

study of Camus, Thomas Hanna, who, significantly, is trained in philosophy and theology, makes these prefatory remarks:

> As one of the greatest of living French novelists, it is Camus' curious
> misfortune that the success of his novels has obscured the fact that he is
> primarily a philosopher who has projected this concern into all of his works.
> Until the scope of his thought is understood it will not be possible to appre-
> ciate fully the power and importance of his total works. . . . Only by under-
> standing Camus first as a philosopher can we fully appraise his literary works,
> for these literary works are part of a more general philosophical position
> and must be related to it.[10]

Hanna's perspective is on the whole a sound one, and what follows is
written in its spirit.

Camus's early philosophizing was not directed primarily at social or
political matters; his concern was, rather, highly personal. He opens *The
Myth of Sisyphus* with a paragraph which shows his problem as personal
and emotional as well as logical:

> There is but one truly serious philosophical problem, and that is suicide.
> Judging whether life is or is not worth living amounts to answering the
> fundamental question of philosophy. All the rest—whether or not the world
> has three dimensions, whether the mind has nine or twelve categories—comes
> afterwards. These are games; one must first answer. And if it is true, as
> Nietzsche claims, that a philosopher, to deserve our respect, must preach by
> example, you can appreciate the importance of that reply, for it will precede
> the definitive act. These are facts the heart can feel; yet they call for careful
> study before they become clear to the intellect.[11]

It is by no means unusual to pose "whether or not life is worth living"
as a philosophical question, but it is surely a bit peculiar to focus on the
question in terms of the problem of suicide. Camus's real interest is not in
the phenomenon of suicide, but rather in the validity of a nihilist
philosophical position. For Camus the modern world is above all marked
off by "the death of God" in Nietzsche's sense. Traditional theological and
philosophical standards which gave meaning to the world and to the life
of man are no longer intellectually available to modern man, or, to be
more precise, what would have to be called, from Camus's point of view,
"clear-thinking modern man." The modern world has become, in a way
which Camus catalogues at length in *The Myth*, a nihilist world. The nihilist position is purported to follow from man's increased awareness of
the irrationality of the universe. When man confronts the world lucidly,
he can find no meaning; he finds instead what Camus, like the existentia-

---

[10]*The Thought and Art of Albert Camus* (Chicago: Regnery, 1958), pp. viii–ix.
[11]From *The Myth of Sisyphus* by Albert Camus, translated by Justin O'Brien.
© Copyright 1955 by Alfred A. Knopf, Inc. Reprinted by the permission of the
publisher and Hamish Hamilton, London.

lists before him, calls "the absurd." If "the absurd" in truth leads to a nihilist position, it must answer the question "Is life worth living?" in the negative and, thus, suicide becomes the proper logical alternative. It is in this sense that suicide becomes the primary philosophical problem—"The subject of this essay is precisely this relationship between the absurd and suicide, the exact degree to which suicide is a solution to the absurd."[12]

The notion of "the absurd" first makes its appearance at the level of feeling; it is a matter of emotional response. From a philosophical point of view, it has, as Camus suggests, "a ridiculous beginning." Man becomes abruptly aware of the absence of sense in the fundamental rules and habits which guide his life. "It happens," says Camus, "that the stage sets collapse."

> Rising, streetcar, four hours in the office or the factory, meal, streetcar, four hours at work, meal, sleep, and Monday Tuesday Wednesday Thursday Friday and Saturday according to the same rhythm—this path is easily followed most of the time. But one day the "why" arises and everything begins in weariness tinged with amazement. "Begins"—this is important. Weariness comes at the end of the acts of a mechanical life, but at the same time it inaugurates the impulse of consciousness. It awakens consciousness and provokes what follows. What follows is the gradual return into the chain or it is the definitive awakening. At the end of the awakening comes in time, the consequence: suicide or recovery.[13]

The condition of being "well adjusted," of being at home in the world, is for Camus a consequence of human mental construction either conscious and deliberate or unconscious and habitual. The absurd arises when it becomes clear that the arrangement of compatibility between man and the world is not truth but construction.

> At the heart of all beauty lies something inhuman, and these hills, the softness of the sky, the outline of these trees at this very minute lose the illusory meaning with which we had clothed them, henceforth more remote than a lost paradise. The primitive hostility of the world rises up to face us across millennia. For a second we cease to understand it because for centuries we have understood in it solely the images and designs that we had attributed to it beforehand, because henceforth we lack the power to make use of that artifice. The world evades us because it becomes itself again. That stage scenery masked by habit becomes again what it is. It withdraws at a distance from us.[14]

Camus does not for a moment pretend that there is anything startling or original about these observations; they have, of course, often been noted by a wide variety of thinkers. But Camus, as we suggested earlier,

[12]Camus, *The Myth of Sisyphus*, p. 5.
[13]Camus, *The Myth of Sisyphus*, p. 10.
[14]Camus, *The Myth of Sisyphus*, p. 11.

is inclined to relate the emotional to the logical, and thus he here introduces an acute epistemological analysis by a description of an emotional reaction. Similarly, his conclusion involves both logic and a commitment to act in a certain way.

Camus's position which I have, perhaps a bit inappropriately, called epistemological is one of the inadequacy and fallibility of the human mind. "Of whom and of what indeed can I say: 'I know that!' This heart within me I can feel, and I judge that it exists. This world I can touch, and I likewise judge that it exists. There ends all my knowledge, and the rest is construction."[15] His reaction to the teachings of natural science is particularly acute:

> You describe [the world] to me and you teach me to classify it. You enumerate its laws and in my thirst for knowledge I admit that they are true. You take apart its mechanism and my hope increases. At the final stage you teach me that this wondrous and multicolored universe can be reduced to the atom and that the atom itself can be reduced to the electron. All this is good and I wait for you to continue. But you tell me of an invisible planetary system in which electrons gravitate around a nucleus. You explain this world to me with an image. I realize then that you have been reduced to poetry: I shall never know. . . . I realize that if through science I can seize phenomena and enumerate them, I cannot, for all that, apprehend the world. Were I to trace its entire relief with my finger, I should not know any more. And you give me the choice between a description that is sure but that teaches me nothing and hypotheses that claim to teach me but that are not sure.[16]

Camus translates a hazy emotional response into a sharply analytical description of the context in which all men operate, or, in language closer to the tone of Camus's remarks, of "the human condition." This context or condition has three parts. There is man, there is the world, and there is that which relates man and the world, that which at once makes the world inscrutable and human mind fallible. This "absurd" situation is for Camus simply given; it is the one truth that is certain; it is the place to start philosophical analysis. Moreover,

> The immediate consequence is also a rule of method. The odd trinity brought to light in this way is certainly not a startling discovery. But it resembles the data of experience in that it is both infinitely simple and infinitely complicated. Its first distinguishing feature in this regard is that it cannot be divided. To destroy one of its terms is to destroy the whole. There can be no absurd outside the human mind. Thus, like everything else, the absurd ends with death. But there can be no absurd outside this world either. And it is by this elementary criterion that I judge the notion of the absurd to be essential and consider that it can stand as the first of my truths. The rule of method alluded to above appears here. If I judge that a thing

[15]Camus, *The Myth of Sisyphus*, p. 14.
[16]Camus, *The Myth of Sisyphus*, p. 15.

is true, I must preserve it. If I attempt to solve a problem, at least I must not by that very solution conjure away one of the terms of the problem. For me the sole datum is the absurd.[17]

Camus suggests three ways of dealing with the absurd: suicide, hope, or living with it. Camus rejects the alternative of suicide because it is an escape from, rather than a solution to, the problem of the absurd; suicide eliminates the problem, it does not solve it. The alternative of hope comes in effect to the same thing; it is, as Camus very acutely suggests, philosophical suicide. Hope is found in an alleged solution to the absurd which lies beyond knowledge. It may be "God" or "history" or "reason," but such a solution again does not solve the problem, it eliminates it by arguments for which there is insufficient evidence. Here Camus is sharply critical of the existentialists who urge a leap into the irrational. The absurd being the only truth, the essence of the human situation, the only proper alternative is to live with it. He later cogently summarized his argument in the introductory passages of *The Rebel:*

> The final conclusion of absurdist reasoning is, in fact, the repudiation of suicide and the acceptance of the desperate encounter between human inquiry and the silence of the universe. Suicide would mean the end of this encounter, and the absurdist reasoning considers that it could not consent to this without negating its own premises. According to absurdist reasoning, such a solution would be the equivalent of flight or deliverance. But it is obvious that absurdism hereby admits that human life is the only necessary good since it is precisely life that makes this encounter possible and since, without life, the absurdist wager would have no basis.[18]

At core Camus's argument is an affirmation of the value of human life, and there is surely nothing very startling about this conclusion. What is important is the *way* in which he argues for this conclusion. He speaks quite consciously as modern man for whom the traditional arguments are unavailable. His discussion is neither idle nor academic; one almost gets the feeling that he is personally trying to decide whether to commit suicide or not. To be able to live without appeal to the transcendental or the suprarational—this is his objective. He tries to show that so-called nihilist premises do not lead to nihilist conclusions, and he speaks therefore directly to those for whom the nihilist premises appear sound.

So far this is but a solution to a personal problem—whether my own life is worth living in the light of the absurd. But it cannot remain merely personal, for to refuse death in the name of the absurd is one thing, but to *live* in the name of the absurd is another. Living is a social problem, and Camus must therefore turn to social philosophy. His efforts are at first

[17]Camus, *The Myth of Sisyphus*, p. 23.
[18]Camus, *The Rebel* (New York: Alfred A. Knopf, Inc., 1956), p. 6.

quite unsure; it is almost as if he experiments in literature. Can society be properly regulated by an abstract set of absolute moral and legal norms? This, it seems to me, is certainly one, if not *the*, important question of his celebrated novel, *The Stranger*. It should be noted that the critics have not read it in these terms, but it seems to me one of the most persuasive indictments of the notion of objective liability in criminal law ever written. The protagonist, a man who could not be more ordinary, finds himself in a set of circumstances which culminate in his killing a man. From the reader's standpoint it is clearly not a case of murder, but from inside the story and particularly from the point of view of the law and its application, it is murder, and the protagonist is sentenced to death. Camus sharply portrays the contrast between life as it is and the objective norms which seek to regulate it.

Can society, on the contrary, be governed by the absurd? Camus's first major play, *Caligula*, is directed at this question. The emperor Caligula starts with the absurdist premise "since there is no right or wrong, everything is permitted" and proceeds to rule by mere personal whim. Camus's dramatic and philosophical suggestion at the end of the play is that everything is not permitted and that the absurd carries within itself what Camus calls "limits."

The problem of the consequences of the absurd becomes for Camus more directly and immediately political with the Nazi occupation. His four remarkable short essays which he called "Letters to a German Friend" are written in this context. The potential consequences of nihilism had become actual, and for Camus the problem was therefore all the sharper. His reaction here is more from the heart than from the mind, but it suggests what is to come. He addresses his "German friend" in part as follows:

> For a long time we both thought that this world had no ultimate meaning and that consequently we were cheated. I still think so in a way. But I came to different conclusions from the ones you used to talk about, which, for so many years now, you have been trying to introduce into history. I tell myself now that if I had really followed your reasoning, I ought to approve what you are doing. And this is so serious that I must stop and consider it, during this summer night so full of promises for us and of threats for you.
>
> You never believed in the meaning of this world, and you therefore deduced the idea that everything was equivalent and that good and evil could be defined according to one's wishes. You supposed that in the absence of any human or divine code the only values were those of the animal world —in other words, violence and cunning. Hence you concluded that man was negligible and that his soul could be killed, that in the maddest of histories the only pursuit for the individual was the adventure of power and his only morality, the realism of conquests. And, to tell the truth, I, believing I thought as you did, saw no valid argument to answer you except a fierce

love of justice which, after all, seemed to me as unreasonable as the most sudden passion.

Where lay the difference? Simply that you readily accepted despair and I never yielded to it. Simply that you saw the injustice of our condition to the point of being willing to add to it, whereas it seemed to me that man must exalt justice in order to fight against eternal injustice, create happiness in order to protest against the universe of unhappiness. Because you turned your despair into intoxication, because you freed yourself from it by making a principle of it, you were willing to destroy man's works and to fight him in order to add to his basic misery. Meanwhile, refusing to accept that despair and that tortured world, I merely wanted men to rediscover their solidarity in order to wage war against their revolting fate.

As you see, from the same principle we derived quite different codes, because along the way you gave up the lucid view and considered it more convenient (you would have said a matter of indifference) for another to do your thinking for you and for millions of Germans. Because you were tired of fighting heaven, you relaxed in that exhausting adventure in which you had to mutilate souls and destroy the world. In short, you chose injustice and sided with the gods. Your logic was merely apparent.

I, on the contrary, chose justice in order to remain faithful to the world. I continue to believe that this world has no ultimate meaning. But I know that something in it has a meaning and that is man, because he is the only creature to insist on having one. This world has at least the truth of man, and our task is to provide its justifications against fate itself. And it has no justification but man; hence he must be saved if we want to save the idea we have of life. With your scornful smile you will ask me: what do you mean by saving man? And with all my being I shout to you that I mean not mutilating him and yet giving a chance to the justice that man alone can conceive.[19]

But what kind of rational defense is to be offered for what Camus here calls "justice"? Clearly no Platonic argument can be relevant for a man who holds "the absurd" as the only truth. Camus had suggested in *The Myth of Sisyphus* that one of the consequences of the absurd was what he called "revolt." This notion of revolt became the principal vehicle of his developing political philosophy. He experimented with it in his plays *The State of Siege* and *The Just Assassins* and in his complex novel *The Plague*, and everywhere he seemed to reach with difficulty and often with something less than clarity a notion that "revolt" implied "limit," or, in other words, some standard of positive value.

In his essay *The Rebel* he takes on this problem squarely. He settles here, again in a way foreign to any Anglo-American philosopher, on the problem of murder. Where suicide, the personal matter, was formerly the problem, he argues, now murder, the social question, is the problem. Camus's argument is complex and difficult, and any summary is likely to

[19]Albert Camus, *Resistance, Rebellion, and Death* (New York: Alfred A. Knopf, Inc., 1961), pp. 27–29.

be rather shallow, but let me with this warning attempt to suggest in a few words what Camus uses many to show. If the absurd leads to the denial of suicide, it affirms the value of life. Such an affirmation means not only refusing to take one's own life, but also refusing to allow anyone else to take it, and, similarly, refusing to take the life of another. From the beginning, then, this refusal or this "revolt" implies a set of limits, but as a matter of history the problem is by no means this simple. Revolt as it occurs historically is revolt against something, that is, revolt against some particular oppression or set of oppressions. Recognition of the absurd leads immediately to the denial of traditional values and to revolt against the historical embodiment of those values, that is, the existing authority, in the name of personal value. Thus, concretely it leads to murder.

Revolt (or, more precisely, "perverted revolt" which Camus calls "rebellion") destroys the old values because they have no value from the absurdist perspective, but as a matter of history seeks to replace them with new values. Thus, murder begins in the name either of the absurd or of new values, and it continues in the name of preserving those new values. The bulk of *The Rebel* is an attempt to describe the perversion of revolt by the creation of the new values of "reason" (in the case of the French Revolution) and "history" (in the case of the Marxist revolution). In short it is an attempt to show the major "revolts" of recent years as "perverted revolt." Revolt in the name of socialism has become, in one of Camus's most memorable phrases, "socialism of the gallows."

But, Camus insists, revolt in the name of life cannot consistently end in murder. This really is the force of *The Rebel:* Revolt when carefully analyzed contains its own limits, not limits which are easily specified, but limits nonetheless. And all this without appeal to the transcendental.

In 1957 Camus published an essay entitled "Reflections on the Guillotine." While the bulk of it is a spine-tingling description of capital punishment in France, it contains also his final and perhaps most succinct statement in support of the rights of man against the state, a subject which had been in many ways his central concern for twenty years. The problem of the modern world is not, says Camus, the sort of murder which the guillotine was invented to punish; that is, "private" murder, a crime against society; but "public" murder, the act of society against the individual. The murders committed by the Nazi state alone are hundreds of times more numerous than all of the "private" murders of the twentieth century. His argument against state-imposed death, what he calls rational murder, hinges on the very fact that he speaks as a modern man. It was once possible, he argues, to reasonably support the death penalty on Christian grounds, for man's judgment even if it were in error could always be superseded by the final judgment of God. But for Camus, modern man has no such excuse:

> For the majority of Europeans, faith is lost. And with it, the justifications faith provided in the domain of punishment. But the majority of Europeans also reject the State idolatry that aimed to take the place of faith. Henceforth in mid-course, both certain and uncertain, having made up our minds never to submit and never to oppress, we should admit at one and the same time our hope and our ignorance, we should refuse absolute law and the irreparable judgment. We know enough to say that this or that major criminal deserves hard labor for life. But we don't know enough to decree that he be shorn of his future—in other words, of the chance we all have of making amends. Because of what I have just said, in the unified Europe of the future the solemn abolition of the death penalty ought to be the first article of the European Code we all hope for.[20]

Here, a bit more explicitly than elsewhere, Camus voices a defense of men against the state, a defense which is in some ways strikingly similar to an argument which might be advanced by a pragmatist. Society has no right to kill in the absence of absolute certainty, first, that it possesses a metaphysical or religious right to do so, and second, that there is no possible doubt in a particular case that there is no error of legal judgment. Given the essentially limited character of human knowledge—both in general, philosophical matters and in the practical details of evidence—neither of these conditions can ever be realized. But Camus's argument is not merely pragmatic; it is a pragmatism enriched by the existential arguments reviewed earlier. Man is not simply the fallible cognitive machine—a sort of inadequately programmed computer—he is also a being aware of imminent death for whom his own fallibility reveals the precious quality of life. It is significant to say that, because we can never be certain that we are completely right, we can never be justified in performing actions as irremedial as taking away a man's life, but it is more significant to affirm simultaneously the value of that life.

Camus's arguments are difficult and by no means always clear or complete. His writing is often beautiful but sometimes merely verbose. But his thought is "to the point" in political philosophy in a way that little else is in our time.

---

[20]Camus, *Resistance, Rebellion, and Death*, pp. 229–230.

Further Readings

Abel, Lionel, "Metaphysical Stalinism," *Dissent*, VIII (2: Spring, 1961), pp. 137–152.

Barrett, William, *Irrational Man: A Study in Existential Philosophy* (Garden City, New York: Doubleday & Company, Inc., 1958).

Cox, Richard H., "Ideology, History and Political Philosophy: Camus' *L'Homme Révolté*," *Social Research*, XXXII (2: Spring, 1965), pp. 71–97.

Gargan, Edward T., "Revolution and Morale in the Formative Thought of Albert Camus," *The Review of Politics*, XXV (4: October, 1963), pp. 483–496.

Hochberg, Herbert, "Albert Camus and the Ethic of Absurdity, *Ethics*, LXXV (2: January, 1965), pp. 87–102.

Kaplan, Abraham, "Existentialism," in Abraham Kaplan, *The New World of Philosophy* (New York: Random House, 1961), pp. 97–128.

Lichtheim, George, "Sartre, Marxism and History," *History and Theory*, III (2: 1963), pp. 222–246.

Micaud, Charles, *Communism and the French Left* (New York: Praeger, 1963).

Novack, George, ed. with Introduction, *Existentialism versus Marxism* (New York: Dell Publishing Co., 1966).

Sartre, Jean-Paul, *Search for a Method* (New York: Alfred A. Knopf, 1963).

Thody, Philip, *Albert Camus: A Study of His Work* (London: Hamish Hamilton; New York: The Macmillan Company, 1957).

Part III

VALUE JUDGMENTS IN POLITICAL THOUGHT

Modern political scientists have attempted to avoid value judgments in the thought that thereby they can more nearly approximate knowledge of reality. Recognizing the restrictive impact of the value judgments of predecessors in their field of study, they have striven for objectivity. This striving has taken the form of a conscious attempt to broaden the field of study and to suspend judgment. By a factual description of what is—that is, by the compilation of facts—they hope to build a basis for a discipline that will lead to valid knowledge of politics. Arnold Brecht described the trend through the early twentieth century in political theory as one "away from 'dogma'—from religious dogma as well as from dogmas of national tradition or of personal conviction—and on to 'reality.'"[1]

The troubled attitude with which modern political scholars write about evaluative statements seems unwarranted. The fact that value judgments are significant data should cause no concern: Value judgments are data just as facts are data, and both are to be treated as

[1]Arnold Brecht, *Political Theory: The Foundations of Twentieth-Century Political Thought* (Princeton, New Jersey: Princeton University Press, 1959), p. 5.

objects of investigation. That both facts and values are perceived by an individual who makes statements about them is a complicating factor, for we must then consider whether every statement—either factual or valuational—is subjective in the selective perception of the person making the statement and therefore presupposes a value judgment. Also, that both facts and value judgments are data and proper objects of scientific investigation does not imply that political thought necessarily contains value assumptions. Whether or not this latter is true must be considered on other grounds, which will shortly be examined.

First, note the distinction between fact and value judgments. Consider the statements, This man is good and This man is six feet tall. Are they fundamentally different kinds of judgments or the same type of judgments? There are three possible answers. The first answer is that all judgments are value judgments. This view, held by philosopher C. I. Lewis, says that even quantitative judgments have intensive value aspects. Second, one can hold that some judgments are value judgments and others are factual judgments. This is the most common position and has been held by many philosophers (for example, Dewitt Parker). Finally, it is possible to hold that all judgments are factual, but it is doubtful that anyone has held strictly to this position.

It matters very little which of the first two positions one assumes. Essentially the same important problem exists in both views, that of determining the value assumptions—tacit or explicit—in a given political theory. It is evident that this problem exists for those holding that there are two kinds of judgments. But the problem of noting important and basic value assumptions exists also for those holding that all judgments are value judgments. This is the important point—rather than that all judgments are value judgments. Hence the distinction between the two approaches is not crucial to political thought.

Another unnecessary concern is that over Hume's famous point that one cannot argue from *is* premises to *ought* conclusions. This is certainly correct. No amount of is statements allows one to infer a conclusion that people ought to do something. That something exists constitutes no justification for its continuance. This situation, however, need not be alarming. Any system can assume an ought statement among its premises. Then one can deduce a conclusion with an *ought* statement. Of course to establish the *ought* premise is another problem— one that must be solved by philosophical criteria such as consistency and study of the reasons given for the premise.

Many political theorists, especially strong empiricists, attempt to write without value assumptions. These value-free advocates face two usual criticisms. First, any political theorist has a certain methodological approach—and this in itself involves the value judgment that this method is best. The most famous example in this regard is the methodology of the logical positivist or behavioralist with its criticized verification theory of meaning. In contrast to this example is the classically oriented political theorist like Strauss who places high value on Plato and Aristotle. A second common criticism arises from the fact that any theory must select certain facts or issues about political life as important. This selection also is in itself a value judgment, namely, whether economic justice, sovereignty, free speech, self-determination, legislative procedures, or some other item is to be of central concern to the particular theorist.

In light of these criticisms and in spite of periodic attempts to work out a value-free approach to political science, the editors contend that all political analysis—from Socrates to Sartre—requires value judgments. If all political treatises are imbued with value statements, then the issue is not how a value-free science can be established; rather, the issues are, first, what value judgments are and must be made, and, second, how the value judgments are to be justified.

15

Gabriel A. Almond

POLITICS, SCIENCE, AND ETHICS*

Gabriel Almond considers the relations between "rationality, science, and ethics" in the light of recent researches and discoveries of the social and psychological sciences. Addressing himself to arguments advanced by William F. Whyte and John H. Hallowell in an earlier controversy on the relationship, Almond criticizes Whyte's view that political scientists "should leave ethics to the philosophers and concern themselves primarily with the description and analysis of political behavior." He distinguishes "concern with detachment and the avoidance of all valuation" from "the scientist's honest concern for objectivity and the methods which are most likely to produce objective results" and asserts that "if science is not to become . . . sterile virtuosity, it must be animated by purpose and devoted to service." Considering the possible view that "men are incapable of rationality" and hence "incapable of ethical behavior, since ethical action is a species of rational action," Almond concludes that when certain "conditions are met, men are capable of that kind of rationality which involves not only the intelligent selection of means, but the intelligent evaluation and modification of ends as well." These preconditions to rationality are "emotional clarity of purpose," availability of "correct data concerning the objective context in which the action is to take place," and "skill in the analysis and interpretation of data." He asserts that the "relationship

*Reprinted by permission of the author and publisher from *American Political Science Review*, XL (2: April, 1946), pp. 283–293.

of science to ethics is not the same for all scientific disciplines" and claims the "practical judgment of 'good and evil' in the area of public policy" as "the special responsibility of the social scientist." "The political scientist and his collaborators in the other social science disciplines," he concludes, "can perform a useful function in judging the relative efficiency and applicability of means." The political scientist may also evaluate the consequences of realizing one value or set of values for other values, and thereby clarify the consequences of particular political choices. Capacity to determine both the efficiency of alternative means and the compatibility of ends is essential to rationality in public policy formation. In his "contribution toward rendering policy formation more rational"—that is, genuinely meet the needs and aspirations of the public—the political scientist is performing an essentially ethical function. His task is to "discover the pathway to 'good' ends. And desiring and influencing so that the 'right path' to the 'good end' is taken, far from being in conflict with his duty as a scientist, is the very essence of his responsibility as a scientist and a man."

1

The recent polemic in the pages of this REVIEW between William F. Whyte and John Hallowell on the relations between politics and ethics raises a familiar and long-standing controversy.[1] Whyte challenges political scientists in the spirit of "scientific detachment" from man's aspirations and strivings, a point of view which attempts to equate the man who follows science as his vocation with science itself. Those aspirations and values which condition and influence the scientist's work, but which are not properly a part of the scientific apparatus, are disposed of as a pastry cook treats that part of the pie dough which does not fit in the tin. Hallowell's reply attacks the logical fallacies of Whyte's argument and discusses some of the implications of this point of view.

It is always justifiable to renew an old controversy if there have been new findings and insights which contribute to a clarification of the issues. The researches and discoveries of the social and psychological sciences during the past decades have thrown some new light on the relations between rationality, science, and ethics. It is rather to bring these findings more sharply to bear upon the controversy than in any spirit of disagreement with the arguments of Hallowell that this article has been written.

[1] Two articles published in *American Political Science Review* a year or two ago stirred a considerable amount of discussion. The first was William F. Whyte, "A Challenge to Political Scientists" (Vol. 37, pp. 692–697, Aug., 1943). The second, by way of a reply, was John H. Hallowell, "Politics and Ethics" (Vol. 38, pp. 639–655, Aug., 1944).

It may be well before proceeding to the main discussion to review briefly the "challenge" of Whyte, and the reply of Hallowell, in order that the progression of the polemic may be clear to the reader. Whyte's arguments may be summarized in the following three points: (1) Too large a proportion of the energies of the political science profession is directed toward the relatively unimportant areas of legal and governmental institutions, and political philosophy. Contrariwise, too little energy is directed toward the study of "informal political processes." (2) More direct contact with politics and politicians is necessary in order to describe the political process adequately. (3) Political scientists ". . . should leave ethics to the philosophers and concern themselves primarily with the description and analysis of political behavior."

We can agree with Whyte's second point without much qualification. Political scientists can, no doubt, learn much from the social anthropologist, and acquire more understanding of political processes through a greater stress on field research in practical politics. But with regard to his first point Whyte appears to be in error, largely because of an ambiguous definition of "politics." There probably has been a disproportionate concentration on legal and administrative problems in political science, but to view these areas as unimportant reflects a regrettable naïveté. One can hardly understand political processes without knowledge of the legal and institutional framework which political movements and pressures are intended to influence. Certainly political processes do not stop at the point where legal and formal political institutions begin. The political process in the narrow sense in which Whyte uses the term is only a part of a larger process. The "struggle for power and prestige" which Whyte views as the essence of politics includes the struggle to influence legislation, administration, and adjudication through which power and prestige and other values may be won. And much valuable work has been done, particularly in recent years, in demonstrating how various types of groups and organizations influence these formal governmental processes.

But it is in his third point that Whyte opens himself to the sharpest criticism. He urges political scientists ". . . to leave ethics to the philosophers and concern themselves primarily with the description and analysis of political behavior." If all Whyte means here is that the value judgments of the political scientists should not be permitted to bias his research and analysis, then there can be no quarrel with him. But one gathers that he means more than this, although, unfortunately, this part of his argument is implicit. He appears to mean that the political scientist should have no ethical purpose animating his work. Thus in an era such as the present he should not be spending his time writing about democracy. Also in his studies of political organization he should not be concerned with eliminating political corruption. Even the description of certain political phenomena as "corruption" Whyte views as a product of the "middle class prejudice" of the political scientist. The manner in which he develops this argument reveals the limitations of his point of view. He endeavors to demonstrate that corruption is neither "good" nor "bad," since machine politics constitutes a channel of advancement for immigrant groups who are at a disadvantage in competition in business and the professions as compared with the more established elements of the population. Consequently, political corruption, though "bad" from the point of view of the "middle classes," may be "good" from the point of view of the immigrant classes of the population. Had Whyte been less inhibited on the score of values and ethical judgments, he might have asked himself whether corruption is really "good" for the immigrant classes. And he might have discovered, as others have discovered before him, that while corruption might be good for those who profit from it, only the merest crumbs in the form of favors and pauperizing charity reach the immigrant masses. Thus he might have concluded that corruption is a totally inadequate way of bringing "power and prestige" to the urban immigrant masses as compared with an efficiently administered system of social legislation and an effectively functioning economy which would assure opportunity to the population as a whole.

In general, Whyte's position with regard to the relation between science and ethics is a product of that "scientificism" which has exercised an unfortunate influence upon the social sciences, particularly since the last war. Hallowell points out quite well that it is an evasion of the scientist's responsibility as a man, even though it parades itself as the only genuine scientific manliness. This concern with detachment and the avoidance of all valuation should not be confused with the scientist's honest concern for objectivity and the methods which are most likely to produce objective results. This unwillingness to be emotionally moved by the conflicts and injustices which move the people whom science is supposed to serve is responsible for those great products of scientific virtuosity which impress the reader or the listener as he might be momentarily impressed by a gifted pianist's playing of a series of cadenzas. Cadenzas are not music. And great displays of methodological or dialectical skill are not science. If science is not to become this type of sterile virtuosity, it must be animated by purpose and devoted to service.

2

Here we are only at the beginning of the problem, and since it is at this point that Whyte and Hallowell join argument, it might be well to summarize the latter's remarks. The summary, of course, does not do justice to the original. He argues: (1) Scientists are continually making value judgments. Behind every work of science, for example, there is an act of choice which rests upon some kind of value determination. Scientists assume the existence of an order of nature, the laws of which can be derived by scientific inquiry and method; (2) The scientific trend represented by Whyte assumes that men are essentially irrational. (Whyte has nowhere stated this explicitly. Hallowell endeavors to refute this by the argument that the scientist who advances this doctrine assumes that he and his readers or listeners are capable of rationality.)

Hallowell's first argument does not in any essential way affect Whyte's position. Whyte might admit that his choice of a problem, even his choice of science as a profession, involves choice or evaluation. He might also admit the metaphysical assumption that there is an order of nature. And still he could assert that the scientist should leave ethics and morals to the philosophers and theologians and confine himself to the analysis of political behavior. It is Hallowell's second point which is the crucial one. For if, as Whyte may believe, human behavior is essentially irrational, then ethical judgments on the part of the scientist are irrelevant. If men are moved by internal and external forces over which they have no control, then social movements and action are mere blind struggles to which neither the scientist nor the philosopher can make a rational or ethical contribution. But Whyte cannot maintain this and at the same time make any claim to rationality himself. His only way out of this dilemma would be to assert that only a small minority, an élite, is capable of rationality. And this position has, as a matter of fact, been urged by persons who have taken a position similar to that of Whyte. Science then comes to have meaning only to the scientist and the small group capable of understanding and utilizing it. It can be of use in enabling him to predict future developments and thereby improve or protect his own position. If Whyte wishes to maintain this "élite" point of view, it is up to him to furnish proof.

The question of man's (and the scientist's) capacity for rationality is the key to the entire argument. For if men are incapable of rationality, they are incapable of ethical behavior, since ethical action is a species of rational action. But neither of our writers has dealt with the question of rationality in any detail. It is here that newer discoveries and insights have thrown light on an age-old controversy.

In a limited sense, all men are capable of rationality if we understand by rationality the capacity to select means leading to desired ends. Any act of conscious choice of an effective means to an end is a rational act. The extent to which this mode of action is employed by individuals, and in different cultures, varies to a considerable degree. In some cultures, for example, traditional action plays a far greater rôle than in our own. In traditional action, not only the ends but the means as well are fixed by custom. But in our culture rational action plays an extremely important rôle. The very facts of social mobility attest to a multitude of conscious choices between means to various ends. And in private life the greater freedom of choice in marriage, in friendship, in housing, occupation, hobbies, and in a host of other relationships and activities reflects the increasing importance of this mode of action in our lives. So that it can hardly be argued in simple terms that men are essentially irrational. The truth of the matter would appear to be that men are both rational and irrational, and typically both at the same time.

The type of rationality which we have been discussing might be called "means rationality." That is, conscious intelligent choice is limited to the action leading to the end or value, and only in a minor way affects the value itself. The value may be the product of "instinct" or "impulse." Rationality may enter into the definition of the value. Typically, all of these and other factors enter into value determination. For example, the value of economic success is a product of tradition. One concentrates his energies toward money-making, because it is the "thing to do." An individual also endeavors to "make money" for the things and satisfactions money can buy. At the same time, one competes with others in "money-making" for the joy of emulation or competition, which some claim has an "instinctive" basis.

However, when the element of rationality or conscious evaluation or choice significantly enters into the definition and determination of the values themselves, we are dealing with a different type of rationality. We might call it "means-end" rationality, or to use Karl Mannheim's expression, "substantial rationality,"[2] or to use a more commonplace expression which has much the same meaning, "enlightened self-interest." An illustration may serve to define this concept more effectively than a formal definition. We might take as examples the contemporary actions of farmers, laborers, and industrialists directed toward breaking the existing price ceilings for their products or services. Through their oganizations, they may direct their energies in a formidably rational manner toward attempting to create that kind of public opinion, and that attitude among public officials, which will permit increases in the particular wages or prices with which they are concerned. The members of the trade union or association may gain an immediate advantage by this means. But should

[2]Karl Mannheim, *Man and Society in the Age of Reconstruction* (New York, 1940), p. 51.

their conduct become generalized, as it is likely to be if they are successful, the short-run advantage would be lost, and a new spiral in the inflationary process would be set in motion. It is only too true, of course, that the consequences of this type of conduct always involve more than those guilty of the responsible actions, and frequently do not immediately and directly affect the guilty at all. But in the long run retribution of a kind comes home to roost. For example, a serious inflation might be a contributing factor to a serious depression which would mean, in effect, unemployment for many laborers and bankruptcy for many farmers and business men. Even worse consequences may in the long run flow from these earlier and later irrational actions, for economic catastrophe breeds movements of political dissatisfaction and desperation. These in turn might lead to excessive nationalism in our foreign policy which might contribute to another world conflict. So that in a sense men who have sought their own short-run interests in what appeared to be "innocent" matters may in the long run bear a share in the responsibility for a renewal of the bloodshed and the costs of war.

What we are dealing with, then, when we speak of "substantial rationality," or "enlightened self-interest," is the use of intelligent choice in the determination of the ends of action as well as in the choice of means. It is, in effect, the capacity to anticipate consequences of action, and to employ the most adequate means in evaluating alternatives. And this leads us logically to our next problem. Under what conditions are men capable of using the most adequate means in evaluating alternative courses of action?

The capacity for "substantial rationality" rests upon a combination of internal and external conditions. From the point of view of individual psychology, there must be relative freedom from unconscious compulsion. It is to the credit of Freud and his followers that they demonstrated the rôle played by unconscious feelings in human conduct. Many students of psychological problems have long given up the Freudian theory that underlying all human conduct are the libidinal and the death instincts or any other combination of definite "basic instincts." From this point of view, for which no satisfactory proof has ever been offered, all behavior is basically irrational or non-rational. Scientific curiosity and interest become "voyeurism," scientific method "anal preoccupation," and the like. All human values are translatable in these terms of the libidinal instinct, or the instinct of destruction, or both in combination. There can be no question of freeing the intellect from the compulsion of these instincts. All values are reduceable to these terms. These unproved hypotheses of Freud and some of his followers have exercised an unfortunate influence on the development of the social sciences. They have proved supports to the attitude of some social scientists that social conflicts are the products of the incurable irrationality of man, and that science can play no rôle in their constructive resolution.

More recent trends in psychology have discarded the biological bias and the instinct theory of Freud, but have retained the concept of the unconscious, and the therapeutic tools developed by psychoanalysis. As defined by such a psychoanalyst as Karen Horney,[3] the unconscious becomes the nervous and emotional "set" acquired by persons through all the influences which have been brought to bear upon them, particularly in the formative period of childhood. Instead of reducing all the traits and tendencies inherent in the biology of man to two "instincts," the assumption is made that man has a variety of biological potentialities, the ends of which are more or less independently valid, and not necessarily derivable from any "basic instincts." Thus the desire of the individual to understand what goes on around him, to act in such a manner as to gain satisfactions of various kinds without impairing his safety, become independently valid ends of action, and not just sublimations of more primitive trends. But as this later psychological tendency is careful to point out, this capacity for what we call rational behavior is only a *potentiality*. Its realization is dependent upon the emotional and nervous condition of the individual. For example, a person who has been rejected in early family life, whose formative years have been spent in a relatively hostile emotional atmosphere, and who has adjusted to this situation by developing into a resentful, withdrawn character, will hardly be capable of thoroughgoing rational behavior in adult life. For in every situation which he meets he will bring his hostile tendencies with him. The efforts which he may make toward friendship, love, occupational satisfaction and success, will be colored by his underlying negative, resentful feelings which will render all of these actions irrational and self-defeating. For, in the field of friendship, one cannot hate and distrust men and at the same time bring them to be fond of one's self, however lonely and needy of response one may become. One can tie persons to one's self by bonds of interest or fear; one can strike up a partnership of resentment with persons of similar tendency; but one cannot win that kind of non-instrumental warmth and affection which all men seek, though many in a twisted and perverse manner. Should such a person seek to make a judgment of a public policy, his choice would be similarly irrational. He would necessarily assume hostility in others. His own feelings would become universal objective data, for an important part of the evidence of how others feel is how we ourselves feel. If such a person should happen

[3]Karen Horney, *The Neurotic Personality of Our Time* (New York, 1937), and *New Ways in Psychoanalysis* (New York, 1939).

to be an industrialist faced with a labor dispute, he would enter the controversy with conflicting ends. On the one hand, as the owner of his enterprise, he would be interested in having a satisfied and productive labor force. On the other hand, as a person motivated by unconscious hostility and resentment, he would be under compulsion to injure and dominate others. Needless to say, under these circumstances an unsatisfactory irrational result would ensue.

In other words, substantially rational behavior is dependent upon a clean and straight intellectual and emotional instrument. It must not be clogged with powerful feelings which are irrelevant to the objective action. There must be an "inner freedom to choose." In positive terms, one must be open to evidence. One must have the capacity to select a policy or an end after having carefully explored the various alternatives and their possible consequences. Necessarily, one will make errors. We can be sure that men will never be able to predict consequences with absolute precision. One can ever strive to perfect the rationality of one's conduct. But rational perfection (which from one point of view is synonymous with ethical perfection) is like beauty—ever beckoning, but ever inaccessible.

In general, the type of character which is capable of substantial rationality is the product of an emotional development in which compulsion has played a minimal rôle. From a positive point of view, it is the product of a constructive fostering of intellectual potentialities which respects the integrity and peculiar qualities of the individual. But this accounts only for the subjective apparatus of rationality, and action involves an objective context. A "proper upbringing" produces only a willingness and a capacity to weigh alternative courses of action. But the execution of a rational action is dependent upon knowledge and understanding of the context of the action.

It was the achievement of Karl Marx that he demonstrated the importance of position in the social structure for the formation of judgments about social phenomena. But as Freud and his followers rode their biological theory out of bounds, Marx and his followers were similarly extremist with their sociological theory. Just as in the case of Freud the individual was defined as the helpless tool of his instincts, so in the case of Marx the individual was defined as the helpless victim of his class interest.[4] Not only this, but the dominant class interest in a society biased the entire apparatus of communication and knowledge, so that a genuine social science (at least in a "class society") was impossible. Although some students of social phenomena continue to operate on the

[4]Charles E. Merriam, *The Rôle of Politics in Social Change* (New York, 1936), p. 13.

assumptions of Marx, some of his constructive insights have been assimilated into the various disciplines. Social scientists now generally recognize that economic and other "interests" bias the judgment of men in general, scientists included. Similarly, many of them recognize that the content of communication is biased by the economic and other interests of those who control the various media. But it is quite a distance from the point of view which holds that economic interest *determines* judgments of social policy to the point of view which holds that these and other interests *affect* such judgments.

We have therefore learned that the data concerning the objective context in which political and social action is fulfilled are biased. But it is difficult to see why persons, where certain conditions are met, cannot correct this bias. In the United States, for example, the means of communication are so numerous and varied in their ownership and direction that it is relatively simple to "correct" for what has been omitted or distorted in the dominant media of communication. It is true, for example, that trade unionists are at the mercy of the press and radio for up to the minute news of labor activity and problems. But any one-sided interpretation can be overcome by direct communication in trade union meetings, or in the labor press. Similarly, bias in the special labor media of communication may be corrected in the non-labor media which reach the trade union as well as the general public. So that the constructive contribution of Marx and others who have dealt with these problems is the recognition of the difficulties of forming objective judgments in a situation in which various "interests" color, select, and distort the evidence which is required if the judgment is to be sound. There is sufficient evidence to prove that not only a "scientific élite," but the rank and file of the population as well, can resist the pressures of propaganda in the dominant conservatively controlled media of communication. As long as the media of communication are sufficiently competitive, rational judgment and action is possible, even though it is rendered more difficult of achievement in a situation of semi-monopolistic control of the more important media in some areas.

Rational judgment and action become possible, then, (1) when the persons involved have an emotional clarity of purpose, and (2) when the correct data concerning the objective context in which the action is to take place are available. A third precondition which has not been stressed here is the factor of skill in the analysis and interpretation of data. Needless to say, there may be clarity of purpose, and correct data, but if skill and experience in evaluating and organizing data are lacking, action may be irrational. One has only to discuss political issues with small children to realize the importance of experience and skill in reasoning and evaluating information in the larger areas of social organization and policy. At the same time, discussion of political issues with small children may similarly illustrate the importance of emotional soundness and clarity, for though they may frequently come out with irrational answers, they sometimes ask disturbingly rational questions. But there is no point in the compass of so brief an article to attempting more than to refer to the problems of skill and method. To the extent that the above conditions are met, men are capable of that kind of rationality which involves not only the intelligent selection of means, but the intelligent evaluation and modification of ends as well.

3

In the contribution of Whyte, political science and ethics are treated as discrete disciplines, having no apparent relationship to one another. Although this is challenged by Hallowell, it will be useful to undertake a further elaboration. The relationship of science to ethics is not the same for all scientific disciplines. The physical[5] and biological sciences, although oriented toward the values of truth and usefulness, are ordinarily not as sciences concerned with problems of public policy. But for the social sciences, and particularly political science, public policy is a primary datum. For the struggles of groups and individuals for control over the instruments of public authority is not only a struggle for power among the leading competitors, but a struggle for public policy. Power, aside from its own satisfactions, is as means to the ends of public policy. The social and political scientist is as much concerned with the analysis of the consequences of different types of public policy as he is concerned with the means employed in the formulation of the policy. And in the analysis of the consequences of the policy it is certainly his job to judge whether a particular policy which has been justified as leading in some manner to the public good actually does so. In this connection, and in specific reply to Whyte, it should be pointed out that the philosopher lacks the knowledge and skill required to deal with these "ethical" problems, while the political scientist, if he is properly trained, has the necessary competence. Rather than leaving "ethics" to the philosophers (who are concerned with these problems only in a doctrinal-historical or logical

[5]This was written before Hiroshima and Nagasaki. The physical scientists these days are deeply involved in problems of public policy, but in a quite different sense from the social scientist. The physicist is not concerned with public policies as scientific data, but as factors affecting his freedom of research. He also views with a growing sense of urgency the effect of his findings on public policy.

sense), practical judgment of "good and evil" in the area of public policy is the special responsibility of the social scientist.

There is no reason why a political scientist who has come to a conclusion that a particular public policy may have dangerous consequences should not make himself articulate on the subject. And if his feelings are strong, there is no reason why he should not become a warm advocate. And there is no reason why warm advocacy and cool objectivity cannot commingle in the same lecture, article, or book. It is true that on the academic platform advocacy is not in place; but the analysis of the consequences of various courses of action is an essential function.

Basically, the reason why the political scientist should be concerned with the consequences of public policy, and particularly with whether the consequences are "good or bad," is that he is a man and partakes of the fate of men. The capacity for warm-hearted sympathy for the fate of individuals, or for groups of men, or for mankind in general, is in no way in conflict with the capacity for scientific objectivity. If his reactions are "healthy," he will be concerned with just these problems which are the matters of social controversy. He will be concerned with the most rational (and therefore the most ethical) solutions of these problems. In the laboratory or in the class-room, he will necessarily operate under the rules of academic freedom which involve a responsibility commensurate with the powers which being on a platform and having an academic status yield. But if he is capable of effective demagogy on the "hustings," where demagogy and not science is in order, then let him speak with whatever eloquence and feeling he can command for the cause which he considers to be good.

Even if the social scientist is unmoved by the events which move his contemporaries (and there are some of us who suffer from this kind of anaesthesia), he may not evade the service which is exacted from him in exchange for his privileges. If not feeling, then "expediency" will indicate that his work must be of some use to his community. It must be related to the community's interests or needs. To be sure, some scientists devote their work to the service of particular "interests," since this yields them the income and prestige with which they are most concerned. They may gain immediate satisfaction and advantage through this means, but by so violating their scientific integrity they bring discredit upon their profession, themselves included. And even in the short run one who perverts his knowledge and skill for the service of a special interest forfeits his right to the highest satisfaction which the pursuit of science can offer—the self-esteem and joy of craftsmanship and creation which only honest work may yield.

If, then, public policy is a primary datum of political science, by what means can that discipline contribute to the success of "good" policy, and the defeat of "bad"?[6] Science cannot create values; these grow out of the needs and aspirations of the people. It can, however, demonstrate how and to what extent alternative public policies contribute to the realization of public values and aspirations. It is a cliché to observe that all groups can agree upon ends if they are stated with sufficient generality. Controversy arises over the question as to which means are the most efficient in leading to these ends. And here the political scientist and his collaborators in the other social science disciplines can perform a useful function in judging the relative efficiency and applicability of means. The political scientist may also play a useful rôle in evaluating the consequences of realizing one value or set of values for other values, and thereby make the consequences of particular political choices clear. It is only when those who exercise public power are capable of determining the efficiency of alternative means, and the compatibility of ends, that rationality in public policy formation becomes possible. The political scientist, by virtue of his training, is qualified to make a contribution toward rendering policy formation more rational—that is, genuinely meet the needs and aspirations of the public. In this sense, his function is an essentially ethical one. For it is his task to discover the pathway to "good" ends. And desiring and influencing so that the "right path" to the "good end" is taken, far from being in conflict with his duty as a scientist, is the very essence of his responsibility as a scientist and a man.

[6]Max Weber, *Gesammelte Aufsätze zur Wissenschaftslehre* (Tübingen, J. C. B. Mohr, 1922), particularly "Wissenschaft als Beruf."

16

Alfred Cobban

ETHICS
AND THE DECLINE
OF POLITICAL THEORY*

Alfred Cobban observes that as the "conditions of social life alter" and
the "words we use, and the ideas they convey, lose old meanings and
acquire new ones," a "continual restatement of political principles is
both necessary and inevitable" if the "tradition of political thinking"
characteristic of Western civilization is to remain alive. Periodically in
Western intellectual history there have been syntheses by great political
thinkers, but "no such synthesis has appeared in our own day or for
some time past." Cobban is much concerned by this lack: "coins can
remain valid currency even when they are worn quite smooth," but
"political ideas need periodical recoining if they are to retain their
value." He thinks that political theory has become an academic discipline "disengaged from political facts," whereas formerly it was "the
work of men intently concerned with practical issues." Men concerned
with practical issues do not strive for "academic impartiality" but rather
strive to arrive at a judgment that one form of political activity is
"better than another." Cobban thinks that "modern political theory has
largely ceased to be discussed in terms of what ought to be" and he
surmises that this change is because political theory "has fallen under

*Reprinted by permission from *Political Science Quarterly*, LXVIII (3:
September, 1953), pp. 321–337, where it was entitled "The Decline of Political Theory."

the influence of two modes of thought which have had a fatal effect on its ethical content": history and science. The historian "sees all ideas and ways of behavior as historically conditioned and transient." His standard of value for an institution is its survival power. The scientist attempts "to show how things happen, and why, in the nexus of cause and effect, they *do* happen": it "is not the function of science to pass ethical judgments." Cobban contends that "rightly or wrongly the human mind demands something more than living from trough to snout." He calls for reintroduction of "the idea of purpose . . . into political thinking"—for resumption of "that 'continuous transformation of morals into politics,' in which, according to Croce, lies 'the real ethical progress of mankind.'"

Political theory is not a progressive science. At least, anyone who puts, say, Aristotle's *Politics* beside the political writings of the twentieth century could be excused if he thought that progress in the subject was imperceptible. A cynic might even argue that everything that is worth saying on political theory has already been said *ad nauseam,* and draw the conclusion that it is time we gave up such wearisome reiteration. But this view would be false, because if political ideas do not progress, their formulation certainly changes. The conditions of social life alter, sometimes more slowly and sometimes more rapidly, in the last few centuries at an increasingly dizzy pace; and as they alter, the words we use, and the ideas they convey, lose old meanings and acquire new ones. For this reason a continual restatement of political principles is both necessary and inevitable—as long, that is, as the tradition of political thinking, which is one of the peculiar characters of Western civilization, remains alive.

It is a tradition with a history of some two and a half millennia, though with one considerable break. Century after century the political ideas of the Western World have undergone progressive modification. The interplay of idea with institution has changed now one and now the other, and the flow of ideas has been punctuated at intervals by the synthesis created by a great political thinker. No such synthesis has appeared in our own day or for some time past, but this is not surprising. Great political thinkers cannot be produced to order, and we would not wail and beat our breasts because there is no contemporary Burke or Bentham. If a general tendency to cease thinking about society in terms of political theory were to be observable, that would be a matter of greater significance than the mere fact that there are no intellectual giants in the field of political theory today. I propose to suggest that there *is* such a tendency.

The view that our cherished political ideas may be capable of dying will naturally meet with opposition, yet there is nothing impossible in such a development. Political ideas are not immortal, however we try to identify them with eternal values. Conscious of our own mortality, we cling all the more to the belief that there must be something presiding over our destinies which is eternal. There may be, but it is not likely to be the little gods of our own creation, whether we call them Imperial Rome, or Divine Right of Kings, or even Democracy. The belief in the permanence of such ideas is only another form of the sophism of the ephemeral—the faith of Fontenelle's rose, which nodded its head and proclaimed in the wisdom of a day that gardeners were immortal, for no gardener had ever died within the memory of a rose. Ideas grow and decay, change into new forms and are reborn. It would be a cause for amazement if the process of continuous transformation were to come to an end while political thinking, as it has existed since fifth-century Athens, still survives.

But does it survive? Conceivably political theory at the present day may *not* be undergoing one of its many metamorphoses, passing through a chrysalis stage before emerging in a new form. It may just be coming to an end. This has happened in the past. Once before in the history of Western civilization a great age of political thought came to an end. The development of Greek political ideas reached its climax in the writings of Plato and Aristotle. In the Hellenistic age attention began to turn away from political theory and into other fields. For a time, with the rise of the National Law school of thought and the elaboration of juristic conceptions by the Roman lawyers, it might have been possible to regard the process as still one of growth and development. But in the Roman Empire politics turned into the struggles of court factions and military dictators, and political thinking as the Greeks understood it ceased.

The experience of the Greco-Roman world is not without relevance to our own time. Some at least of the conditions which accompanied this earlier decline and fall of political theory are repeated today. It is a commonplace that state activity is irresistibly expanding. More and more of the activities of society are falling under the control of bureaucracy and therefore are to some extent outside political control. Great military machines are being created, to the support of which more and more of the wealth of society has to be diverted. These are as yet, it is true, the servants and not the masters of the civil power, but so the legions were in Rome for a long time. This is an age of revolutions, like the age of Marius and Sulla and Caesar, and revolutions are apt to end in military dictators; in more than a few countries they begin with them as well. The knowledge of this tendency is perhaps one reason why it has hitherto failed to operate in Soviet Russia. In Nazi Germany also the Army was never able to challenge the party successfully.

Possibly in the new form of party organization a technique has been found for averting military dictatorship and the rule of pretorian guards to which the Roman Empire degenerated. But the substitution of the party machine for the military machine is not necessarily a great improvement. It means the rule of a small oligarchy, with political life concentrated in the internal struggles of its factions. Both bureaucracy and party seem also in practice to involve the emergence of a super-bureaucrat or party chief, or both rolled in one, in whom ultimate power is concentrated, and who is himself semideified as the incarnation of the state, like the Roman emperors. Since the majority of the population are naturally outside the chosen circle of bureaucracy or party there is also a need, as long as a degree of political consciousness survives in any part of this excluded majority, for a machinery of repression, a system of delation and espionage, political police, concentration camps or prisons and the rule of universal suspicion—such as Tacitus described in dreadful detail in his imaginative account of the last years of Tiberius, and Camille Desmoulins borrowed for a description of France under the Terror.

It may be said that this picture represents only half of the world, and that is doubtless so. But are some of these tendencies completely absent anywhere? Contemporaries naturally notice differences. Historians, looking back on an age, are often more struck by similarities. The most fundamental trends in any period are those which exist at the same time in the most diverse and apparently opposed camps. If I were asked what are the deepest underlying tendencies of our age I should look for those which are common to both sides of the Iron Curtain. I should look for something which communist Russia and capitalist America have in common. At bottom, it seems to me that there are more similarities than either side would be very pleased to admit, and that they are sufficient to make the parallel with the ancient world a fair one, though obviously it must not be pushed too far.

The parallel is also noticeable with respect to the decline of political theory. In the period when Caesarism was rising, the ideas associated with the old Roman conception of *libertas* were falling. The connection between new conditions of society and the decline of political thinking may be obscure, but it would be dangerous to suggest that there is none. The rule of *senatus populusque romanus* led to anarchy when an empire had to be governed instead of a city. Rome was faced with the choice of abandoning the political principles by which it had achieved greatness, or seeing the Roman world degenerate into a chaos of warring states. Its solution was the Empire, in which, however, the classic political theories of the city-state could find no place, any more than the institutions by which they had achieved some measure of realization. For political theory to exist, it seems to me, there must be an active political life. One does not expect to find it flourishing among Australian aboriginal tribes, in the Russia of Ivan or Peter, the Paraguay of the Jesuits or the empire of the Caesars.

Are there signs—I do not say more—that our own political ideas may be coming to their end as those of the ancient city-states did? It would be absurd to suppose that one wants a continual stream of new political ideas, or old ones new-fashioned; but I suggest that there has been rather a long interval since there was last any original political thinking. It is necessary to go back to the eighteenth century to find it. This, I admit, is a sweeping statement, which it would require considerable space to attempt to justify.

But let me present one consideration. The dominant political idea in the modern world is democracy. Most of the contradictions of contemporary politics find their place under the democratic umbrella, but broad as that is they jostle one another, and moreover the umbrella seems to be leaking badly. And where are the political theorists of democracy today? Instead of a rational theory it has become a sort of incantation. It is the "open sesame" of political treasure hunters everywhere. The world is full of would-be Aladdins chanting "democracy." The masses, at least in those countries which have no experience of democracy, are waiting in a state of mystic faith on the revelation that the word is to produce. Where at least the idea has been known longer, expectations are not so high. Is it unfair to suggest that there is even a certain degree of disillusionment, a feeling that the traditional conceptions of democracy do not answer our greatest problems?

Liberal democratic principles ceased to evolve in the nineteenth century: in general, the world of practice is apt to be a generation, sometimes a century, behind the world of original thought. But the nineteenth century failed to refashion and think out anew, for the benefit of its successors, the ideas that it was living on. It provided, admittedly, an intellectual ancestry for nationalism and Fascism and communism, but that is another story. Liberal democratic principles ceased to evolve then, but the world did not stop at that point, and it has become a very different place since. Meanwhile democracy, for lack of thought, has ceased to be a living political idea. It has become a shibboleth, and not even serviceable as such. A password is no good when all the hostile camps use it indiscriminately. For the most part it has ceased to be discussed seriously and in relation to the concrete problems of practical politics. It has largely become a meaningless formula. Politicians, like the princess in the fairy tale condemned to the oracular utterance of frogs, seem scarcely able to open their mouths without some platitude flopping out, wet and flabby and slightly repulsive, but is this political theory? If it is, no wonder that practical men prefer to ignore it. Coins can remain valid currency even when they are worn quite smooth. Political ideas need periodical recoining if they are to retain their value.

It may be said that this is not a fair argument, that practical politics has always been conducted on the basis of platitudes. A Burke was the exception, his fellow member for Bristol, whose political principles were summed up in "I say ditto to Mr. Burke," the norm; but at least he had a Burke to say ditto to, and besides Burke a great body of informed and serious public discussion existed on the rights and wrongs of political behavior. Where will the average politican find a discussion of theoretical questions on the same level today?

Of course, there have been writers in the last few decades who have had something significant to say about the contemporary political situation, but the same conclusion about the decline of political theory seems to emerge from a study of their work. I am thinking of such writers as Ferrero, Bertrand de Jouvenel, Russell, E. H. Carr, Reinhold Niebuhr, Lasswell, Hans Morgenthau and others. The thing that impresses them most about political life is the state as power. They envisage power as a kind of electric force, now diffused and now concentrated, which not merely runs through society but is its very essence. "The laws of social dynamism," says Lord Russell, "are only capable of being stated in terms of power." The wretched individual atoms of which society is composed are massed together, hurled violently about, disintegrated by power, which they did not create and cannot control.

Traditional political theory, in so far as it has failed to recognize this fact, is regarded as no more than a beautiful fairy tale. To quote Reinhold Niebuhr,

> It may be possible, though it is never easy, to establish just relations between individuals within a group by moral and rational suasion and accommodation. In inter-group relations this is practically an impossibility. The relations between groups must therefore always be predominantly political rather than ethical, that is, they will be determined by the proportion of power which each group possesses at least as much as by any rational and moral appraisal of the comparative needs and claims of each group.[1]

According to Niebuhr the tragedy of the human spirit is "its inability to conform its collective life to its individual ideals." This is the reason why men "invent romantic and moral interpretations of the real facts, prefer-

---

[1] *Moral Man and Immoral Society* (New York, 1933), pp. 22–23.

ring to obscure rather than reveal the true character of their collective behavior." In other words, it is the dilemma of "moral man and immoral society." Man, when he became a social and political animal, sacrificed his individual morality to the egoism that is the accompaniment of social life. The complaint is not a new one: it was the theme of Rousseau's *Discourse on Inequality*. But for the modern thinker, unlike Rousseau, there is no resolution to the tragedy of society. Humanity is caught in a cul-de-sac. In such a situation absolute pessimism is unavoidable. There is no possibility of creating, as Rousseau set out to do in the opening chapter of the *Contrat social*, a society in which justice can be allied with utility and power with freedom. There is no hope of establishing rational or ethical control.

In a different way the same conclusion was reached by Ortega y Gasset. He wrote:

> we live at a time when man believes himself fabulously capable of creation, but he does not know what to create. Lord of all things, he is not lord of himself. He feels lost amid his own abundance. With more means at his disposal, more knowledge, more technique than ever, it turns out that the world to-day goes the same way as the worst of worlds that have been; it simply drifts.[2]

All this is degrees of pessimism below Machiavelli. The author of the *Prince* saw society at the mercy of arbitrary power, but believed that somehow out of evil would come good; the tyrant would serve social ends that a better ruler might not be able to fulfill. We have lost the innocence of a Machiavelli now and do not look for moral good to be born of political evil. Political pessimism is deeper than it has been perhaps since St. Augustine wrote the *De Civitate Dei*. Indeed, for a century and a half pessimism has slowly been infecting the intellectual world. That is a process I have no space to trace, though it has, I believe, a close connection with the decay in political ideas that has been contemporaneous with it.

The decline of political theory may thus be regarded as a reflection of the feeling that ethical values have no place in the field of social dynamics and power politics. This, I believe, is the real significance of "the revolt of the masses": it means the rise to control of those who live their lives without theory, to whatever class they may happen to belong. Another term for it is the rule of the expert, I mean the technician, the *Fachmann*, to use the German word for an especially German disease. Twenty years ago Ortega y Gasset saw what it meant. "Anyone who wishes," he said, "can observe the stupidity of thought, judgement and

[2]*The Revolt of the Masses* (London, 1932), p. 47.

action shown to-day in politics, art, religion and the general problems of life and the world by the 'men of science,' and of course, behind them, the doctors, engineers, financiers, teachers and so on."[3] The politician who merely repeats platitudes is no worse than his own experts; he is not to be singled out for criticism. And how can he be held responsible for failing to translate political theory into practice if there is no theory to be translated?

There is another way of looking at the decline of political thought. Professor Toynbee sees our civilization going the way of previous civilizations, and consoles himself with the idea that the death of a civilization may be the birth of a religion. Ferrero put it differently. Mysticism, he said, is a form of escapism from the horror of illegitimate power. One seems to remember the early Christian invocation: "The poet has said, 'O lovely city of Cecrops', wilt thou not say, 'O lovely city of God'?" And a modern poet repeats the cry:

> Man, frustrated and sleep-forsaken,
> Gloom-regarding from inward sight,
> Sees the city of God unshaken
> Steeply stand in unworlded white;
> Sees, adrift from his faith-lost learning,
> Sun-remote from terrestrial thought,
> Power, envisioned by earth's discerning,
> Peace, by moral aspiring wrought.[4]

A nobly phrased restatement of an ideal that appeared to men in a former time of troubles, but one that belongs to a nonpolitical age. Religious revival *may* be a way out, but it is not a political way. And will it be the resurgent idealism to give substance to our hopes, or merely a narcotic to our discontents? The religious approach to political problems is also not without its dangers. The Nazi Revolution of Destruction gained greatly in force by being able to drape itself with the robes of chiliastic aspiration.

In this analysis—though that is to dignify a brief indication of some contemporary tendencies, as I see them, with too ambitious a title—I may seem to be bent on a pessimistic interpretation of the modern world; but what I have said so far is only a one-sided view of the current situation. To take it as the whole truth would be to despair of the political community prematurely. If it is true that political theory has ceased to develop, is this a sign that political life is in fact coming to an end and that we are entering a nonpolitical age, as the ancient world did? Here one must appeal to a broader view of the facts. The differences are far

---

[3]*The Revolt of the Masses* (London, 1932), p. 124.

[4]From *Collected Poems* by Siegfried Sassoon. Copyright 1936, Copyright renewed 1964 by Siegfried Sassoon. Reprinted by permission of the Viking Press, Inc.

greater than the similarities. If there are signs that the world is moving in the direction of universal empire, there is no reason to believe that it will reach that goal before the present age of catastrophes has been long continued. Bureaucracy is not yet the major reality of government in any Western country; nor are pretorian guards or political parties yet our masters rather than our servants. In short, there seems no reason to believe that if there has been a decline of political theory this is the necessary result of the appearance of a social and political situation in which it no longer has any valid *raison d'être*. If this is so, the only alternative explanation is to suppose that it is declining because of some internal condition, and not because of the inevitable pressure of objective fact. Perhaps something has gone wrong with political thinking itself. I believe that it has, and that it is even possible to suggest a diagnosis.

If the decline of political theory is to be explained by some inherent misdirection in contemporary thinking about politics, the remedy might appear to be to work out, on abstract grounds, the proper way of thinking about politics. This method has certain attractions. It can be used to justify practically any form of political theory that appeals to us; because naturally the conclusions we arrive at will be determined by the assumptions we start from, and we are not in much danger of starting from assumptions that do not appeal to us.

However, I propose not to adopt this line of approach. Fortunately, we have not to *invent* political theory; that was invented long ago. If there is a right way of considering its problems, I think we should be modest enough to believe that it might possibly be the way of all the greater political thinkers of the past; that is, if there is a way which so many, and such diverse, theorists have in common. I think there is. In the first place we have the simple, obvious fact that they all wrote with a practical purpose in mind. Their object was to influence actual political behavior. They wrote to condemn or support existing institutions, to justify a political system or persuade their fellow citizens to change it: because, in the last resort, they were concerned with the aims, the purposes of political society. Even Machiavelli does not merely describe the way in which things are done, without also indicating the way in which, and to what ends, he thinks they *ought* to be done. At the opposite extreme, Plato's *Republic* may represent an ideal to which the human race—perhaps happily—cannot attain, but in his mind it was no mere Cloud-Cuckoo-Land of fantasy.

Political theory in the past, I suggest, was essentially practical. The political theorist, in his way, was a party man, and party men themselves used not to be afraid to season their practice with the salt of theory. One of the striking differences between political discussion in, say, the eighteenth century and at the present day is that politicians have on the whole ceased to discuss general principles. This is not stated as a criticism, but as a fact which needs explaining, and I think one clue to the explanation has already appeared. The study of political theory, I have just said, was formerly the work of men intently concerned with practical issues. It has become instead an academic discipline, written in various esoteric jargons almost as though for the purpose of preventing it from being understood by those who, if they did understand it, might try to put it into practice. It has entered the high realm of scholarship, and, as Whitehead has pointed out, some modern forms of scholarship, at least, reproduce the limitations which dominated thought in the Hellenistic epoch. "They canalize thought and observation," he says, "within predetermined limits, based upon inadequate metaphysical assumptions dogmatically assumed."[5]

Political theory has in this way become disengaged from political facts. Even worse, it has become disengaged on principle, as it has seldom if ever been in the past. The academic political theorist of today may study the great political thinkers of the past, but in the name of academic impartiality he must carefully abstain from doing the kind of thing that they did. I put it forward as a hypothesis that this may conceivably be one source of the decline of political theory.

The view that the connection between political theory and practical politics is a condition of the survival of theory deserves a more elaborate discussion than it can be given here. But if it were to be accepted, then there is an important corollary to be noticed. The implication is that the issues with which political theory has been concerned in the past were not chosen arbitrarily, or as a result of some theoretical argument, and that theory was able to come to grips with the practical world because its discussions were determined by the actual conditions and problems of the day. For example, John Stuart Mill lived in an age when new social problems called for measures of state action which conflicted with established ideals of individual liberty: his thought derives its value from the fact that he devoted himself to the task of attempting to reconcile the two demands. Bentham's lifework was to establish a theoretical basis for the legislative and administrative reforms that were urgently needed in *his* day. Burke, faced in Great Britain, America, Ireland, France with a challenge to the existing bases of political allegiance, attempted to provide an alternative to the new democratic principle of the sovereignty of the people. Rousseau, conscious of the moral collapse of divine-right monarchy, offered a new justification for the rightful powers of govern-

---

[5]A. N. Whitehead, *Adventures of Ideas* (London, 1933), p. 151.

ment. Montesquieu, earlier, had seen the defects of absolutism, but his alternative was a return to the aristocratic organization of society, and the limitation of all power by law. Locke provided a political theory for a generation which had overthrown divine right and established parliamentary government. Hobbes and Spinoza, in an age of civil wars, maintained that sovereignty meant all or nothing. And so we might continue, till we reached in the end—or rather the beginning—Plato and Aristotle, attempting to prescribe remedies for the diseases of the city-state. Among recent political thinkers, it seems to me that one of the very few, perhaps the only one, who followed the traditional pattern, accepted the problems presented by his age, and devoted himself to the attempt to find an answer to them was Harold Laski. Though I am bound to say that I do not agree with his analysis or his conclusions, I think that he was trying to do the right kind of thing. And this, I suspect, is the reason why, practically alone among political thinkers in Great Britain, he exercised a positive influence over both political thought and action.

If political theory *has* become generally disengaged from practice, and if this is one cause of its decline, it will be worth while asking why this has happened. The bias of the academic approach away from action is not a new thing, and it can hardly provide an adequate explanation by itself. An answer which goes a little deeper can be found, I think, again by a comparison with traditional political thought. The object of this was to arrive at the judgment that one form of political activity was better than another. Academic impartiality between what it believed to be good and bad it neither sought nor attained. Because its aim was to influence action, it had to consider the forces that move men, and these are not the products of abstract analysis but of the passions. And since not all passions could be regarded as conducive to a good end, it had to be the passions under the guidance of ethical motivation. In other words, politics was essentially a branch of morals, or ethics. It is not my object here to discuss the problems of ethical theory. What I want to do is to suggest that modern political theory has largely ceased to be discussed in terms of what ought to be; and the reason, I believe, is that it has fallen under the influence of two modes of thought which have had a fatal effect on its ethical content. These, and they have come to dominate the modern mind, are history and science.

The historian naturally sees all ideas and ways of behavior as historically conditioned and transient. Within itself, history has no standard of value but success, and no measure of success but the attainment of power, or survival for a little longer than rival individuals or institutions have survived. Moreover, history is the world studied under the category of what is past: however much we may proclaim that all history is contemporary, its nature is to be a field into which practice cannot penetrate. The paradox of history is that though its writing is a contemporary action, with practical consequences, the historian puts this fact in the back of his mind and tries to behave as though it were not so. By itself, in political theory, history can produce only the crudest Machiavellianism. If all historians are not little Machiavellis, it is only because they take their political ideals from some other source and carry them into their history. This is, fortunately, almost unavoidable, though it might sometimes be a good thing if they were a little more conscious of the ideals they are in fact applying and inculcating through their histories. This is yet another problem which can be raised but not discussed here. It is sufficient to say that at least there is a tendency among modern historians to regard the passing of ethical judgment as an illegitimate process against which historical discipline should be a safeguard. In so far as it is a successful safeguard it is also one against thinking about the problems of political theory at all.

The influence of historical thought did not stop at this. History acquires more positive, and more dangerous, implications, when it is made into a philosophy of history. This was particularly the achievement of Hegel and Marx. The dominant trend in both Hegelianism and Marxism was to associate ethics with the historical process—by which I do not mean the grand pattern of the universe, which I suspect was not revealed even to Hegel or Marx, but the little corner of the fabric which came under their immediate notice, the few strands which they took for the pattern of the whole. Even if Hegel and Marx themselves did not intend this result, in those who followed them there was an uneasy slip from saying, "This is what will be", into saying, "This is what ought to be." The result was to base moral judgments on temporary and limited historical phenomena. Hegelian and Marxist politics, therefore, have had the ultimate effect of setting up a politics devoid of ethical foundations. In this way they played an important part in creating a breach between modern political practice and the traditions of political thinking in the West.

The influence of history over the modern mind is, however, challenged by that of science. Particularly in the forms of mathematics and psychology, science has influenced political thinking practically from the beginning; though of course the scientific bases on which earlier political theories were sometimes built are about as closely related to modern science as the voyages of Sinbad the Sailor are to modern geographical discovery. This did not prevent Plato and Aristotle from being great political theorists. It is only in recent times that a general belief has grown up in the possibility and desirability of studying politics by the methods that have achieved such remarkable results in the natural sciences. This belief is embodied in the now common term, political science. I do not ask, is political science possible? It must be, it exists. But what is it? The object of science is to show how things happen, and why, in the nexus of cause and effect, they *do* happen. There is no reason why political phenomena, as well as any other phenomena, should not be treated in this way so long as we do not mistake the result for political theory and expect it to answer questions which in the nature of things it cannot answer. What I mean is simply that it is not the function of science to pass ethical judgments. That statement can hardly be questioned. I imagine that any scientist would indignantly repudiate the suggestion that his scientific thought entered into the category of what ought to be. The political theorist, on the other hand, is essentially concerned with the discussion of what ought to be. His judgments are at bottom value judgments. The kind of opinion he offers is that one line of political action is ethically preferable to another, not merely that it is more efficient, whatever that may mean; and surely we have seen enough in our day to know that the difference between political systems is not merely a difference between relative degrees of efficiency.

In case I am thought to be unjust to the political scientist, let me give what seems a fair description of the way in which he envisages his task. It is fallacious, says a recent writer, to suggest that the only way of understanding politics is to participate in it: we do not teach the principles of geometry by a manual training course in carpentry. Political science is a body of knowledge, which must be taught and learned like any other body of knowledge. What this definition neglects is the fact that the degree of moral disinterestedness possible in natural science is impossible in the field of political theory. The political scientist, in so far as he wishes to remain a scientist, is limited to the study of techniques. His subject may be compared to eighteenth-century German cameralism, which was a political theory by bureaucrats, about bureaucrats, for bureaucrats. Mostly, what is called political science, I must confess, seems to me a device, invented by university teachers, for avoiding that dangerous subject politics, without achieving science. Taking it at the highest valuation, political science can give us guidance of the greatest possible importance in achieving the objects we want to achieve; it cannot help us to decide what those objects should be, or even what they are. And to believe that we are all agreed on them and therefore do not need to discuss them is surely, in the light of contemporary events, the wildest utopianism. In the last resort science, like history, leaves us, as Ortega y Gasset put it, to drift: we have a magnificent technical equipment for going somewhere, without anywhere to go.

The image of political life which emerges from the prevailing tendencies in political thought is not a pleasing one. The state appears as a ship in the sea of politics, with no port of embarcation or destination inscribed on its papers, manned by a pressed crew, whose whole endeavor is devoted to the task of keeping the vessel afloat in uncharted waters, with little to help them save their own traditional seamanship, and the records of earlier captains and crews who have for all time been tossed on the seas in the same endless, meaningless motion. A depressing picture, I think, perhaps dreamed up by some remote philosopher who has seen the ships scudding by from the lanternroom of a dead lighthouse, dead because he has carefully extinguished the light.

Luckily we need not take the picture too seriously: it is only an analogy, and analogies are the camouflage of loose thinking. The sea is, of course, the sea of politics. But the state is itself the community as a political organization, the bond that holds it together; the life it lives is also politics. And how is the ship distinguishable from the crew? The state is no mere wooden artifact inhabited by men; it *is* men as political animals. And sea, ship and crew move on together for they are the same. How can we envisage ourselves as inhabiting the ship of state in the sea of politics when the ship is ourselves and the element it moves in our own political being, and *we* rouse the storms and *we* still the waters?

One thing is missing from the picture. It is missing from contemporary politics also. This, as I have said, is the idea that the ship is going anywhere. A sense of direction is lacking, a feeling of purpose. That, I think, is what the decay of political theory means in ordinary terms to the ordinary man. Does it matter? If we were all of us, all our time, porkers not even from the sty of Epicurus, perhaps it would not: our purpose would be set by something outside ourselves, and it would be just as well that it should not be revealed to us in disturbing detail. Such, of course, may be the facts of the case; but rightly or wrongly the human mind demands something more than living from trough to snout. In the absence of a more or less rational theory to justify its sense of political obligation and the rightful powers of government, it will fall victim to an irrational one. If it cannot have, say, Locke on *Toleration*, it will have, say, Hitler on *Mein Kampf*. That is what the decline of political theory means in practice.

One last word. The analysis I have made is perhaps moderately pessimistic; but it is not intended to lead to the conclusion that in political thinking we have reached the terminus, the end of that line. The reasons that I have given for its decline are in themselves even encouraging, since there are signs that they may be only temporary aberrations. Historians are in revolt against philosophies of history: ethics is sapping the lack of morale of professors of history. Hegelian politics is already dead. Marxist politics is increasingly revealed as a dialectical apologia for the pursuit of power for its own sake. The inadequacy, in relation to the broader issues of political society, of the scientific study of administrative methods, constitutional devices, electoral statistics and the like—I hope it will not be thought that within their own field I am attempting to deny the value of the techniques of political science—is gradually becoming apparent.

For a century and a half the Western democracies have been living on the stock of basic political ideas that were last restated toward the end of the eighteenth century. That is a long time. The nineteenth century did pretty well on them, but provided no restatement for its successors. The gap thus formed between political facts and political ideas has steadily widened. It has taken a long time for the results to become evident; but now that we have seen what politics devoid of a contemporary moral and political theory means, it is possible that something may be done about it. After a generation's experience of drifting directionless on a stormy sea the need of recovering a sense of direction, and therefore control, is beginning to be felt. And if political theory revives, if the idea of purpose is reintroduced into political thinking, we may take up again the tradition of Western political thought, and in doing so resume that "continuous transformation of morals into politics, which still remains politics," in which, according to Croce, lies "the real ethical progress of mankind."

Further Readings

Almond, Gabriel A., Lewis A. Dexter, William F. Whyte, and John H. Hallowell, "Politics and Ethics: A Symposium," *American Political Science Review,* XL (2: April, 1946), pp. 283–312.

Braybrooke, David, V. Sacheri and Fredrich Olafson, "Ethics and Politics— A Symposium," *Proceedings of Inter-American Philosophical Convention,* Quebec (June, 1967), pp. 150–182.

Brecht, Arnold, *Political Theory; The Foundations of Twentieth-Century Political Thought* (Princeton, N.J.: Princeton University Press, 1959), Chap. III.

Jacob, Philip E. and James J. Flink, with the collaboration of Hedvah L. Shuchman, "Values and Their Function in Decision-Making," *American Behavioral Scientist,* 5 (9, supplement: May, 1962), pp. 1–38.

Waldo, Dwight, " 'Values' in the Political Science Curriculum," in Roland Young, ed., *Approaches to the Study of Politics* (Evanston, Ill.: Northwestern University Press, 1958), pp. 96–111.

Also see the bibliography on politics and values in *American Political Science Review,* XLIX (1: March, 1955), p. 216.

Part IV

THE CONDITION
AND PROSPECT
OF POLITICAL THOUGHT

Western civilization has had countless significant political philosophers. From the time of Socrates to the time of Sartre political philosophers have nearly always been on the scene. Some believe that times of political crisis necessarily bring forth great political thinkers who respond suggesting cures for the illnesses of their times. Yet, in spite of the many and continuous crises of the twentieth century, it is claimed by such writers as Laslett, Easton, Dahl, Cobban, and others, that political philosophy is dead. Just as God was killed by his own kind, that is, by certain theologians, so political philosophy allegedly has been killed by its kind, the philosophical analysts—the logical positivists and the Ordinary Language School. The culprits did this alleged slaying by setting up systems which reduced ethical theories to nonsensical statements. Since political philosophy is grounded on ethics, political philosophy falls along with ethics. As Cobban says, this decline "may . . . be regarded as a reflection of the feeling that ethical values have no place in the field of social dynamics and power politics." And Easton notes that "values can be reduced to emotional responses. . . ."

If, however, one contends, as Berlin does, that ethical values are neither nonsensical and completely subjective, nor merely emotive, then political philosophy not only lives, but lives necessarily because questions of value about the state, democracy, rights, liberty, equality, justice, and so forth, must be answered anew in each generation. Hence it is alleged by Berlin and others that political philosophy is not dead, and that what we have witnessed is the death of the ability of analytic philosophy to deal with critical political problems.

Berlin's conclusion is full of common sense and worthy of support: "Neo-Marxism, neo-Thomism, nationalism, historicism, existentialism, anti-essentialist liberalism and socialism, transpositions of doctrines of natural rights and natural law into empirical terms, discoveries made by skilful application of models derived from economic and related techniques to political behaviour, and the collisions, combinations and consequences in action of these ideas, indicate not the death of a great tradition, but, if anything, new and unpredictable developments." Otherwise, all these are much ado about nothing. Political thought in both its dimensions appears to be neither dead nor in its death throes.

17

David Easton

THE DECLINE
OF MODERN
POLITICAL THEORY*

David Easton indicts contemporary political thought both for living "parasitically on ideas a century old" and for failing to develop "new political syntheses." He attributes both the condition and the failure to the kind of historical interpretation common in contemporary political thought. "The history of political values has led theorists to concentrate on the relation of values to the milieu in which they appear rather than on the task of attempting to create new conceptions of values commensurate with men's needs." Therein they have "given up theory's traditional task of reformulating the content of values." Also, "To the extent that political theory today deals with causal theory, it consists almost exclusively of historical commentaries describing applied political principles of the great theorists." Professor Easton calls for corrective action helping to analyze old and formulate new political values and conceptualizing the basic areas for empirical research in political science. This corrective action should both synthesize and codify the limited generalizations we have in the various fields of political science into a theory that lends itself to verification or invalidation and attempt the "more massive task of elaborating a usable conceptual framework for the whole body of political science."

*Reprinted by permission of the author and publisher from *Journal of Politics*, XIII (1: February, 1951), pp. 36–58.

Dr. Easton extended his analysis of the "malaise" of political science and the role of political theory in that malaise in a subsequent book entitled *The Political System: An Inquiry into the State of Political Science* (New York: Alfred A. Knopf, Inc., 1953). In still later books he joined those who heeded his call for corrective action: *A Framework for Political Analysis* (Englewood Cliffs, N. J.: Prentice-Hall Inc., 1965) and *A Systems Analysis of Political Life* (New York: John Wiley & Sons, Inc., 1965).

THE ELEMENTS OF A POLITICAL THEORY

Why is it that today in political theory we must turn to the past in order to find inspiration and genuine freshness? An axiom in political theory has always declared that political ideas flourish in the soil of social conflict and change. When we view the social upheavals in ancient Greece, the political and religious conflicts of the sixteenth and seventeenth centuries, and the turmoil preceding the French Revolution, and compare this with the profound theory that was generated in each case, this axiom appears to ring true. We too live in a period of fundamental change and widespread conflict and yet our civilization seems to be the exception that proves the rule. Contemporary political thought lives parasitically on ideas a century old and, what is more discouraging, we see little prospect of the development of new political syntheses. It is said that the social sciences await a new Aristotle or a new social Newton. For political theory, if present prospects are any indication of the actual turn of future events, this wait will be in vain, for we are not preparing the soil out of which revolutionary creative thinking can arise.

My remarks below are designed to show that this poverty of political theory can be attributed in large part to the kind of research in the field, during the last fifty years at least. With certain exceptions to be noted, research during this period has been devoted primarily to a form of historical analysis that, by its nature, inhibited any desire to restore theory to its natural and traditional rôle.[1] Specifically, two reasons account for this impoverishment of theory. In the first place, this kind of historical analysis has played a major part in destroying a species of mental activity that has prevailed in literate civilizations and which emerges out of universal human needs. By its existence such mental activity bore witness to the value of pondering about the actual direction of human affairs and of offering for the serious consideration of all men

[1]George H. Sabine, "What Is a Political Theory," *The Journal of Politics,* I, No. 1 (February, 1939), p. 1; and Westel Woodbury Willoughby, "The Value of Political Philosophy," *Political Science Quarterly,* 15, No. 1 (March, 1900), pp. 75–95.

some ideas about the desirable course of events. My first point will therefore be that the kind of historical interpretation with which we are today familiar has driven from theory its only unique function, that of creatively constructing a valuational frame of reference.

In the second place, the accepted historical approach has unwittingly helped to divert the attention and energies of political theorists from the task of building systematic theory about political behavior and the operation of political institutions. Economics, for example, or sociology, both attempt to give unity and coherence to their empirical research by constructing a general theory for the whole discipline. Political science, on the other hand, has largely ignored this task. Since theory at its most general level has always been the province of the branch of political science we call political theory, the latter must at least share the responsibility for failing to stimulate inquiry into an empirical or causal frame of reference.

Political theory must carry this double burden of guilt because of the fact that traditionally, although this is seldom recognized or acknowledged, it deals with two major orders of knowledge, facts and values. Although it has always shown a primary concern for values, we would be seriously misled about the nature of a political theory if we did not recognize that in practice it does depend upon factual statements about political relations. If theory is to show a regard for its factual statements equivalent to that shown to its value judgments, then it must turn to the task of systematizing its empirical base. Since my subsequent discussion will depend on an unambiguous understanding of the rôles that factual statements as well as value judgments play in a political theory, their preliminary examination is necessary.

It is patent that no political theory has ever been purely speculative in the sense of arising full-blown out of a mind uncontaminated by facts. Speculations of the best political theorists have always been founded on acute observations of the contemporary political scene and a knowledge of human history. At the base of each political theory, therefore, there are certain propositions which use facts referring either to contemporary or historical events. The presence of these factual statements need not detain us long for no one denies their existence in a political theory. They allege that certain events took place at certain times and places or that given political circumstances have existed. These statements are subject to checking in the same way as any historical fact.

There is, however, a quite different class of statement characteristic of political theory. This kind refers not to what *is* but to the state of affairs that men would like to see come into existence. They are consciously value-orientated statements. They describe the way in which the desired social order should be organized, if the values adopted by the theorist are to be realized. This mode of expression embraces three diverse kinds of propositions that must be distinguished in order to understand the tasks that political theory has set for itself. In the first place, it implies the choice of a constellation of values or preferences which the political theorist uses as a criterion to appraise social policy. When abstracted and systematically examined, I shall speak of this aspect as value theory. In the second place, these value-oriented statements also imply that the means advocated by the theorist for realizing his values will be adequate for the attainment of the kind of political order he prefers. Now, in order to demonstrate that a selected means will be hospitable to given ends, the theorist must assume that he can show a universal, that is, a highly probable, connection between the means he would use and the end he desires. That is, in order to prove that the use of means B will achieve the goal A, there must be an assumption that, under the given conditions whenever B occurs, it is more probable than less that A will follow. Otherwise, there would be no reasonable assurance that the advocacy of the given means would produce the desired results. In effect, then, the theorist must be assuming the existence and validity of still a third kind of proposition; namely, a generalized causal theory about the relations of facts. Only on the basis of this causal theory is he able to specify with some assurance how his objectives can be achieved. We can conveniently identify this variety of proposition by calling the descriptive statements, factual statements; the assumed relations between facts, pure or causal theory; the interrelated statements of preferences, value theory; and the propositions designed to apply facts and implicit causal theory to the fulfillment of given ends, applied principles.

To illustrate concretely that a political theory is composed of this variety of propositions we can turn for a moment to Locke in his second treatise *Of Civil Government*. There can be no question that Locke makes observations of political facts that rest on his knowledge of history and of his own time, and, therefore, we do not need to dwell on the factual statements. Similarly, the presence of a value theory is beyond question. The very concept of natural law and derivative natural rights in which Locke's reasoning, like that of his age, is imbedded, indicates the existence in this treatise of a systematic value theory. But what is not always so clearly discerned or understood is that Locke also offers his reader a systematic application of theoretical knowledge to show the best way of organizing political life for the pursuit of a moral life, and that, in doing this, he must be making certain implicit assumptions in the realm of causal theory. Having claimed to show that a given means would produce a specified result, such as the preservation of one's natural rights, he could have proved this, if called upon, only by asserting a universal connection between relevant facts. For example, at one point he says that to obtain a political order that will secure men in their natural rights, the legislative must be separated from the executive power. But to have any reliability for this applied principle, Locke must be assuming that, if called upon, he could prove that such a minimum "separation" of powers does prevent the abuse of authority. Presumably, he might turn to the whole constitutional history of England, culminating in the Whig revolution, as evidence for the validity of this assumption. But the assumption that there is an invariant relation between the division of powers and the impartial formulation and execution of the laws is nothing less than a causal theory. This implicit causal theory stands out sharply in Locke's own words, even though the statement is cast in the form of an application of knowledge. "And that because it may be too great a temptation to human frailty, apt to grasp at power, for the same persons who have the power of making laws to have also in their hands the power to execute them, whereby they may exempt themselves from obedience to the laws they make, and suit the law, both in its making and execution, to their private advantage, and thereby come to have a distinct interest from the rest of the community, contrary to the end of society and government."[2] This is clearly a seventeenth century way of saying that there is an invariant relation between constitutionalism and the structure of political institutions. It is simply one illustration of what becomes apparent upon the examination of any political theory. Every such theory consists of this variety of propositions: factual, value, causal, and applied.

VALUE THEORY

Having thus suggested the empirical or factual in addition to the unquestioned valuational aspect of a political theory, I shall turn first to its value side. An examination of some classic Anglo-Saxon works in theory over the last half-century, such as those by Allen, A. J. Carlyle, Dunning, McIlwain, Sabine, and Lindsay, will uncover the source of the contemporary decline in constructive value theory. Scrutiny of their works reveals that they have been motivated less by an interest in analyzing and formulating new value theory than in retailing information about the meaning, internal consistency, and historical development of contemporary and past political values. There are, of course, others who are genuine exceptions, such as Dewey, Barker, Croce, and Laski, among others. Nevertheless, in spite of the fact that the latter theorists did treat

[2] John Locke (Second Essay), *Of Civil Government* (London: J. M. Dent & Sons, Ltd., 1924), Chap. XII, p. 190.

the value question more seriously, they are a mere handful among the vast majority that confines itself to historical interpretation.

As it has been practiced by that majority, the historical approach has managed to crush the life out of value theory. The historical treatment of political ideas need not in itself produce this result. Rather, it is the kind of history that has seized the minds of theorists in the last half-century that must bear the blame. The history of political values has led theorists to concentrate on the relation of values to the milieu in which they appear rather than on the task of attempting to create new conceptions of values commensurate with men's needs. Political theorists have been devoting themselves to what is essentially an empirical rather than a value problem, at least in terms of the traditional disjunction between facts and values. In doing so they have assimilated value theory into empirical or causal social science and have thereby given up theory's traditional task of reformulating the content of values.

Although there is this unity in the disregard for creative theory, considerable differences do exist in the general approach which each theorist has adopted towards the relation of values to historical conditions. There are at least four main points of view. Identification of these will serve to bring out the intrinsic nature of the prevailing historical approaches and thereby the main reasons for their undermining of theory. For example, those whom I would describe as the institutionalists, such as Carlyle or McIlwain, usually treat the history of ideas as the study of epiphenomena; as mere froth on the ocean, as it were, that has little effect on the movement of the waves. For them, political theory involves a discussion of the kind of ideas that have emerged to help rationalize political interests and institutional development. They come close to a contemporary notion that such ideas are myths, justifying behavior but hardly instrumental in determining political activity. Others, on the other hand, whom I would name the interactionists, such as Allen, and quite inconsistently, at times even Carlyle, would insist that ideas do play a vital rôle in political life, interacting with institutions as a significant variable in the whole process of social change. For them, the task of political theory is to unveil the actual rôle of ideas at each historical juncture. A third category of theorists, such as Dunning, to some extent Sabine, and most scholars in part at least, whom I would be inclined to call the materialists if all the other implications of the concept were not imputed to these writers, approach political theory with the objective of uncovering the historical and cultural conditions that gave rise to the prevailing political conceptions of an age. Here they join the sociology of knowledge in seeking to understand ideology in terms of the total cultural matrix. This third group of theorists represents nothing more than the most general statement of the problem of the relation of ideas to the social environment, of which the first two classes are special cases.

Finally, there are those like A. D. Lindsay who differ markedly from the others. They do not concern themselves primarily with an objective description of past systems of political ideas for the sake of revealing their function in the historical process. Instead, they begin with the deliberate choice of contemporary values and then seek to understand their meaning more fully by examining their growth through a special tradition, such as the Machiavellian or the democratic. They use history to illuminate the meaning and to establish the worth of contemporary political values, whereas the historian of political ideas tends to emphasize the objective appraisal of their growth. In effect, this kind of political theorist assumes, in Burke's traditionalistic vein, that the political values that have evolved through trial and error of a civilization over the centuries have thereby acquired a sanctity and truth which no re-analysis can fundamentally impair or radically modify.

Although no one political theorist mentioned has consistently pursued one or the other of these approaches exclusively, this in no way impairs the homogeneity of their outlook. All are historicist in their fundamental orientation.[3] They do not use the history of values as a device to stimulate their own thoughts on a possible creative redefinition of political goals. Their fundamental outlook prevents this. In the interstices of their work lurks the prevailing conceptions of social science, that all a social scientist can legitimately say about moral categories is that they are a product of the historical situation. In this view, the only meaningful task for the social scientist is to try to understand the factual conditions that have given rise to a particular ideology or system of values. Aside from another consideration, since personal values are conditioned in this way, it becomes a futile task for any theorist to go very far beyond the political ideals current in his own day and age. The formulation of a system of personal values, therefore, cannot be attempted within the bounds of social science. This frame of mind has inhibited the historicist from attempting a radical reconstruction of his inherited system of values.

Lindsay has unwittingly demonstrated this in the first chapter of his *The Modern Democratic State*.[4] There he maintains that the theorist at his best must confine himself to an attempt to understand the "operative

[3]For a systematic explication of historicism from the point of view of a defender of social science, see K. R. Popper, *The Open Society and Its Enemies* (London: G. Routledge & Sons, 1945), 2 vols., which deals with historicist political theory. A series of articles by the same author in *Economica*, New Series, 11 (1944) and 12 (1945), appraises historicist methodology.

[4]A. D. Lindsay, *The Modern Democratic State* (New York: Oxford University Press, 1943).

ideals" which have governed each era, especially those of our own day. The very title of the work indicates its limitations in this respect. He does not intend or pretend to enquire into a democratic theory that may serve future generations as well as our own; he restricts himself to the *modern* democratic ideas. "This volume," he writes, "is not about a general ideal called democracy but an historical type called the modern democratic state. . . ."[5] He devotes himself to the explanation of what he conceives to be the true meaning of contemporary political ideals in terms of which men seem to act, as they have been handed down and modified through the centuries.

The historical interpretation of values associated today with historicism has led to two unanticipated consequences. The first relates to practical affairs in political life and the second to social research in the universities. In the first place, from the point of view of practical affairs, historicism has carried political theory far from the original practical problems that gave it birth as a discipline in ancient Greece and which were the prevailing drive behind it, until the middle of the nineteenth century, at least, ending perhaps with Hegel and Marx.[6] In this long span of time, political theory was more than a mere offshoot of political history or the sociology of knowledge. In that long epoch, political theory, like the rest of political science, began and adhered to an elemental question to which the people, as laymen, have always sought an answer; namely, what criteria ought one to use in evaluating the variety of social programs offered by groups competing for political power. The initial concern of political science, and this is what distinguishes it *par excellence* from the other social sciences, has always been with social policy that arises out of political struggle. There are innumerable questions that require answers if one is to understand the way in which policy is formulated and executed, but in the whole field of political science, political theory by tradition has chosen as part of its task to try to propose standards within the frame of which practical policy might be adopted.

Towards the end of the nineteenth century, however, interest in the reformulation of values and in conceptions of a good political order declined, and the reasons are not hard to find. They are a composite, on the one hand, of the growth of the relativistic attitude towards values as it emerged from Hume and was crystallized for the social sciences by Max Weber; and on the other, of the political situation between 1848 and 1918. As long as men thought it possible to arrive at some standard or values in terms of which a future political order could be conceived, there

[5]Lindsay, *The Modern Democratic State*, p. 1.
[6]Leo Strauss, "On Classical Political Philosophy," *Social Research*, 12, No. 1 (February, 1945), pp. 98–117.

was sufficient incentive for a creative examination of past political ideas, but once the conclusion was drawn that all values are the expression of individual or group preferences and that these preferences in turn reflect the life experience of the individual or group, then the impetus for the creative study of values seemed to disappear. If the preferences of each person or of each historical epoch were neither better nor worse than those of another, then it seemed, if not a waste of time, at least a purely aesthetic and therefore politically meaningless task for scholars to devote themselves to the creative elaboration of value systems. Since this conclusion was manifestly illogical, as I shall try to show later, and could never be seriously adhered to in practice, the adoption of a relativistic conception of values need not in itself have led to the decline of critical appraisals of values. Yet, however illogical this conclusion was, since its truth was accepted, its effect was to turn political theorists to a study of the source, origin, and historical importance of these normative ideas. Their hitherto creative functions promptly evaporated.

The true reason, however, for the disappearance of these functions was not the emergence of moral relativism. The decline of interest in creative values and the growth of moral relativism were two concomitant results of a third factor; namely, the particular historical circumstances of the time. With the subsequent change of these conditions, any historical justification for the refusal publicly to redefine value frameworks must now be considered destroyed. In the nineteenth and early twentieth centuries there was undoubtedly sufficient agreement in western Europe for the indifference to value reformulation to have little important meaning in every day political affairs. There were no cleavages in ethical opinion that could so sharply divide antagonistic groups as to require a choice among fundamentally irreconcilable and competing values. But with the growth of fascism at the end of the first World War and the subsequent spread of totalitarianism in the West, the fact that Nietzsche had foreseen decades earlier, namely, that men can act on the basis of widely divergent ethical standards, has become all too apparent. This must gradually lead to a reconsideration of the need not only to analyze but also to question in a creative spirit, as was done in the earlier centuries, prevailing political values and their institutional implications. The fact is that, unlike the nineteenth century, we do feel the need for some guidance for our conduct in practical matters. In our period of conflicting value patterns, reinforced by almost irreconcilable power relations, the mere adoption of the values of our ancestors begins to pall unless they are seriously subjected, before acceptance, to critical analysis and imaginative reconstruction.

In the second place, not only for practical political matters, but for social research as well, is it inadequate to accept blindly a historicist approach? By the beginning of the twentieth century, particularly under the impact of Weber's ideas, the social scientist had accepted as axiomatic and unquestionable, what he had learned as a callow student; namely, that political values must be vigorously excluded from empirical research. The assumption here was and still is, not only that it is desirable to disassociate one's moral views from one's empirical analysis, but that this is also a possible achievement. Most of contemporary social science continues within this framework. It was thought sufficient to construct a theoretical framework in purely amoral causal terms. The adoption of a value frame of reference, it was and is still felt, would either distract the empirical worker from his main interest in observing human behavior or distort his results, since the wish easily becomes father to the thought.[7]

Today, of course, since the research of Karl Mannheim and the whole field of the sociology of knowledge, it has become as indisputable as the converse was to Weber, that whatever effort is exerted, values cannot be shed in the way a person removes his coat. They are an integral part of personality and as long as we are human, we can assume that our mental sets and preferences will be with us. Under these circumstances, our value framework becomes of crucial significance for what is generally viewed as empirical research. It influences the kind of problem we select for research and the way in which we interpret results. It helps to determine whether the factual problems involved in trying to pursue a set of social policies in political life will be investigated by the social scientist. For unless the latter is constantly aware that he himself does make value decisions, and that his research is inevitably immersed in an ethical perspective, he is apt to forget that social science lives in order to meet human needs. By shying away from his own rôle as a value builder, as well as analyzer, the research worker is less apt to identify the crucial problems of human life in society that require examination. In part, this search for an amoral science and its correlative hostility to a creative redefinition of values accounts for the feeling today that social science lives isolated in an ivory tower.[8]

In more than one case, such indifference to value assumptions has led the social scientist into research that turned out to have less relevance and meaning for society than otherwise might have been the case. This is not purely a hypothetical statement but can be adequately documented. However, since this would go beyond the space available here, I would

---

[7]The classic statement of this position appears in Max Weber, *The Methodology of the Social Sciences* (Glencoe, Illinois: The Free Press, 1949).

[8]Robert S. Lynd, *Knowledge for What?* (Princeton: Princeton University Press, 1939).

simply refer to an article in which I have attempted to show how one social scientist, in sincerely claiming and trying to pursue amoral research for at least a decade, had on the contrary unconsciously adopted the value frame of reference of Pareto's elitism.[9] There can be little doubt that this accounted in no small measure during the first period of his research for the fact that his conclusions failed to take into account the whole of the power relations in society.

The unanticipated consequences of historicism, therefore, have been, first, to detract political scientists from asking the question of "knowledge for what" and, second, even in the face of Mannheim's efforts, to trap some of them into believing that social objectivity is a necessity for good research. A way is needed to overcome these unfavorable consequences. I would urge that this path leads to the training of social scientists in the analysis and reconstruction of their value systems. To provide this training within the social sciences, however, it would first be necessary to re-establish political theory in its earlier and natural place within political science.

In turning now to show that this is not only a necessary but also a possible and fruitful enterprise, I certainly do not intend to disparage empirical investigations into the factors that give rise to and mould our values. This is an area of study in its own right and although historicist political theory has failed to develop an appropriate set of conceptual tools to do justice to this problem, at least it is seeking to throw light on a significant and still obscure question. Furthermore, in order to demonstrate that a return to the tradition of creative theory is possible, I do not intend to minimize the utility of raising the crucial and disputed issue of the nature of values themselves. However, whether they are objective principles, or whether they are periphrastic modes for expressing what are essentially indicative moods, as pragmatism implies,[10] or whether our preferences are goal-oriented psychological responses to our experiences, is not vital to our present problem. I propose instead to make the traditional assumption of social science; that is, that values are personal responses fixed by our life-experience. In making this assumption, I am aware of the fact that I am adopting a conception of values which is least favorable for the defense of a doctrine of creative valuational thought. I am, however, deliberately operating on this assumption because, if the

---

[9]David Easton, "Harold Lasswell: Policy Scientist for a Democratic Society," *The Journal of Politics*, 12, No. 3 (August, 1950), p. 450.

[10]See recent new approaches to a "science of values" in E. Fromm, *Man for Himself* (New York: Rinehart and Company, 1947); F. S. C. Northrop, *The Logic of the Sciences and the Humanities* (New York: The Macmillan Company, 1947); and Ray Lepley, *Verifiability of Value* (New York: Columbia University Press, 1944).

need for creative thought can be justified in these terms, it must by this very fact be reasonable and convincing to those who begin with other premises about the nature of values. And furthermore, any attempt to revive constructive value theory that did not accept this minimum assumption would be confronted with a prior overwhelming task of attempting to wean social science away from its deep-seated convictions about the nature of values.

My premise is least easily defended because it is on this very ground that social scientists have traditionally argued, not for but against the introduction of values into the classroom. If values are purely emotional responses, then no one set of values can claim to have a higher truth than any other set. In merely logical terms, fascism has as great a claim to truth as democracy. Regardless of the relativistic nature of these values, however, the fact is, as I have already indicated, in our own historical period we do need some serious political guidance, in the broadest and most sophisticated terms; and by "we," I mean the politician as well as the humble citizen. We could leave this task purely to the most perceptive of the statesmen. But clearly this would be a continuation of the earlier practice of social scientists in shirking a task that falls within the ambit of their competence. Those social scientists who are most closely associated with analyzing the content of past value systems are in a strategic position for contributing to a reformulation of contemporary theory. The fact that any such reformulation might not be able to aspire to some ultimate truth because it is just the way in which one individual happens to look upon the possible course of events is quite irrelevant here. We are all seeking to define our situation in the world both with regard to past occurrences and future prospects and goals. If a group of social scientists can aid us in this task, then there is little reason why the purely historically conditioned self-image of an amoral social science, conjured up during the special conditions of the nineteenth century, should be perpetuated today.

The task of the social scientist has been too sharply and artificially divorced from that of the politician. The function of the latter, it is said, is to sense human purposes and to reconcile them into a viable political order, whereas the task of the social scientist is to accumulate data about the relation of facts.[11] But this distinction is only partly true. Between these two tasks there lies yet a third which by oversight has been assigned to no one. This is the function of sensitively responding to the urgent problems of society and to the emerging social needs so that it

[11]For the classic elaboration of this position we must turn again to Max Weber in his essays, "Politics as a Vocation" and "Science as a Vocation" in H. H. Gerth and C. Wright Mills, *From Max Weber* (New York: Oxford University Press, 1946).

becomes possible to articulate a sophisticated system of values that will help both the citizen and the statesman to define their situation. Such a definition requires a conjunction of three elements: a statement of the actual situation, a statement of goals, both long-run and proximate, and a statement of the means to achieve these goals. Clearly, these three elements describe exactly the constituent elements of traditional creative theory. In other words, creative theory has been as much an institution for adjustment to society as political parties, the family, and similar human devices. The decline of creative theory has meant the disappearance of an important institution which in the past has helped to give determinate content and direction to felt but unarticulated human needs. My point is that the enterprise of defining the situation in evaluational terms is a legitimate one for the political theorist because as a social scientist, he is in close touch with the data of empirical relations, and as a value theorist, he is directly involved with human goals. Neither the politician nor the citizen is normally as well equipped.

Given my premise about the nature of values, the task of defining the situation in value terms must be considered an art rather than a science. If this is true, one can seriously question the place that the creative theorist can have in a university, at least among the social sciences. The answer here is threefold. In the first place, now that the sociology of knowledge has taught us that values are implicit in all research, it has become incumbent on the social scientist to excise his values and hold them up for inspection, as I have already suggested. But anyone who has had any experience in this operation knows that it is not always easy to uncover hidden assumptions of values, that in the process of bringing them to consciousness they seem to change subtly or take unexpected forms and, finally, that once they are presented as an objective datum, the holder of these ideas is apt to change them quite deliberately. This is possible especially if the social scientist becomes aware of the implications of his thought, since, as in the case already cited, it is quite possible that his value system might have implications which once known, repel him. While it is true that the creative reworking of values, as values are conceived for present purposes, is a task of art, nevertheless it is in practice so vital to the meaningfulness of social research that no alternative is left but to expose the political scientist at an early stage to the way in which the art has been practiced in the past. It is true that today political scientists are exposed to the value-creating theorist of the past; however, they are not really introduced to his art. Instead they circle *about* his art, seeking to explain empirically the form it takes, but seldom trying to understand it as an imitable attempt at value construction.

Failure to realize the function that value-creation plays in empirical research means that the choices of political scientists, like other social scientists, will be moulded not by the conscious adoption of a set of values, but by the implicit and intuitive acceptance of a value framework which they have accidentally acquired. Clearly this conflicts with our first principles as social scientists, that is, to be strictly aware of our operations so that the validity of the results can be known in terms of the way they were derived. By the denigration of this creative function as a meaningless pursuit for social scientists, historical interpretation as we know it today has thereby contributed to social blindness in empirical research. New vision and clarity for research is possible if the political scientist is trained to appraise his values critically. Only in this way can he be certain that his research is relevant and significant for human goals, as he conceives them. In the need for such training lies one justification for a resurgence of creative value theory.

In the second place, there is no *a priori*, as contrasted to a simply traditionalistic reason, why the political scientist needs to confine himself only to the task of seeking to understand political relations as they exist. Indeed, as I have already pointed out, the attempt to do this over the last hundred years has led to the increasing isolation of social science from the source of its original impetus, that is, from the attempt to understand the goals of society so that human needs, at the very least as they are conceived by each age, might be satisfied. Creative political theory in the past was engaged in the task of attempting to organize for each age its own conceptions of its needs, both proximate and long-run. But when political theory became converted to historicism it neglected its earlier function of linking knowledge of political facts to political goals. The revival of creative theory will provide once again a bridge between the needs of society and the knowledge of the social sciences. For this reason creative as against historicist theory finds a legitimate place in the field of political science. By reasserting the intrinsic tie between all social research and political policy, it will serve to entice the social sciences out of their recent isolation into the society which they are designed to serve.

My third point I need only to mention as it is clear from the earlier discussion. Creative theory as part of social science will help both statesmen and citizens to define their situation, thereby serving to clarify for them the grounds of political action. It is part of the same institutional justification applying to social science as a whole.

With these clear tasks confronting political theory there is little wonder that the historicist studies of past theories should prove so inadequate to us today. None of these studies is directed in a forthright manner to the questioning of old or the creation of new political syntheses.

CAUSAL THEORY

I shall turn now to the second reason for the decline of political theory in the last half-century; namely, its indifference to causal theory. From the point of view of causal theory, which I use as a synonym for systematic empirically-oriented theory about political behavior, the term, political theory, is a sad misnomer for the field of knowledge it embraces. It misleads one into expecting that political theory will deal with genuine systematic theory. As everyone knows, little theory, if any, finds its way into this field. In fact, the manifest lack of such causal theory has induced a sociological theorist to argue that as "a *theoretically distinctive* conceptual scheme of purely *empirical* social science which is not sociological, economic, anthropological, or psychological, I cannot see that there is such a thing as political theory."[12] The neglect of theory in this second sense accounts in no small measure for the chasm that separates political theory from the whole body of contemporary research into political behavior and institutions.

If political theory had performed its task well, it would now be in the forefront of empirical research to light the way; in practice, it stumbles along behind. It has been delinquent in this respect, not because it offered poor theories about political behavior, but because it has never been guided by an image of itself as a truly theoretical organ for political science. Instead, as I have already shown, political theory in spite of its name has approached the study of political activity, as distinct from political goals, primarily through a discussion of means to ends. The creative political theorists of the past have traditionally passed judgment on the best means for the attainment of the goals they espoused. By formulating goals and then specifying the means thereto, political theorists have really been attempting to create an applied science of politics adapted to these values. To the extent that political theory today deals with causal theory, it consists almost exclusively of historical commentaries describing the applied political principles of the great theorists.

The weakness of political theory in its causal aspects does not arise, therefore, solely from the emergence of historicism. Even during the great epochs of its creativeness it failed to develop genuine theoretical causal knowledge, the nature of which I shall later describe more fully. Abortive as these earlier attempts at an applied science were, they at least were trying to perform a necessary task for political science. They were trying to describe the institutional means necessary to achieve the

[12]Talcott Parsons, *Essays in Sociological Theory* (Glencoe, Illinois: The Free Press, 1949), p. 13.

specified goals. But with the growth of historicism, political theorists were led to abandon even these inadequate efforts at an applied science. Historicist theory replaced these efforts with so-called objective accounts for their development and internal consistency. As with value theory proper, the genuine questioning of existing institutions yielded to the acceptance of the status quo, usually with minor modifications that never threatened any fundamental change.

As I have suggested, the essential shortcomings of political theory in relation to empirical research stem not solely from the impact of historicism but initially from the very nature of the way it has always looked at political facts. An analysis of political theory at any stage of its development reveals that it has always set the cart to draw the horse. It has been able to offer little causal theory which could permit the construction of a meaningful applied science. If the discussion of means to ends is to pass beyond the level of uncommon common sense, if, in other words, the recommendations of political scientists for the attainment of specific objectives are to be of greater value than the proposals for political reform proffered by the informed Washington columnist or the gifted statesman, then these proposals must arise from a well-grounded body of theoretical knowledge about political behavior and the functioning of political institutions. This does not mean that the political theorist needs to refrain from offering whatever advice he can on the basis of the kind of generalized data that he does possess; but it does suggest that he must become conscious of the fact that his advice cannot pass beyond the rank of exceptional common sense unless it is drawn from a general theory of political behavior.

Political *theory* is not by itself responsible, however, for the scarcity of causal theory. In a sense, its condition accurately reflects the low level of theoretical development of our discipline as a whole. Careful examination of the vast body of data in political science, which would require too lengthy a diversion at this point, would lead to the conclusion that, with significant exceptions, it consists of an agglomeration of empirical observations and of broad generalizations that are difficult to comprehend. Comprehension eludes us because the meaning of the terms is often so imprecise and the nature of the relationships between the isolated variables is often so indistinct as to reduce these generalizations to the order of first insights. While undoubtedly these insights often do show a high level of imagination at work, in too many cases they do not transcend the level of first principles, self-evident to men of common sense. In addition, it is the rule rather than the exception to find in political research, numerous factual assumptions about human behavior that are seldom brought to the surface for critical examination. Thus, even if political theory had consciously set itself the task of examining the empirical literature in political science with the avowed purpose of discovering a systematic pattern, the mass of poorly formulated knowledge at present available would not readily have yielded fruitful results.

Where some attempt has been made in the last half-century to develop a theory of political behavior, political theorists, who ought to have been the first to seize upon these efforts for comment and development, have tended as a group to ignore them. That is, the little systematic theory attempted has been the product of the enterprise of persons who were not primarily concerned with traditional theory. I am thinking, for example, of Mosca, well-known now in the United States, in whose writings there is elaborated the basic framework of the elitist theory;[13] or of Lasswell, in whose writings there is a reworking of that framework in more precise terms;[14] or of Michels who offers a less elaborate version in relation to political parties;[15] or, more recently, of Herbert Simon who is developing a narrow-gauge theory of decision-making for public administration.[16]

During the last fifty years, in only two cases of which I am aware, in the United States at least, can it be said that professional *political theorists* considered it profitable and advisable to attempt to formulate a general theoretical structure as a guide for empirical research. These are George Catlin, who made an abortive attempt in the thirties to emulate physics and economic theory by building a deductively formulated theory for political science as a whole;[17] and C. J. Friedrich, who has sought to cast the study of political institutions within the framework of a theory of power.[18] Unfortunately, as stimulating as both attempts have been, the transition from the theory to the facts has proved so difficult as to discourage further precise research.

I am, of course, assuming that it is possible to discover uniformities in human, and in particular, in political behavior which can be used as a basis for predictions. I am also suggesting that the blind search for such uniformities undirected by a more general theory leads to a crude empiricism in which facts are piled upon facts until all sense of purpose is

[13]Gaetano Mosca, *The Ruling Class* (New York: McGraw-Hill Book Company, Inc., 1939).

[14]Harold D. Lasswell, *Politics, Who Gets What, When, How* (New York: McGraw-Hill Book Company, Inc., 1936).

[15]Robert Michels, *Political Parties* (New York: Hearst's International Library Co., 1915).

[16]Herbert A. Simon, *Administrative Behavior* (New York: The Macmillan Company, 1947).

[17]G. E. G. Catlin, *Principles of Politics* (New York: The Macmillan Company, 1930).

[18]Carl J. Friedrich, *Constitutional Government and Democracy* (Boston: Little, Brown and Company, 1941), esp. chap. I.

lost. Furthermore, when I speak of theory I have in mind three kinds of generalizations and it seems to me that political theory might appropriately devote itself to two of these. There are, first of all, singular generalizations, which I would not dignify with the name, theory. These are statements of observed uniformities between the two isolated and easily identified variables. Since from such a statement, few deductions can be made that go beyond the actual observed uniformity, this places singular generalizations at the lowest level of theoretical thought. What I call "Gosnell's generalization" is an illustration of this kind of proposition.[19] Derived from a careful experiment in voting behavior, it states that nonpartisan stimulation of voting will increase the number of people who vote, given certain specified conditions. Such generalizations are without doubt the least difficult to obtain and yet there are relatively few such rigorously formulated propositions available in the whole literature of political science. One suspects that this dearth is due less to the nature of the subject matter than to the inclinations and traditions of political scientists.

At a higher, intermediary level stands synthetic or narrow-gauge theory. Theory, in this sense, consists of a set of interrelated propositions which are designed to synthesize the data contained in an unorganized body of single generalizations. But in the process of synthesis, the theory that is developed goes beyond the actual data included in the original cluster of generalizations. It becomes possible to understand not only the phenomena to which these generalizatons originally related, but also other phenomena which had hiterto been shrouded in doubt. Consider the "iron law of oligarchy" as an illustration of this kind of theory. It arose initially as the result of the desire of Michels to indicate in a brief form the fact that all organizations with specific ends, containing human beings of the kind we know in western Europe, tend to concentrate power into the hands of a few. The so-called "law," therefore, emerges out of an attempt to synthesize a considerable number of empirical observations relating to party organizations. By transcending the limits of his observations in this one case, Michels was able to generalize and apply this law to all social groups organized to fulfill specific ends, including the political order itself. It is a theory, therefore, since it has broader implications than the actual facts which it was designed to draw together. If it is true, we should be able to deduce that even in a direct democracy, after Rousseau, the bulk of power would still not reside in the hands of the people. If true, it might also help to explain the source of political apathy and other related problems.

[19]Harold F. Gosnell, *Getting Out the Vote* (Chicago: The University of Chicago Press, 1927).

At the highest level, there stands broad gauge theory or the conceptual framework within which a whole discipline is cast. Theory of this order is designed to help select the specific variables that are vital to an understanding of the problems which a discipline seeks to solve. The more developed this framework is, the more precisely will these variables be identified and related. It is conceivable that some day in the social sciences such a framework might reach the stage of maturity of theory in physics, for example. In the latter science, from a few basic premises it has proved possible to formulate deductively a whole body of intermediate theory and from this, in turn, to predict the occurrence of empirical events. From such predictions the ultimate validity of the parent conceptual theory is then either affirmed or denied.

At the present stage of development, with the exception of economics, the attainment of such advanced theory in social science is still in the realm of pious aspiration. But even in the case of this exception, the deductively formulated theory has proved so unsatisfactory that it has led some people to argue that it may never be possible in social science. Nevertheless, one cannot deny that behind all empirical research there are certain basic assumptions with regard to the major variables in the field and their relations and that one way of promoting the maturation of a discipline is to raise these assumptions to the point of consciousness for purposes of careful examination.

To my knowledge, George Catlin is the only political theorist who in recent years has elaborated such a deductive system for politics. It achieved few results, however, because it proved so abstract that it could never be reduced to reality with any degree of precision. Lasswell, in his *Politics: Who Gets What, When, How* conceivably was striving towards the same goal, but I think it could be demonstrated upon analysis that he has provided us with a synthetic narrow-gauge theory rather than a conceptual framework useful for the whole of political science.

I am not suggesting, of course, that it is either probable or possible that political theory could provide us today with a body of theory that even approaches in architectural form or intrinsic explanatory value the theories of such natural sciences as physics, chemistry, or biology. To pose as our immediate goal the attainment of the methodological rigor and precise formulations of the physical sciences, which are centuries ahead of the social sciences in their theoretical and factual maturity, would be to fall victim to scientism, that is, to the premature and slavish imitation of the physical sciences.[20] All social research cannot yet be conducted with the methodological rigor familiar to the natural sciences or in terms

[20]F. A. von Hayek, "Scientism and the Study of Society," *Economica*, New Series, 9 (1942), 10 (1943), and 11 (1944).

of the systematic frameworks resembling the model of physics. There is yet to appear an advocate of scientism who in his published research has measured up to his own *a priori* scientific standards, simply because in most areas of social science this is either impossible or, where possible, the financial and other resources to do the massive research necessary are not available. If political science were to insist upon universal adherence to methodological rigor at the present time as the only kind of adequate research, there is little doubt that, in attending so mechanically to form, all life and wisdom would be squeezed from even the existing insights into political behavior.[21] Contemporary knowledge in political science can be criticized not because it fails to measure up to the rigorous canons of unadulterated science but because it does not use the more modest methods and techniques that are at present available in the social sciences as a whole and that have proved exceedingly fruitful in research.

However, in spite of this real backwardness in political science, these criticisms ought not to be understood as an indirect depreciation of existing knowledge. On the contrary, in spite of its methodological innocence, traditional political science has attracted and continues to attract to its approach some of the brilliant minds of each generation. In consequence it could not help but offer us penetrating insight into the nature of the political process and the operation of political institutions; nor could it fail to identify crucial variables that must be examined more systematically. Twenty-five years ago such knowledge was at the forefront of the social sciences. Today it is still vital. But we have now reached a point when it is possible to take what are essentially insights, to refine them, and to begin to examine them more rigorously. It is not a matter of discarding or spurning the results of what has come to be called traditional political research. It is a matter, wherever possible, of using the available knowledge as the point of departure for the next stage of development. Our knowledge of method for the study of human behavior has now made it mandatory and feasible, in preparation for this next period, to attack the problems of reformulating our knowledge into more systematic narrow-gauge theories and, if possible, into an integrated theoretical framework for the whole of political science.

The burden of my argument is, then, that in addition to its task of helping to analyze old and formulate new political values, political theory ought to devote itself to the equally vital job of conceptualizing the basic areas for empirical research in political science. It ought to undertake this in two concurrent and parallel ways: first, by synthesizing and codifying

[21]The work of G. Lundberg is only one of many examples of such excessive insistence on methodological rigor that can be cited from sociology.

the limited generalizations we have in the various fields of political science and by so formulating the resulting theory that it lends itself to verification or invalidation and, second, by attempting the more massive task of elaborating a usable conceptual framework for the whole body of political science. In this way it would be possible for political theory to assimilate itself to the main current of empirical research in political science, and thereby to revivify itself after the unrewarding historical study to which it has been devoted in the last fifty years. Historical study would thereby recede from its present place of paramount importance to the more humble position of a useful device for nourishing the mind both with regard to creative values and causal theory.

18

Isaiah Berlin

DOES POLITICAL THEORY STILL EXIST?*

Professor Berlin points out in consideration of the question he poses that there are only "two good reasons for certifying the demise of a discipline": (1) "its central presuppositions, empirical, or metaphysical, or logical, are no longer accepted" and (2) "new disciplines have come to perform the work originally undertaken by the older study." He considers the ways in which we answer questions that occur to us, and perceives two which have afforded clear answers, and denominates these methods "very generally" as "empirical and formal." But neither of these methods can be used wholly satisfactorily in treating "philosophical" questions, "one of the surest hallmarks" of which is "that we are puzzled from the very outset, that there is no automatic technique, no universally recognized expertise, for dealing with such questions." Among the "obstinately philosophical" questions are those that necessarily entail questions of value. Some count such questions illegitimate, but why, asks Professor Berlin, are they illegitimate? They are questions about something that puzzles us. He contends that unless political theory is "conceived in narrowly sociological terms," it differs from empirical enquiry in being concerned with questions such as what is specifically human and why and whether specific categories, such as purpose or of belonging to a group, are indispensable to understand-

*Reprinted by permission of the publisher from Peter Laslett and W. G. Runciman, eds., *Philosophy, Politics and Society* (Second Series; New York: Barnes and Noble, Inc., 1962), pp. 1–33.

ing what men are. Hence it would be concerned inevitably with the source, scope, and validity of certain human goals and could not, from the very nature of its interests, avoid evaluation. He thinks that in this broader conception he is thoroughly committed not only to the analysis of, but also to conclusions about the validity of, ideas of the good and the bad, the permitted and the forbidden, the harmonious and the discordant problems any discussion of liberty or justice or authority or political morality is sooner or later bound to encounter. As Professor Berlin puts his case, "no amount of careful empirical observation and bold and fruitful hypothesis will explain to us what those men see who see the state as a divine institution, or what their words mean and how they relate to reality; nor what those believe who tell us that the state was sent upon us only for our sins; or those who say that it is a school through which we must go before we are adult and free and can dispense with it; or that it is a work of art; or a utilitarian device; or the incarnation of natural law; or a committee of the ruling class; or the highest stage of the self-developing human spirit; or a piece of criminal folly." Moreover, he asserts, unless imaginative insight informs our understanding of "what notions of man's nature (or absence of them) are incorporated in these political outlooks, what in each case is the dominant model, we shall not understand our own or any human society."

Professor Berlin's commentary upon his topic throws much light upon our ways of thinking and their cross-fertilization. He concludes political theory is and will continue to be very much with us.

1

Is there still such a subject as Political Theory?[1] This query, put with suspicious frequency in English speaking countries, questions the very credentials of the subject: it suggests that political philosophy, whatever it may have been in the past, is to-day dead or dying. The principal symptom which seems to support this belief is that no commanding work of political philosophy has appeared in the twentieth century. By a commanding work in the field of general ideas I mean at the very least one that has in a large area converted paradoxes into platitudes or vice versa. This seems to me no more (but also no less) than an adequate criterion of the characteristic in question.

[1]The original version of this article appeared in French in the *Revue Française de Science Politique*, Vol. XI, no. 2, 1961. It has since been revised by the author whose thanks are due to Professor S. N. Hampshire, Professor H. L. A. Hart, Professor F. Rossi Landi, Mr. P. L. Gardiner, Mr. G. Warnock, and most of all to Mr. M. W. Dick, for reading and commenting on it in its earlier form.

But this is scarcely conclusive evidence. There exist only two good reasons for certifying the demise of a discipline: one is that its central presuppositions, empirical, or metaphysical, or logical, are no longer accepted because they have (with the world of which they were a part) withered away, or because they have been discredited or refuted. The other is that new disciplines have come to perform the work originally undertaken by the older study. These disciplines may have their own limitations, but they exist, they function, and have either inherited or usurped the functions of their predecessors: there is no room left for the ancestor from whom they spring. This is the fate that overtook astrology, alchemy, phrenology (positivists, both old and new, would include theology and metaphysics). The postulates on which these disciplines were based were either destroyed by argument or collapsed for other reasons; consequently they are to-day regarded merely as instances of systematic delusion.

This type of systematic parricide is, in effect, the history of the natural sciences in their relation to philosophy, and so has a direct bearing upon the question before us. The relevant consideration is this: there exist at least two classes of problems to which men have succeeded in obtaining clear answers. The first have been so formulated that they can (at least in principle, if not always in practice) be answered by observation and by inference from observed data. These determine the domains of natural science and of everyday common sense. Whether I ask simple questions about whether there is any food in the cupboard, or what kind of birds are to be found in Patagonia, or the intentions of an individual; or more complicated ones about the structure of matter, or the behaviour of social classes or international markets; I know that the answer, to have any genuine claim to truth, must rest on someone's observation of what exists or happens in the spatio-temporal world. Some would say "organized observation." I should be inclined to agree: observation is an activity, and part and parcel of the intention and the conceptual world of the observer. But differences on this issue, while they are crucial for the philosophy of science and the theory of knowledge, do not affect my argument. All the generalizations and hypotheses and models with which the most sophisticated sciences work, can be established and discredited ultimately only by the data of inspection or introspection.

The second type of question to which we can hope to obtain clear answers is formal. Given certain propositions called axioms, together with rules for deducing other propositions from them, I can proceed by mere calculation. The answers to my questions will be valid or invalid according to whether the rules that I accept without question as part of a given discipline, have been correctly used. Such disciplines contain no statements based on observation of fact, and therefore are not nowadays expected to provide information about the universe, whether or not they are used in providing it. Mathematics and formal logic are, of course, the best known examples of formal sciences of this type, but heraldry, chess, and theories of games in general, are similar applications of the formal methods which govern such disciplines.

These two methods of answering questions may be, very generally, denominated empirical and formal. Among the characteristics of both are at least these:

1. That even if we do not know the answer to a given question, we know what kinds of methods are appropriate in looking for the answer; we know what kinds of answers are relevant to these questions, even if they are not true. If I am asked how the Soviet system of criminal law functions or why Mr. Kennedy was elected President of the United States, I may not be able to answer the question, but I know within what region the relevant evidence must lie, and how an expert would use such evidence to obtain the answer; I must be able to state this in very general terms, if only to show that I have understood the question. Similarly, if I am asked for the proof of Fermat's theorem, I may not be able to give it, indeed I may know that no one has yet been able to provide it, but I also know what kinds of demonstration would count as answers to this problem, even though they may be incorrect or inconclusive, and discriminate these from assertions which are irrelevant to the topic. In other words, in all these cases, even if I do not know the answer, I know where to look for it, or how to identify an authority or expert who knows how to set about looking for it.

2. This means, in effect, that where the concepts are firm, clear and generally accepted, and the methods of reasoning, arriving at conclusions, etc., are agreed between men (at least the majority of those who have anything to do with these matters) there and only there is it possible to construct a science, formal or empirical. Wherever this is not the case—where the concepts are vague or too much in dispute, and methods of argument and the minimum qualifications that constitute an expert are not generally agreed, where we find frequent recriminations about what can or what cannot claim to be a law, an established hypothesis, an undisputed truth, and so on, we are at best in the realm of quasi-science. The principal candidates for inclusion into the charmed circle, who have not succeeded in passing the required tests, are the occupants of the large, rich and central, but unstable, volcanic and misty region of "ideologies." One of the rough and ready tests for finding out which region we are in, is whether a set of rules, accepted by the great majority of experts in the subject, and capable of being incorporated in a

text-book, can be applied in the field in question. To the degree to which such rules are applicable, a discipline approaches the coveted condition of an accepted science. Psychology, sociology, semantics, logic, perhaps certain branches of economics, are in a no-man's-land, some nearer, some further from the frontier which demarcates, less or more clearly, the frontiers of the established sciences.

3. But besides these two major categories, there arise questions which fall outside either group. It is not only that we may not know the answers to certain questions, but that we are not clear how to set about trying to answer them—where to look—what would constitute evidence for an answer and what would not. When I am asked "Where is the image in the mirror?" or "Can time stand still?" I am not sure what kind of question it is that is being asked, or whether indeed it makes any sense at all. I am in not much better plight with some traditional questions which have probably been asked since the dawn of thought, such as: "How did the world begin?", and, following that, "What happened before the beginning?" Some say that these are not legitimate questions; but then what makes them illegitimate? There is something that I am trying to ask; for I am certainly puzzled by something. When I ask "Why can I not be in two places at once?" "Why can I not get back into the past?" or, to move to another region, "What is justice?" or "Is justice objective, absolute, etc.?" or again "How can we ever be sure that an action is just?"—no obvious method of settling these questions lies to hand. One of the surest hallmarks of a philosophical question—for this is what all these questions are—is that we are puzzled from the very outset, that there is no automatic technique, no universally recognized expertise, for dealing with such questions. We discover that we do not feel sure how to set about clearing our minds, finding out the truth, accepting or rejecting earlier answers to these questions. Neither induction (in its widest sense of scientific reasoning) nor direct observation (appropriate to empirical enquiries), nor deduction (demanded by formal problems), seem to be of help. Once we do feel quite clear about how we should proceed, the questions no longer seem philosophical.

The history—and indeed the advance—of human thought (this is perhaps a truism) have, in fact, largely consisted in the gradual shuffling of all the basic questions that men ask into one or the other of two well-organized compartments—the empirical and the formal. Wherever concepts grow firm and clear and acquire universal acceptance, a new science, natural or formal, comes into being. To use a simile that I cannot claim to have invented, philosophy is like a radiant sun that, from time to time, throws off portions of itself; these masses, when they cool down, acquire a firm and recognizable structure of their own and acquire independent careers as tidy and regular planets; but the central sun continues on its path, and does not seem to dimish in mass or radiance. The "status" and vitality of philosophy is another matter, and seems to be directly connected with the extent to which it deals with issues that are of concern to the common man. The relation of philosophy to opinion and conduct is a central question both of history and sociology, too large to be considered here. What concerns us is that philosophy in one state of development may turn into a science in the next.

It is no confusion of thought that caused astronomy, for example, to be regarded as a philosophical discipline in, say, the times of Scotus Erigena, when its concepts and methods were not what we should to-day regard as firm or clear, and the part played by observation in relation to *a priori* teleological notions (e.g. the yearning of each body to realize the full perfection of its nature) made it impossible to determine whether the amalgam that went under the name of the knowledge of celestial bodies was empirical or formal. As soon as clear concepts and specific techniques developed, the science of astronomy emerged. In other words, astronomy in its beginning could not be relegated to either compartment, even if such compartments as the empirical and the formal had been clearly distinguished; and it was, of course, part of the "philosophical" status of early mediaeval astronomy that the civilization of that time (Marxists would say "the superstructure") did not permit the distinction between the two compartments to be clearly demarcated.

What, therefore, is characteristic of specifically philosophical questions is that they do not (and some of them perhaps never will) satisfy conditions required by an independent science, the principal among which is that the path to their solution must be implicit in their very formulation. Nevertheless, there are some subjects which clearly are near the point of taking flight and divorcing themselves from the main body in which they were born, much as physics and mathematics and chemistry and biology have done in their day. One of these is semantics; another is psychology; with one foot, however reluctantly, they are still sunk in philosophical soil; but they show signs of a tendency to tear themselves loose and emancipate themselves, with only historical memories to tell them of their earlier, more confused, if in some respects richer, years.

2

Among the topics that remain obstinately philosophical, and have, despite repeated efforts, failed to transform themselves into sciences, are some that in their very essence involve value judgements. Ethics, æsthetics, criticism explicitly concerned with general ideas, all but the most technical types of history and scholarship, still live at various points of this limbo, unable or unwilling to emerge by either (the empirical or the formal) door. The mere fact that value judgements are relevant to an intellectual pursuit is clearly not sufficient to disqualify it from being a recognized science. The concept of normal health certainly embodies a valuation, and although there is sufficient universal consensus about what constitutes good health, a normal state, disease and so on, this concept, nevertheless, does not enter as an intrinsic element into the sciences of anatomy, physiology, pathology, etc. Pursuit of health may be the strongest sociological and psychological (and moral) factor in creating and promoting these sciences; it may determine which problems and aspects of the subject have been most ardently attended to; but it is not referred to in the science itself, any more than the uses of history or logic need be mentioned in historical or logical works. If so clear, universally accepted, "objective," a value as that of desirable state of health is extruded from the structure of the natural sciences, this fact is even more conspicuous in more controversial fields. The attempts, from Plato to our own day (particularly persistent and numerous in the eighteenth century) to found objective sciences of ethics and æsthetics on the basis of universally accepted values, or of methods of discovering them, have met with little success; relativism, subjectivism, romanticism, scepticism with regard to values, keep breaking in. What, we may ask at this point, is the position of political theory? What are its most typical problems? Are they empirical, or formal, or neither? Do they necessarily entail questions of value? Are they on the way to independent status, or are they by their very nature compelled to remain only an element in some wider body of thought?

Among the problems which form the core of traditional political theory are those, for instance, of the nature of equality, of rights, law, authority, rules. We demand the analysis of these concepts, or ask how these expressions function in our language, or what forms of behaviour they prescribe or forbid and why, or into what system of value or outlook they fit, and in what way. When we ask, what is perhaps the most fundamental of all political questions—"Why should anyone obey anyone else?", we ask not "Why do men obey"—something that empirical psychology, anthropology and sociology might be able to answer; nor yet "Who obeys whom, when and where, and determined by what causes?" which could perhaps be answered on the basis of evidence drawn from these and similar fields. When we ask why a man should obey, we are asking for the explanation of what is normative in such notions as authority, sovereignty, liberty, and the justification of their validity in political arguments. These are words in the name of which orders are issued, men are

coerced, wars are fought, new societies are created and old ones destroyed—expressions which play as great a part as any in our lives to-day.
What makes such questions *prima facie* philosophical is the fact that no
wide agreement exists on the meaning of some of the concepts involved.
There are sharp differences on what constitute valid reasons for actions
in these fields; on how the relevant propositions are to be established or
even rendered plausible; on who or what constitutes recognized authority
for deciding these questions; and there is consequently no consensus on
the frontier between valid public criticism and subversion, or freedom and
oppression and the like. So long as conflicting replies to such questions
continue to be given by different schools and thinkers, the prospects of
establishing a science in this field, whether empirical or formal, seem
remote. Indeed, it seems clear that disagreements about the analysis of
value concepts, as often as not, spring from profounder differences, since
the notions of, say, rights or justice or liberty will be radically dissimilar
for theists and atheists, mechanistic determinists and Christians, Hegelians and empiricists, romantic irrationalists and Marxists, and so forth. It
seems no less clear that these differences are not, at least *prima facie*,
either logical or empirical, and have usually and rightly been classified as
irreducibly philosophical.

This carries at least one important implication. If we ask the Kantian
question, "In what kind of world is political philosophy—the kind of
discussion and argument in which it consists—in principle possible?" the
answer must be "Only in a world where ends collide." In a society dominated by a single goal there could in principle only be arguments about
the best means to attain this end—and arguments about means are technical, that is, scientific and empirical in character: they can be settled by
experience and observation or whatever other methods are used to discover causes and correlations; they can, at least in principle, be reduced
to positive sciences. In such a society no serious questions about political
ends or values could arise, only empirical ones about the most effective
paths to the goal. And indeed, something amounting to this was, in effect, asserted by Saint-Simon and Comte; and, on some interpretations
of his thought, by Marx also, at any rate after "prehistory," i.e. the class
war, is over, and man's true "history"—the united attack on nature to
obtain goods upon whose desirability the whole of society is agreed—has
begun. It follows that the only society in which political philosophy in
its traditional sense, that is, an enquiry concerned not solely with elucidation of concepts, but with the critical examination of presuppositions
and assumptions, and the questioning of the order of priorities and ultimate ends, is possible, is a society in which there is no total acceptance
of any single end. There may be a variety of reasons for this: because

no single end has been accepted by a sufficient number of persons; because no one end can be regarded as ultimate, since there can, in principle, exist no guarantee that other values may not at some time engage men's reason or their passions; because no unique, final end can be found —inasmuch as men can pursue many distinct ends, none of them means to, or parts of, one another; and so on. Some among these ends may be public or political; nor is there any reason to suppose that all of them must, even in principle, be compatible with one another. Unless political philosophy is confined to the analysis of concepts or expressions, it can be pursued consistently only in a pluralist, or potentially pluralist, society. But since all analysis, however abstract, itself involves a critical approach to the assumptions under analysis, this distinction remains purely academic. Rigid monism is compatible with philosophical analysis only in theory. The plight of philosophy under depotism in our own times provides conclusive concrete evidence for this thesis.

3

Let me try to make this clearer. If we could construct a society in which it was believed universally (or at least by as many people as believe that the purpose of medicine is to promote or maintain health and are agreed about what constitutes health) that there was only one overriding human purpose: for example, a technocratic society dedicated to the single end of the richest realization of all human faculties; or a utilitarian society dedicated to the greatest happiness of men; or a Thomist or communist or Platonic or anarchist, or any other society which is monistic in this sense—then plainly all that would matter would be to find the right roads to the attainment of the universally accepted end.

This statement needs to be qualified in at least two respects. The schema is in the first place artificially over-simplified. In practice, the kind of goal that can command the allegiance of a society—happiness, power, obedience to the divine will, national glory, individual self-realization, or some other ultimate pattern of life, is so general that it leaves open the question of what kind of lives or conduct incarnate it. No society can be so "monolithic" that there is no gap between its culminating purpose and the means towards it—a gap filled with secondary ends, penultimate values, which are not means to the final end, but elements in it or expressions of it; and these in their turn incarnate themselves in still more specific purposes at still lower levels, and so on downwards to the particular problem of everyday conduct. "What is to be done?" is a question which can occur at any level—from the highest to the lowest: doubts and disputes concerning the values involved at any of these levels, and the relationships of these values to one another can arise at any point.

These questions are not purely technical and empirical, not merely problems about the best means to a given end, nor are they mere questions of logical consistency, that is, formal and deductive: but properly philosophical. To take contemporary examples: what is claimed for integration of negroes and whites in the Southern states of the United States is not that it is a means towards achieving a goal external to itself—social justice or equality—but that it is itself a form of it, a value in the hierarchy of values. Or again "one vote one man," or the rights of minorities or of colonial territories, are, likewise, not simply questions of machinery—a particular means of promoting equality which could, in theory, be equally well realized by other means, say by more ingenious voting devices—but, for those who believe in these principles, are intrinsic ingredients in the ideal of social equality, and consequently to be pursued as such, and not solely for the sake of their results. It follows that even in a society dominated by a single supreme purpose, questions of what is to be done, especially when the subordinate ends come into conflict, cannot be automatically answered by deductive reasoning from accepted premises, aided by adequate knowledge of facts, as certain thinkers, Aristotle at times, or Bertrand Russell in his middle phase, or a good many Catholic casuists, seem to have assumed.

Moreover, and this is our second qualification, it might well be the case that although the formulæ accepted by a society were sacred and immutable, they might carry different—and perhaps incompatible—meanings for different persons and in different situations; philosophical analysis of the relevant concepts might well bring out sharp disagreements. This has been the case conspicuously where the purpose or ideal of a society is expressed in such vague and general terms as the common good, or the fulfilment of the law of God, or rights to life, liberty and the pursuit of happiness and the like.

Nevertheless, and in spite of these qualifications, the stylized model of a society whose ends are given once and for all, and which is merely concerned with discovery of means, is a useful abstraction. It is useful because it demonstrates that to acknowledge the reality of political questions presupposes a pluralism of values—whether ultimate ones, or on the lower slopes of the hierarchy of values, recognition of which is incompatible with a technocratic or authoritarian everything-is-either-an-indisputable-end-or-a-means, monistic structure of values. Nor is the monistic situation entirely a figment of theory. In critical situations where deviation from the norm may involve disastrous consequences—in battles, surgical operating rooms, revolutions, the end is wholly concrete, varying interpretations of it are out of place and all action is conceived as a means towards it alone. It is one of the stratagems of totalitarian régimes to represent all situations as critical emergencies, demanding ruthless elimination of all goals, interpretations, forms of behavior save for one absolutely specific, concrete, immediate end, binding on everyone, which calls for ends and means so narrow and clearly definable that it is easy to impose sanctions for failing to pursue them.

To find roads is the business of experts. It is therefore reasonable for such a society to put itself into the hands of specialists of tested experience, knowledge, gifts and probity, whose business it is, to use St.-Simon's simile, to conduct the human caravan to the oasis the reality and desirability of which are recognized by all. In such a society, whatever its other characteristics, we should expect to find intensive study of social causation, especially of what types of political organization yield the best results, that is, are best at advancing society towards the overriding goal. Political thought in such a society would be fed by all the evidence that can be supplied by the empirical sciences of history, psychology, anthropology, sociology, comparative law, penology, biology, physiology and so forth. The goal (and the best ways of avoiding obstacles to it) may become clearer as the result of careful studies of human thought and behaviour; and its general character must not at any stage be obscure or doubtful; otherwise differences of value judgement will creep into the political sciences as well, and inject what can only be called philosophical issues (or issues of principle) incapable of being resolved by either empirical or formal means. Differences of interpretation of fact—provided these are uncontaminated by disagreements about the ends of life—can be permitted; but if political theory is to be converted into an applied science, what is needed is a single dominant model—like the doctor's model of a healthy body—accepted by the whole, or the greater part, of the society in question. The model will be its "ideological foundation." Although such a model is a necessary condition for such a science, it may not, even then, begin to be a sufficient one.

It is at this point that the deep division between the monists and pluralists becomes crucial and conspicuous. On one side stand Platonists and Aristotelians, Stoics and Thomists, positivists and Marxists, and all those who seek to translate political problems into scientific terms. For them human ends are objective: men are what they are, or change in accordance with discoverable laws; and their needs or interests or duties can be established by the correct (naturalistic, or transcendental, or theological) methods. Given that we can penetrate past error and confusion by true and reliable modes of investigation—metaphysical insight or the social sciences, or some other dependable instrument—and thereby establish what is good for men and how to effect this, the only unsolved problems will be more or less technical:. how to obtain the means for securing these ends, and how to distribute what the technical means provide in a socially and psychologically best manner. This, in the most general terms, is the ideal both of the enlightened atheists of the eighteenth century and the positivists of the nineteenth; of some Marxists of the twentieth, and of those Churches which know the end for which man is made, and know that it is in principle attainable—or at least is such that the road towards it can be discerned—here, below.

On the other side are those who believe in some form of original sin or the impossibility of human perfection, and therefore tend to be sceptical of the empirical attainability of any final solution to the deepest human problems. With them are to be found the sceptics and relativists and also those who believe that the very efforts to solve the problem of one age or culture alter both the men who strive to do so and those for whose benefit the solutions are applied, and thereby create new men and new problems, the character of which cannot to-day be anticipated, let alone analysed or solved, by men bounded by their own historical horizons. Here, too, belong the many sects of subjectivists and irrationalists; and in particular those romantic thinkers who hold that ends of action are not discovered, but are created by individuals or cultures or nations as works of art are, so that the answer to the question "What should we do?" is undiscoverable not because it is beyond our powers to find the answer, but because the question is not one of fact at all, the solution lies not in discovering something which is what it is, whether it is discovered or not—a proposition or formula, an objective good, a principle, a system of values objective or subjective, a relationship between a mind and something non-mental—but resides in action: something which cannot be found, only invented—an act of will or faith or creation obedient to no pre-existent rules or laws or facts. Here too stand those twentieth century heirs of romanticism, the existentialists, with their belief in the free self-commitment by individuals to actions or forms of life determined by the agent choosing freely; such choice does not take account of objective standards, since these are held to be a form of illusion or "false consciousness," and the belief in such figments is psychologically traced to fear of freedom—of being abandoned, left to one's own resources—a terror which leads to uncritical acceptance of systems claiming objective authority, spurious theological or metaphysical cosmologies which undertake to guarantee the eternal validity of moral or intellectual rules and principles. Not far from here, too, are fatalists and mystics, as well as those who believe that accident dominates history, and other irrationalists; but also those indeterminists and those troubled rationalists who doubt the possibility of discovering a fixed human nature obedient to invariant laws; especially those for whom the proposition that the future needs of men and their satisfaction are predictable does not fit into an idea of human nature which entails such concepts as will, choice, effort, purpose, with their presupposition of the perpetual opening of new paths of action—a presupposition which enters into the very definition of what we mean by man. This last is the position adopted by those modern Marxists who, in the face of the cruder and more popular versions of the doctrine, have understood the implications of their own premises and principles.

4

Men's beliefs in the sphere of conduct are part of their conception of themselves and others as human beings; and this conception in its turn, whether conscious or not, is intrinsic to their picture of the world. This picture may be complete and coherent, or shadowy or confused, but almost always, and especially in the case of those who have attempted to articulate what they conceive to be the structure of thought or reality, it can be shown to be dominated by one or more models or paradigms: mechanistic, organic, aesthetic, logical, mystical, shaped by the strongest influence of the day—religious, scientific, metaphysical or artistic. This model or paradigm determines the content as well as the form of beliefs and behaviour. A man who, like Aristotle, or Thomas Aquinas, believes that all things are definable in terms of their purpose, and that nature is a hierarchy or an ascending pyramid of such purposive entities, is committed to the view that the end of human life consists in self-fulfilment, the character of which must depend on the kind of nature that a man has, and on the place that he occupies in the harmonious activity of the entire universal, self-realizing enterprise. It follows that the political philosophy, and, more particularly, the diagnosis of political possibilities and purposes of an Aristotelian or a Thomist, will *ipso facto* be radically different from that of, let us say, someone who has learned from Hobbes or Spinoza or any modern positivist that there are no purposes in nature, that there are only causal (or functional or statistical) laws, only repetitive cycles of events, which may, however, within limits, be harnessed to fulfil the purposes of men; with the corollary that the pursuit of purposes is itself nothing but a product in the human consciousness of natural processes the laws of which men can neither significantly alter nor account for, if by accounting is meant giving an explanation in terms of the goals of a creator who does not exist, or of a nature of which it is meaningless to say that it pursues purposes—for what is that but to attempt to apply to it a subjective human category, to fall into the fallacy of animism or anthropomorphism?

The case is similar with regard to the issue of freedom and authority. The question, "Why should I obey (rather than do as I like)?" will be (and has been) answered in one way by those who, like Luther, or Bodin, or the Russian Slavophils and many others whose thoughts have been deeply coloured by biblical imagery, conceive of life (although in very different fashions) in terms of the relations of children to their father, and of laws as his commands, where loyalty, obedience, love, and the presence of immediate authority, are all unquestioned, and surround life from birth to death as real and palpable relationships or agencies. This question will be answered very differently by the followers of, say, Plato, or Kant (divided by a whole heaven as these thinkers are) who believe in permanent, impersonal, universal, objective truths, conceived on the model of logical or mathematical or physical laws, by analogy with which their political concepts will be formed. Yet other, and wholly dissimilar, sets of answers will be determined by the great vitalistic conceptions, the model for which is drawn from the facts of growth as conceived in early biology, and for which reality is an organic, qualitative process, not analysable into quantitative units. Others again will originate in minds dominated by the image of some central force, thrusting forward in many guises, like some gnostic or Brahmin notion of perpetual self-creation; or be traceable to a concept drawn from artistic activity, in which the universe is seen not as an unconscious, quasi-biological process of the spirit or the flesh, but as the endless creation of a demiurge, in which freedom and self-fulfilment lie in the recognition by men of themselves as involved in the purposive process of cosmic creation—a vision fully revealed only to those beings to whom the nature of the world is disclosed, at least fragmentarily, through their own experience as creators (something of this kind emanated from the doctrines of Fichte, Schelling, Carlyle, Nietzsche and other romantic thinkers, as well as Bergson and in places Hegel, and, in his youth, Marx, who were obsessed by æsthetico-biological models); some among these, anarchists and irrationalists, conceive of reality as freedom from all rules and set ideals—fetters, even when they are self-imposed, upon the free creative spirit—a doctrine of which we have heard, if anything, too much. The model itself may be regarded as the product of historical factors: the social (and psychological) consequences of the development of productive forces, as Marx taught, or the effects in the minds of individuals of purely psychological processes which Freud and his disciples have investigated. The study of myths, rationalizations, ideologies and obsessive patterns of many kinds, has become a great and fertile preoccupation of our time. The fundamental assumption underlying this approach is that the "ideological" model has not been arrived at by rational methods, but is the product of causal factors; it may disguise itself in rational dress, but, given the historical, or economic, or geographical, or psychological situation, must, in any case, have emerged in one form or another.

For political thinkers, however, the primary question is not that of genesis and conditions of growth, but that of validity and truth: does the model distort reality? Does it blind us to real differences and similarities and generate other, fictitious ones? Does it suppress, violate, invent, deceive? In the case of scientific (or common-sense) explanations or hypotheses, the tests of validity include increase in the power of accurate (or more refined) prediction or control of the behaviour of the subject matter. Is political thought practical and empirical in this sense? Machiavelli, and in differing degrees Hobbes, Spinoza, Helvétius, Marx, at times speak as if this were so. This is one of the interpretations of the famous doctrine of the unity of theory and practice. But is it an adequate account of the purpose or achievements of—to take only the moderns—Locke or Kant or Rousseau or Mill or the liberals, the existentialists, the logical positivists and linguistic analysts and Natural Law theorists of our own day? and if not, why not?

To return to the notion of models. It is by now a commonplace that the data of observation can be accommodated to almost any theoretical model. Those who are obsessed by one model can accept facts, general propositions, hypotheses and even methods of argument, adopted and perfected by those who were dominated by quite a different model. For this reason, political theory, if by theories we mean no more than causal or functional hypotheses and explanations designed to account only for what happens—in this case for what men have thought or done or will think or do—can perfectly well be a progressive empirical enquiry, capable of detaching itself from its original metaphysical or ethical foundations, and sufficiently adaptable to preserve through many changes of intellectual climate its own character and development as an independent science. After all, even mathematics, although bound up with—and obstructed by—metaphysics and theology, has nevertheless progressed from the days of the Greeks to our own; so too have the natural sciences, at any rate since the seventeenth century, despite vast upheavals in the general *Weltanschauungen* of the societies in which they were created.

But I should like to say once again that unless political theory is conceived in narrowly sociological terms, it differs from political science or any other empirical enquiry in being concerned with somewhat different fields; namely with such questions as what is specifically human and what is not, and why; whether specific categories, say those of purpose or of belonging to a group, or law are indispensable to understanding what men are; and so, inevitably, with the source, scope and validity of certain human goals. If this is its task, it cannot, from the very nature of its interests, avoid evaluation; it is thoroughly committed not only to the analysis of, but to conclusions about the validity of, ideas of the good and the bad, the permitted and the forbidden, the harmonious and the discordant problems which any discussion of liberty or justice or authority or political morality is sooner or later bound to encounter. These central conceptions, moral, political, æsthetic, have altered as the all-inclusive metaphysical models in which they are an essential element have themselves altered. Any change in the central model is a change in the ways in which the data of experience are perceived and interpreted. The degree to which such categories are shot through with evaluation will doubtless depend on their direct connexion with human desires and interests. Statements about physical nature can achieve neutrality in this respect; this is more difficult when the data are those of history, and nearly impossible in the case of moral and social life, where the words themselves are inescapably charged with ethical or æsthetic or political content.

To suppose, then, that there have been or could be ages without political philosophy, is like supposing that as there are ages of faith, so there are or could be ages of total disbelief. But this is an absurd notion: there is no human activity without some kind of general outlook: scepticism, cynicism, refusal to dabble in abstract issues or to question values, hard boiled opportunism, contempt for theorizing, all the varieties of nihilism, are, of course, themselves metaphysical and ethical positions, committal attitudes. Whatever else the existentialists have taught us, they have made this fact plain. The idea of a completely *Wertfrei* theory (or model) of human action (as contrasted, say, with animal behaviour) rests on a naïve misconception of what objectivity or neutrality in the social studies must be.

5

The notion that a simile or model, drawn from one sphere, is necessarily misleading when applied to another, and that it is possible to think without such analogies in some direct fashion—"face-to-face" with the facts—will not bear criticism. To think is to generalize, to generalize is to compare. To think of one phenomenon or cluster of phenomena is to think in terms of its resemblances and differences with others. This is by now a hoary platitude. It follows that without parallels and analogies between one sphere and another of thought and action, whether conscious or not, the unity of our experience—our experience itself—would not be possible. All language and thought is, in this sense, necessarily "metaphorical." The models, once they are made conscious and explicit, may turn out to be obsolete or misleading. Yet even the most discredited among these models in politics—the social contract, patriarchalism, the organic society and so forth, must have started with some initial validity to have had the influence on thought that they have had.

No analogy powerful enough to govern the concepts or generations of men can have been wholly specious. When Jean Bodin or Herder or the Russian Slavophils or the German sociologist Tönnies transfer the notion of family nexus to political life, they remind us of aspects of relationships between men united by traditional bonds or bound by common habits and loyalties, which had been misrepresented by the Stoics or Machiavelli or Bentham or Nietzsche or Herbert Spencer. So, too, assimilation of law to a command issued by some constituted authority in any one of the three types of social order distinguished by Max Weber, throws some light on the concept of law. Similarly, the social contract is a model which to this day helps to explain something of what it is that men feel to be wrong when a politician pronounces an entire class of the population (say, capitalists or Negroes) to be outside the community—not entitled to the benefits conferred by the state and its laws. So, too, Lenin's image of the factory which needs no supervision by coercive policemen after the state has withered away; Maistre's image of the executioner and his victims as the cornerstone of all authority, or of life as a perpetual battlefield in which only terror of supernatural power keeps men from mutual extermination; the state's role as traffic policeman and night watchman (Lassalle's contemptuous description of the Liberal ideal); Locke's analogy of government with trusteeship; the constant use by Burke and the entire Romantic movement of metaphors drawn from organic growth and decay; the Soviet model of an army on the march, with its accompanying attributes and values, such as uncritical loyalty, faith in leadership, and military goals such as the need to overtake, destroy, conquer some specified enemy—all these illuminate some types of social experience.

The great distortions, the errors and crimes that have sought their inspiration and justification in such images, are evidence of mechanical extrapolation, or over-enthusiastic application of what, at most, explains a sector of life, to the whole. It is a form of the ancient fallacy of the Ionian philosophers, who wanted a single answer to the question: "What are all things made of?" Everything is not made of water, nor fire, nor is explained by the irresistible march towards the world state or the classless society. The history of thought and culture is, as Hegel showed with great brilliance, a changing pattern of great liberating ideas which inevitably turn into suffocating straitjackets, and so stimulate their own destruction by new, emancipating, and at the same time, enslaving conceptions. The first step to the understanding of men is the bringing to consciousness of the model or models that dominate and penetrate their thought and action. Like all attempts to make men aware of the categories in which they think, it is a difficult and sometimes painful activity, likely to produce deeply disquieting results. The second task is to analyse the model itself, and this commits the analyst to accepting or modifying or rejecting it, and, in the last case, to providing a more adequate one in its stead.

It is seldom, moreover, that there is only one model that determines our thought; men (or cultures) obsessed by single models are rare, and while they may be more coherent at their strongest, they tend to collapse more violently when, in the end, their concepts are blown up by reality—experienced events, "inner" or "outer," that get in the way. Most men wander hither and thither, guided and, at times, hypnotized by more than one model, which they seldom trouble to make consistent, or even fragments of models which themselves form a part of some none too coherent or firm pattern or patterns. To drag them into the light makes it possible to explain them and sometimes to explain them away. The purpose of such analysis is to clarify; but clarification may expose shortcomings and subvert what it describes. That has often and quite justly been charged against political thought, which, at its best, does not disclaim this dangerous power. The ultimate test of the adequacy of the basic patterns by which we think and act is the only test that common sense or the sciences afford, namely, whether it fits in with the general lines on which we think and communicate; and if some among these in turn are called into question, then the final measure is, as it always must be, direct confrontation with the concrete data of observation and introspection which these concepts and categories and habits order and render intelligible. In this sense, political theory, like any other form of thought that deals with the real world, rests on empirical experience, though in what sense of "empirical" still remains to be discussed.

6

When one protests (as we ourselves did above) that the application of such (social or political) models or combinations of overlapping models, which at most hold a part of our experience, causes distortion when applied beyond it; how do we set about to justify this charge? How do we know that the result is distortion? We usually think this because the universal application of a simile or a pattern—say that of the general will, or the organic society, or basic structure and superstructure, or the liberating myth—seems to those who reject it to ignore something that they know directly of human nature and thereby to do violence to what we are, or what we know, by forcing it into the Procrustean bed of some rigid dogma; that is to say, that we protest in the name of our own view of what men are, have been, could be.

How do we know these things? How do we know what is and what is not an adequate programme for human beings in given historical circumstances? Is this knowledge sociological, or psychological? Is it empirical at all, or metaphysical and even theological? How do we argue with those whose notions are different from ours? Hume, Helvétius, Condorcet, Comte, are clear that such knowledge must be based on empirical data and the methods of the natural sciences, all else is imaginary and worthless.

The temptation to accept this simple solution was (and is) very great. The conflict of the rival explanations (or models) of social and individual life had, by the late eighteenth century, grown to be a scandal. If one examines what answers were offered, let us say, between the death of Newton and the birth of Darwin, to a central political question—why anyone should obey anyone else—the babel of voices is appalling, perhaps the most confused in recorded history. Some said that I should obey those rules or institutions submission to which alone would fulfil my nature, with the rider that my needs and the correct path to their satisfaction were clear only to those privileged observers who grasped at least some part of the great hierarchy of being. Others said that I should obey this or that authority or law because only in that way could I (without aid of experts) fulfil my "true" nature, or be able to fit into a harmonious whole. Some supposed this whole to be static; others taught that it was dynamic, but could not agree on whether it moved in recurrent cycles, or a straight, or spiral, or irregular evolutionary line, or by a series of oscillations leading to "dialectical" explosions; or again, whether it was teleological or functional or causally determined.

Some conceived the ultimate universal pattern in mechanistic, others in organic, others still, in æsthetic terms. There were those who said that men must obey because they had promised to do so, or others had promised on their behalf; or that they were behaving as if they had promised and this was tantamount to having promised, whether they admitted this or no; or, if this seemed unconvincing, that it were best that they should behave as if they had so promised, since otherwise no one would know where he was and chaos would ensue. Some told men to obey because they would be happier if they did, or because the majority, or all men, would be happier; or because it was God's will that they should obey, or the will of the sovereign, or of the majority, or of the best or wisest, or of history, or of their state, or their race, or their culture, or their church.

They were told also that they must obey because the natural law laid down that they must do so, but there were differences about how the precepts of natural law were to be discovered, whether by rational or by empirical means, or by intuition, and again, by common men or only by the experts; the experts in their turn were identified by some with natural scientists, by others with specialists in metaphysics or theology, or perhaps in some other discipline—mass psychology, mystical revelation, the laws of history, of economics, of natural evolution, of a new synthesis of all or some of these. Some people supposed that truth in these matters could be discovered by a faculty which they called moral sense, or common sense or the perception of the fitness of things, or that it consisted in what they had been told by their parents or nurses or was to be found in accepted views which it was mere perversity to question, or came from one or other of many sources of this sort which Bentham mocks at so gaily and effectively. Some (and perhaps these have always been the majority) felt it to be in some degree subversive to raise such questions at all.

This situation caused justified indignation in a country dominated by free enquiry and its greatest triumph, Newtonian science. Surely this monstrous muddle could be cleared away by the strong new broom of scientific method—a similar chaos had, after all, not so long ago prevailed in the natural sciences too. Galileo and Newton—and the light of reason and experiment—had silenced for ever the idle chatter of the ignoramus, the dark muttering of the metaphysician, the thunder of the preacher, the hysterical shrieks of the obscurantist. All genuine questions were questions of discoverable fact—*calculemus*, Condorcet declared, was to be the motto of the new method; all problems must be so reformulated that inspection of the facts—aided by mathematical techniques—would answer them decisively, with a clear, universally valid, empirical statement of verifiable fact.

7

Nevertheless, attempts by the *philosophes* of the eighteenth century to turn philosophy, and particularly moral and political philosophy, into an empirical science, into individual and social psychology, did not succeed.

They failed over politics because our political notions are part of our conception of what it is to be human, and this is not solely a question of fact, as facts are conceived by the natural sciences; nor the product of conscious reflection upon the specific discoveries of anthropology or sociology or psychology, although all these are relevant and indeed indispensable to an adequate notion of the nature of man in general, or of particular groups of men in particular circumstances. Our conscious idea of man—of how men differ from other entities, of what is human and what is not human or inhuman—involves the use of some among the basic categories in terms of which we perceive and order and interpret data. To analyse the concept of man is to recognize these categories for what they are. To do this is to realize that they are categories, that is, that they are not themselves subjects for scientific hypotheses about the data which they order.

The analogy with the sciences which dominates the pre-Kantian thinkers of the eighteenth century—Locke, Hume and Condillac, for example, is a typical misapplication of a model that works in one sphere to a region where it will obscure at least as much as it illuminates.

Let me try to make this more specific. When the theological and metaphysical models of the Middle Ages were swept away by the sciences of the seventeenth and eighteenth centuries, they disappeared largely because they could not compete in describing, predicting, controlling the contents of the external world with new disciplines. To the extent to which man was regarded as an object in material nature the sciences of man—psychology, anthropology, economics, sociology and so on—began to supplant their theologico-metaphysical predecessors. The questions of the philosophers were affected by this; some were answered or rendered obsolete: but some remained unanswered. The new human sciences studied men's actual habits; they promised, and in some cases, provided, analyses of what men said, wanted, admired, abhorred; they were prepared to supply empirical evidence for this, or experimental demonstration; but their efforts to solve normative problems were less successful. They tried to reduce questions of value to questions of fact—of what caused what kind of men to feel or behave as they did in various circumstances. But when Kant or Herder or Dostoevsky or Marx duly rejected the encyclopædists' answers, the charge against them was not solely that of faulty observation or invalid inference; it was that of a failure to recognize what it is to be a man, that is, failure to take into account the nature of the framework—the basic categories—in terms of which we think and act and assume others to think and act, if communication between us is to work.

In other words, the problem the solutions of which were found insufficient is not in the usual sense empirical, and certainly not formal, but something that is not adequately described by either term. When Rousseau (whether he understood him correctly or not) rejected Hobbes's account of political obligation on the ground that Hobbes seemed to him to explain it by mere fear of superior force, Rousseau claimed not that Hobbes had not seen certain relevant empirical, psychologically discoverable, facts, nor that he had argued incorrectly from what he had seen— but that his account was in conflict with what, in thinking of human beings as human, and distinguishing them, even the most degraded among them, not only in explicit thought, but in our feelings and in our action, from beings that we regard as inhuman or non-human, we all know men to be. His argument is not that the facts used to construct Hobbes's model had gaps in them, but that the model was inadequate in principle; it was inadequate not because this or that psychological or sociological correlation had been missed out, but because it was based on a failure to understand what we mean by motive, purpose, value, personality and the like.

When Kant breaks with the naturalistic tradition, or Marx rejects the political morality of Bentham, or Tolstoy expresses a low opinion of the doctrines of Karl Marx, they are not complaining merely of empirical ignorance or poor logic or insufficient experimental evidence, or internal incoherence. They denounce their adversaries mainly for not understanding what men are and what relationships between them—or between them and outside forces—make them men; they complain of blindness not to the transient aspects of such relations, but to those constant characteristics (such as discrimination of right from good for Kant, or, for Marx, systematic self-transmutation by their own labour) that they regard as fundamental to the notion of man as such. Their criticisms relate to the adequacy of the categories in terms of which we discuss men's ends or duties or interests, the permanent framework in terms of which, not about which, ordinary empirical disagreements can arise.

What are these categories? How do we discover them? If not empirically, then by what means? How universal and unchanging are they? How do they enter into and shape the models and paradigms in terms of which we think and respond? Do we discover what they are by attention to thought, or action, or unconscious processes, and how do we reconcile these various sources of knowledge? These are characteristically philosophical questions, since they are questions about the all but permanent ways in which we think, decide, perceive, judge, and not about the data of experience—the items themselves. The test of the adequate working of the methods, analogies, models which operate in discovering and classifying the behaviour of these empirical data (as natural science and common sense do) is ultimately empirical: it is the degree of their success in forming a coherent and enduring conceptual system.

To apply these models and methods to the framework itself by means of which we perceive and think about them, is a major fallacy by the analysis of which Kant transformed philosophy. In politics it was committed (by Hume and Russell, for example) when enquiry into the empirical characteristics of men was confounded with the analysis of the notion of man (or "self" or "observer" or "moral agent" or "individual" or "soul," etc.) in terms of which the empirical characteristics were themselves collected and described. Kant supposed these categories to be discoverable *a priori*. We need not accept this; this was an unwarranted conclusion from the valid perception that there exist central features of our experience that are invariant and omnipresent, or at least much less variable than the vast variety of its empirical characteristics, and for that reason deserve to be distinguished by the name of categories. This is evident enough in the case of the external world: the three-dimensionality of (psychological, common sense) space, for example, or the solidity of things in it, or "the irreversibility" of the time order, are among the most familiar and inalienable kinds of characteristics in terms of which we think and act. Empirical sciences of these properties do not exist, not because they exhibit no regularities—on the contrary they are the very paradigm of the concept of regularity itself—but because they are presupposed in the very language in which we formulate empirical experience. That is why it seems absurd to ask for evidence for their existence, and imaginary examples are enough to exhibit their structure; for they are presupposed in our commonest acts of thought or decision; and where imaginary examples are, for the purpose of an enquiry, as good as, or even better than, empirical data drawn from actual experience, we may be sure that the enquiry is not, in the normal sense, an empirical one. Such permanent features are to be found in the moral and political and social worlds too: less stable and universal, perhaps, than in the physical one, but just as indispensable for any kind of intersubjective communication, and therefore for thought and action. An enquiry that proceeds by examples, and is therefore not scientific, but not formal, that is deductive, either, is most likely to be philosophical.

There is an ultimate sense, of course, in which such facts as that space has three dimensions, or that men are beings who demand reasons or make choices, are simply given: brute facts and not *a priori* truths; it is not absurd to suppose that things could have been otherwise. But if they had been (or will one day be) other than they are now, our entire conceptual apparatus—thought, volition, feeling, language, and therefore our very nature, would have been (or will be) different in ways that it is impossible or difficult to describe with the concepts and words available to us as we are to-day. Political categories (and values) are a part of this all but inescapable web of ways of living, acting and thinking, a network liable to change only as a result of radical changes in reality, or through dissociation from reality on the part of individuals, that is to say, madness.

8

The basic categories (with their corresponding concepts) in terms of which we define men—such notions as society, freedom, sense of time and change, suffering, happiness, productivity, good and bad, right and wrong, choice, effort, truth, illusion (to take them wholly at random)—are not matters of induction and hypothesis. To think of someone as a human being is *ipso facto* to bring all these notions into play: so that to say of someone that he is a man, but that choice, or the notion of truth, mean nothing to him, would be eccentric: it would clash with what we mean by "man" not as a matter of verbal definition (which is alterable at will), but as intrinsic to the way in which we think, and (as a matter of "brute" fact) evidently cannot but think.

This will hold of values too (among them political ones) in terms of which men are defined. Thus, if I say of someone that he is kind or cruel, loves truth or is indifferent to it, he remains human in either case. But if I find a man to whom it literally makes no difference whether he kicks a pebble or kills his family, since either would be an antidote to *ennui* or inactivity, I shall not be disposed, like consistent relativists, to attribute to him merely a different code of morality from my own or that of most men, or declare that we disagree on essentials, but shall begin to speak of insanity and inhumanity; I shall be inclined to consider him mad, as a man who thinks he is Napoleon is mad; which is a way of saying that I do not regard such a being as being fully a man at all. It is cases of this kind, which seem to make it clear that ability to recognize universal—or almost universal—values, enters into our analysis of such fundamental concepts as "man," "rational," "sane," "natural," etc.—which are usually thought of as descriptive and not evaluative—that lie at the basis of modern translations into empirical terms of the kernel of truth in the old *a priori* Natural Law doctrines. It is considerations such as these, urged by neo-Aristotelians and the followers of the later doctrines of Wittgenstein, that have shaken the faith of some devoted empiricists in the complete logical gulf between descriptive statements and statements of value, and have cast doubt on the celebrated distinction derived from Hume.

Extreme cases of this sort are of philosophical importance because they make it clear that such questions are not answered by either empirical observation or formal deduction. Hence those who confine themselves to observation of human behaviour and empirical hypotheses about it, psychologists, sociologists, historians, however profound and original they may be, are not, as such, political theorists, even though they may have much to say that is crucial in the field of political philosophy. That is why we do not consider such dedicated empiricists as the students, say, of the formation and behaviour of parties or élites or classes, or of the methods and consequences of various types of democratic procedure, to be political philosophers or social theorists in the larger sense.

Such men are in the first place students of facts, and aspire to formulate hypotheses and laws like the natural scientists. Yet as a rule these thinkers cannot go any further: they tend to analyse men's social and political ideas in the light of some overriding belief of their own—for example, that the purpose of all life is or should be the service of God, however interpreted; or on the contrary that it is the pursuit of experimentally discoverable individual or collective satisfaction; or that it lies in the self-realization of a historical (or psychological or æsthetic) pattern, grasp of which alone can explain men to themselves and give meaning to their thoughts and action; or, on the contrary, that there exists no human purpose; or that men cannot but seek conflicting ends; or cannot (without ceasing to be human) avoid activities that must end in self-frustration, so that the very notion of a final solution is an absurdity. In so far as it is such fundamental conceptions of man that determine political doctrines (and who will deny that political problems, e.g. about what men and groups can or should be or do, depend logically and directly on what man's nature is taken to be?), it is clear that those who are governed by these great integrating syntheses bring to their study something other than empirical data.

If we examine the models, paradigms, conceptual structures that govern various outlooks whether consciously or not, and compare the various concepts and categories involved with respect, for example, to their internal consistency or their explanatory force, then what we are engaged upon is not psychology or sociology or logic or epistemology, but moral or social or political theory, or all these at once, depending on whether we confine ourselves to individuals, or to groups, or to the particular types of human arrangements that are classified as political, or deal with them all in one. No amount of careful empirical observation and bold and fruitful hypothesis will explain to us what those men see who see the state as a divine institution, or what their words mean and how they relate to reality; nor what those believe who tell us that the state was sent upon us only for our sins; or those who say that it is a school through which we must go before we are adult and free and can dispense with it; or that it is a work of art; or a utilitarian device; or the incarnation of natural law; or a committee of the ruling class; or the highest stage of the self-developing human spirit; or a piece of criminal folly. But unless we understand (by an effort of imaginative insight such as novelists usually possess in a higher degree than logicians) what notions of man's nature (or absence of them) are incorporated in these political outlooks, what in each case is the dominant model, we shall not understand our own or any human society: neither the conceptions of reason and nature which governed Stoics or Thomists or govern the European Christian Democrats to-day; nor the very different image which is at the heart of the holy war in which the national-Marxist movements in Africa or in Asia, are or may soon be marching; nor the very different notions that animate the liberal and democratic compromises of the West.

It is by now a platitude to say that understanding human thought and action is in large measure understanding what problems and perplexities they strive with. When these problems, whether empirical and formal, have been conceived in terms of models of reality so ancient, widely accepted and stable, that we use them to this day, we understand the problems and difficulties and the attempted solutions without explicit reference to the governing categories; for these, being common to us and to cultures remote from us, do not obtrude themselves on us; stay, as it were, out of sight. In other cases (and this is conspicuously true of politics) the models have not stood still: some of the notions of which they were compounded are no longer familiar. Yet unless we have the knowledge and imagination to transpose ourselves into states of mind dominated by the now discarded or obsolescent model, the thoughts and actions that had them at their centre will remain opaque to us. It is failure to perform this difficult operation that marks much of the history of ideas, and turns it into either a superficial literary exercise, or a dead catalogue of strange, at times almost incomprehensible, errors and confusions.

This may not matter too much in the empirical and formal disciplines, where the test of a belief is, or should be, verification or logical coherence: and where one can accept the latest solutions, and reject the falsified or incoherent solutions of the past without bothering (if one is incurious) to understand why they were ever held. But philosophical doctrines are not established or discredited in this final fashion: for they are concerned with—indeed they owe their existence to—problems that cannot be settled in these ways. They are not concerned with specific facts, but with ways of looking at them; they do not consist of first order propositions concerning the world. They are second or higher order statements about whole classes of descriptions of, or responses to, the world and man's activities in it; and these are in turn determined by models, networks of categories, descriptive, evaluative, and hybrids compounded of the two, in which the two functions cannot be disentangled even in thought—categories which if not eternal and universal, are far more stable and widespread than those of the sciences; sufficiently continuous, indeed, to constitute a common world which we share with mediæval and classical thinkers.

Ionian cosmology, the biology of Aristotle, Stoic logic, Arab algebra, Cartesian physics, may be of interest to historical specialists, but need not occupy the minds of physicists or biologists or mathematicians who are solely interested in the discovery of new truth. In these studies there is genuine progress: what is past is largely obsolete. But the political philosophy of Plato or Aristotle or Machiavelli, the moral views of the Hebrew prophets or of the Gospels or of the Roman jurists or of the mediæval Church—these, whether in the original or in the works of their modern expositors, are incomparably more intelligible and more relevant to our own preoccupations than the sciences of antiquity. The subject matter of these disciplines—the most general characteristics of men as such, that is, as beings engaged in moral or social or spiritual activities— seems to present problems which preserve a considerable degree of continuity and similarity from one age and culture to another. Methods of dealing with them vary greatly; but none have as yet achieved so decisive a victory as to sweep all their rivals into oblivion. The inadequate models of political thought evidently have, by and large, perished and been forgotten; the great illuminating models are still controversial today, stir us still to adherence or criticism or violent indignation.

We might take as examples Professor Karl Popper's denunciation of Plato's political theory or Irving Babbitt's philippics against Rousseau, Simone Weil's violent distaste for the morality of the Old Testament, or the frequent attacks made to-day on eighteenth-century positivism or "scientism" in political ethics.[2] Some of the classical constructions are in conflict with one another, but, inasmuch as each rests on a vivid vision of permanent human attributes and is capable of satisfying some enquiring minds in each generation, no matter how different the circumstances of time and place, the models of Plato, or of Aristotle, or of Judaism, Christianity, Kantian liberalism, romanticism, historicism, all survive and contend with each other to-day in a variety of guises. If men or circumstances alter radically, or new empirical knowledge is gained which will revolutionize our conception of man, then certainly, some of these edifices

---

[2] What thinker to-day entertains violent emotions towards the errors of Cartesian physicists or mediæval mapmakers?

will cease to be relevant and will be forgotten like the ethics and meta-physics of the Egyptians or the Incas. But so long as men are as they are, the debate will continue in terms set by these visions and others like them: each will gain or lose in influence as events force this or that aspect of men into prominence. One thing alone is certain, that save to those who understand and even feel what a philosophical question is, how it differs from empirical or formal question (although this difference need not be explicitly present to the mind, and overlapping or borderline questions are frequent enough) the answers—in this case the main political doc-trines of the West—may well seem intellectual fancies, detached philoso-phical speculations and constructions without much relation to acts or events.

Only those who can to some degree re-enact within themselves the states of mind of men tormented by questions to which these theories claim to be solutions, or at any rate the states of mind of those who may accept the solutions uncritically but would, without them, fall into a state of insecurity and anxiety—only these are capable of grasping what part philosophical views, and especially political doctrines, have played in history, at any rate in the West. The work of the logicians or physicists of the past has receded because it has been superseded. But there is something absurd in the suggestion that we reject Plato's political doc-trines or Kant's æsthetics or ethics because they have been "superseded." This consideration alone should prevent facile assimilation of the two cases. It may be objected to this line of argument that we look upon old ethical or political doctrines as still worth discussion because they are part of our cultural tradition—that if Greek philosophy, biblical ethics, etc., had not been an intrinsic element in Western education, they would by now have been as remote from us as early Chinese speculation. But this merely takes the argument a step backwards: it is true that if the general characteristics of our normal experience had altered radically enough—through a revolution in our knowledge or some natural upheaval which altered our reactions—these ancient categories would probably by now have been felt to be as obsolete as those of Hammurabi or the epic of Gilgamesh. That this is not so is doubtless due partly to the fact that our experience is itself organized and "coloured" by ethical or political categories that we have inherited from our ancestors, ancient spectacles through which we are still looking. But the spectacles would long ago have caused us to blunder and stumble and would have given way to others, or been modified out of recognition as our physical and biological and mathematical spectacles have been, if they had not still performed their task more or less adequately: which argues a certain degree of continuity in at least two millennia of moral and political consciousness.

9

We may be told that whatever we may maintain about the sources, motives or justification of our beliefs, the content of what adherents of divers philosophies believe tends to be similar if they belong to the same social or economic or cultural milieu or have other—psychological or physiological—characteristics in common. The English philosophers, T. H. Green and J. S. Mill, preached philosophically contradictory doctrines: Green was a quasi-Hegelian metaphysician, Mill a Humean empiricist, yet their political conclusions were close to one another's; both were humane Victorian liberals with a good deal of sympathy for socialism. This, we shall further be told, was because men are conditioned to believe what they believe by objective historical factors—their social position, or the class structure of their society and their position in it, although their own (erroneous) rationalizations of their beliefs may be as widely different as those of Mill and Green.

So, too, it has been said, the outlook—the "operational ideas"—of Fascists and Communists display a surprising degree of similarity, given the extreme opposition and incompatibility of the official axioms from which these movements logically start. Hence the plausibility of some of the methods of the "sociology of knowledge," whether Marxist or Paretian or psycho-analytic, and of the various eclectic forms which, in the hands of Weber, Mannheim and others, this instrument has acquired. Certainly such theorists have cast light on the obscure roots of our beliefs. We may be conditioned to believe what we believe irrationally, by circumstances mainly beyond our control, and perhaps beyond our knowledge too. But whatever may in fact causally determine our beliefs, it would be a gratuitous abdication of our powers of reasoning—based on a confusion of natural science with philosophical enquiry—not to want to know what we believe, and for what reason, what the metaphysical implications of such beliefs are, what their relation is to other types of belief, what criteria of value and truth they involve, and so what reason we have to think them true or valid. Rationality rests on the belief that one can think and act for reasons that one can understand, and not merely as the product of occult causal factors which breed "ideologies," and cannot, in any case, be altered by their victims. So long as rational curiosity exists—a desire for justification and explanation in terms of motives and reasons, and not only of causes or functional correlations or statistical probabilities— political theory will not wholly perish from the earth, however many of its rivals, such as sociology, philosophical analysis, social psychology, political science, economics, jurisprudence, semantics, may claim to have dispelled its imaginary realm.

It is a strange paradox that political theory should seem to lead so shadowy an existence at a time when, for the first time in history, literally the whole of mankind is violently divided by issues the reality of which is, and has always been, the sole *raison d'être* of this branch of study. But this, we may be sure, is not the end of the story. Neo-Marxism, neo-Thomism, nationalism, historicism, existentialism, anti-essentialist liberalism and socialism, transpositions of doctrines of natural rights and natural law into empirical terms, discoveries made by skilful application of models derived from economic and related techniques to political behaviour, and the collisions, combinations and consequences in action of these ideas, indicate not the death of a great tradition, but, if anything, new and unpredictable developments.

19

Harry Eckstein

THE CONDITION
AND PROSPECT
OF POLITICAL THOUGHT*

Harry Eckstein's article is in part a report and in part "interpretive
commentary" upon a three-day conference in February of 1955 at
Northwestern University on "Political Theory and the Study of Poli-
tics." Participants in the conference in addition to Professor Eckstein
and members of Northwestern's Department of Political Science were
David Easton, Cortez Ewing, Carl Friedrich, Frank Grace, Pendleton
Herring, Norman Jacobson, Thomas Jenkin, Evron Kirkpatrick, Robert
McCloskey, Austin Ranney, Lindsay Rogers, Mulford Sibley, David
Smith, John Stewart, Kenneth Thompson, Frederick Watkins, and
Sheldon Wolin. Roy Macridis of Northwestern University, who organized and chaired the conference, stated that Eckstein's "report indicates the most significant aspects of the discussion and highlights
the false distinction between 'behaviorists' and 'theorists.' At the same
time it meets squarely the issue of the role of political philosophy in
graduate instruction in political science." The report reflects the principal views on the questions at issue. Its virtue is that it affords the
fruit of a discourse among scholars of various views on these questions.

The issues which arose during the discussions of the conference fall fairly
conveniently into three compartments.

*Reprinted by permission of the author and publisher from *American Political Sci-
ence Review*, L (2: June, 1956), pp. 475–487, where it was entitled "Political Theory
and the Study of Politics: A Report of a Conference."

First, we obviously had to settle, with reasonable clarity, what we were talking about: what "political philosophy" is, what "political science" is, and whether they are really distinguishable. The basic issue of the conference was to determine the relevance of the one to the study of the other, and if we had decided that they were really the same thing, there would simply have been no problems for us to discuss. On the whole, we felt that a valid, if not necessarily sharp, distinction was to be made between the "philosophical" and the "scientific" approaches to the study of politics and that we were not discussing absurd or tautological issues. We agreed, however, that all types of political inquiry involve the construction of *theory,* implicit or explicit, and that the title "political theory" has been unjustifiably appropriated by the historians of political thought.

Second, what is the point of studying the political philosophies of the past? Why insist that they be part of the equipment of the professional political scientist? Ought we not to stop "hesitating to forget our founders" and relegate them to the general education courses, where all good obsolete Greats properly belong? Needless to say, these questions, less aggressively phrased, took up most of our discussions. Needless to say also, they resolved themselves into two categories of questions. That is to say, the utility of political philosophy might be found either in the intrinsic ability of the best of past political thought to sharpen the wits of contemporary political thinkers, much as any difficult intellectual exercise sharpens the mind and deepens the imagination, or in the ability of political philosophy to serve as a thought-saving device by providing the political scientist with a rich source of concepts, models, insights, theories, and methods.

Third, what should be the role of contemporary political philosophers in the field—not of teachers of the history of political philosophy, but of people who still devote themselves to creative political philosophy?

The conference did not reach agreement on all of these large issues, nor did we succeed in isolating all the subsidiary problems they pose. But our discussions at least touched on all of them.

THE END OF THE STUDY OF POLITICS

Most of the disagreements which arose during the discussions of the conference arose from certain fundamentally different ideas about the "end" of the study of politics. It is very difficult to state precisely in what sense our ideas on this subject differed; certainly we never had a sharply focussed debate on it. But there were perceptible differences in mood among the members, a certain something in the "climate of opinion" which was omnipresent, if only as an undercurrent, in the debates we did have. In sharply focussing the issue, therefore, there may be some distortion of what was actually said at the conference.

For the sake of clarity, it may be useful to deal with the various shades of opinion which gradually emerged on the subject in terms of a dichotomy of views. On the one hand, there were certain people who would probably not object to being called behaviorists if I confess to loose usage of the term; these people seemed to feel that the main task of contemporary political science (its historic mission, as it were) is to transform the field of political studies into a genuine scientific *discipline*. What this means will be discussed more concretely below. On the other hand, there were certain people (anti-behaviorists, again loosely speaking) who felt that the end of the study of politics was something they called political *wisdom*, and that wisdom about (or in) politics could not be achieved at all, or that it could not be best achieved, by the sort of discipline the behaviorists seemed to want. The vast majority of the members of the conference, however, steered a careful, even if at times ambiguous, middle course between these extremes.

What troubled the "behaviorists," of course, was the extreme eclecticism and individualism of effort in political science. The field seemed to them to lack all the characteristics of a discipline, especially the constant accumulation of tested theories, a high degree of meaningful communication among its practitioners, and a high degree of cooperative research activity. This, they felt, makes us different not only from the natural scientists (a difference which might be justified on the basis of differences in subject-matter and practicable research techniques), but also from other social scientists, especially economists and sociologists, and for this they felt there was no justification at all. But exactly why does political science have so extraordinarily little "discipline"? The diagnosis of the behaviorists is a familiar one. We do not accumulate, communicate, and cooperate sufficiently because we have no common language, no common problems, no significant methodological agreement *in the field as a whole;* and we lack these highly desirable things because we do not have a comprehensive and shared model (or conceptual scheme) of the political process which could guide our researches and give them a collectively coherent structure. Our task, therefore, is to unify and to systematize our field; at any rate, this, if not the ultimate end of the study of politics, should be our immediate goal.

Obviously, however, the behaviorists were not willing to buy discipline at the price of "wisdom." Therefore, when the "anti-behaviorists" opposed them with pleas for wisdom they clearly had something rather special in mind, something which can be roughly put as follows (and it can only be put "roughly"): (1) Wisdom is to be found not in "explanation" but in "understanding." "Explanation," the anti-behaviorists felt, involves the systematic collection of data and the rigorous application of theoretical procedures (hypothesizing and testing, presumably) to the data, generally in accordance with a set of arbitrary rules which, properly observed, result in something called "verified theory." The whole process, in short, is a mechanical sort of game rather than genuinely intellectual, speculative activity. In its most repulsive form, it is "scientism," which was defined by one member as the use of mathematical procedures for the manipulation of political data. "Understanding," on the other hand, goes to the very core of experience; it involves, presumably, some deeper, perhaps more intuitive grasp of the meaning of reality. It is more likely to grow out of a flash of insight than a long evening with the logarithm table; it is certainly more likely to be found in an aphorism than in a conceptual scheme. One can get "understanding" only from a sensitive, critical, imaginative mind, not from a mere human IBM machine. (2) Wisdom, moreover, penetrates certain kinds of experience which a "scientific" discipline either could not or would not touch and which may be the most important in our field. There is, in the first place, the field of moral speculation. Morality cannot be factored out of politics or the study of politics, if only because the very function of politics is to formulate imperatives and to back them with collective force. There is, again, the field of immediate practical activity. We cannot wait for the scientific machinery to grind out rigorously tested results before we act. Action is thrust upon us; policies have to be made, usually on the basis of something less than total knowledge and absolutely systematic calculation. Nor should the student of politics wash his hands of the chances he has to influence practical activity simply because he is not in command of a commonly shared theoretical system. At the very least, he has sufficient knowledge and experience to justify his influence. And one may even suspect that "wisdom," in the rather vague sense used here (a good grasp of data, keenness of mind, highly-developed critical power), is more likely to be useful in practical activity than any systematically formulated theories would be, even if we had them.

In a sense, all this means simply that the behaviorists wanted to *train*, the anti-behaviorists to *cultivate* people engaged in the study of politics. But the vast majority—the "Marsh" of our Assembly—felt that the distinction between discipline and wisdom is a false one. They believed that we not only could but must have the best of both possible worlds. And this feeling seemed to grow out of genuine reasons rather than equivocation or politeness toward the extremists in the group.

In the first place, the moderates agreed on the desirability of "discipline" in the field, if by discipline is meant the cooperative and progressive accumulation of tested theories and a high degree of meaningful communication among the practitioners of political science. They did not, however, agree that the field was unprogressive and inchoate now. We do make progress, even though we may not be as self-conscious of it as people in other social sciences. What, after all, constitutes progress in a field like political science? It involves: first, increasing refinement in the definition of problems (learning what sort of questions to ask and not to ask); second, increasing conceptual precision; third, the accumulation of specific hypotheses about specific political systems and political behavior in general; fourth, the systematic conceptual analysis of the field; and fifth, the application of useful concepts, theories, and techniques from other fields to our subject-matter. One can easily cite long lists of recent works which make "progress" in all of these senses: e.g., Weldon's analysis of the epistemological status of certain traditional problems in political philosophy, a whole spate of books (by Lasswell and deJouvenel, among a good many others) on "power," Goguel and Williams' analyses of the French political system, David Easton's diagnostic study of the current state of political science, the impressive use of psychological techniques by the authors of *The Authoritarian Personality* (who, to be sure, are not professional political scientists), DeGrazia's use of anomie theory in *The Political Community*—one could go on for pages. And one need scarcely mention the accumulation of concepts and theories, the increasing refinement of techniques, the checking and rechecking of old theories, and the constant cross-fertilization of the field achieved by the best of the political "behaviorists" themselves.

The moderates, therefore, disagreed first of all with the behaviorists' diagnosis of the condition of the field. They disagreed also with their apparent desire for the organization of our work on the basis of some authoritarian conceptual scheme. They felt, in short, that eclecticism was desirable. No single line of approach, no conceptual map, however large its scale, could ever exhaust the richness of any field, least of all a field as rich as politics. If we all agreed on a single line of approach, we should soon find ourselves mistaking the map for reality and feel that we had progressed when we had translated familiar facts into unfamiliar jargon. The sense of being in on a mystery, which distinguishes most of the economists and some sociologists from ourselves, may not be an altogether unmixed blessing, particularly if it involves the identification of "science" with the rules of some esoteric methodological and conceptual game. The moderates felt, as Mill felt, that only pseudo-progress could be achieved by rigid conformity of any sort.

What then distinguished the moderates from the anti-behaviorists? The essential difference between them was that the moderates were unwilling to strip the field of all "scientific" pretensions and to concede that insights are superior to systems and aphorisms superior to correlations. The moderates felt simply that insights need to be subjected to rigorous analysis and that no aphorism can stand on its own two feet merely because it issues from a sensitive mind. Hence, of course, their insistence on eclecticism: the simultaneous cultivation of what the anti-behaviorists called "understanding" and "explanation," i.e., insight and discipline. They also felt that no real distinction was to be made between wisdom and science; that, in effect, the anti-behaviorists were using a value-laden term merely to conceal a profound anti-scientific bias.

These views led to three fundamentally different positions on the subject of the conference. One group felt that political philosophy probably does no one any great harm, but that it does very little good, either, so far as the condition of political science is concerned. Another group felt that political philosophy comprises all that is genuinely admirable and useful in the field. The third felt that political philosophy should have a major place in our departments precisely because it can play a useful role in political "science" itself.

POLITICAL PHILOSOPHY AND POLITICAL SCIENCE

What we called "political philosophy" is generally called "political theory" in the departments of political science. As I have said, we all agreed that this involves a mistaken use of the word "theory." Theorizing plays a role in all kinds of inquiries, even inquiries which pretend to do nothing more than collect data. After all, criteria of selection imply judgments of significance, and what are judgments of significance if not theories? Thus, we agreed that the theorist-behaviorist dichotomy, which seems to be taken seriously by most political scientists, is naive at best and dangerous at worst; dangerous, in the sense that a sharp separation between "theory" and "empirical" inquiry is likely to lead to both bad theorizing and bad empirical work.

What then did we mean by "political philosophy"? In the first place, we meant the great political speculations of the past, the works of people generally taught in our political theory courses. We were aware, of course, that it is arbitrary in the extreme to label as "philosophy" anything written before the First World War and to withhold the term from almost everything written thereafter. We decided on this meaning of the term, nevertheless, simply because we wanted to discuss the value of studying the Greats who had written on our subject.

Many members of the conference, however, thought that there was a more serious distinction to be made between political science and political philosophy. Political science, of course, is concerned with the analysis of actual political behavior. Political philosophy, we felt, could be distinguished from it on at least three reasonable grounds: subject, scope, and criteria of validity.

So far as subject is concerned, political philosophy is distinguished chiefly by the fact that it deals not only with matters of fact but also with matters of norm: either moral theory in the abstract or questions of immediate practical activity. Political philosophy, in short, is "concerned with ends as well as means"—one of the most frequently used phrases at the conference. In addition to moral theory, political philosophy also involves another kind of speculative activity, not strictly part of political science but highly relevant to it. This sort of speculative activity we might perhaps call "meta-theory": theory about theory. The term refers to something I have difficulty in putting very precisely, but anyone who has followed the trend in the contemporary philosophy departments will know what I mean. Modern philosophy seems increasingly to have given up the historic work of philosophy, the search for substantive truth. It seems increasingly to concentrate on commenting upon what the people who do search for substantive truth are doing: the language they use, the methods they employ, the epistemological and metaphysical implications of their activities, and so forth. Someone has said—and with some justification—that modern philosophers (in Britain and America) are "clever dilettantes who criticize the work of dull specialists." But this is not meant to poke fun at "meta-theory," which can obviously be extremely useful in the development of science. Meta-theory, in the sense the term is used here, includes analysis of the sort of problems one can fruitfully raise, the sort of language (concepts) one should or should not employ, the "ultimate implication" of substantive research findings, methodological analyses, general criticisms of research procedures and findings, and, not least, the overall programmatic analysis of a field, "programmatic" referring to the sort of analyses which are meant to lead to research rather than to present research findings. Weldon's *Vocabulary of Politics* and much of the work done by the Social Science Research Council's committees are fairly familiar cases in point.

So far as scope is concerned, political philosophy is characterized chiefly by system-building, i.e., the construction of comprehensive theories of politics. The line cannot be drawn precisely because we have no convenient measures of partialness and comprehensiveness. But one can at least illustrate the extremes. On one extreme would be, let us say, a theory explaining the defeat of the British Labor party in 1951; obviously such a theory is not likely to involve the ordering of a very great range of political experience. On the other hand would be theories like Marx's analysis of the state and the determinants of political power, which obviously involve the ordering of almost the whole of political experience and call for a judgment as to what is significant and insignificant in experience as such. Bentley's analysis of the process of government might also be cited on the Marxian extreme, despite his claim to have devised merely a basis for research, and Bentley is especially worth noting here because he is a political analyst to whom the philosophers and the scientists can clearly lay an equal claim, the former on the basis of both the scope and the meta-theoretical aspects of his work.

When we came to "criteria of proof" as a factor distinguishing political science and philosophy, we found ourselves in much muddier waters. Some of us felt that anything validated by correspondence is "science" and anything validated by anything else (or not validated at all—"above validation," perhaps) is philosophy. This would, of course, put moral theory in the realm of philosophy, since one certainly does not test moral theory by correspondence, if one tests it at all. Similarly, meta-theory would be philosophy since it, in a sense, is merely theory about testing itself.

The chief task of the conference was, of course, to discuss the utility of political philosophy in each of the two senses I have outlined: the study of the Greats, and the study of "comprehensive" political theories, theories of political obligation (moral theories) and meta-theoretical writings on political science.

THE UTILITY OF POLITICAL PHILOSOPHY

No one disputed that the Greats were worth studying for their *intrinsic interest*. Even the most extreme behaviorists felt that no one need apologize for being interested in the history of thought in our field. They considered the history of political thought to be as worthwhile as any other sort of history. It could no doubt give a great deal of amusement; it was probably as mentally stimulating as chess and as aesthetically pleasing as great art. We agreed that we did not want to breed philistines and that anything amusing, anything mentally stimulating, anything aesthetically pleasing needs no further defense. The question was, of course, whether the history of political thought was anything more than amusing to people who find their amusement in such things. What precisely would be lost if we surrendered our Greats to the history, philosophy, and General Education departments, as have most of the other fields? The behaviorists certainly would not have been very sad to see Plato and Locke deported to other jurisdictions, but the others felt that the loss would be both sad and harmful, most of all to the behaviorists them-selves—and not only because they felt that moral theory, whatever its "scientific" status, was ultimately inseparable from political theory. The following are some other more important reasons:

1. Even if a good grasp of political philosophy cannot be immediately converted into brilliant scientific results, the majority of us felt that analysis of the Greats at least sharpens the wits, deepens the imagination, and refines one's critical powers—and that even the dullest specialist can use all the wits, imagination, and critical powers he can develop. There is no real distinction to be made between a cultivated mind and a trained mind, since some speculative ability is required in even the most routine of behavioral inquiries and practical activities. The majority of us felt that the attitude which underlies the British examination for the Administra-tive Class was entirely right; there were very few Ilexes and Opimians among us.[1] One member of the conference who had had a great deal of administrative experience in Washington felt that, even on the lower bureau levels, men who had a broad grounding in "liberal arts" subjects showed greater capacity and, above all, greater adaptability than men trained mainly in a specialty. Most of us agreed that if the generalizing mind is desirable in a government bureau, it is even more desirable in a scholarly discipline. And most of us felt that speculative and critical abilities are not simply natural gifts, but talents to be developed by contact with great speculative and critical works. This, however, consti-tutes a defense of the liberal arts in general, not of political philosophy in particular.

2. Secondly, most of us felt that there is a need in any field for people who do not fully share the assumptions and attitudes of the orthodox "scientists." Every social organization has a tendency to isolate and punish the eccentric, to compel conformity to its dominant conceptions of ultimate truth and ultimate value, and frequently for good reasons. But

[1]Miss Iles (in T. L. Peacock's *Gryll Grange*): "The poor young men . . . are not held qualified for a profession unless they have overloaded their understanding with things of no use in it. . . ."

The Rev. Dr. Opimian: "Very true. Brindly would not have passed as a canal-maker, nor Edward Williams as a bridge-builder. I saw the other day some examina-tion papers which would have infallibly excluded Marlborough from the army and Nelson from the navy. . . . Fancy Watt being asked how much Joan of Naples got for Avignon when she sold it to Pope Clement the Sixth."

Compare, on the other hand, the remark of Mr. Flosky (in *Nightmare Abbey*), who speaks for the "wisdom" party (Flosky is a parody on Coleridge, a political philosopher in good standing): "My dear Miss O'Carroll, it would have given me great pleasure to have said anything that would have given you pleasure; but if any person living could make report of having obtained any information on any subject from Ferdinando Flosky, my transcendental reputation would be ruined forever."

the majority of the conference was sufficiently of the classical liberal persuasion to feel that too much success in this respect is self-defeating. No one can be sure that the scientific assumptions of today will not turn out to be the metaphysical nonsense of tomorrow; but we can be fairly certain that it is almost always the non-conformist who breaks new ground and makes "progress." One way to prevent the over-routinization of new and temporarily dominant ideas is, of course, to keep the history of ideas constantly in mind; if nothing else, this will engender a healthy perspective toward the authoritarian tendencies which generally afflict every field of inquiry at every stage of its development. Another way to prevent it is to present the student with a variety of different approaches to the analysis of the same subject; and this, in lieu of a sufficient number of eccentrics in our departments, can be accomplished by studying the eccentrics who fill Professor Sabine's book. Thus, while some of the behaviorists agreed that the study of political philosophy is useful as long as we do not have a real discipline of political science, the rest felt that it would be particularly useful when and if we ever got a discipline worthy of the name.

3. The majority felt, however, that there is a still stronger argument to be made for retaining the history of political ideas as a central part of the field. This argument rests on the very nature of the social as distinguished from the natural sciences. The study of society must be historical and "dynamic" precisely because the social sciences do not deal with a closed universe into which nothing new ever intrudes and in which a fixed mechanism plays itself out into a constant uniformity of motion. Most of us were on the side of Heraclitus and Hegel: "Everything is and is not, for everything is fluid, is constantly changing, constantly coming into being and passing away." Whether the natural sciences also deal with a dynamic universe the conference, unlike Engels, did not dare to discuss; but we felt reasonably certain, at any rate, of the need for dynamic models and theories in the social sciences.

Consistently with this attitude, we felt that the impression of unreality many of us get from sister-fields like economics and sociology is due to the prevalence of static models in these fields. Nor did we think it accidental that static models should be so prevalent in them. We agreed with one of the members that the emphasis on methodological rigor in these fields results in an exaggerated preoccupation with the "here and now" and hence with static analyses of static social situations. Political philosophy, even if it cannot claim the logical rigor of economic theory or the empirical comprehensiveness of the Yankee City series, at least accommodates the "intelligent" analysis of the real essence of our subject, dynamic change in time. We felt, of course, that a rigorous dynamic approach to social behavior may some day be worked out by the behaviorists. But the majority felt that the work of the economists, sociologists, and our own behaviorists offered no immediate hope of this and that there was such an affinity between systematic rigor and static analysis that there was every prospect of disappointment in the future. Hence, at least in the short run—and probably also in the long run—a healthy emphasis on dynamic analysis presupposes an equally healthy emphasis on political philosophy, as distinguished from the sort of thing the behaviorists wanted.

4. There is still another argument to be made for political philosophy on the basis of the dynamic historical nature of political science—and here we come much closer to the "cash value" of political philosophy to the behaviorists. The documents which comprise the history of political thought are simply one of the sources (many sources) on which we can construct knowledge of politics of the past. They are not absolutely reliable documents; they are certainly not compendia of the sort of information about the past all of us want. Hence the tendency of the rigid behaviorists to neglect the past for the here and now: we simply cannot do in the past what *The Authoritarian Personality* has done in the present. But this is a fault which documents in political philosophy share with all other historical documents, and even perhaps with contemporary documents. After all, Plato's *Dialogues* and Aristotle's *Politics* may contain more information relevant to the general analysis of political behavior than all the voting statistics compiled and sifted for Erie county. The problem of checking and evaluating the information contained in the documents of political philosophy merely involves the application of historiographical techniques. That does not mean that the problem is easy to solve in every case; it does mean that a discipline for coping with it exists—a discipline, incidentally, in which most of us unfortunately have no technical training. The point is that political behavior in the past is an indispensable datum for the analysis of political behavior as such; hence we must make the best we can of the sources we have on past political behavior, and the history of political thought is one of these sources. There may be better ones, but in historical research one must use everything one can get.

5. Moreover, the history of political thought, not least because of the moral consciousness of the political philosophers, may be particularly informative on a matter of obviously central importance in the field: political ideologies. Most of us agreed that political activities and political attitudes are inseparably related aspects of the same phenomena. Conceptions of "legitimacy," the myths in men's minds, the way in which they view the world and the way in which they translate their world-views

into political "directives" are absolutely fundamental to the correct analysis of political behavior. Even our behaviorists were not behaviorists in the more narrow sense of the term.

But here a disagreement emerged among the members of the conference which was never successfully resolved, even among the moderates. Do the highly refined ideologies which constitute our History of Political Thought courses really and accurately reflect ideologies which have actually influenced behavior? Do the sort of people whom Max Weber called *Kathedersozialisten* really have the same sort of attitudes as the people who actually go to the barricades? If we agreed on anything here, it was on the point that no general judgment could be made on the matter; every case must be treated on its own merits. We felt that probably all political philosophies (above all American political philosophies) reflect popular ideologies; that the consciousness of even the most free-floating intellectual is conditioned by the consciousness of his society; and that this social consciousness can manifest itself not only in conformity with an ideology but also in revolt against it. Hence, the majority of us felt that all political philosophies are potentially useful sources of politically significant ideologies.

We also felt, however, that the unsophisticated identification of political philosophy and politically significant ideology is full of dangers. The fact that Rousseau's political thought has both democratic and totalitarian implications (if it does) does not mean, *ipso facto*, that they are the sources of British socialism or that British Socialists think like Green, Bradley, and Bosanquet. Hence, positing a one-one relationship between "political philosophy" and politically significant "ideology" is, perhaps more often than not, merely a way of avoiding difficult historical research.

Many of us felt that, in most cases, we have available infinitely better sources of politically significant ideologies than the cream of political thought, and that neither the political behaviorists nor the political "theorists" have scratched even the surface of these sources—although the historians have, usually for purposes different from ours. The "behaviorists" have not extracted the juice from the sources because they are too current-events-conscious and frequently lack a decent training in historiography. The "theorists" have neglected them because they lack adequate training in empirical research techniques and because they are not genuinely interested in political behavior. There is, consequently, a vast territory of politically significant information which lies fallow, mainly because we seem unable to reach a reasonable compromise between the study of Plato and the study of local government in Illinois.

Many members of the conference felt that the priority of research in ideologies should be given to these sources (legal documents, novels, letters, memoirs, pamphlets, handbills) rather than to the Greats. Others, however, felt that the Greats were at least a source of what we want and that the evaluation of their "relevance" posed no problems intrinsically different from the problems posed by the other sources.

6. If political philosophy is valuable as a source of data, it is also valuable as a source of ideas for analyzing the data. The history of political thought is indisputably a gold-mine of concepts, models, hypotheses, and methods which may turn out to be useful even in the analysis of contemporary political behavior.

What really disturbed us on this subject was not whether political philosophy is useful but why the reservoir of potentially useful ideas in the history of political thought is not being used more. After all, if we want a "cumulative" discipline we need not begin entirely from scratch; we need only use whatever is useful in past thought on politics. The reason we rarely do this is plain and has already been mentioned: the fact that the behaviorists have a generally insufficient interest and preparation in the history of political thought and the fact that the historians of political thought hardly ever do anything but expound the history of political ideas.

This is the real core of the difficulty, and the real reason, many of us felt, why it was necessary to have a conference on the relevance of political philosophy to political science at all. Their relevance to one another seemed beyond question to the majority at the conference. And if the majority is right, the problem of the conference is ultimately a political rather than an intellectual problem: how to persuade the practitioners in the field to develop a healthy interest and to acquire a healthy preparation in both political science and philosophy. It should be added that we did not feel that this is simply a matter of persuading the behaviorists to take their Aristotle out of the basement. It would also involve persuading the political "philosophers" to stoop to the grimy work of empirical analysis occasionally. Our villain, in the final analysis, and not surprisingly, was simply the "behaviorist"-"theorist" dichotomy.

THE ROLE OF THE CONTEMPORARY POLITICAL PHILOSOPHER

But what of the contemporary political philosopher, i.e., the man who is less interested in expounding the history of political "theories" than in adding to them? What sort of work might he do? And, above all, in what special ways can he be useful to the political "scientists" other than those in which all political "theories" are useful to them?

1. The anti-behaviorists felt, on the whole, that he should perform two roles. First, he should undertake the never-ending task of ethical and moral reflection: ethical reflection toward the definition and critique of ultimate imperatives, moral reflection toward the definition of actions which can approach the imperatives in practical activity. In effect, he should address himself to the matter of ends and means, to the problems of choice in practical activity rather than the analysis of behavior as a given. His function, in this sense, is to be a source of directives for society in general. Second, he should use his critical powers, experience, and general knowledge—his "wisdom"—in commenting upon contemporary political experience: analyzing broad trends in political development, criticizing the activities of statesmen, trying to penetrate the inner meaning, as it were, of contemporary political life.

2. The moderates felt that the chief task of the contemporary political philosopher was to provide a constant flow of theoretical ideas and concepts to those more interested in empirical work; ideas and concepts, however, which have no claim to "wisdom" other than their utility and testability in "scientific" analysis. They felt that it was perhaps not entirely necessary for every practitioner in the field to possess both a highly-developed theoretical imagination and a rigorous command of empirical research methods. Instead, there might well be some sort of rational division of labor. At any rate, the moderates could not see why certain political scientists should not devote their efforts chiefly to speculation, provided that they were sufficiently aware of the problems and difficulties arising in empirical analysis to make their ideas useful to the behaviorists.

3. Interestingly enough, the behaviorists, more than anyone else, insisted on the system-building and meta-theoretical functions of the contemporary political philosopher. It is not difficult to see why they should insist on system-building. After all, if the immediate task of political science is to transform itself into a unified discipline, we need someone to perform the unifying function: someone to construct the authoritative model of the political process and program for research which would govern our future activities, to coin the interrelated concepts, to chart the map, and to base the system on the relevant work already done in detail. This would be the unique function of the political philosophers. They would be sources not of moral directives but of scientific directives. Here, of course, the behaviorists and anti-behaviorists might join hands—as usual, the extremists turn out to be not so entirely different from one another—for the wise philosopher of the anti-behaviorists would be peculiarly fitted to play the unifying role in the field. But perhaps this is not entirely fair, since the behaviorists would vehemently insist that even the

wisest of conceptual schemes is merely a program for research and can have no claim to validity in and of itself.

Even more important, the behaviorists insisted that the political philosophers should play a more constructive role as "critics" of the work of the political scientists, i.e., that they should increasingly assume the position which modern philosophy in general is assuming toward the substantive fields. There should be less expounding of the ancients and more keeping the moderns up to the mark. The contemporary political philosopher should be constantly engaged in the critical analysis of the political scientist's concepts, the methods he uses, the models which seem to govern his work, and the consistency of his findings and reasonings. He should constantly clarify the basic assumptions of the behaviorist's work and its "larger" implications. This is the service in which he can most help the work of political science and find a justifiable niche for himself in our academic departments. He should, in short, be a methodologically and linguistically sophisticated critic, in constant process of refining the products of empirical activity.

CONCLUSION

At the end of the conference, many of us felt that a real problem confronting us was revealed by our discussions. *How and why had the political "philosophers" and the political "scientists" managed to drift so far apart in their work when most of them were so eager to concede that they had much to learn from one another?* It would be tedious and not very useful to go into all the possible explanations. The important thing is not to hold post mortems—which might after all only widen the breach— but to begin making some attempts to bring the two closer together. Some of us believed that the most promising step at present would be to attempt some sort of collaborative analysis of the area in which political science and philosophy touch most closely on one another, i.e., the field of politically significant "ideologies." However this may be, it is hoped that this report will stimulate further thought in tackling this problem of collaborative work between "philosopher" and "scientist."

Further Readings

Dahl, Robert A., "Political Theory: Truth and Consequences," *World Politics*, XI (1: October, 1958), pp. 89–102.

Easton, David, "The Decline of Modern Political Theory," *Journal of Politics*, XIII (1: February, 1951), pp. 36–58.

Germino, Dante, "The Revival of Political Theory," *Journal of Politics*, XXV (3: August, 1963), pp. 437–460.

Laslett, Peter, ed., *Philosophy, Politics and Society* (New York: The Macmillan Company, 1956).

INDEX

Absurd, 265–268
Acton, Lord, 31
Almond, G., 117, 120, 151, 276
Analytic political philosophy
    criticism of, 175ff.
    nature of, 97, 162ff.
Aquinas, St. Thomas, 100, 336, 338, 340,
    357
Aristotle, 3–4, 9, 21, 24, 26, 32, 44, 46–47,
    58, 65–66, 110, 113, 115–116, 136,
    140, 223, 259–260, 275, 290–291,
    299–300, 308, 337–338, 340, 352,
    368, 370
Augustine, S., 45, 99, 113

Barker, E., 43
Bay, C., 137ff.
Behavioralism
    criticisms of, 96, 137ff., 361, 371
    nature of, 93–96, 118ff., 360, 371
Bentham, J., 25, 108, 113, 115, 298, 349
Bergson, H., 219, 341
Berlin, I., 306, 328–329
Bodin, J., 5, 109, 116, 341, 344
Brogan, D., 34, 121
Burke, E., 43, 114, 298, 313, 344
Butler, Bishop, 15, 32, 43

Camus, A., 100–101, 256–257, 260–269,
    280–281
Cassirer, E., 110, 224
Catlin, G., 1, 4, 21–22, 47, 121, 323, 325
Causal factors in political theories, 12,
    16, 75ff., 321ff.
Cobban, A., 289–290, 307
Comte, A., 50, 225, 335, 346

Dahl, R., 118–119, 137, 145–147, 153,
    305
Darwin, C., 347

Descartes, R., 59, 162, 225, 230, 233, 238
Dewey, J., 12, 20, 23, 41, 219, 311
Durkheim, E., 25, 29, 121, 189

Easton, D., 6, 25–26, 37, 93, 103, 124,
    211–215, 219–224, 226–227, 307
Ethics, 38, 79ff., 132, 276ff.
Engels, F., 248, 250
Eulau, H., 5–6, 138, 143
Existentialism, 100–101, 230–255, 256–
    271
    and Marxism, 230

Facts, 12, 16, 19, 86
Freud, S., 26, 31, 33, 121, 283–284, 341
Functionalism
    nature of, 98–99, 186ff.

Galileo, 135, 347
Grazia, A. de, 125
Greece, 307, 314
Green, T., 110

Hallowell, J., 276–280, 286
Hegel, F., 3, 19–20, 26, 100, 106–107,
    110, 113–114, 116, 225, 230, 233,
    235–240, 247, 251, 258, 260, 300,
    367
Heidegger, M., 49, 101, 263
Historicism, 46ff., 72ff., 317
Hobbes, T., 3, 5, 9, 24, 27, 32–33, 35, 37,
    44, 104, 108, 113, 115–116, 136, 299,
    340, 342, 349
Hooker, T., 113
Hume, D., 19, 33, 44, 115–116, 140, 162,
    225, 249, 274, 346–347

Jaspers, K., 101, 224, 238–239
Jefferson, T., 13, 15, 18–19
Jouvenel, B. de, 33

Kant, I., 167, 169–170, 230, 233, 238, 341–342, 348, 350
Kaplan, A., 30
Kierkegaard, S., 100, 212, 230, 234, 239, 247, 251–252, 262–263
Kirk, R., 114

Laski, H., 40, 104, 115, 299, 311
Laslett, P., 305
Lasswell, H., 27–28, 30–31, 115, 120, 130, 294, 323, 325
Leibniz, G., 20, 162
Lenin, N., 23, 111, 115, 223, 249, 344
Lindsay, A., 121, 313
Locke, J., 2, 9, 11, 73, 112–113, 115–117, 233, 299, 302, 310–311, 342, 344, 347, 365
Lukacs, G., 217, 242, 246, 248

Machiavelli, 3, 21, 26, 31–32, 105–116, 136, 294, 297, 300, 342, 344
Mannheim, K., 27, 142, 218, 281, 316
Marx, K., 2–3, 9, 23, 26, 30, 32, 37, 45, 73, 80, 101–102, 105–106, 111–114, 116, 121, 171, 189ff., 230–231, 233, 237–240, 244, 247, 249–250, 253–254, 284–285, 300, 314, 335, 338
Materialism, 249n., 250n.
Matson, F., 218
Merriam, C., 28, 31, 120, 124–125, 134
Merton, R., 25, 193
Methodology, 91ff.
Michels, R., 29, 121, 323–324
Mill, J., 79, 114, 116, 298, 342, 356, 362
Models, 82ff., 342ff.
Morgenthau, H., 28, 35–36, 294
Mosca, G., 121, 323

Natural rights, 259
Neumann, F., 121
Newton, I., 135, 308, 347
Nietzsche, F., 225, 263–264, 315, 341, 344

Pareto, V., 25–26, 121, 317
Parsons, T., 25, 27, 36–37
Plato, 27, 39, 46, 52, 58, 60, 66, 68, 80, 100, 108, 140, 155, 223, 260, 275, 297, 299–300, 336, 338, 341, 354–355, 365, 369
Political behavior, 119
Political philosophy
  classical, 58ff.
  nature of, 2, 8ff., 46, 47ff., 363–368

Political science
  definition, 2, 5, 24, 27
  difference from political philosophy, 2
Political systems, 6
Political theory
  decline of, 258, 289ff., 303ff.
  logical structure, 13, 16, 17, 112
  nature of, 7ff., 22ff., 70ff., 308ff., 328
Political thought
  nature of, 2
Politics, 23, 26
Popper, K., 27, 40
Positivism, 50, 56ff.
Power
  politics as, 5, 28ff.
Pragmatism, 20

Rousseau, J., 24, 27, 33, 44, 66, 105–106, 109, 113–114, 116, 233, 294, 298, 324, 342, 349
Runciman, W., 188ff.
Russell, B., 28, 31, 294, 337, 350

Sabine, G., 1, 7, 8, 22, 47, 73, 108, 311, 365
Sartre, J., 100–101, 216, 230–231, 262–263, 275, 307
Schopenhauer, A., 18
Science, 54, 128
  and ethics, 277ff.
Smith, A., 30, 106
Socrates, 8, 52, 63, 66, 68, 115, 136, 262, 275
Sorel, G., 14
Spinoza, B., 226, 299, 342
Systems analysis, 197, 211ff. (critique)

Tawney, R., 115
Thoreau, H., 91
Thorson, T., 256
Tocqueville, A. de, 121, 136
Toynbee, A., 25–26, 44
Truman, D., 28–29, 120, 126–127

Values, 12, 18, 50, 273ff., 311

Washington, G., 27
Weber, M., 25, 27, 32, 54, 121, 316, 344, 356, 369
Weldon, T., 3, 97, 113, 162ff., 175ff., 362
Whitehead, A., 49, 218–219
Wittgenstein, L., 351